SEIKAI TRILOGY

BANNER OF THE STARS

THE SHAPE OF BONDS

VOL. 2

Original Story by
HIROYUKI MORIOKA

Manga by
Toshihiro Ono

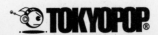

HAMBURG // LONDON // LOS ANGELES // TOKYO

SEIKAI TRILOGY

Count Jinto Lin of the Hyde Star System is a lander, catapulted to the status of Abh nobility in the wake of a political deal. The agreement, struck between his father, the president of Planet Martine, and the Humankind Empire Abh, transformed Jinto's life and subjected the young count to the unending consternation of his own people and the vagaries of interstellar politics.

For years, the races of humankind have resented the genetic disposition and technical superiority of the Abh—genetically enhanced humans who have blossomed into an ageless, space-faring race. As Abh dominance over galactic trade increased, the other human worlds began to form alliances to oppose the further expansion of the Abh Empire and even regain trading rights over worlds conquered by the Abh. Though genetically different from his Abh compatriots, Jinto is embroiled in their burgeoning conflict. The tension between the Humankind Empire Abh and the rest of the human worlds finally erupted into full-scale, interstellar war three years ago when the alliances attacked and destroyed the Abh Patrol Ship Gosroth.

At this time, Jinto Lin's life became entwined with that of Lafiel, the granddaughter of the Abh Empress Ramaj and a pilot trainee on the patrol ship Gosroth. Assigned to transport Jinto to Lakfakalle to continue his education at the Imperial academy, the Gosroth entered history as the first casualty of humankind's most devastating war. The attack on the Gosroth forced Lafiel to abandon ship with Jinto in the hope that she'd be able to evade the assault force and carry her charge and the Gosroth's data logs to the Imperial Capital of Lakfakelle.

STORY SO FAR

In need of fuel, the two young officers diverted their ship to the barony of Febdash, only to become subject to the jealousy of the domain's minor noble. All too willing to use Lafiel as leverage to improve his social status, the Baron Fedbash threatened Lafiel's mission and imprisoned the young Count Hyde. In order to complete her mission, Lafiel found it necessary to escape, and in doing so killed the young Baron and freed his vassals.

Resuming course for the capital, Jinto and Lafiel were chased by the forces of their enemy, the United Mankind. In order to escape, the two fugitives crash-landed on the occupied Planet Clasbul, which was struggling to adjust to the presence of the occupying army. Trapped on the surface, Jinto and Lafiel worked together to ensure their mutual safety and escape with the ship's data logs. The harrowing experience created for them an unbreakable bond of friendship.

While Abh forces successfully liberated Clasbul from the United Mankind, Jinto's homeworld in the Hyde System fell to enemy forces. The resulting battle exhausted the military might of all sides, and both the Abh and the United Mankind turned their attention to training officers and constructing massive fleets of formidable interstellar warships.

Three years have passed since Lafiel and Jinto's escape from Planet Clasbul. Lafiel is now captain of her own Assault Ship, the Basroil, and has requested the services of Jinto Lin as her supply officer...

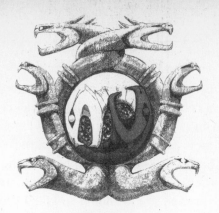

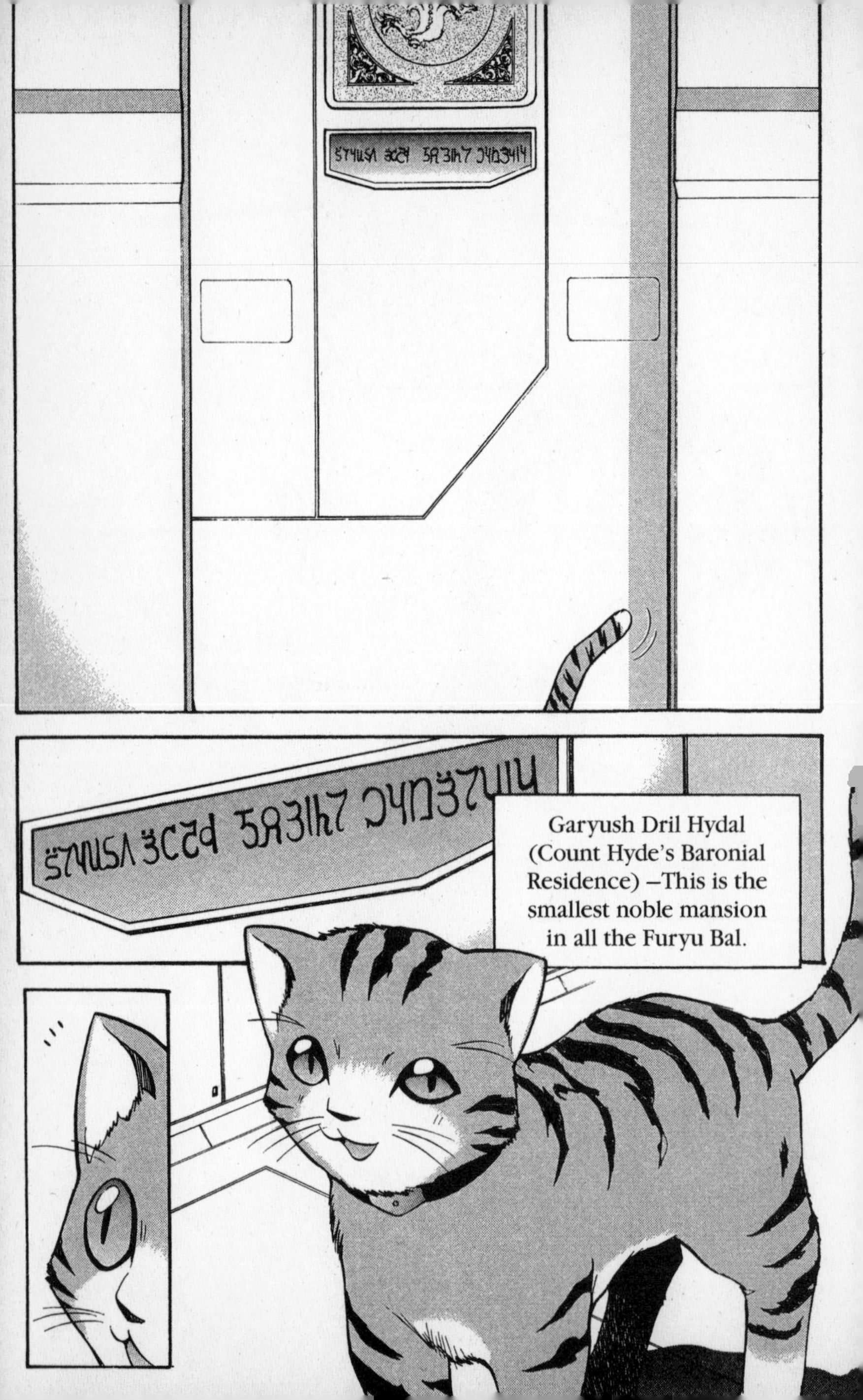
Garyush Dril Hydal (Count Hyde's Baronial Residence) –This is the smallest noble mansion in all the Furyu Bal.

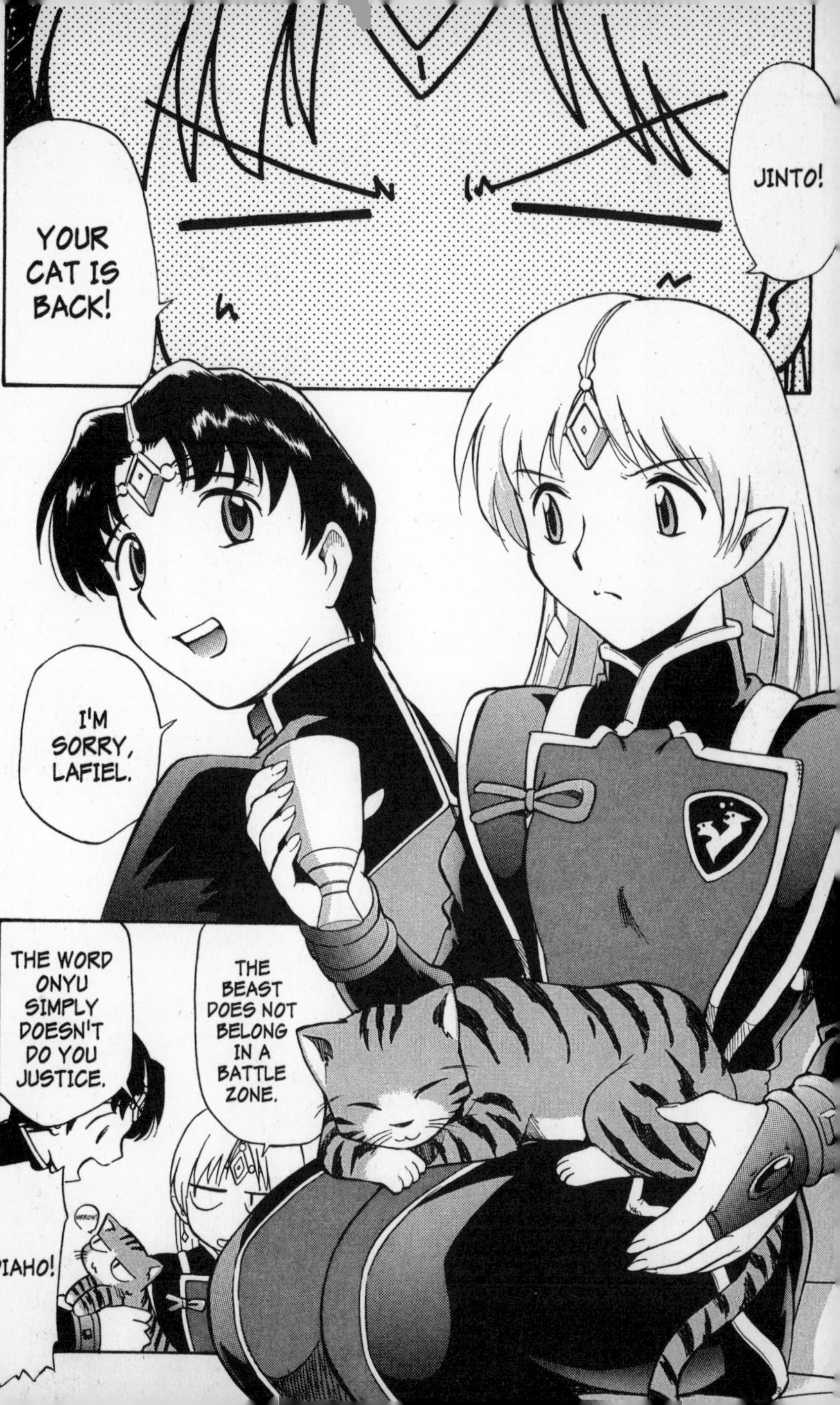

JINTO!
YOUR CAT IS BACK!
I'M SORRY, LAFIEL.
THE BEAST DOES NOT BELONG IN A BATTLE ZONE.
THE WORD ONYU SIMPLY DOESN'T DO YOU JUSTICE.
MRROW!
DIAHO!

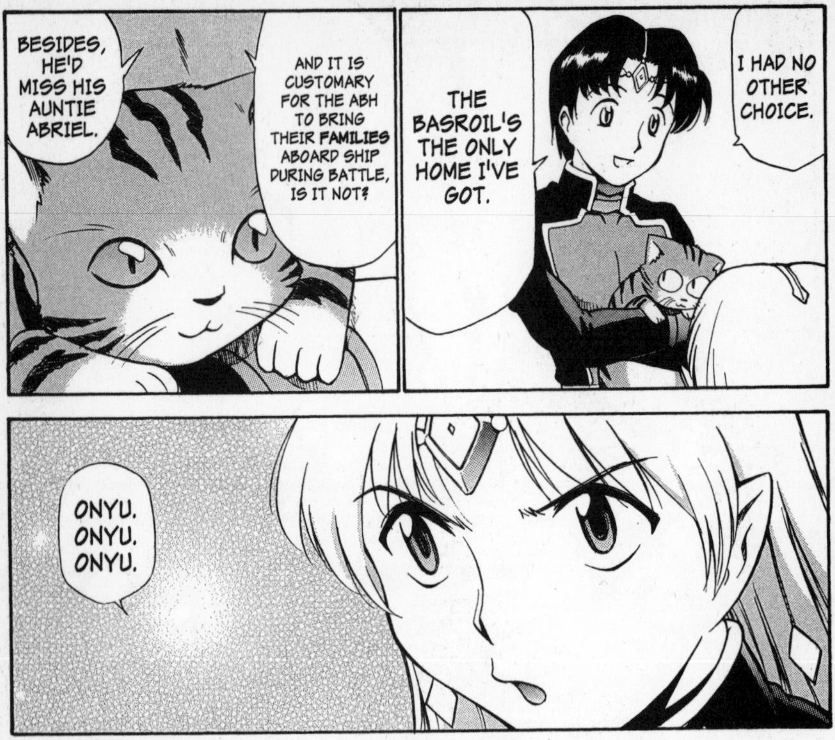
I HAD NO OTHER CHOICE.
THE BASROIL'S THE ONLY HOME I'VE GOT.
AND IT IS CUSTOMARY FOR THE ABH TO BRING THEIR **FAMILIES** ABOARD SHIP DURING BATTLE, IS IT NOT?
BESIDES, HE'D MISS HIS AUNTIE ABRIEL.
ONYU. ONYU. ONYU.

Author's Note: When Lafiel was a child, she believed Diaho's grandmother, Holia, supplied half of her genes.

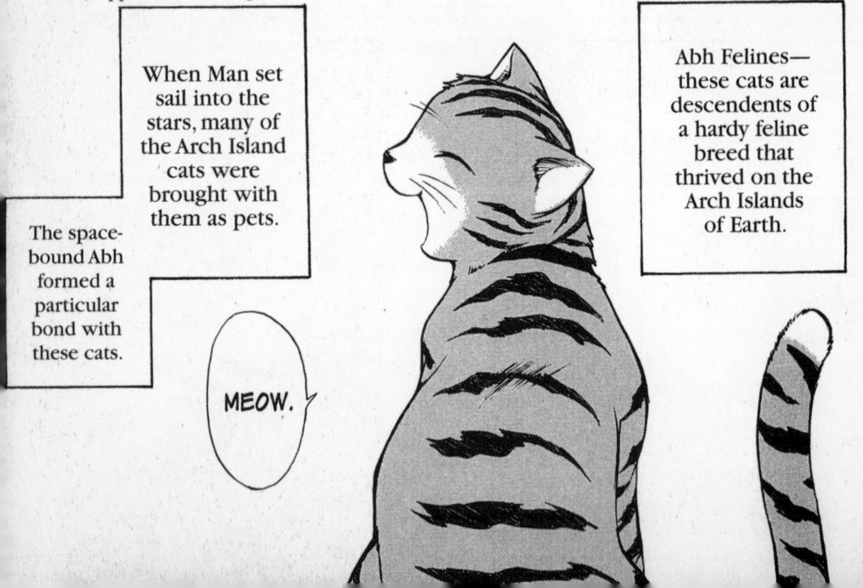
Abh Felines—these cats are descendents of a hardy feline breed that thrived on the Arch Islands of Earth.
When Man set sail into the stars, many of the Arch Island cats were brought with them as pets.
The space-bound Abh formed a particular bond with these cats.
MEOW.

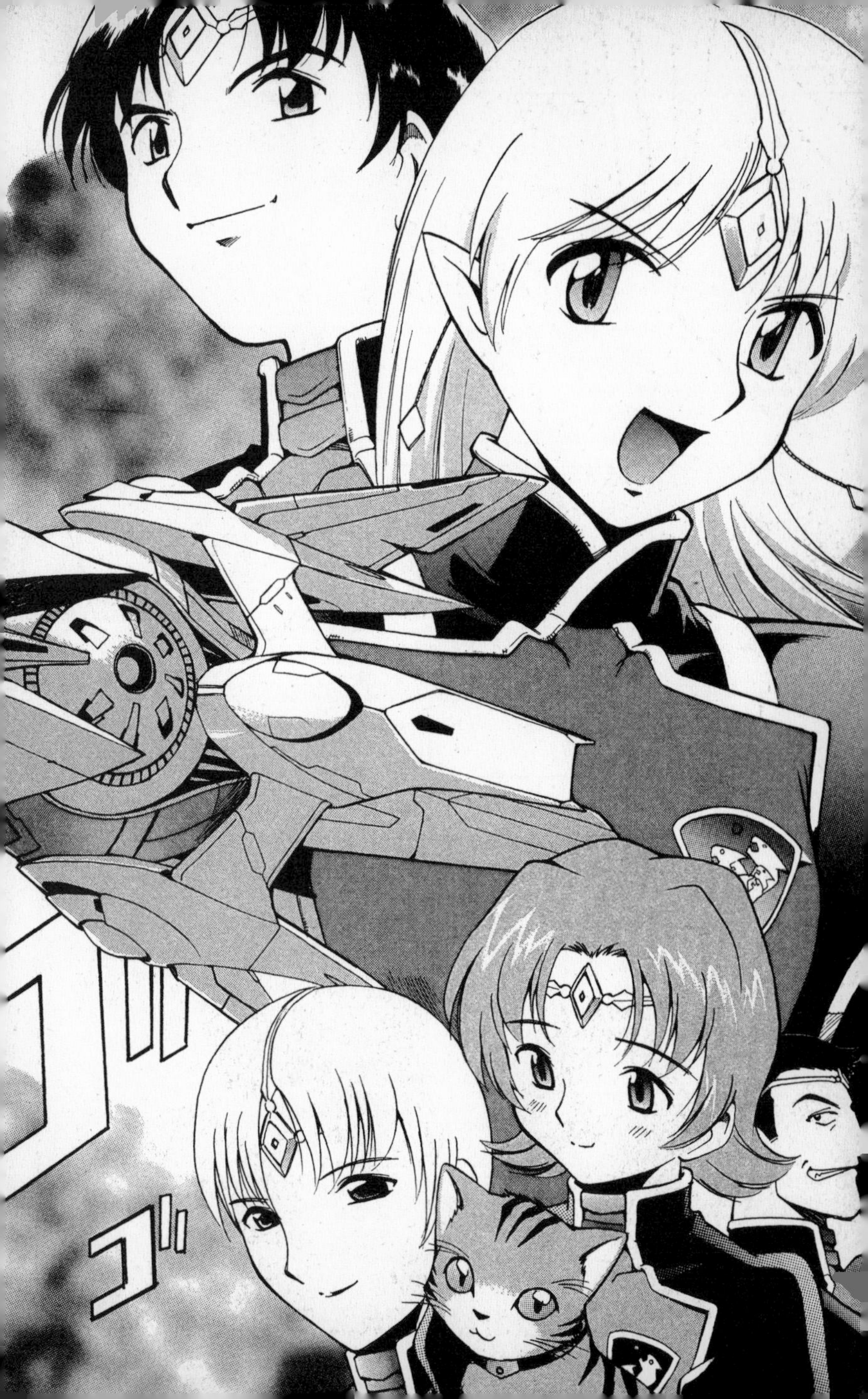
ゴ
ゴ

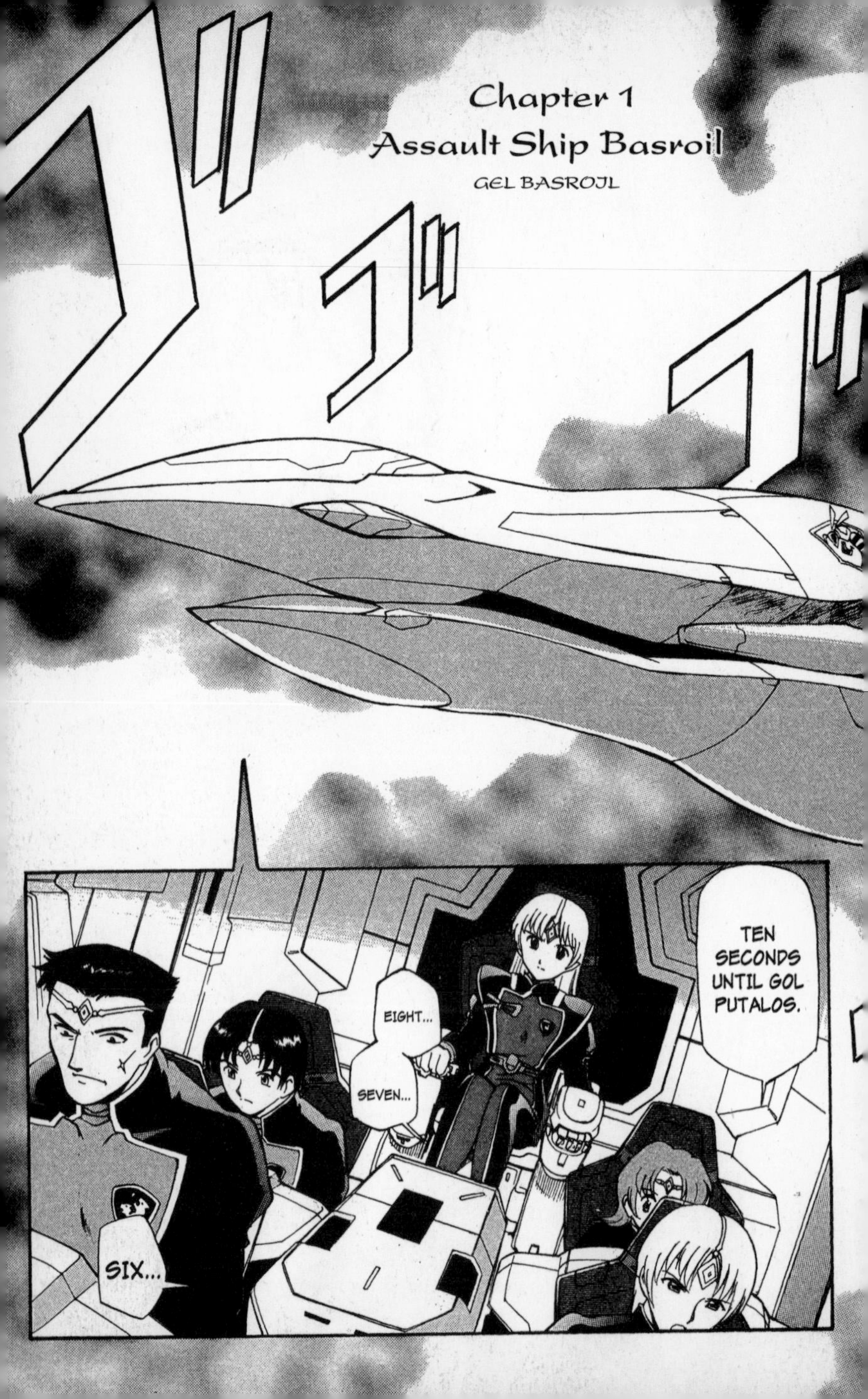
Chapter 1
Assault Ship Basroil
GEL BASROJL
TEN SECONDS UNTIL GOL PUTALOS.
EIGHT...
SEVEN...
SIX...

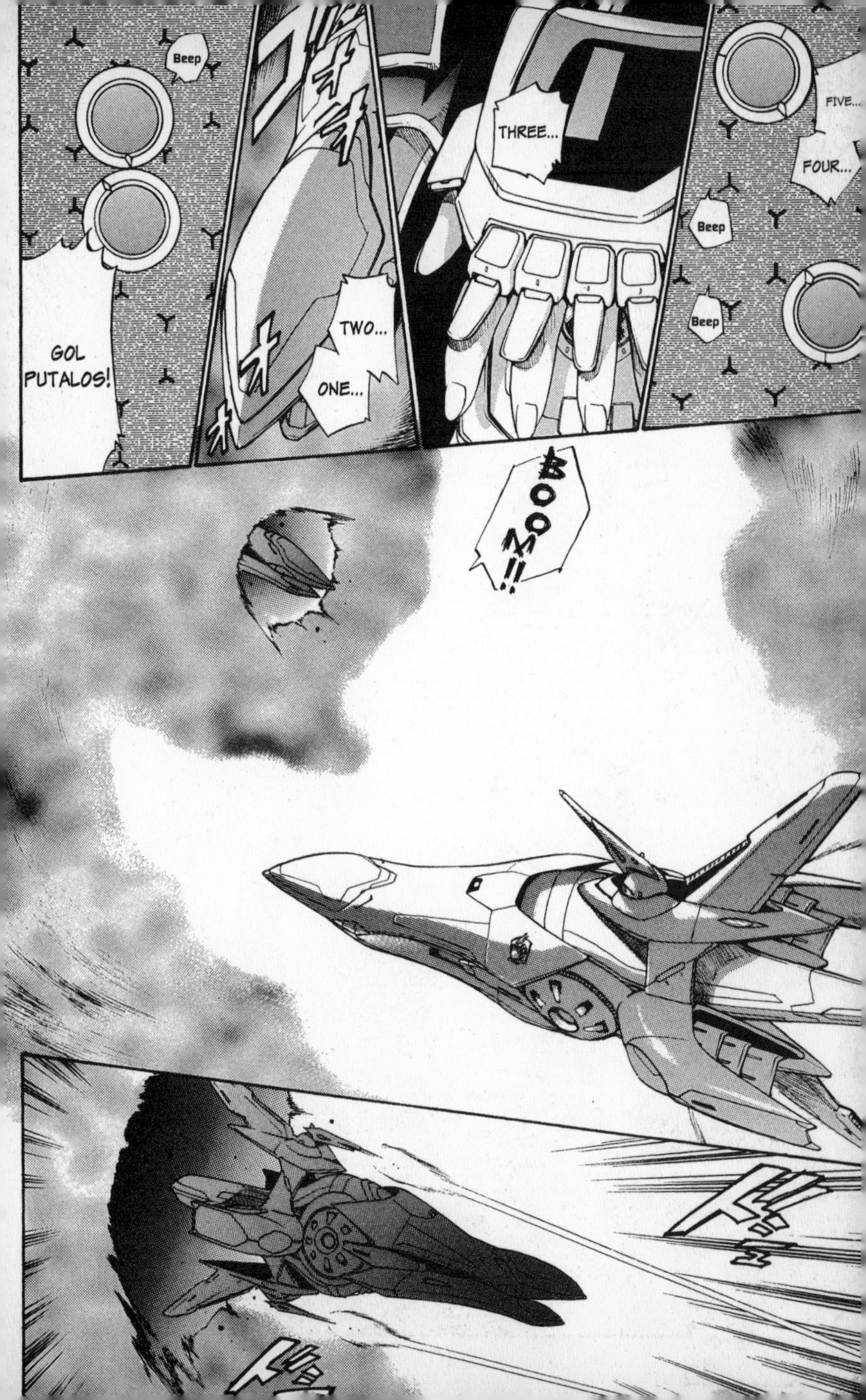
FIVE...
FOUR...
Beep
Beep
THREE...
TWO...
ONE...
Beep
GOL PUTALOS!
BOOM!!

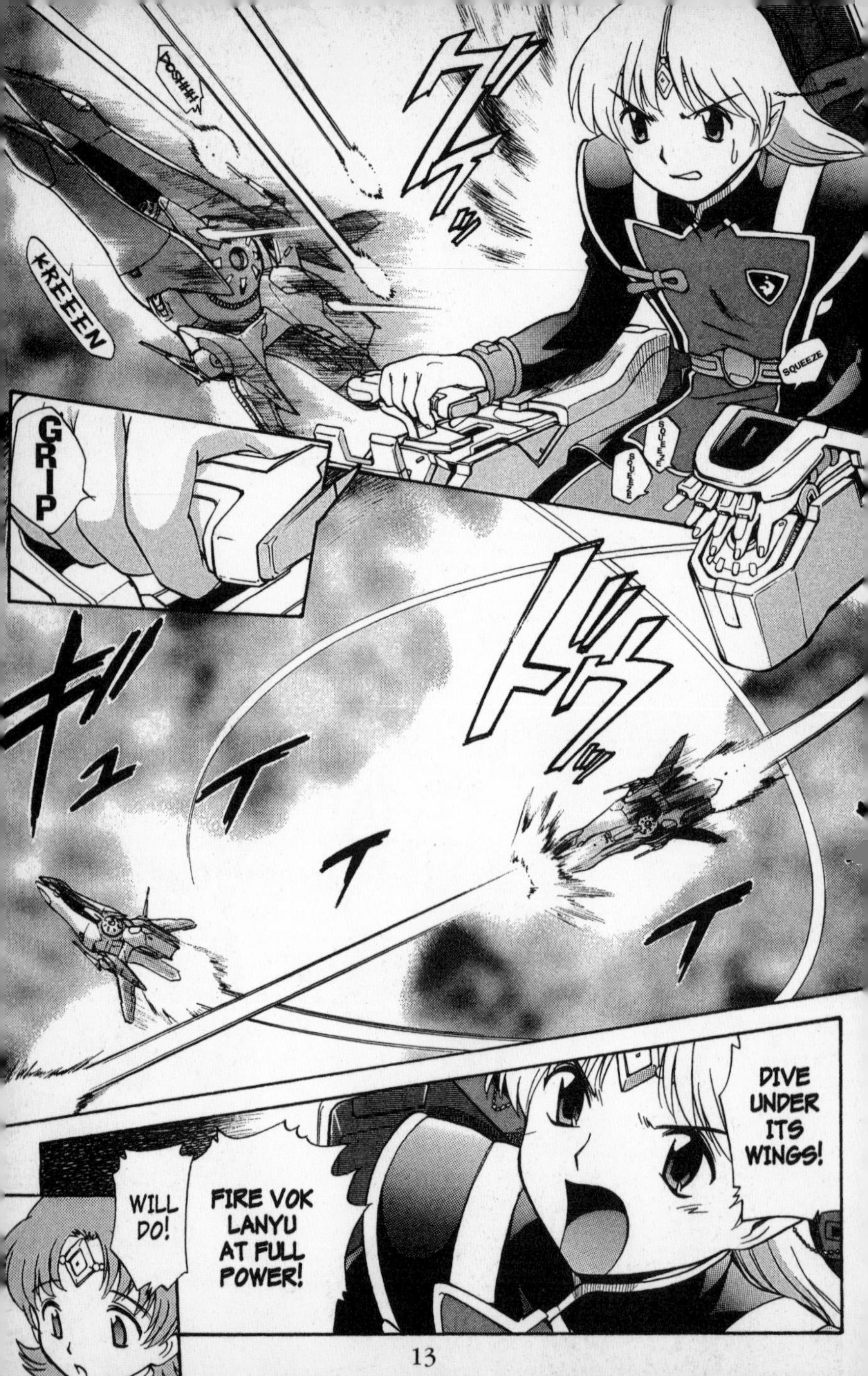
POSHHH
KREEEN
SQUEEZE
SQUEEZE
SQUEEZE
GRIP
DIVE UNDER ITS WINGS!
FIRE VOK LANYU AT FULL POWER!
WILL DO!

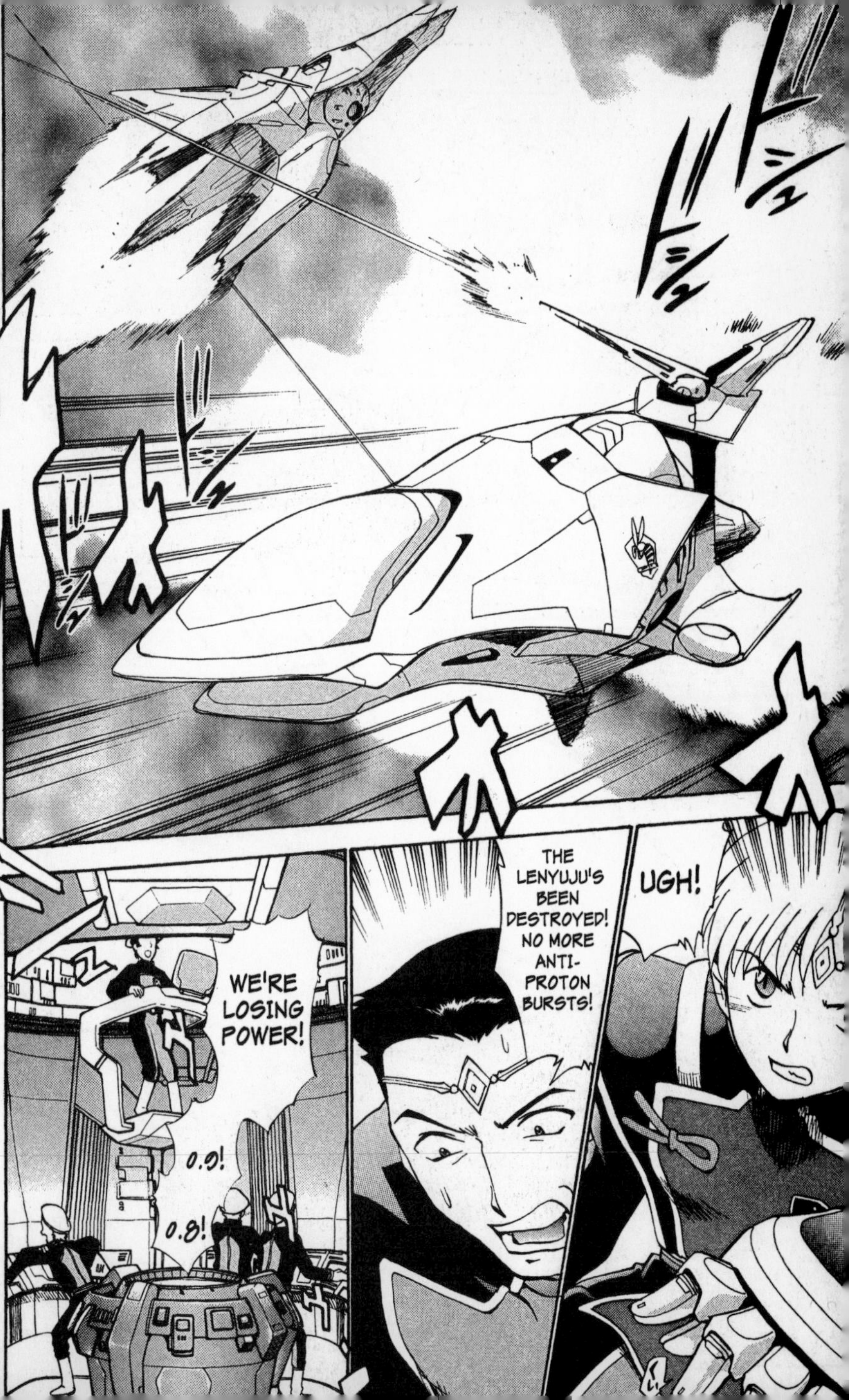
UGH!
THE LENYUJU'S BEEN DESTROYED! NO MORE ANTI-PROTON BURSTS!
WE'RE LOSING POWER!
0.9!
0.8!

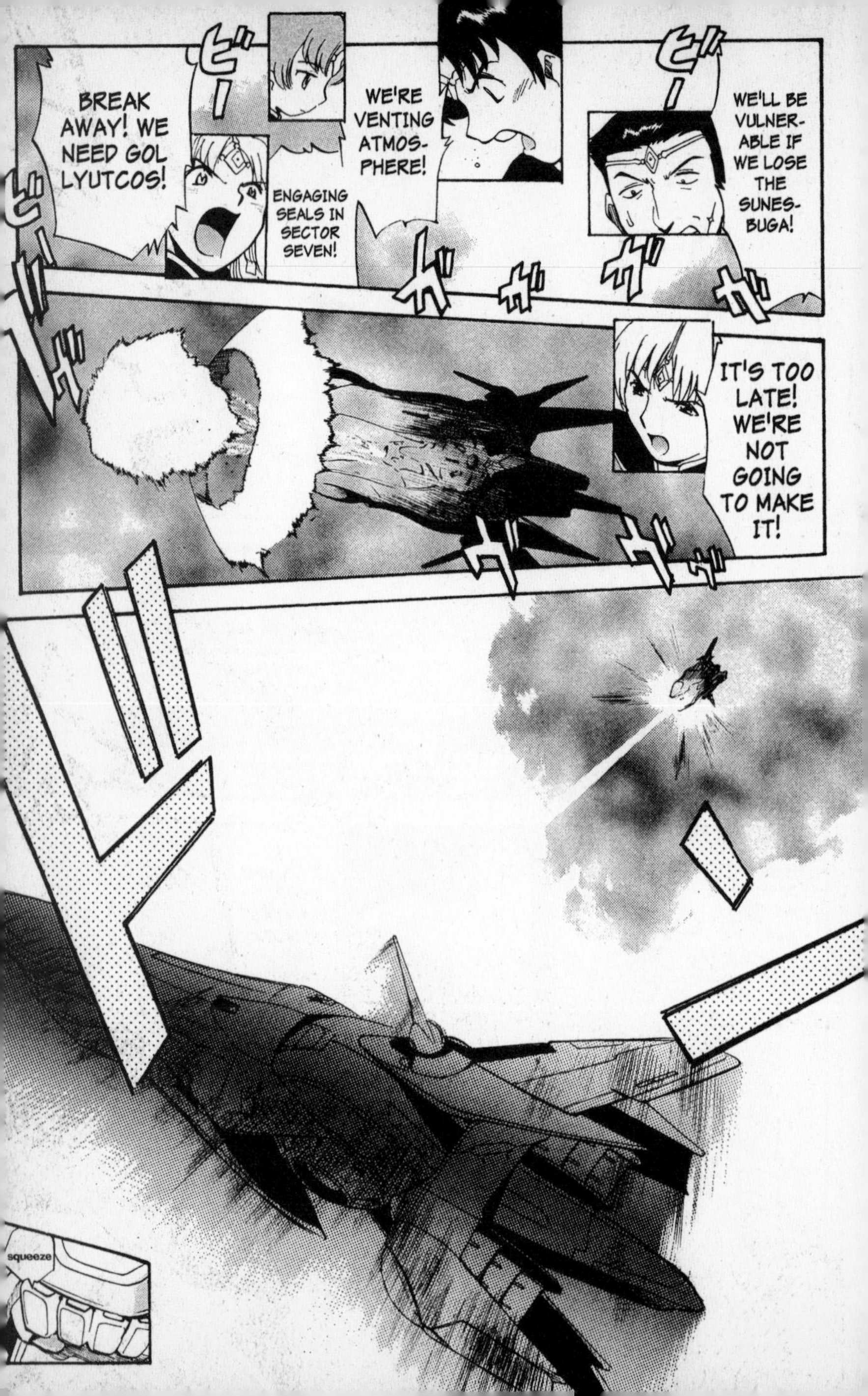
WE'LL BE VULNER-ABLE IF WE LOSE THE SUNES-BUGA!
WE'RE VENTING ATMOS-PHERE!
ENGAGING SEALS IN SECTOR SEVEN!
BREAK AWAY! WE NEED GOL LYUTCOS!
IT'S TOO LATE! WE'RE NOT GOING TO MAKE IT!
squeeze

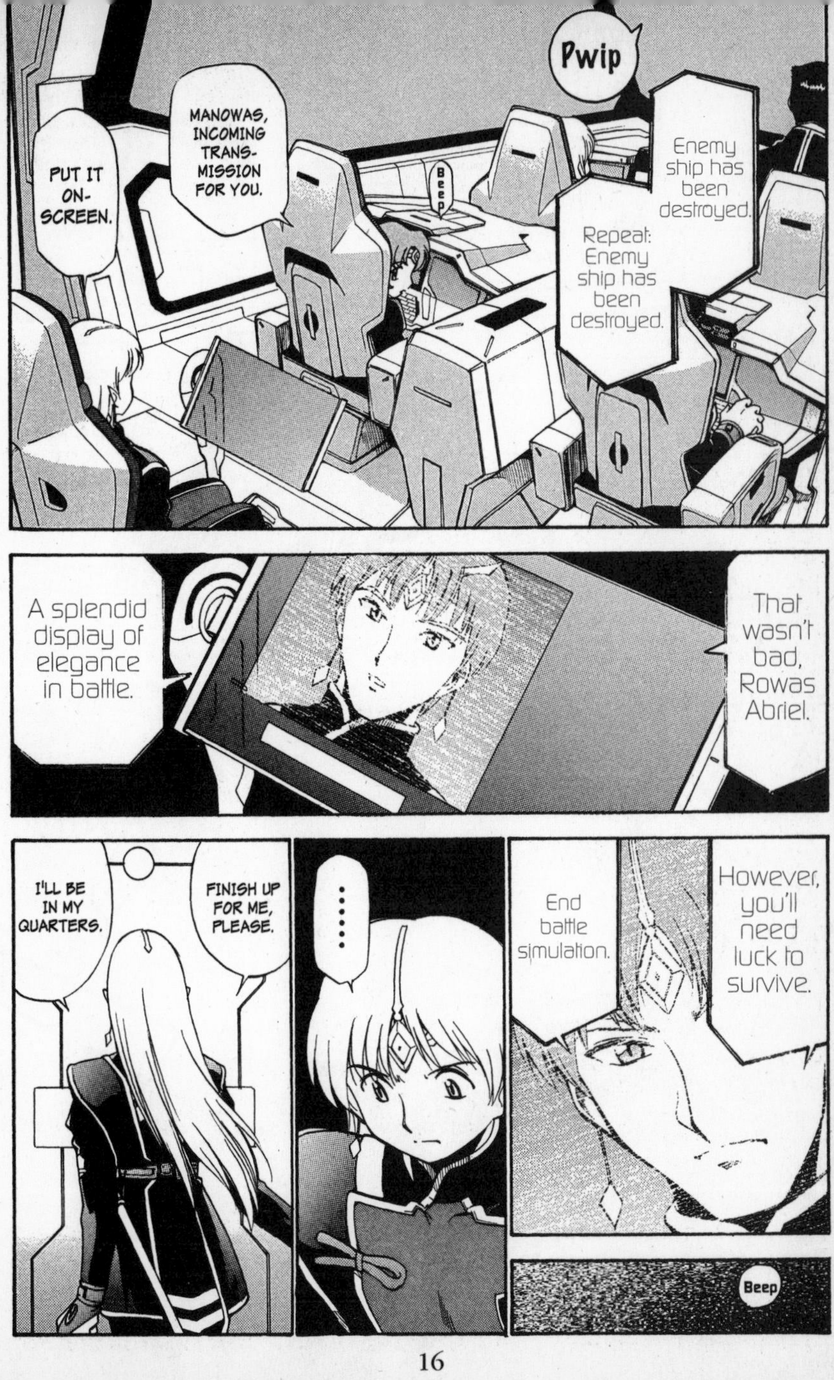
Pwip
Enemy ship has been destroyed.
Repeat: Enemy ship has been destroyed.
Beep
MANOWAS, INCOMING TRANS-MISSION FOR YOU.
PUT IT ON-SCREEN.
That wasn't bad, Rowas Abriel.
A splendid display of elegance in battle.
However, you'll need luck to survive.
End battle simulation.
Beep
......
FINISH UP FOR ME, PLEASE.
I'LL BE IN MY QUARTERS.

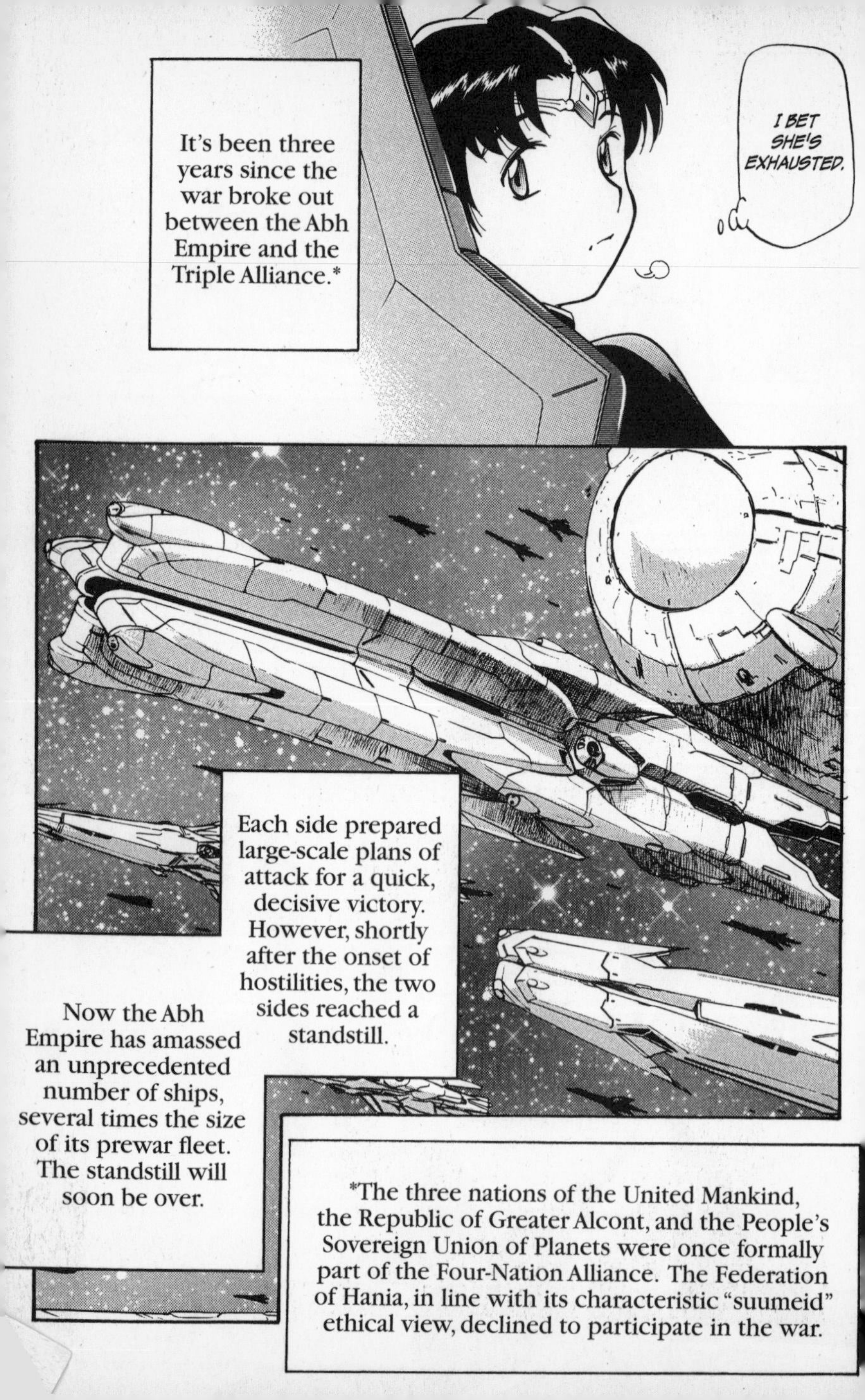
I BET SHE'S EXHAUSTED.
It's been three years since the war broke out between the Abh Empire and the Triple Alliance.*
Each side prepared large-scale plans of attack for a quick, decisive victory. However, shortly after the onset of hostilities, the two sides reached a standstill.
Now the Abh Empire has amassed an unprecedented number of ships, several times the size of its prewar fleet. The standstill will soon be over.

*The three nations of the United Mankind, the Republic of Greater Alcont, and the People's Sovereign Union of Planets were once formally part of the Four-Nation Alliance. The Federation of Hania, in line with its characteristic "suumeid" ethical view, declined to participate in the war.

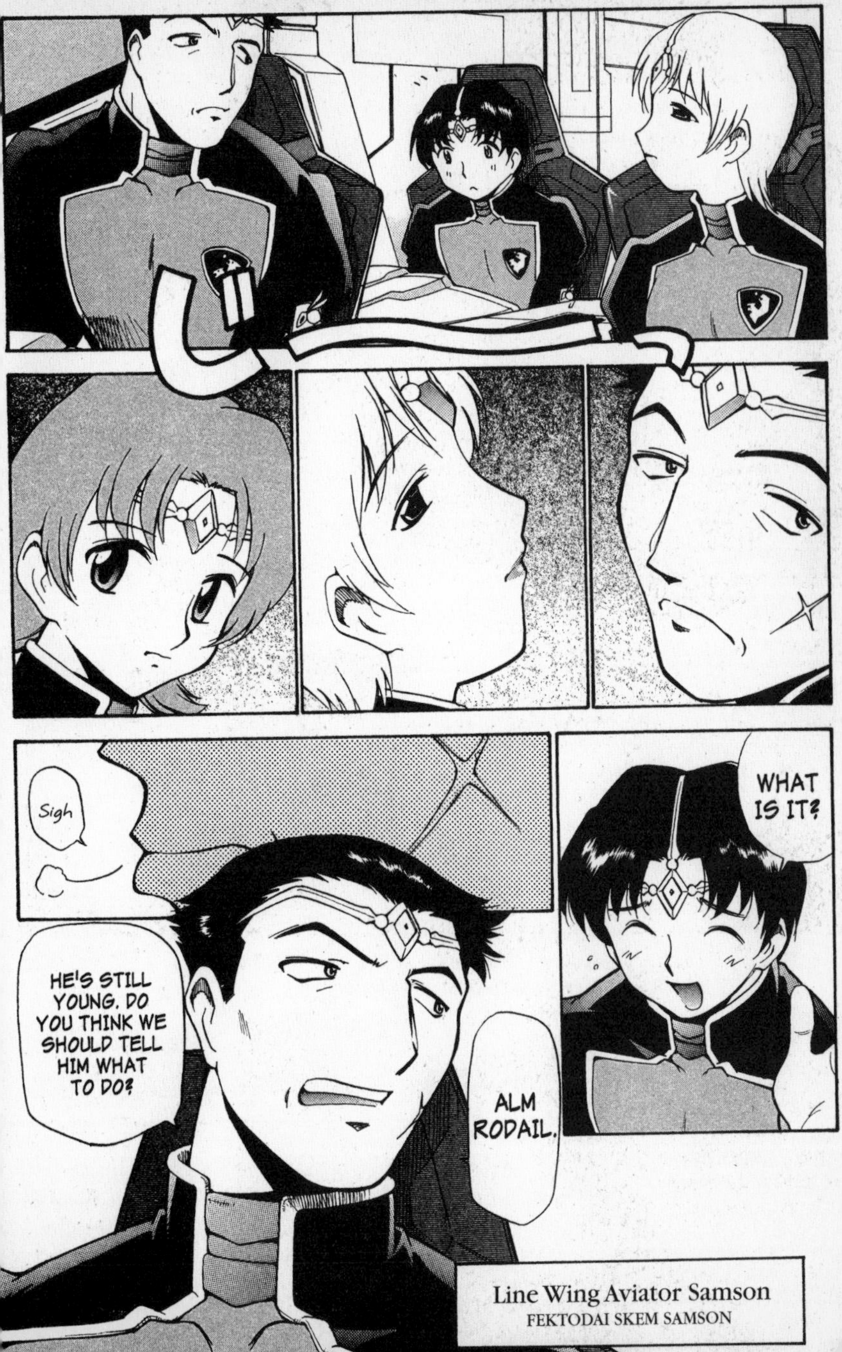
WHAT IS IT?
Sigh
ALM RODAIL.
HE'S STILL YOUNG. DO YOU THINK WE SHOULD TELL HIM WHAT TO DO?
Line Wing Aviator Samson
FEKTODAI SKEM SAMSON

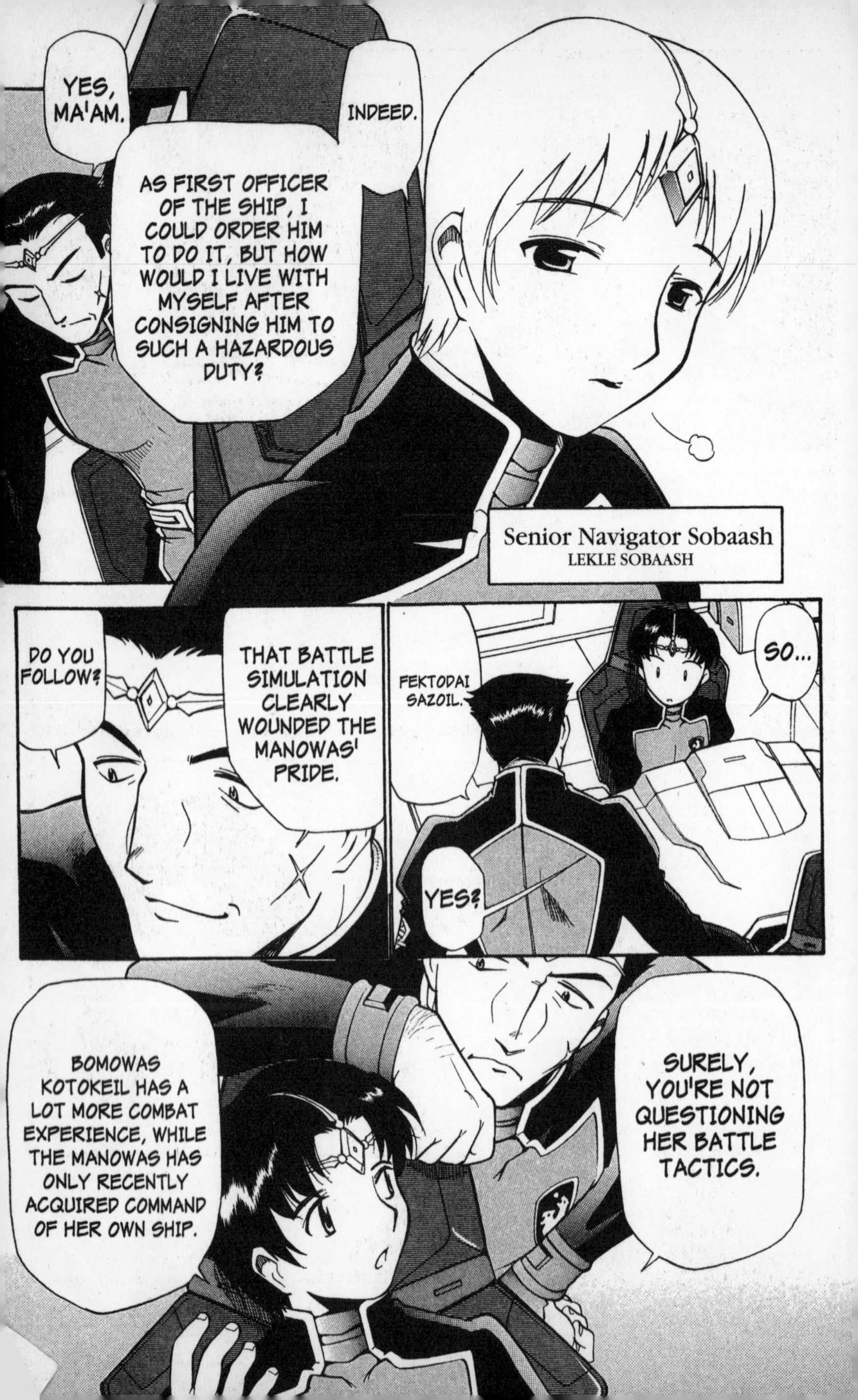
INDEED.
YES, MA'AM.
AS FIRST OFFICER OF THE SHIP, I COULD ORDER HIM TO DO IT, BUT HOW WOULD I LIVE WITH MYSELF AFTER CONSIGNING HIM TO SUCH A HAZARDOUS DUTY?
Senior Navigator Sobaash
LEKLE SOBAASH
SO...
FEKTODAI SAZOIL.
YES?
THAT BATTLE SIMULATION CLEARLY WOUNDED THE MANOWAS' PRIDE.
DO YOU FOLLOW?
SURELY, YOU'RE NOT QUESTIONING HER BATTLE TACTICS.
BOMOWAS KOTOKEIL HAS A LOT MORE COMBAT EXPERIENCE, WHILE THE MANOWAS HAS ONLY RECENTLY ACQUIRED COMMAND OF HER OWN SHIP.

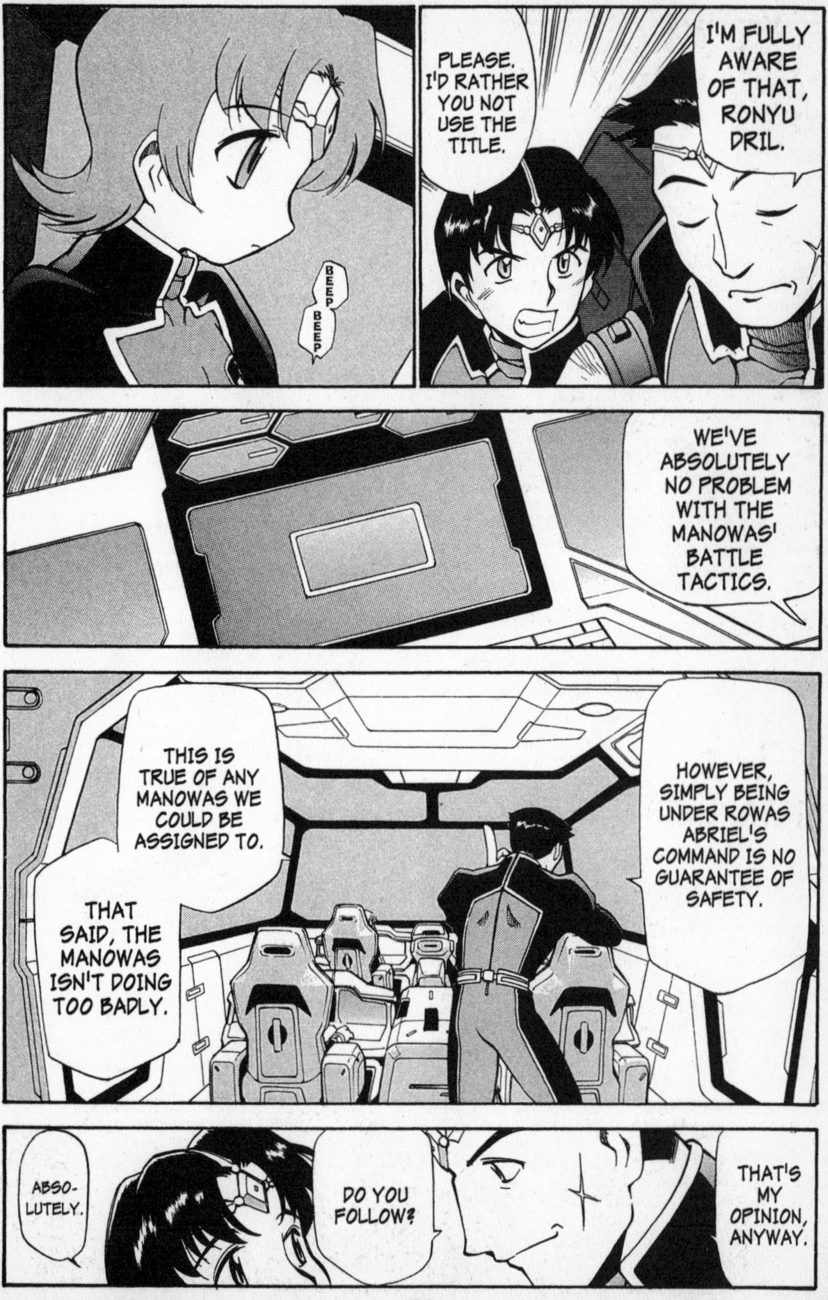
I'M FULLY AWARE OF THAT, RONYU DRIL.
PLEASE. I'D RATHER YOU NOT USE THE TITLE.
BEEP BEEP
WE'VE ABSOLUTELY NO PROBLEM WITH THE MANOWAS' BATTLE TACTICS.
HOWEVER, SIMPLY BEING UNDER ROWAS ABRIEL'S COMMAND IS NO GUARANTEE OF SAFETY.
THIS IS TRUE OF ANY MANOWAS WE COULD BE ASSIGNED TO.
THAT SAID, THE MANOWAS ISN'T DOING TOO BADLY.
THAT'S MY OPINION, ANYWAY.
DO YOU FOLLOW?
ABSO-LUTELY.

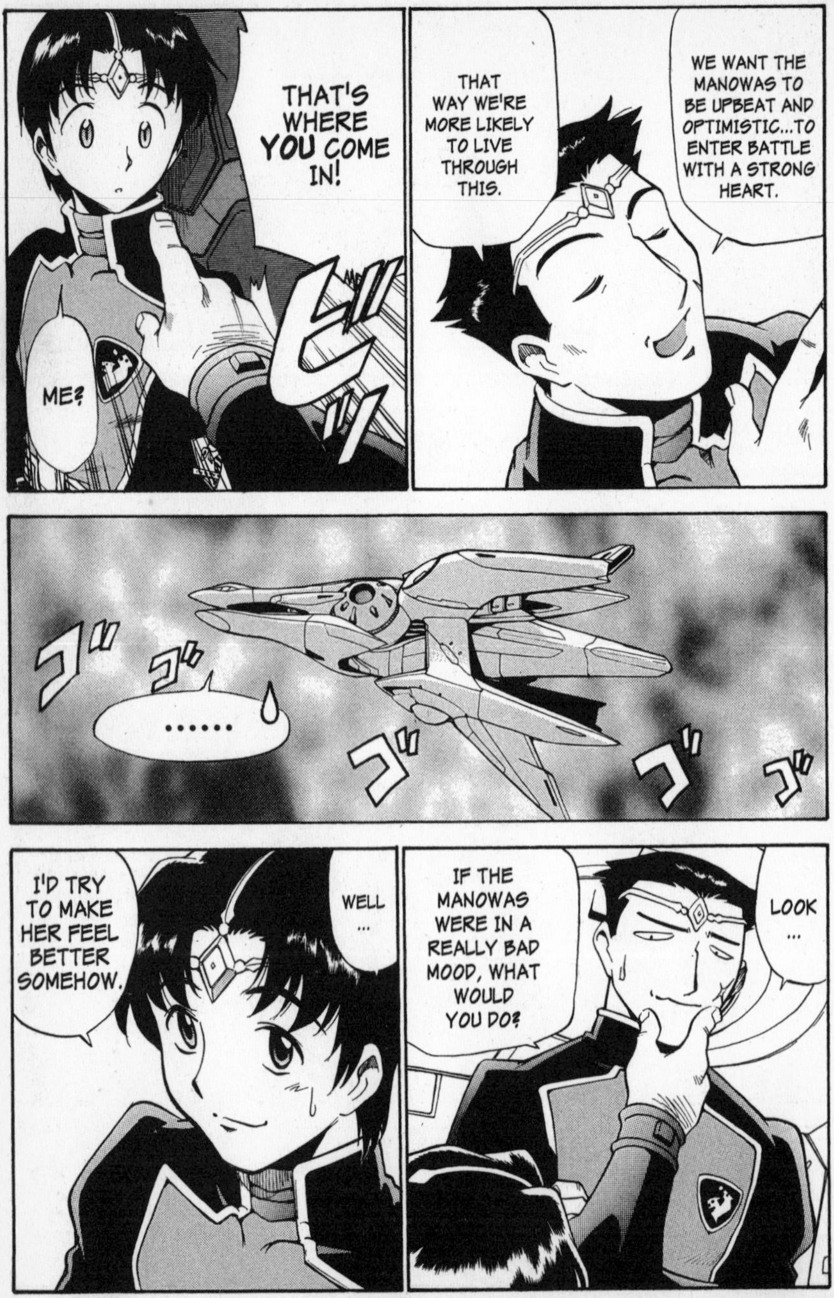
WE WANT THE MANOWAS TO BE UPBEAT AND OPTIMISTIC...TO ENTER BATTLE WITH A STRONG HEART.
THAT WAY WE'RE MORE LIKELY TO LIVE THROUGH THIS.
THAT'S WHERE YOU COME IN!
ME?
......
LOOK ...
IF THE MANOWAS WERE IN A REALLY BAD MOOD, WHAT WOULD YOU DO?
WELL ...
I'D TRY TO MAKE HER FEEL BETTER SOMEHOW.

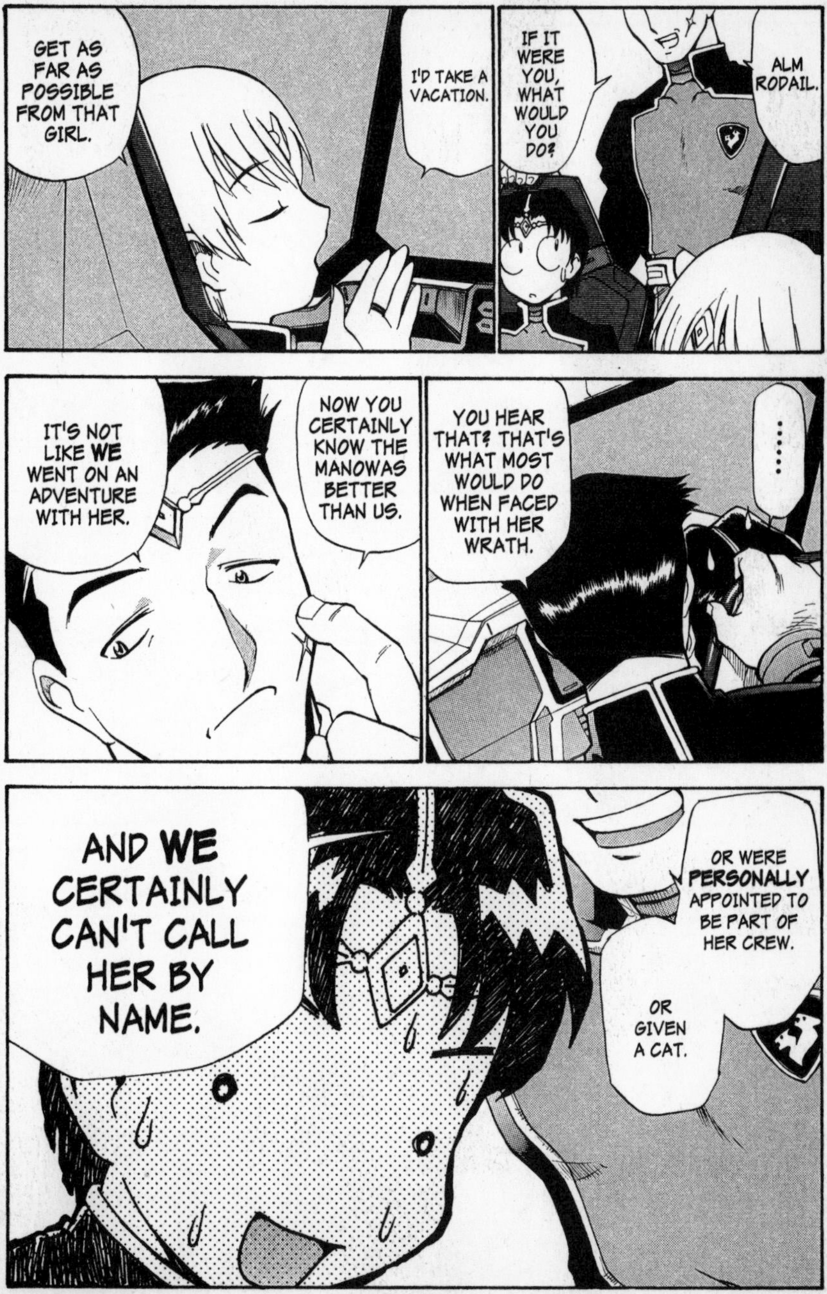
ALM RODAIL.
IF IT WERE YOU, WHAT WOULD YOU DO?
I'D TAKE A VACATION.
GET AS FAR AS POSSIBLE FROM THAT GIRL.
......
YOU HEAR THAT? THAT'S WHAT MOST WOULD DO WHEN FACED WITH HER WRATH.
NOW YOU CERTAINLY KNOW THE MANOWAS BETTER THAN US.
IT'S NOT LIKE WE WENT ON AN ADVENTURE WITH HER.
OR WERE PERSONALLY APPOINTED TO BE PART OF HER CREW.
OR GIVEN A CAT.
AND WE CERTAINLY CAN'T CALL HER BY NAME.

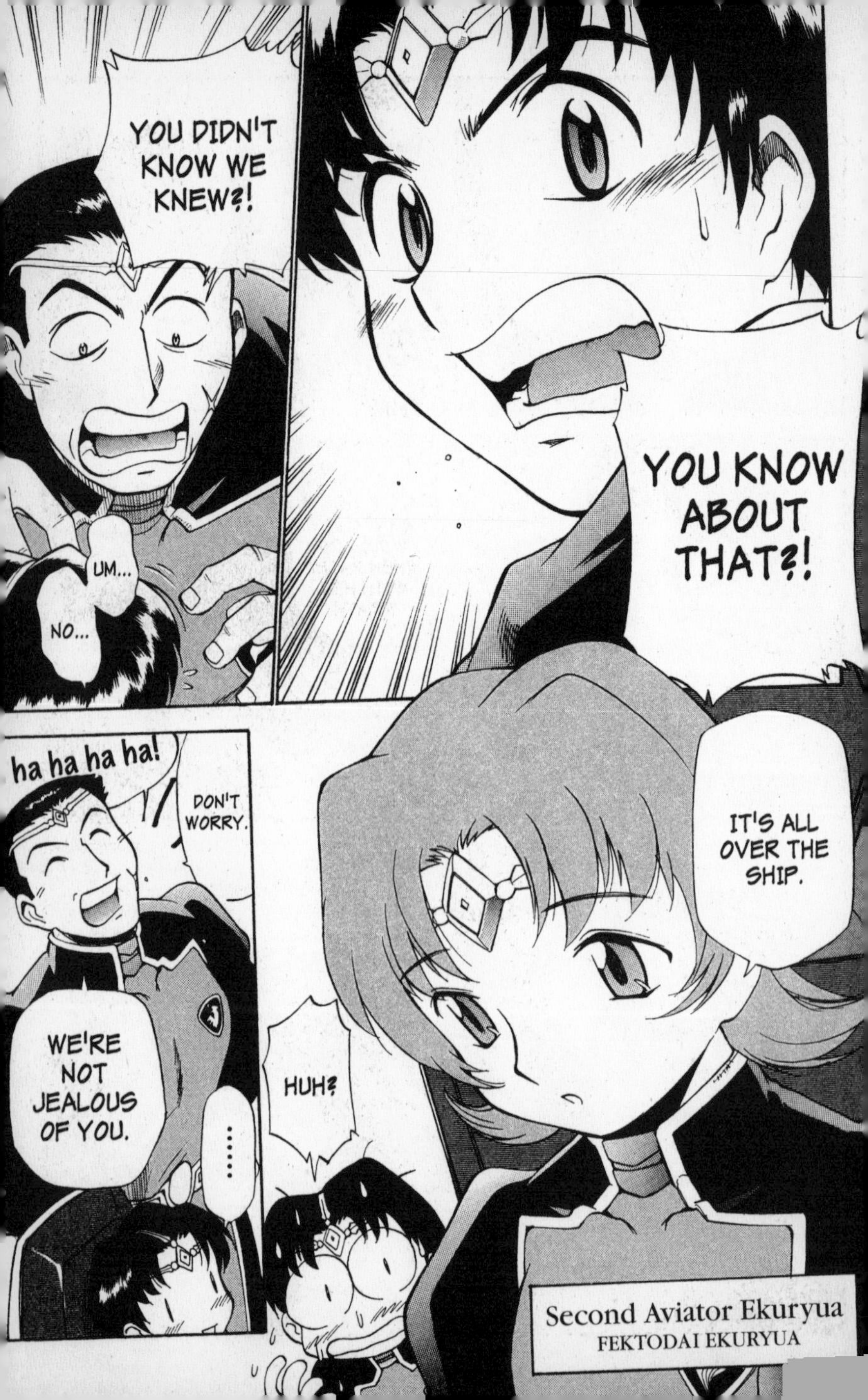
YOU KNOW ABOUT THAT?!
YOU DIDN'T KNOW WE KNEW?!
UM...
NO...
IT'S ALL OVER THE SHIP.
HUH?
Second Aviator Ekuryua
FEKTODAI EKURYUA
ha ha ha ha!
DON'T WORRY.
WE'RE NOT JEALOUS OF YOU.
......

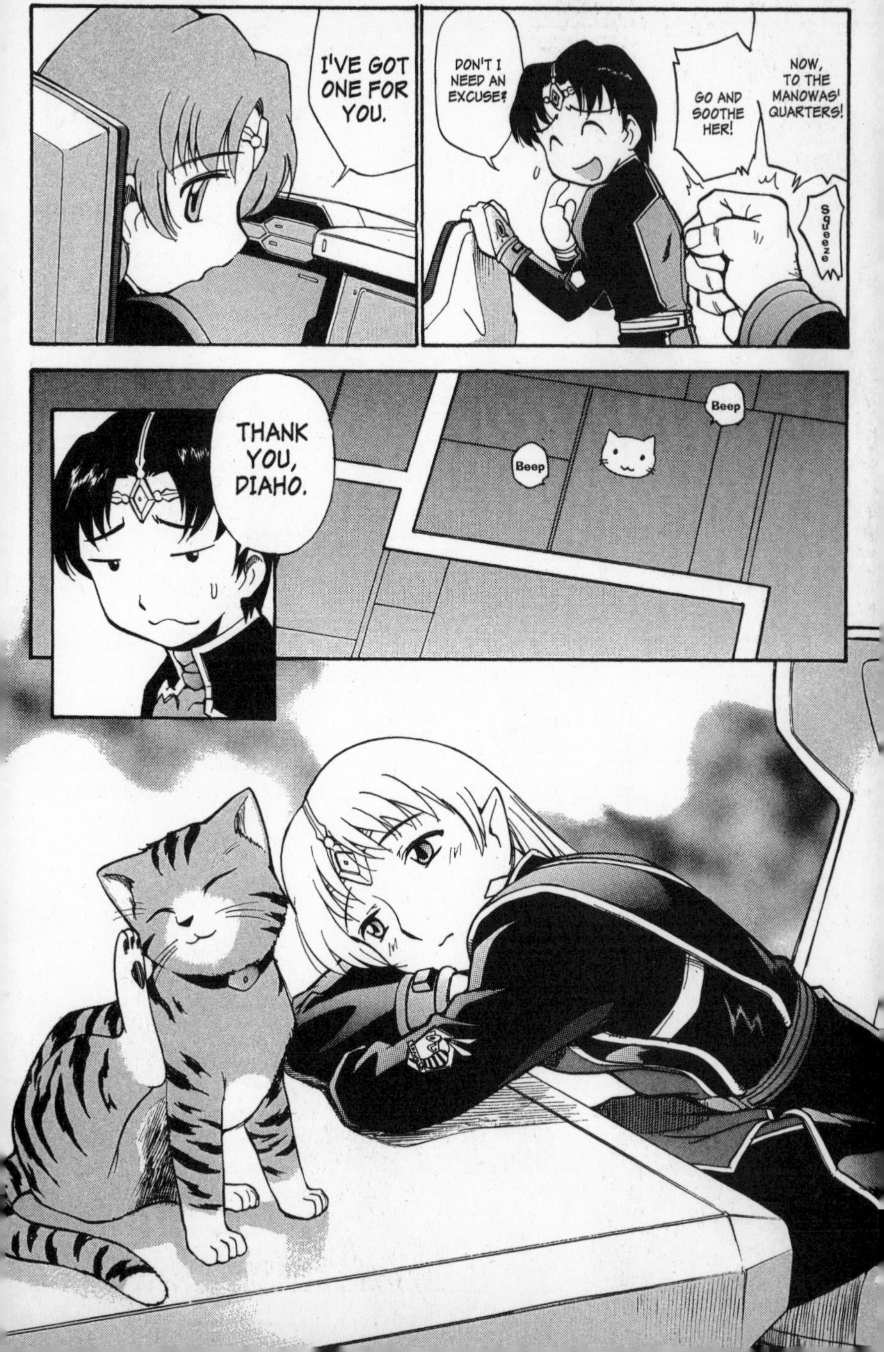
NOW, TO THE MANOWAS' QUARTERS!
GO AND SOOTHE HER!
Squeeze
DON'T I NEED AN EXCUSE?
I'VE GOT ONE FOR YOU.
Beep
Beep
THANK YOU, DIAHO.

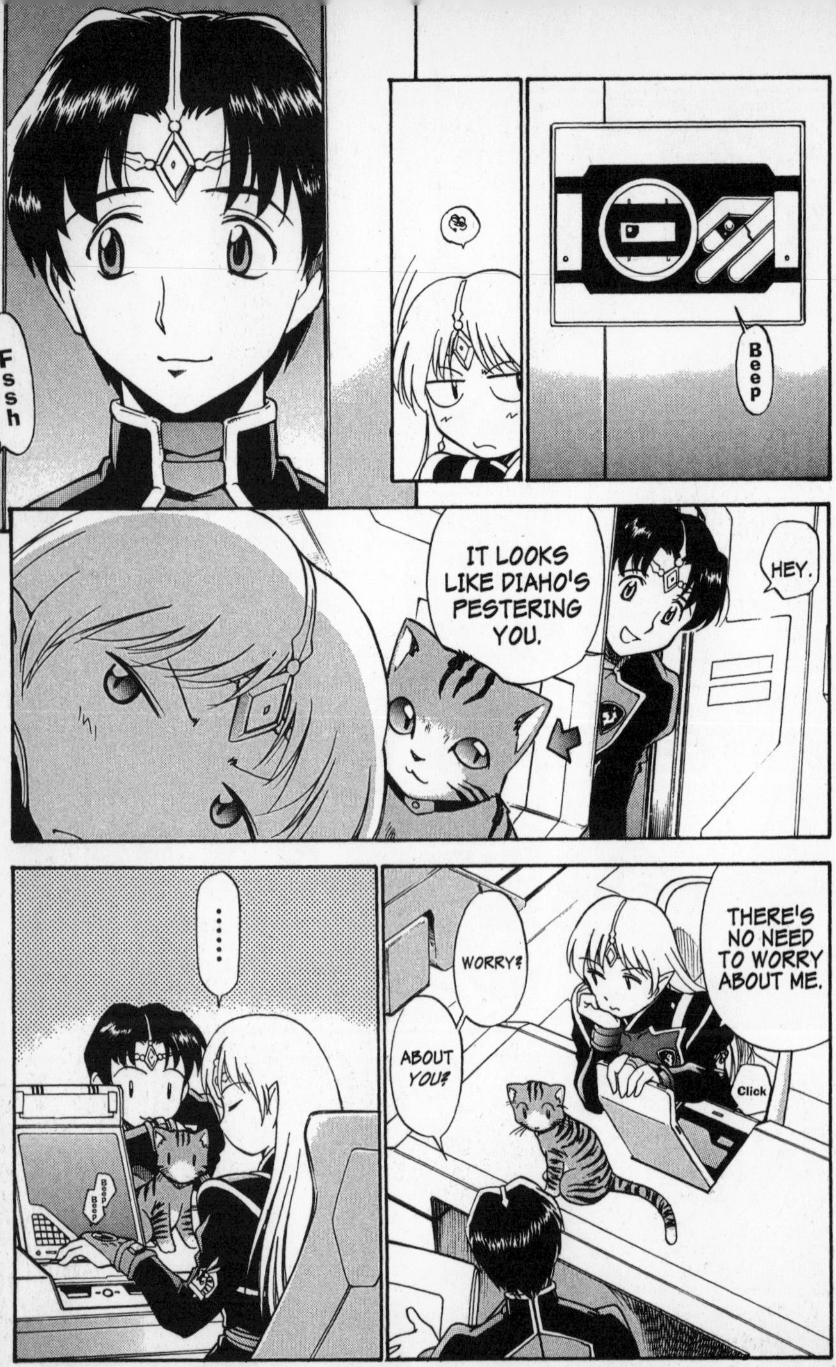
Beep
Fssh
HEY.
IT LOOKS LIKE DIAHO'S PESTERING YOU.
THERE'S NO NEED TO WORRY ABOUT ME.
Click
WORRY?
ABOUT YOU?
......
Beep Beep

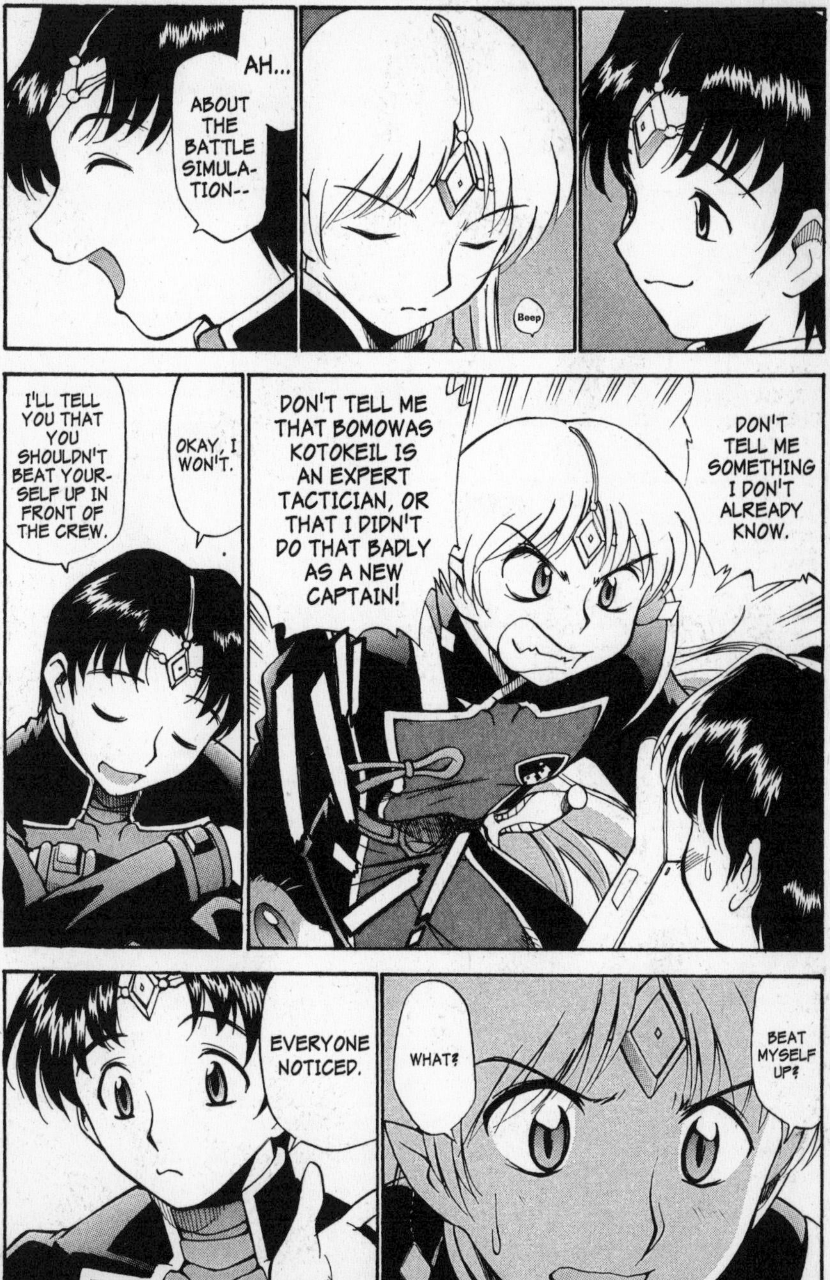
Beep
AH...
ABOUT THE BATTLE SIMULATION--
DON'T TELL ME SOMETHING I DON'T ALREADY KNOW.
DON'T TELL ME THAT BOMOWAS KOTOKEIL IS AN EXPERT TACTICIAN, OR THAT I DIDN'T DO THAT BADLY AS A NEW CAPTAIN!
OKAY, I WON'T.
I'LL TELL YOU THAT YOU SHOULDN'T BEAT YOURSELF UP IN FRONT OF THE CREW.
BEAT MYSELF UP?
WHAT?
EVERYONE NOTICED.

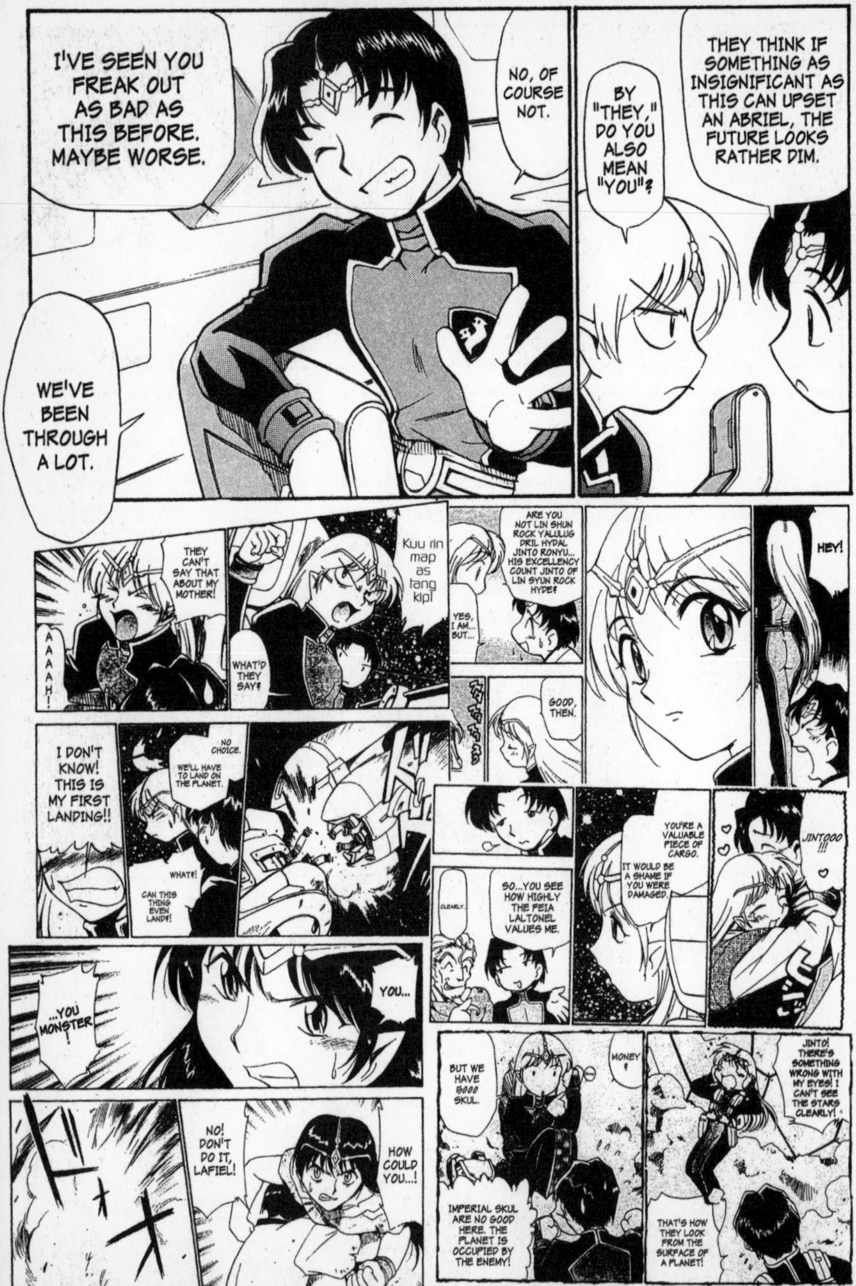
THEY THINK IF SOMETHING AS INSIGNIFICANT AS THIS CAN UPSET AN ABRIEL, THE FUTURE LOOKS RATHER DIM.
BY "THEY," DO YOU ALSO MEAN "YOU"?
NO, OF COURSE NOT.
I'VE SEEN YOU FREAK OUT AS BAD AS THIS BEFORE. MAYBE WORSE.
WE'VE BEEN THROUGH A LOT.
HEY!
ARE YOU NOT LIN SHUN ROCK YALULUG DRIL HYDAL JINTO RONYU... HIS EXCELLENCY COUNT JINTO OF LIN SYUN ROCK HYDE?
YES, I AM... BUT...
GOOD, THEN.
Kuu rin map as tang kip!
WHAT'D THEY SAY?
THEY CAN'T SAY THAT ABOUT MY MOTHER!
AAAAAH!
NO CHOICE.
WE'LL HAVE TO LAND ON THE PLANET.
WHAT?!
CAN THIS THING EVEN LAND?!
I DON'T KNOW! THIS IS MY FIRST LANDING!!
JINTOOO!!!
YOU'RE A VALUABLE PIECE OF CARGO.
IT WOULD BE A SHAME IF YOU WERE DAMAGED.
SO...YOU SEE HOW HIGHLY THE FEIA LALTONEL VALUES ME.
CLEARLY.
YOU...
...YOU MONSTER!
JINTO! THERE'S SOMETHING WRONG WITH MY EYES! I CAN'T SEE THE STARS CLEARLY!
THAT'S HOW THEY LOOK FROM THE SURFACE OF A PLANET!
MONEY?
BUT WE HAVE 5000 SKUL.
IMPERIAL SKUL ARE NO GOOD HERE. THE PLANET IS OCCUPIED BY THE ENEMY!
HOW COULD YOU...!
NO! DON'T DO IT, LAFIEL!

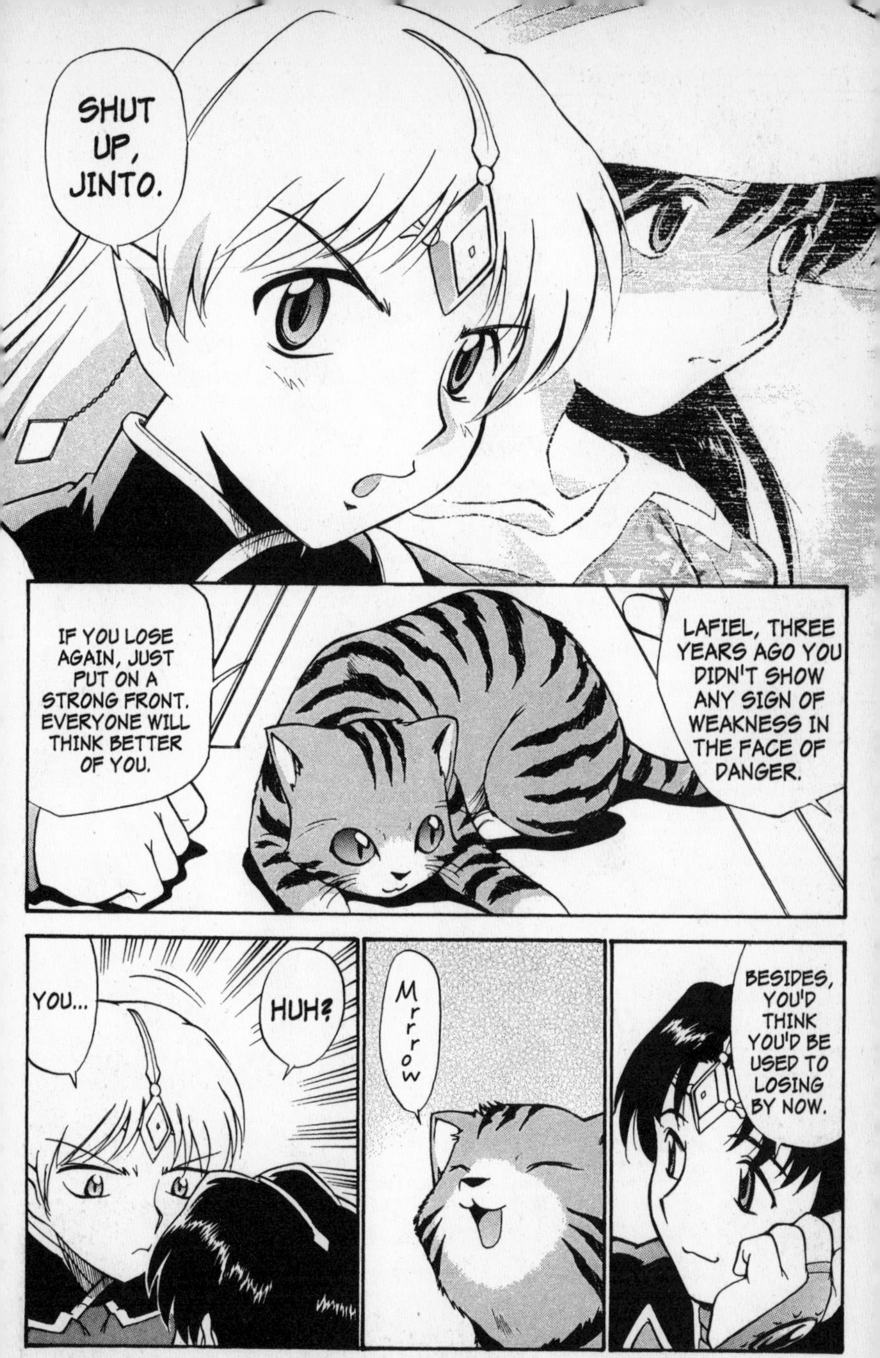
SHUT UP, JINTO.
LAFIEL, THREE YEARS AGO YOU DIDN'T SHOW ANY SIGN OF WEAKNESS IN THE FACE OF DANGER.
IF YOU LOSE AGAIN, JUST PUT ON A STRONG FRONT. EVERYONE WILL THINK BETTER OF YOU.
BESIDES, YOU'D THINK YOU'D BE USED TO LOSING BY NOW.
Mrrrow
HUH?
YOU...

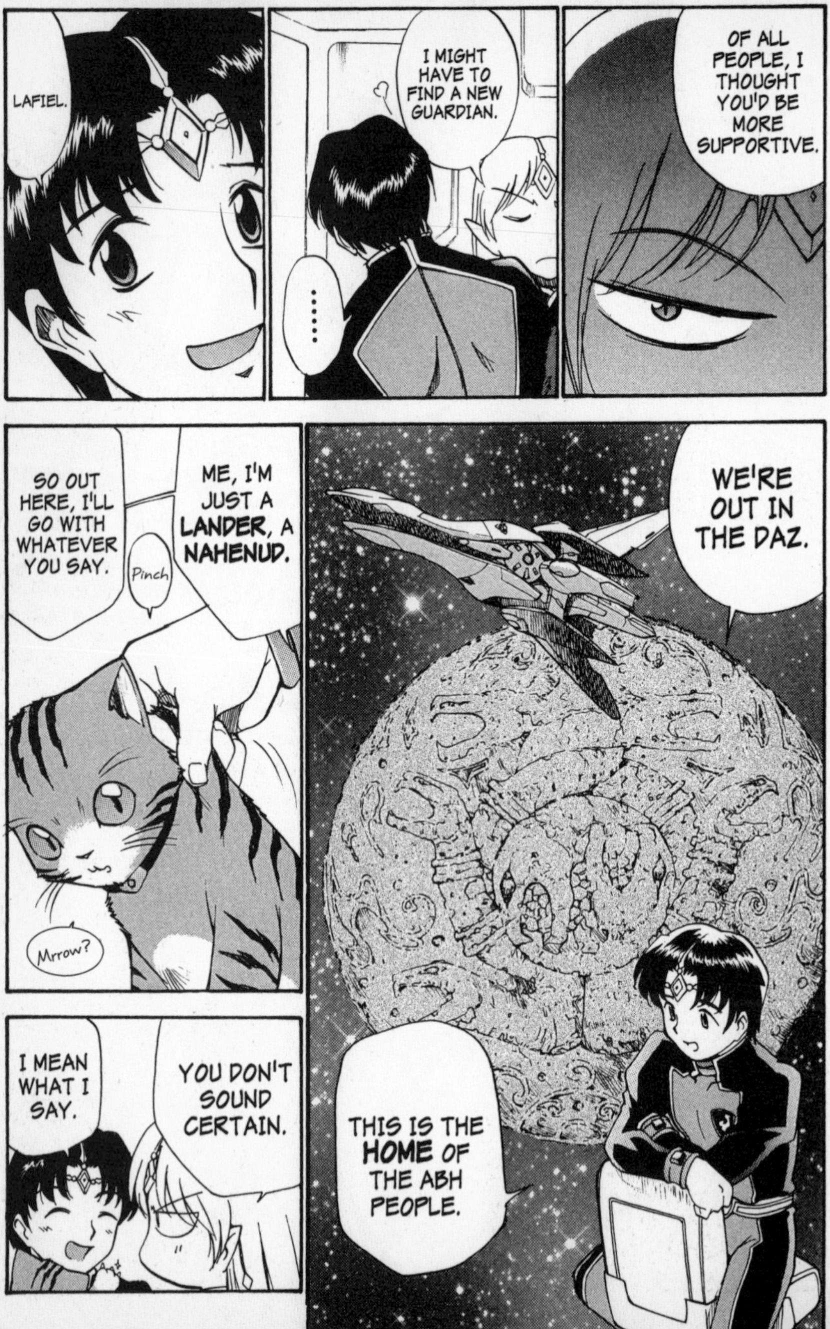
OF ALL PEOPLE, I THOUGHT YOU'D BE MORE SUPPORTIVE.
I MIGHT HAVE TO FIND A NEW GUARDIAN.
......
LAFIEL.
WE'RE OUT IN THE DAZ.
THIS IS THE **HOME** OF THE ABH PEOPLE.
ME, I'M JUST A **LANDER**, A **NAHENUD.**
Pinch
SO OUT HERE, I'LL GO WITH WHATEVER YOU SAY.
Mrrow?
YOU DON'T SOUND CERTAIN.
I MEAN WHAT I SAY.

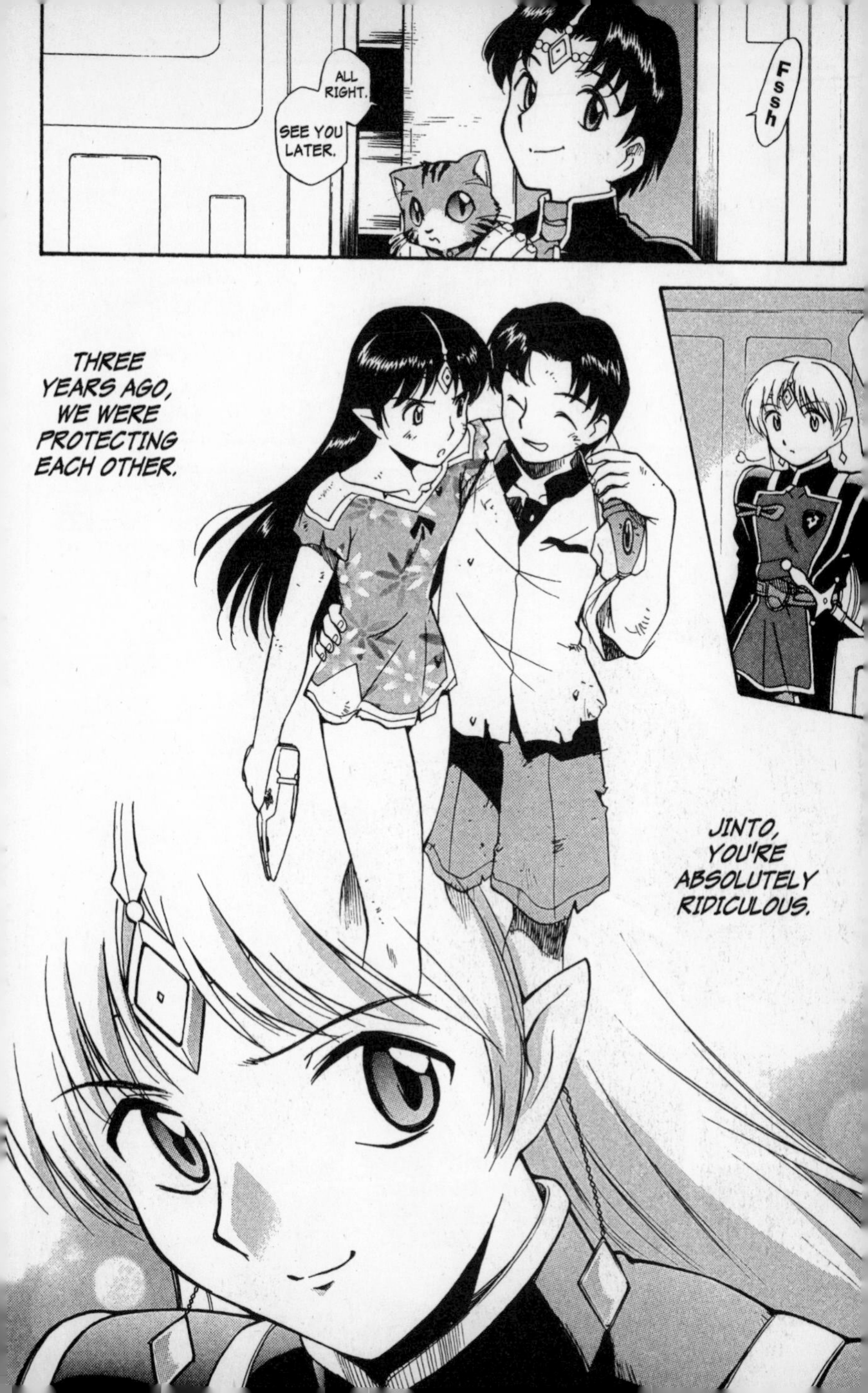
Fssh
ALL RIGHT.
SEE YOU LATER.
JINTO, YOU'RE ABSOLUTELY RIDICULOUS.
THREE YEARS AGO, WE WERE PROTECTING EACH OTHER.

Chapter 2
Operation Phantom Flame

KUFAZET LENJV

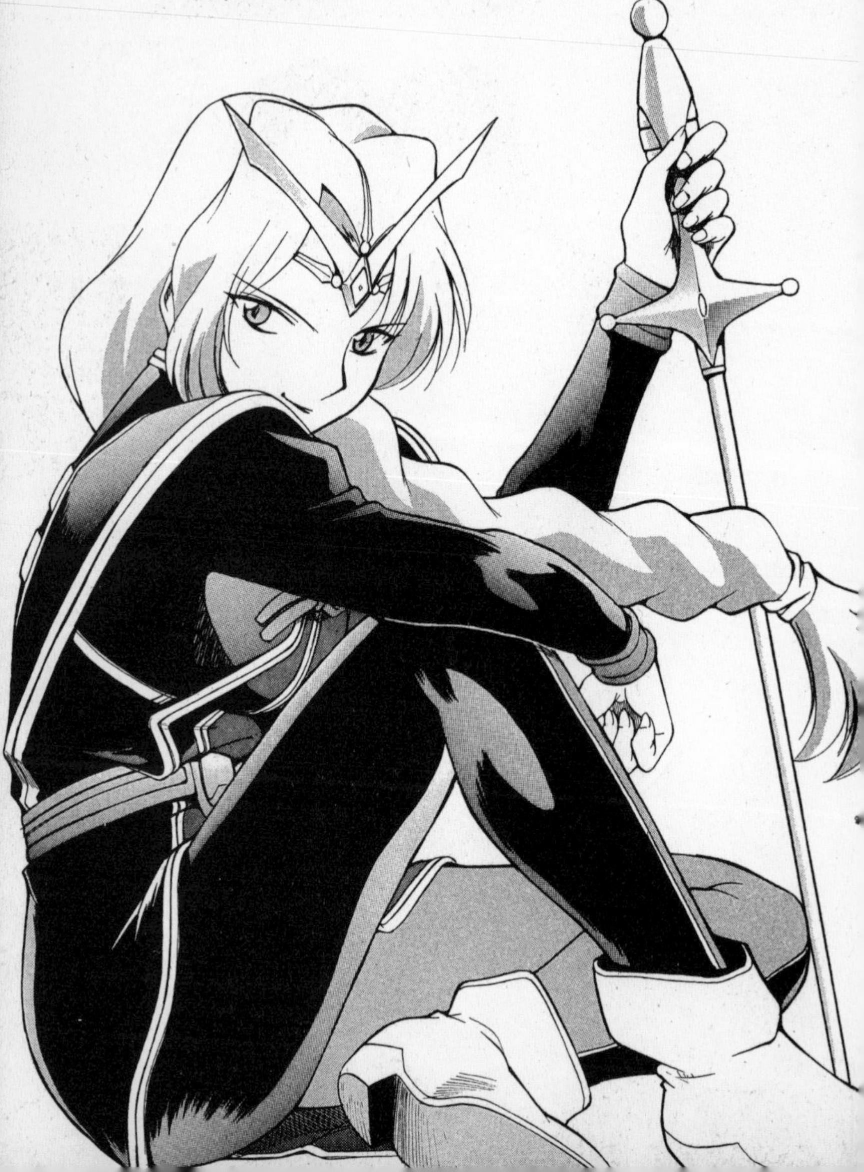

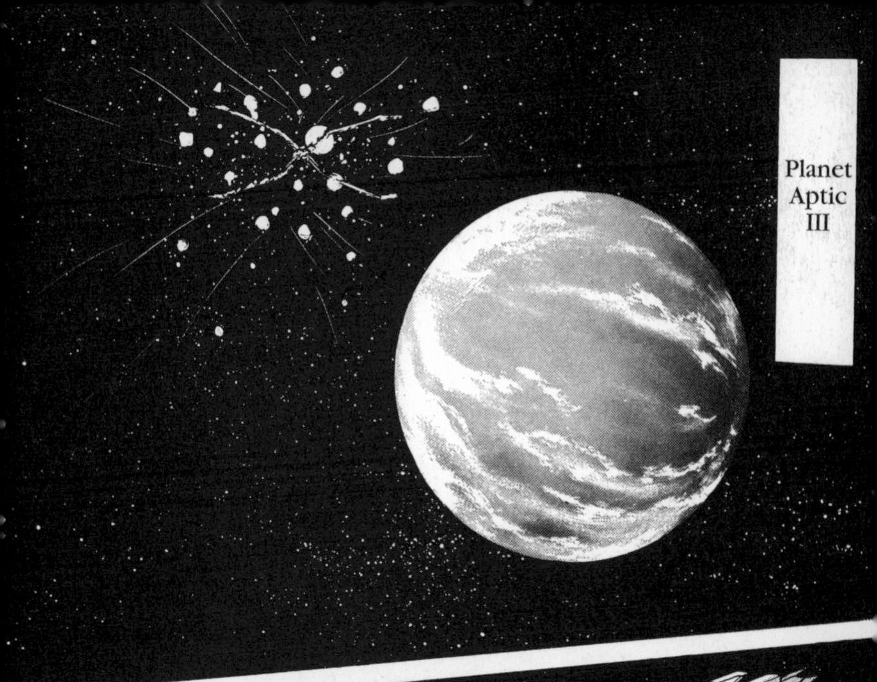
Planet
Aptic
III

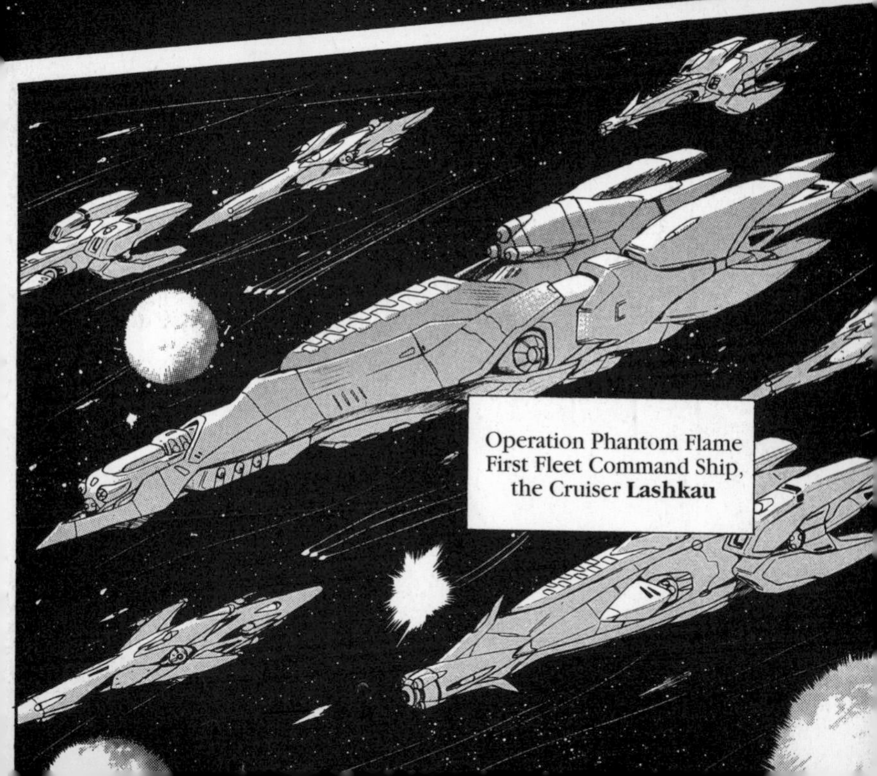
Operation Phantom Flame
First Fleet Command Ship,
the Cruiser **Lashkau**

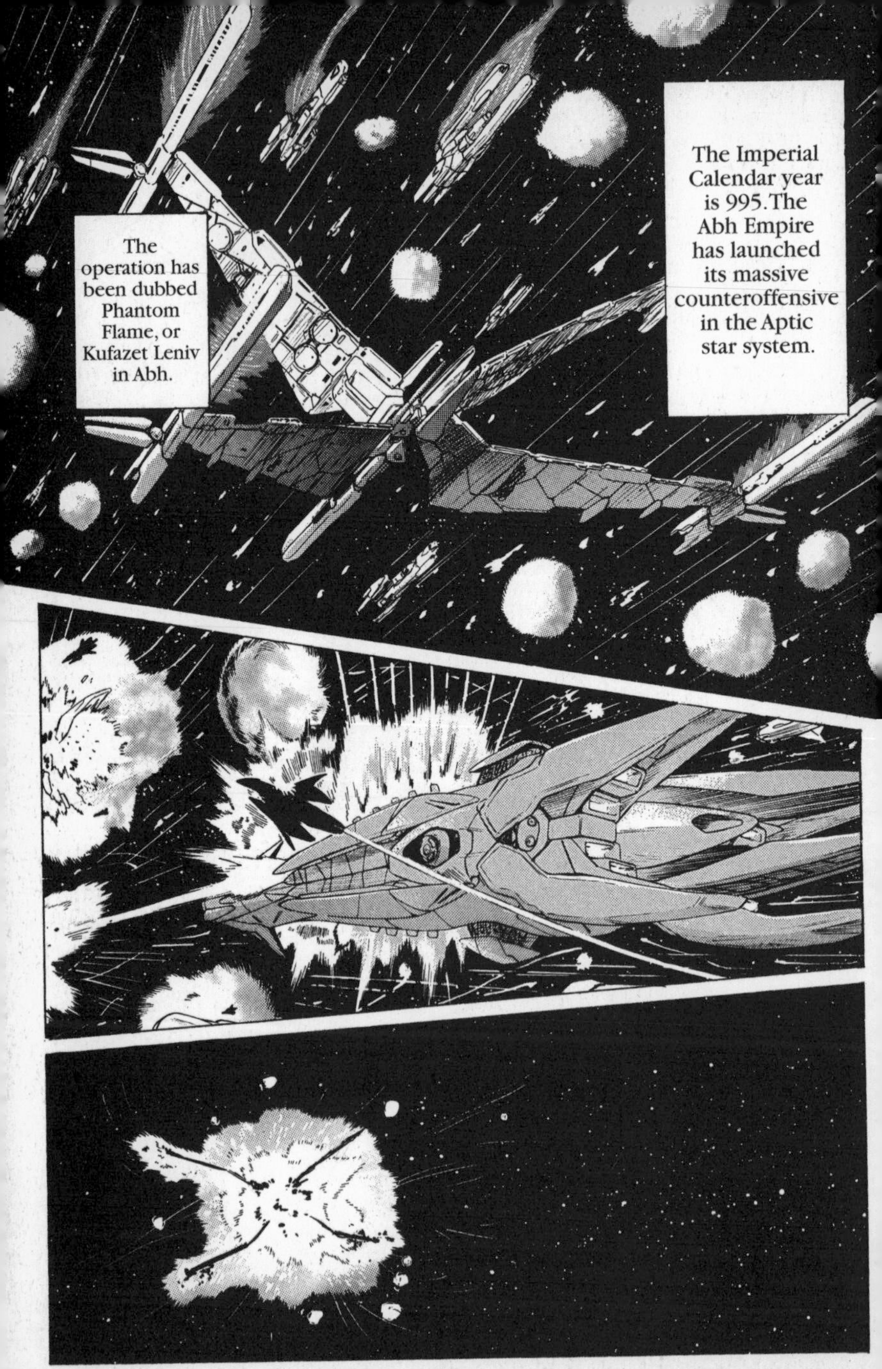
The Imperial Calendar year is 995. The Abh Empire has launched its massive counteroffensive in the Aptic star system.
The operation has been dubbed Phantom Flame, or Kufazet Leniv in Abh.

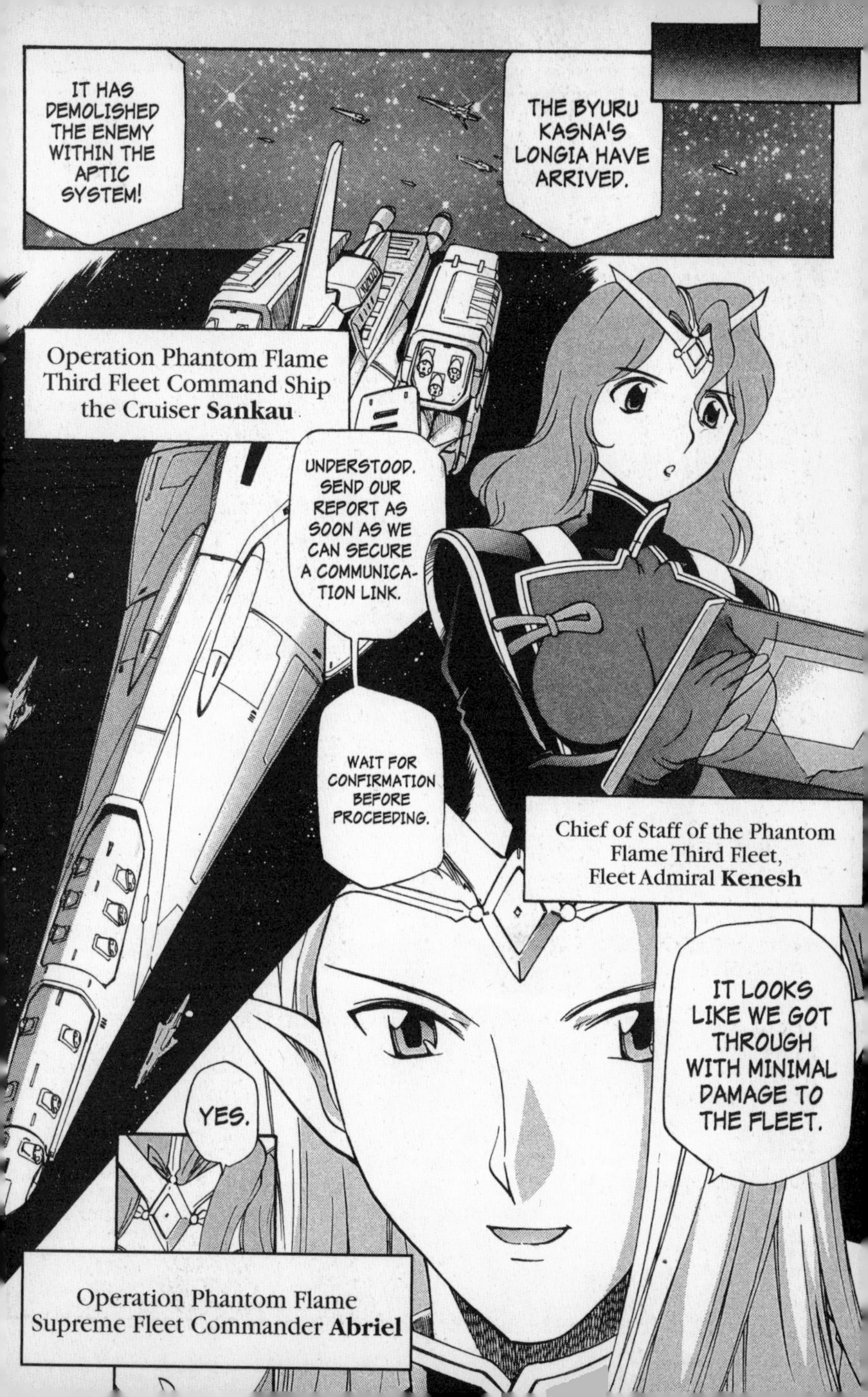
THE BYURU KASNA'S LONGIA HAVE ARRIVED.
IT HAS DEMOLISHED THE ENEMY WITHIN THE APTIC SYSTEM!
Operation Phantom Flame Third Fleet Command Ship the Cruiser **Sankau**
UNDERSTOOD. SEND OUR REPORT AS SOON AS WE CAN SECURE A COMMUNICATION LINK.
WAIT FOR CONFIRMATION BEFORE PROCEEDING.
Chief of Staff of the Phantom Flame Third Fleet, Fleet Admiral **Kenesh**
IT LOOKS LIKE WE GOT THROUGH WITH MINIMAL DAMAGE TO THE FLEET.
YES.
Operation Phantom Flame Supreme Fleet Commander **Abriel**

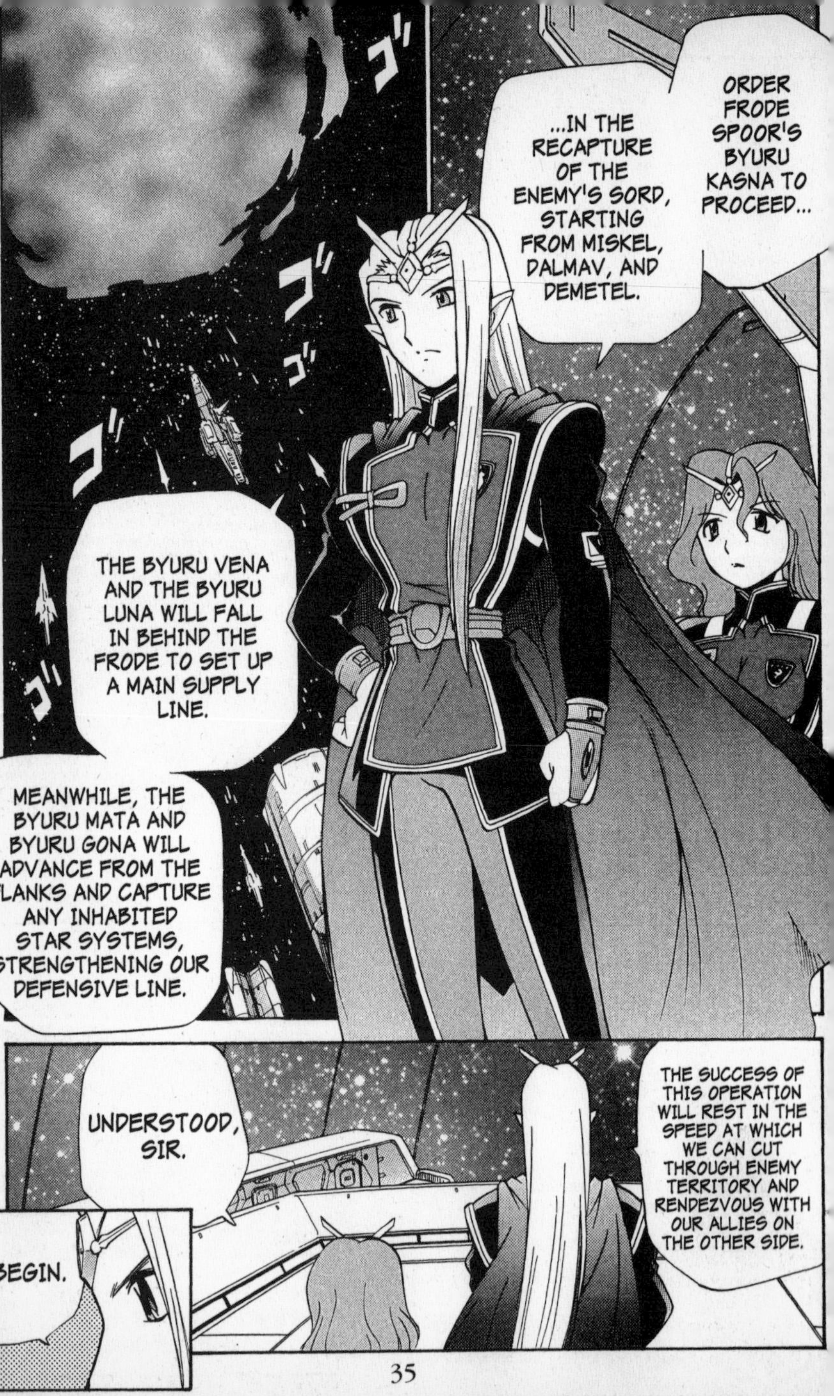
ORDER FRODE SPOOR'S BYURU KASNA TO PROCEED...
...IN THE RECAPTURE OF THE ENEMY'S SORD, STARTING FROM MISKEL, DALMAV, AND DEMETEL.
THE BYURU VENA AND THE BYURU LUNA WILL FALL IN BEHIND THE FRODE TO SET UP A MAIN SUPPLY LINE.
MEANWHILE, THE BYURU MATA AND BYURU GONA WILL ADVANCE FROM THE FLANKS AND CAPTURE ANY INHABITED STAR SYSTEMS, STRENGTHENING OUR DEFENSIVE LINE.
THE SUCCESS OF THIS OPERATION WILL REST IN THE SPEED AT WHICH WE CAN CUT THROUGH ENEMY TERRITORY AND RENDEZVOUS WITH OUR ALLIES ON THE OTHER SIDE.
UNDERSTOOD, SIR.
BEGIN.

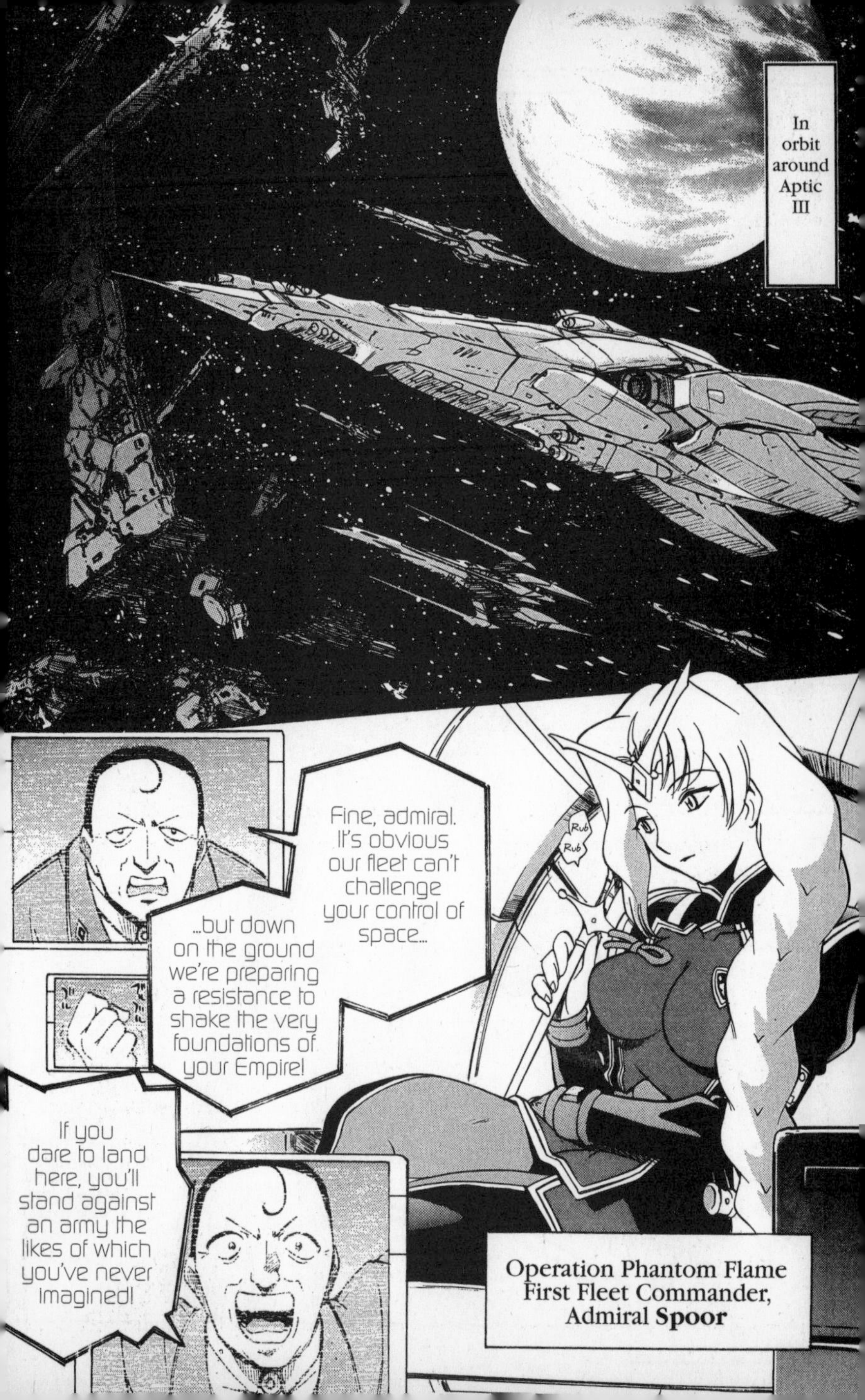
In orbit around Aptic III
Rub Rub
Operation Phantom Flame First Fleet Commander, Admiral Spoor
Fine, admiral. It's obvious our fleet can't challenge your control of space...
...but down on the ground we're preparing a resistance to shake the very foundations of your Empire!
If you dare to land here, you'll stand against an army the likes of which you've never imagined!

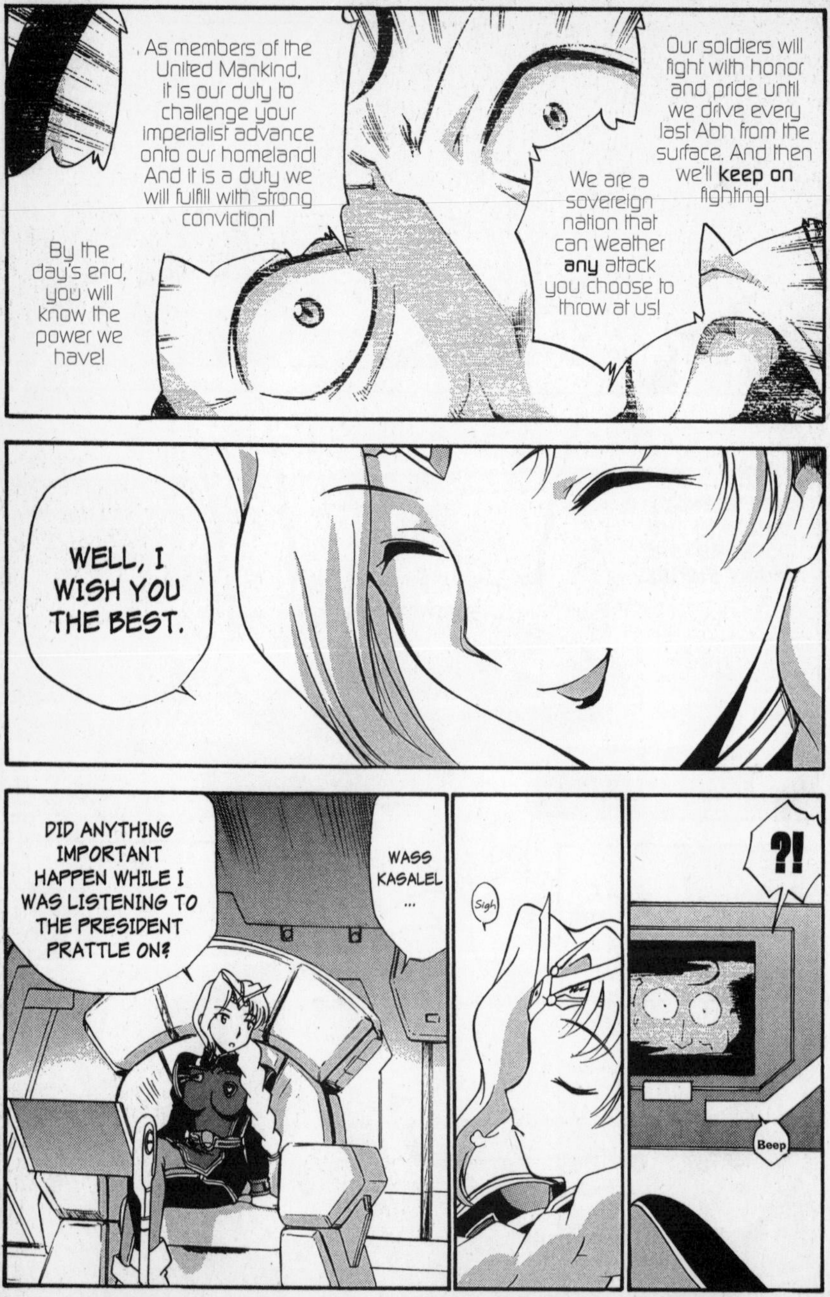
Our soldiers will fight with honor and pride until we drive every last Abh from the surface. And then we'll **keep on** fighting!
We are a sovereign nation that can weather **any** attack you choose to throw at us!
As members of the United Mankind, it is our duty to challenge your imperialist advance onto our homeland! And it is a duty we will fulfill with strong conviction!
By the day's end, you will know the power we have!
WELL, I WISH YOU THE BEST.
?!
Beep
Sigh
WASS KASALEL ...
DID ANYTHING IMPORTANT HAPPEN WHILE I WAS LISTENING TO THE PRESIDENT PRATTLE ON?

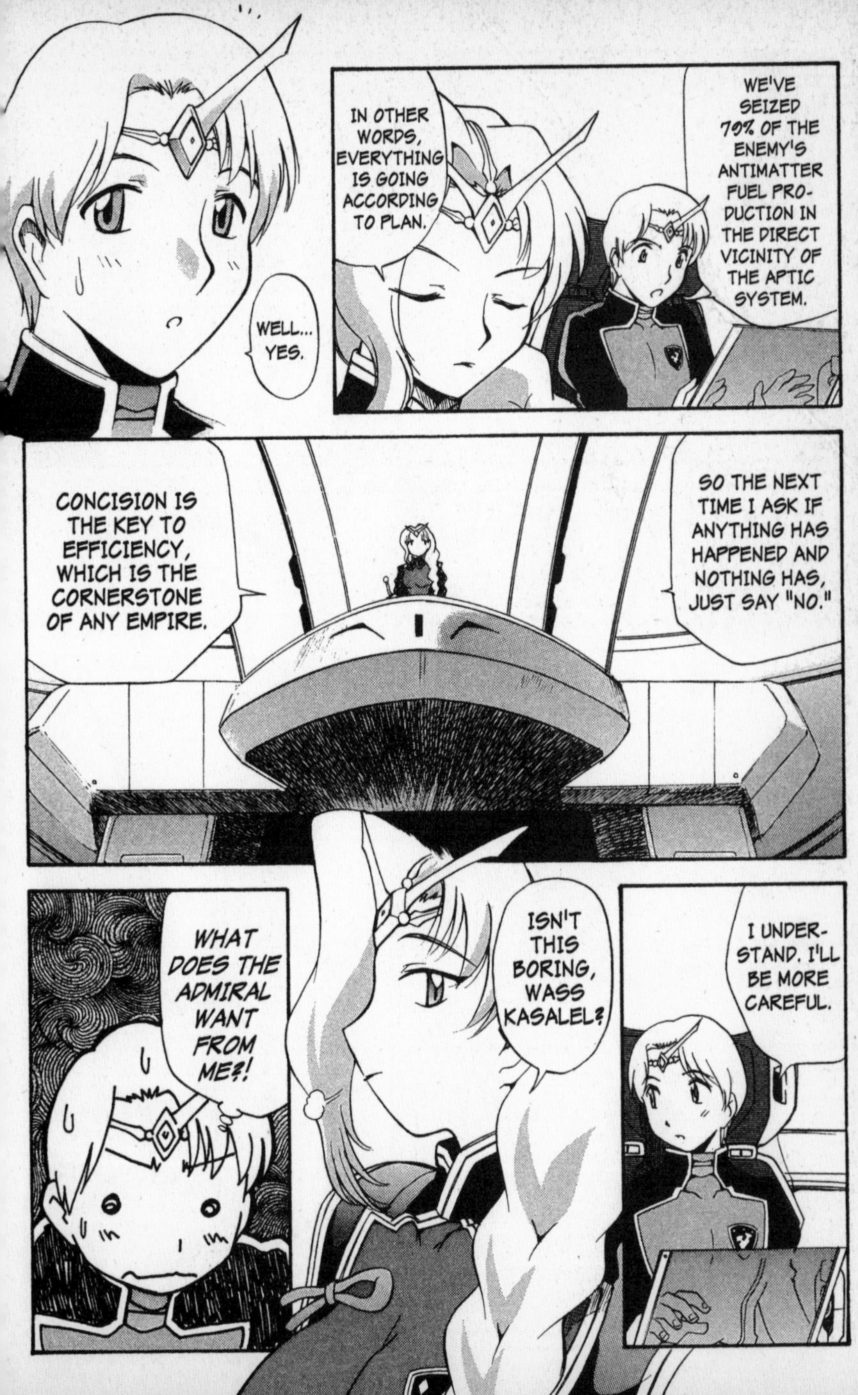
WE'VE SEIZED 70% OF THE ENEMY'S ANTIMATTER FUEL PRODUCTION IN THE DIRECT VICINITY OF THE APTIC SYSTEM.
IN OTHER WORDS, EVERYTHING IS GOING ACCORDING TO PLAN.
WELL... YES.
SO THE NEXT TIME I ASK IF ANYTHING HAS HAPPENED AND NOTHING HAS, JUST SAY "NO."
CONCISION IS THE KEY TO EFFICIENCY, WHICH IS THE CORNERSTONE OF ANY EMPIRE.
I UNDERSTAND. I'LL BE MORE CAREFUL.
ISN'T THIS BORING, WASS KASALEL?
WHAT DOES THE ADMIRAL WANT FROM ME?!

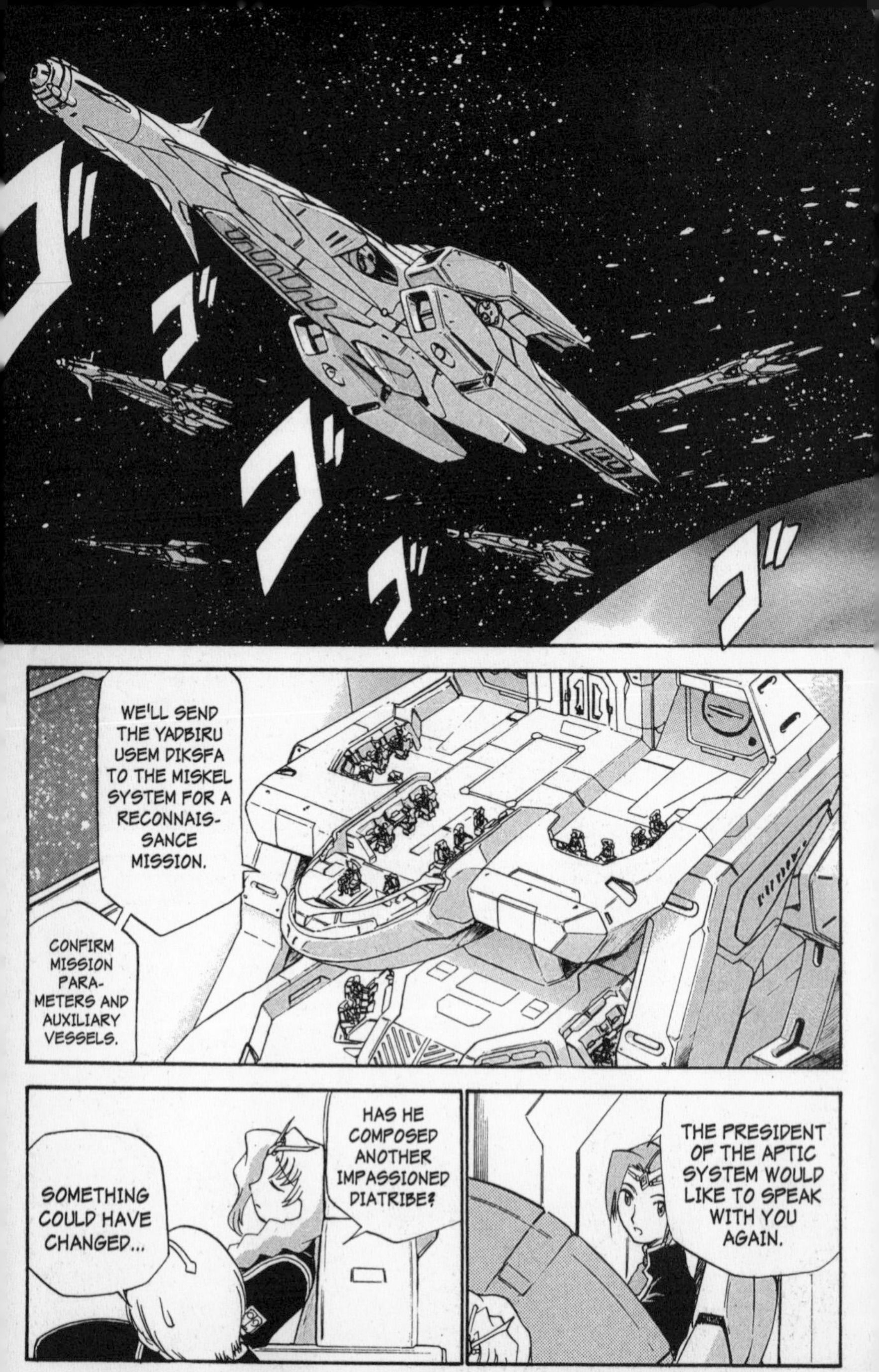
ゴゴゴゴゴ
WE'LL SEND THE YADBIRU USEM DIKSFA TO THE MISKEL SYSTEM FOR A RECONNAIS-SANCE MISSION.
CONFIRM MISSION PARA-METERS AND AUXILIARY VESSELS.
THE PRESIDENT OF THE APTIC SYSTEM WOULD LIKE TO SPEAK WITH YOU AGAIN.
HAS HE COMPOSED ANOTHER IMPASSIONED DIATRIBE?
SOMETHING COULD HAVE CHANGED...

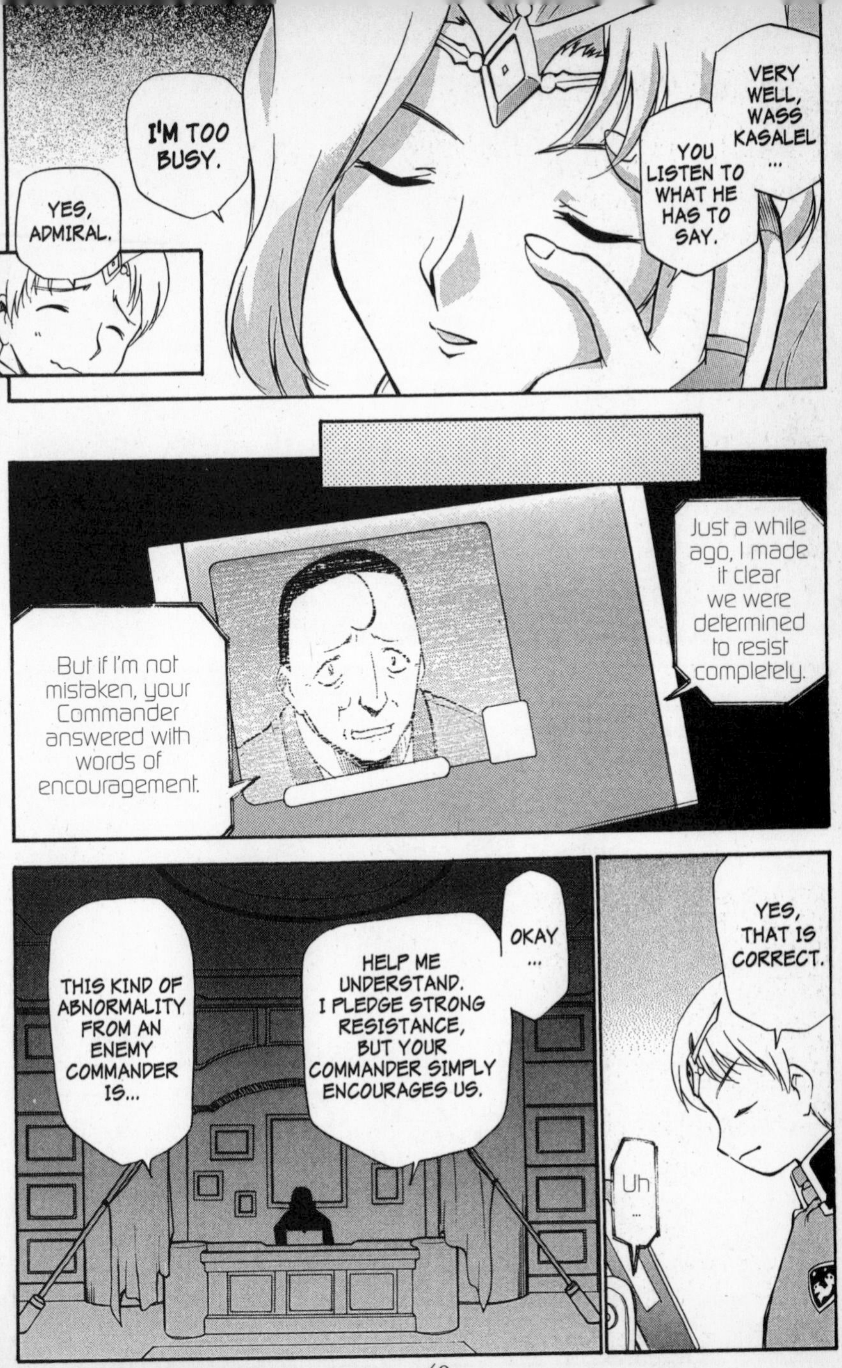
VERY WELL, WASS KASALEL ...
YOU LISTEN TO WHAT HE HAS TO SAY.
I'M TOO BUSY.
YES, ADMIRAL.
Just a while ago, I made it clear we were determined to resist completely.
But if I'm not mistaken, your Commander answered with words of encouragement.
YES, THAT IS CORRECT.
Uh ...
OKAY ...
HELP ME UNDERSTAND. I PLEDGE STRONG RESISTANCE, BUT YOUR COMMANDER SIMPLY ENCOURAGES US.
THIS KIND OF ABNORMALITY FROM AN ENEMY COMMANDER IS...

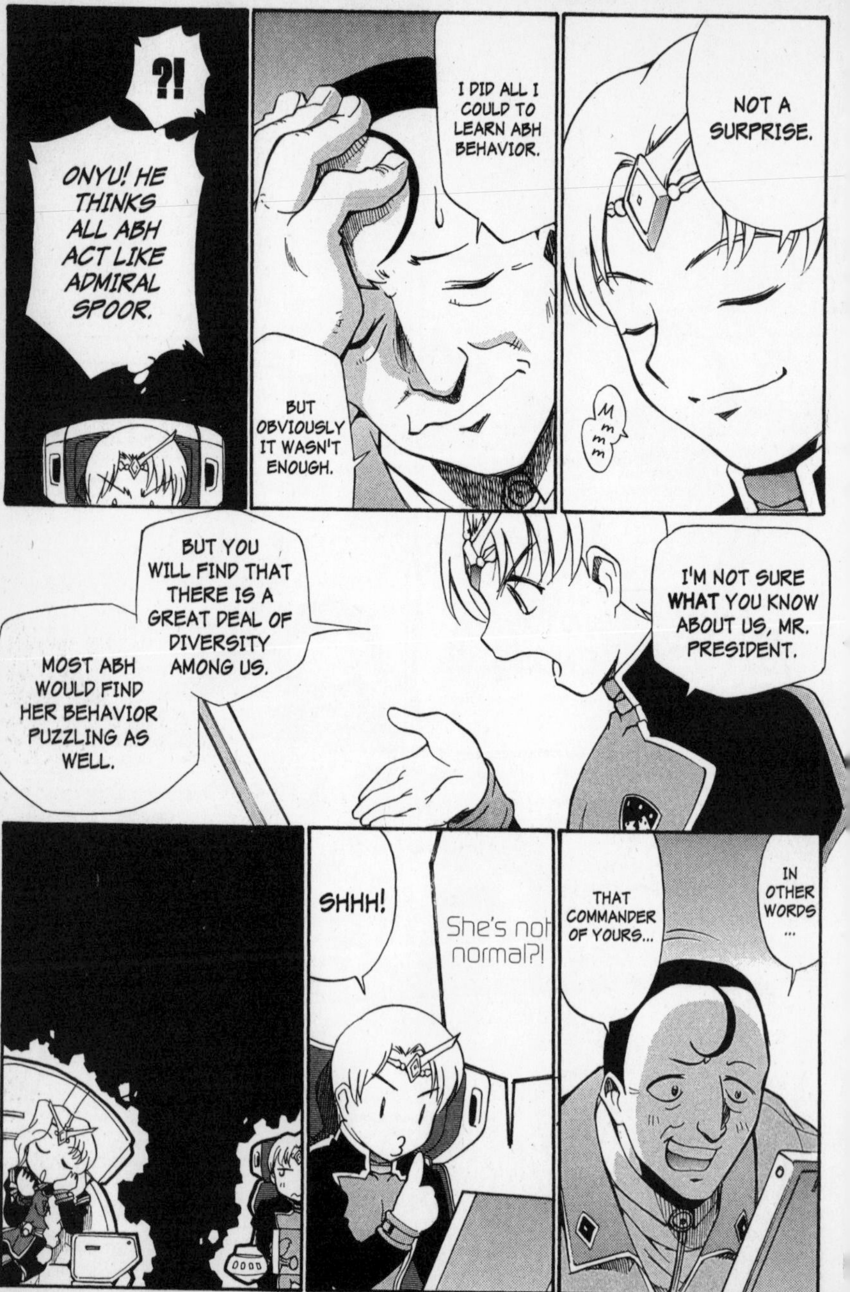
NOT A SURPRISE.
Mmmm
I DID ALL I COULD TO LEARN ABH BEHAVIOR.
BUT OBVIOUSLY IT WASN'T ENOUGH.
?!
ONYU! HE THINKS ALL ABH ACT LIKE ADMIRAL SPOOR.
I'M NOT SURE WHAT YOU KNOW ABOUT US, MR. PRESIDENT.
BUT YOU WILL FIND THAT THERE IS A GREAT DEAL OF DIVERSITY AMONG US.
MOST ABH WOULD FIND HER BEHAVIOR PUZZLING AS WELL.
IN OTHER WORDS...
THAT COMMANDER OF YOURS...
She's not normal?!
SHHH!

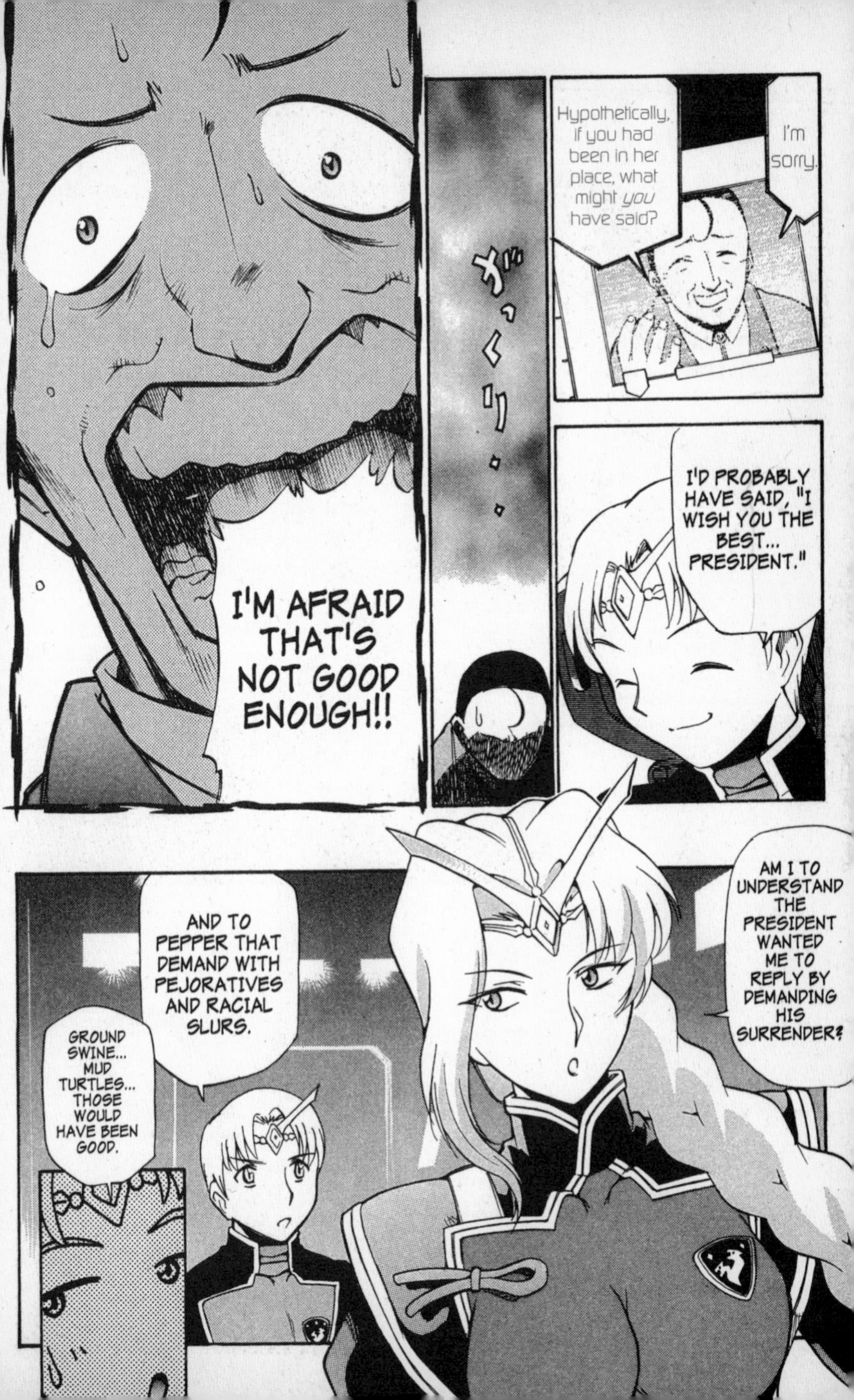
I'm sorry.
Hypothetically, if you had been in her place, what might *you* have said?
I'D PROBABLY HAVE SAID, "I WISH YOU THE BEST... PRESIDENT."
ぎっくり。。
I'M AFRAID THAT'S NOT GOOD ENOUGH!!
AM I TO UNDERSTAND THE PRESIDENT WANTED ME TO REPLY BY DEMANDING HIS SURRENDER?
AND TO PEPPER THAT DEMAND WITH PEJORATIVES AND RACIAL SLURS.
GROUND SWINE... MUD TURTLES... THOSE WOULD HAVE BEEN GOOD.

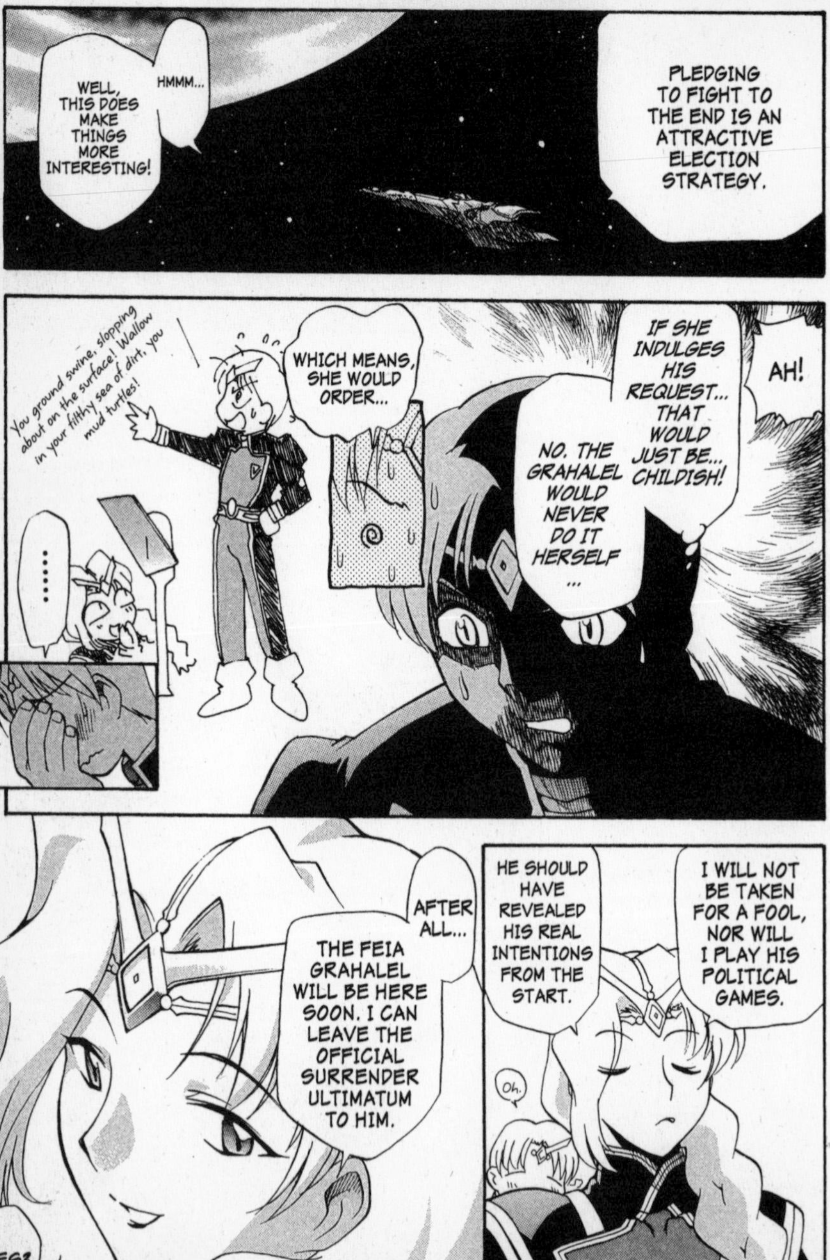
PLEDGING TO FIGHT TO THE END IS AN ATTRACTIVE ELECTION STRATEGY.
HMMM...
WELL, THIS DOES MAKE THINGS MORE INTERESTING!
AH!
IF SHE INDULGES HIS REQUEST... THAT WOULD JUST BE... CHILDISH!
NO. THE GRAHALEL WOULD NEVER DO IT HERSELF ...
WHICH MEANS, SHE WOULD ORDER...
You ground swine, slopping about on the surface! Wallow in your filthy sea of dirt, you mud turtles!
......
I WILL NOT BE TAKEN FOR A FOOL, NOR WILL I PLAY HIS POLITICAL GAMES.
HE SHOULD HAVE REVEALED HIS REAL INTENTIONS FROM THE START.
Oh.
AFTER ALL...
THE FEIA GRAHALEL WILL BE HERE SOON. I CAN LEAVE THE OFFICIAL SURRENDER ULTIMATUM TO HIM.
YES?

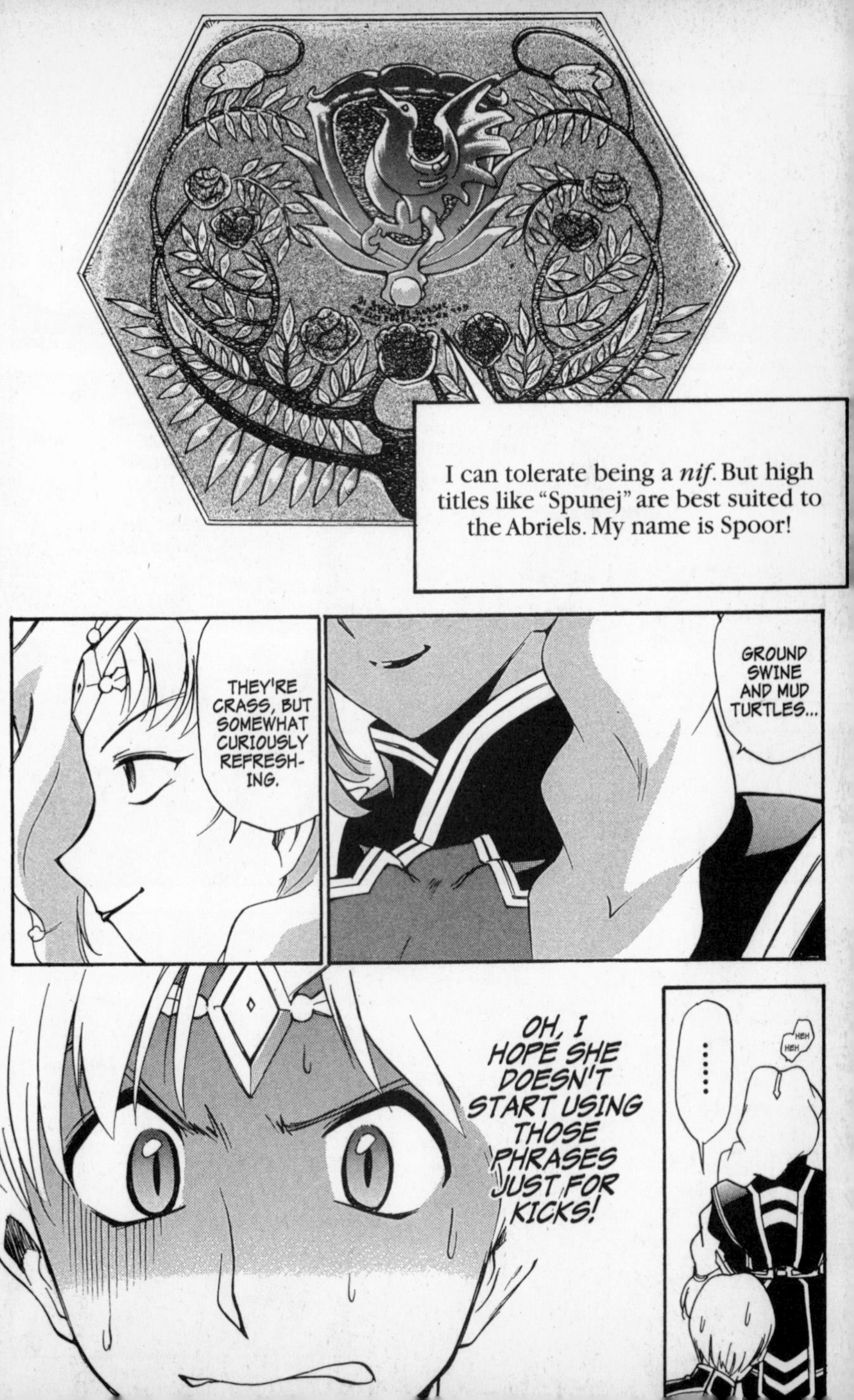
I can tolerate being a *nif*. But high titles like "Spunej" are best suited to the Abriels. My name is Spoor!
GROUND SWINE AND MUD TURTLES...
THEY'RE CRASS, BUT SOMEWHAT CURIOUSLY REFRESH-ING.
HEH HEH
......
OH, I HOPE SHE DOESN'T START USING THOSE PHRASES JUST FOR KICKS!

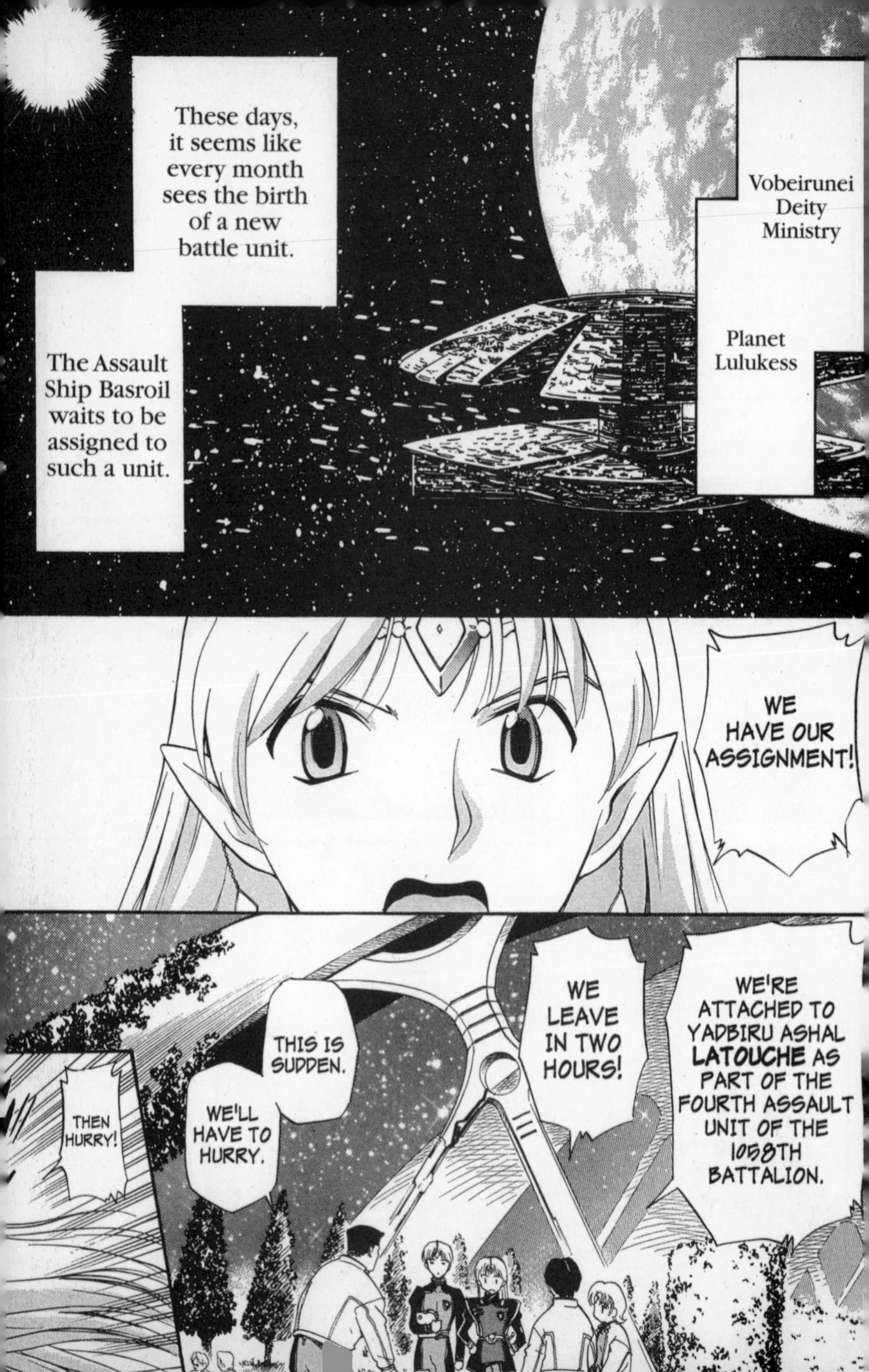
Vobeirunei Deity Ministry
Planet Lulukess
These days, it seems like every month sees the birth of a new battle unit.
The Assault Ship Basroil waits to be assigned to such a unit.
WE HAVE OUR ASSIGNMENT!
WE'RE ATTACHED TO YADBIRU ASHAL LATOUCHE AS PART OF THE FOURTH ASSAULT UNIT OF THE 1058TH BATTALION.
WE LEAVE IN TWO HOURS!
THIS IS SUDDEN.
WE'LL HAVE TO HURRY.
THEN HURRY!

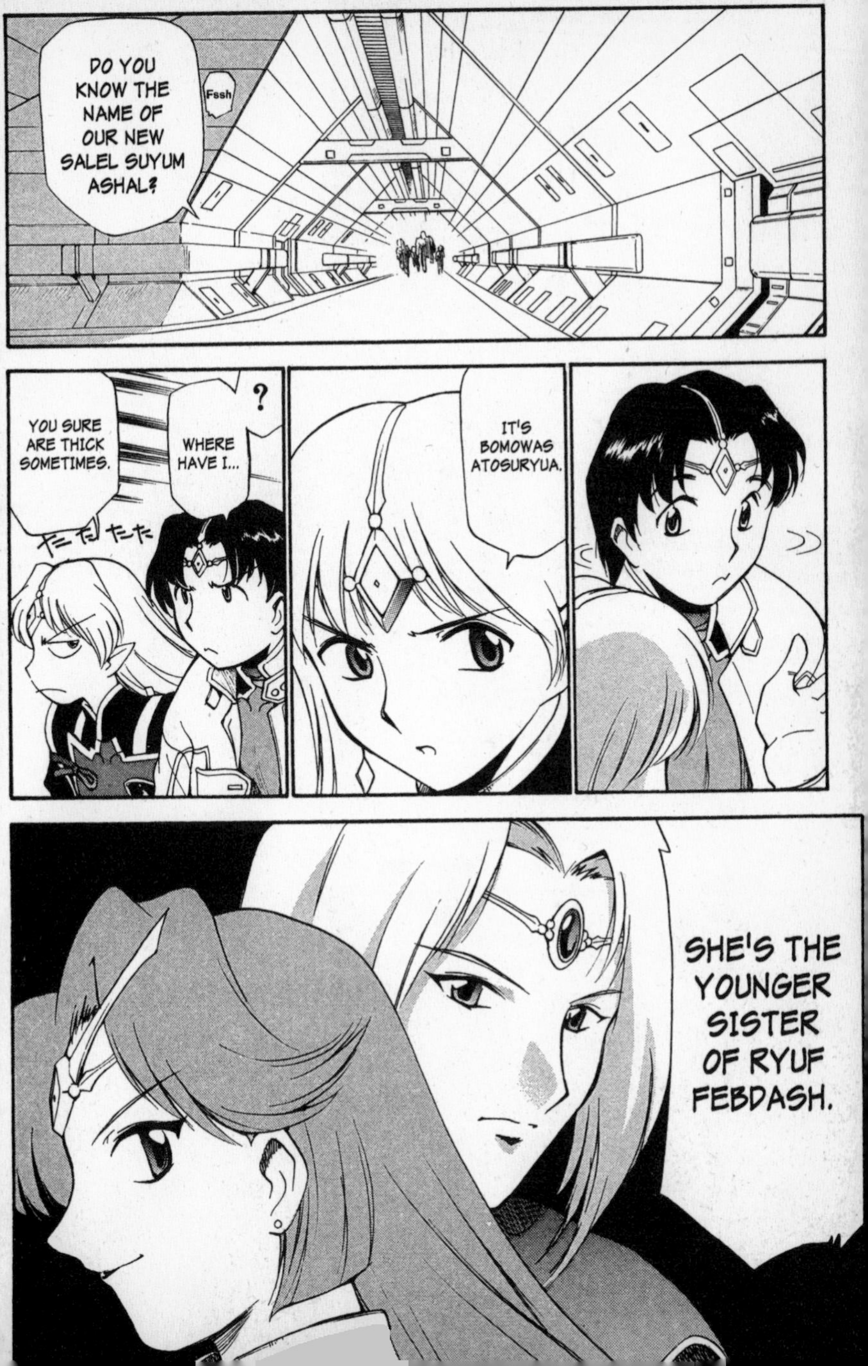
DO YOU KNOW THE NAME OF OUR NEW SALEL SUYUM ASHAL?
Fssh
IT'S BOMOWAS ATOSURYUA.
?
WHERE HAVE I...
YOU SURE ARE THICK SOMETIMES.
SHE'S THE YOUNGER SISTER OF RYUF FEBDASH.

Chapter 3
Hecto-Commander Atosuryua

BOMOWAS ATOSURYUA

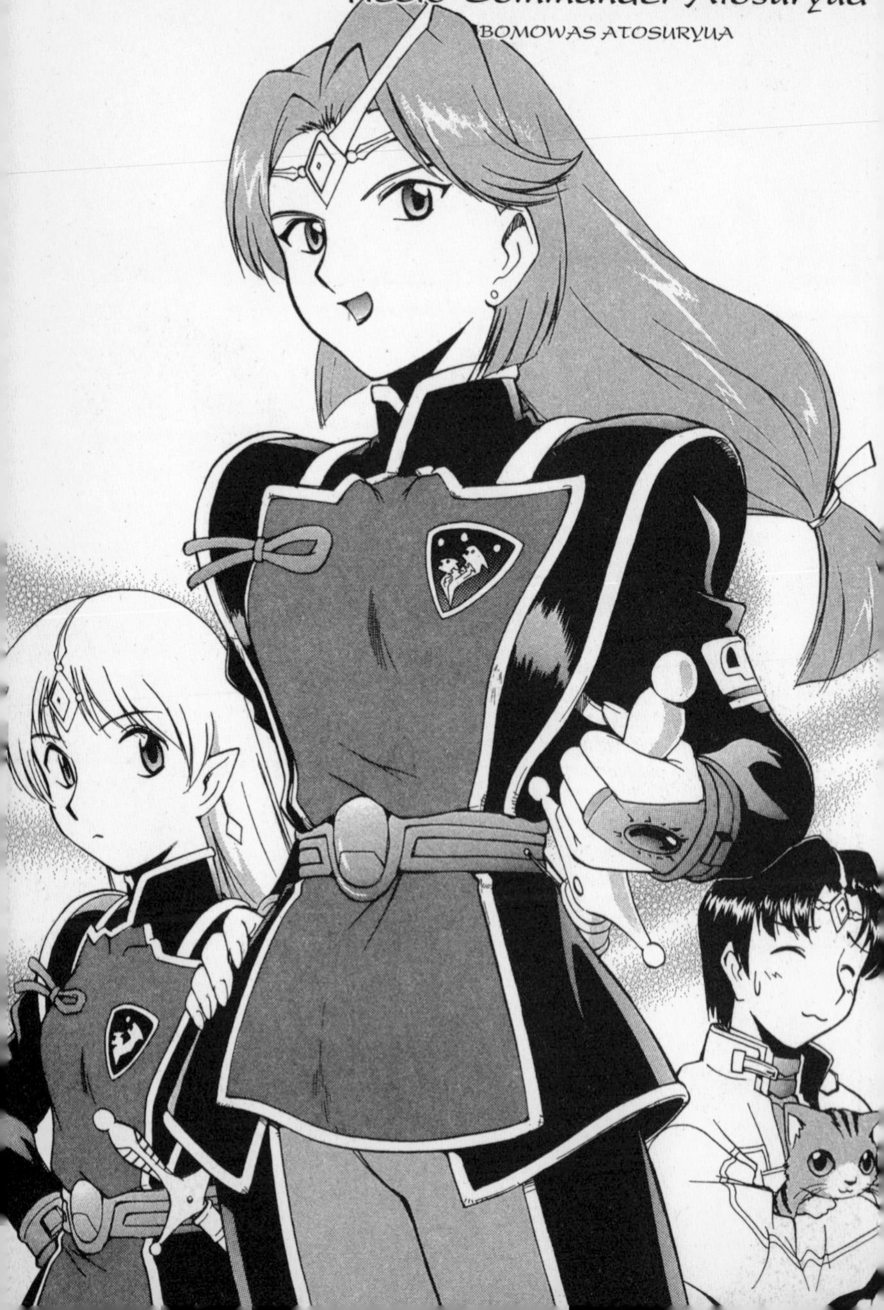

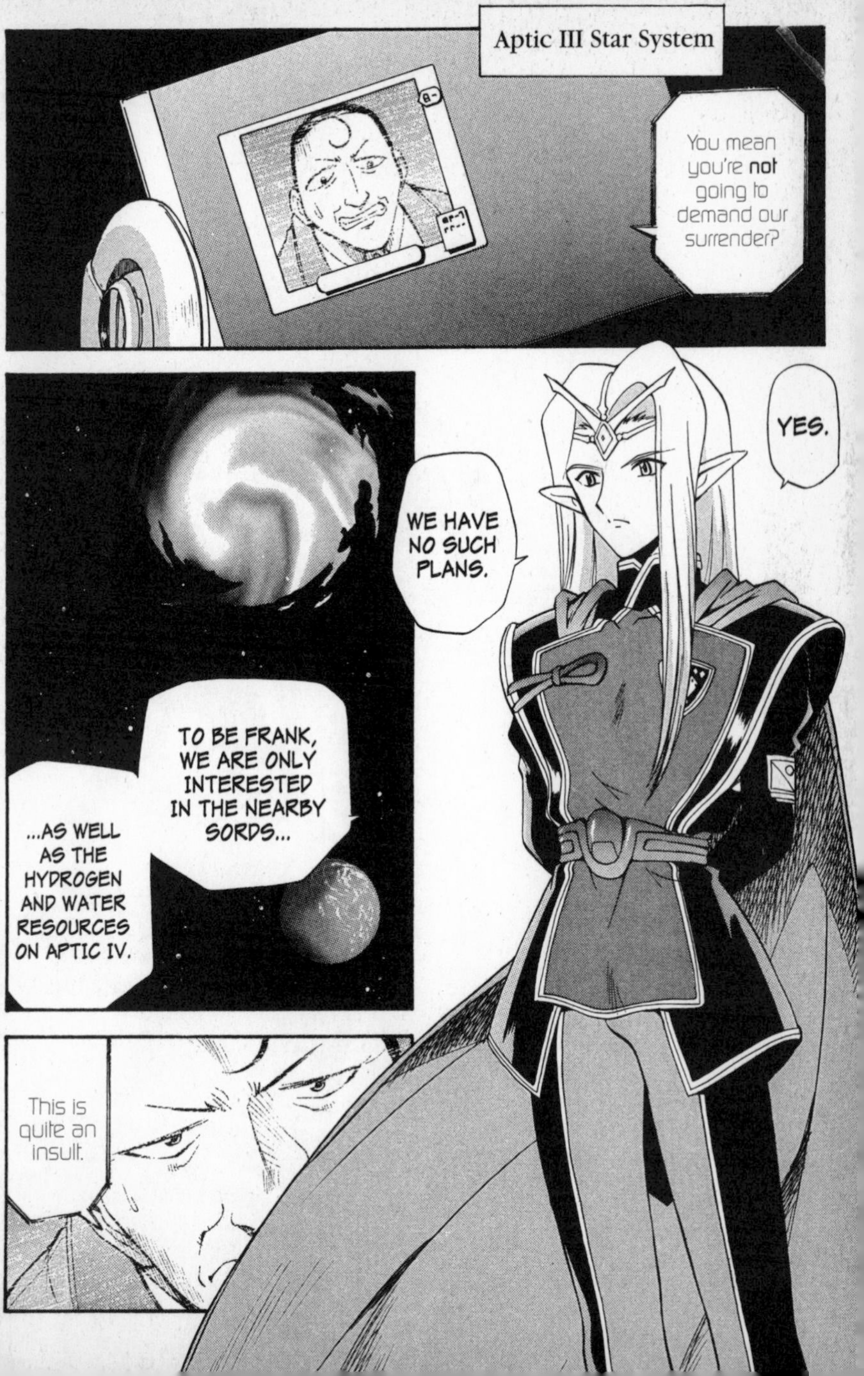
Aptic III Star System
You mean you're **not** going to demand our surrender?
YES.
WE HAVE NO SUCH PLANS.
TO BE FRANK, WE ARE ONLY INTERESTED IN THE NEARBY SORDS...
...AS WELL AS THE HYDROGEN AND WATER RESOURCES ON APTIC IV.
This is quite an insult.

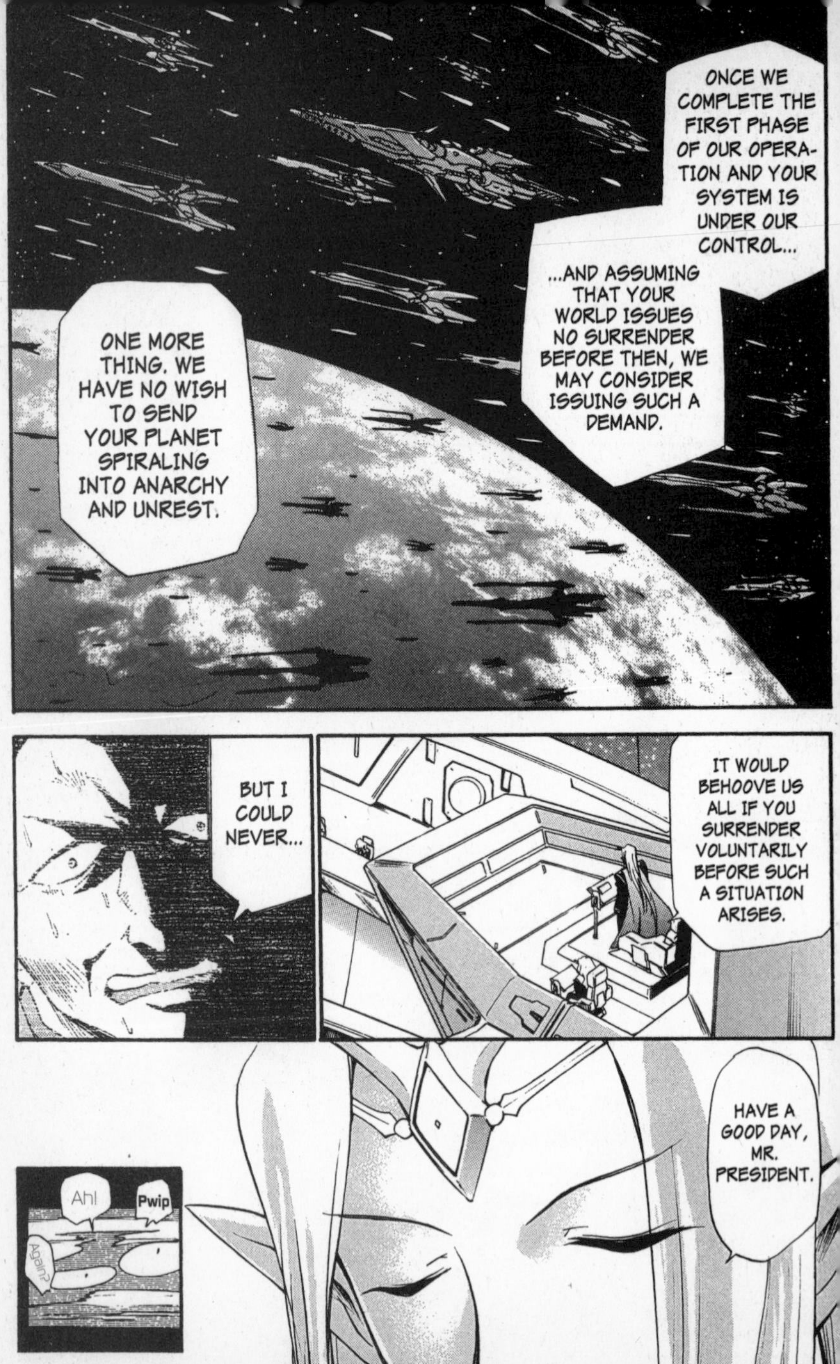
ONCE WE COMPLETE THE FIRST PHASE OF OUR OPERATION AND YOUR SYSTEM IS UNDER OUR CONTROL...
...AND ASSUMING THAT YOUR WORLD ISSUES NO SURRENDER BEFORE THEN, WE MAY CONSIDER ISSUING SUCH A DEMAND.
ONE MORE THING. WE HAVE NO WISH TO SEND YOUR PLANET SPIRALING INTO ANARCHY AND UNREST.
IT WOULD BEHOOVE US ALL IF YOU SURRENDER VOLUNTARILY BEFORE SUCH A SITUATION ARISES.
BUT I COULD NEVER...
HAVE A GOOD DAY, MR. PRESIDENT.
Pwip
Ah!
Again?

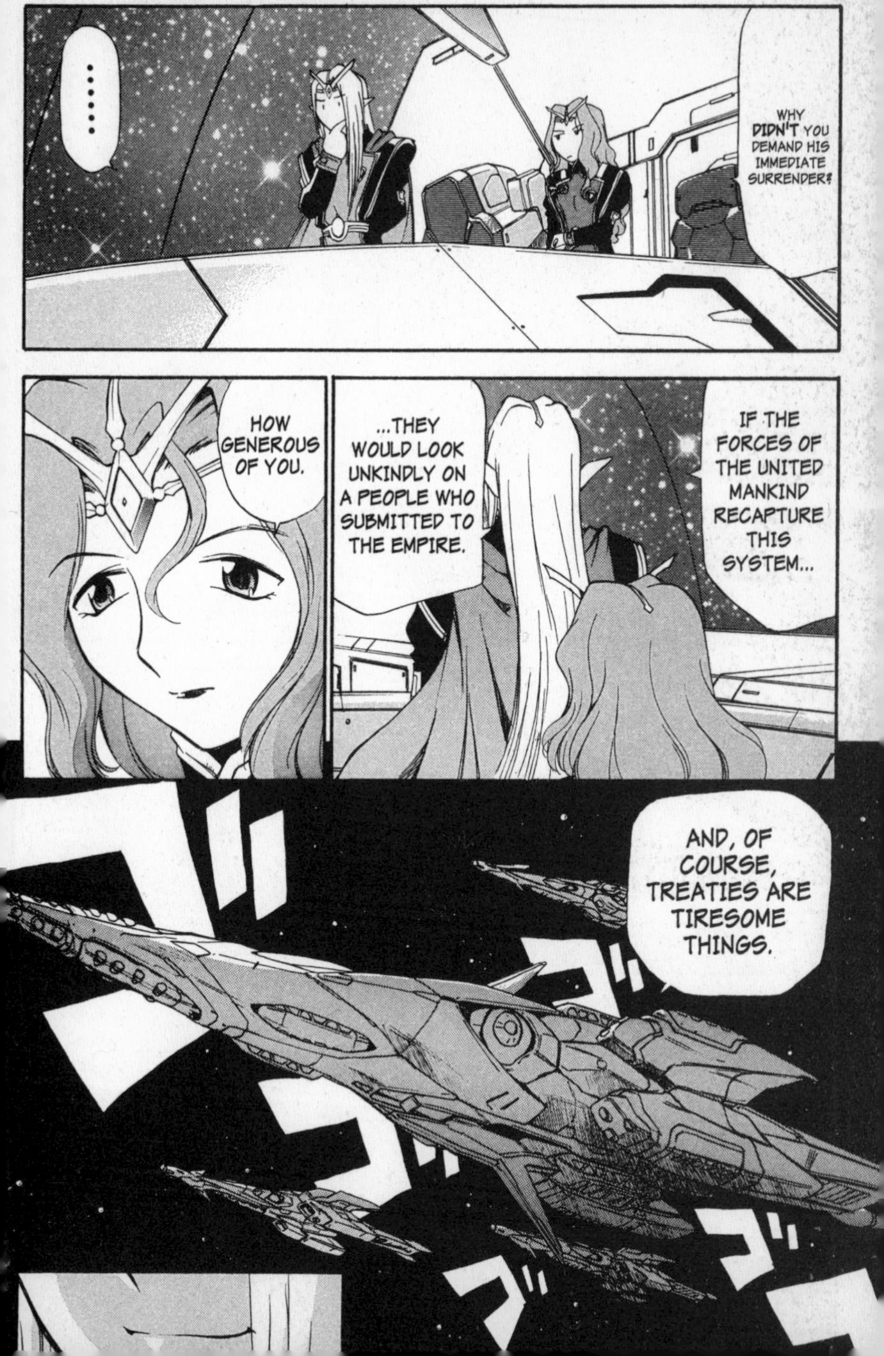
WHY DIDN'T YOU DEMAND HIS IMMEDIATE SURRENDER?
......
IF THE FORCES OF THE UNITED MANKIND RECAPTURE THIS SYSTEM...
...THEY WOULD LOOK UNKINDLY ON A PEOPLE WHO SUBMITTED TO THE EMPIRE.
HOW GENEROUS OF YOU.
AND, OF COURSE, TREATIES ARE TIRESOME THINGS.

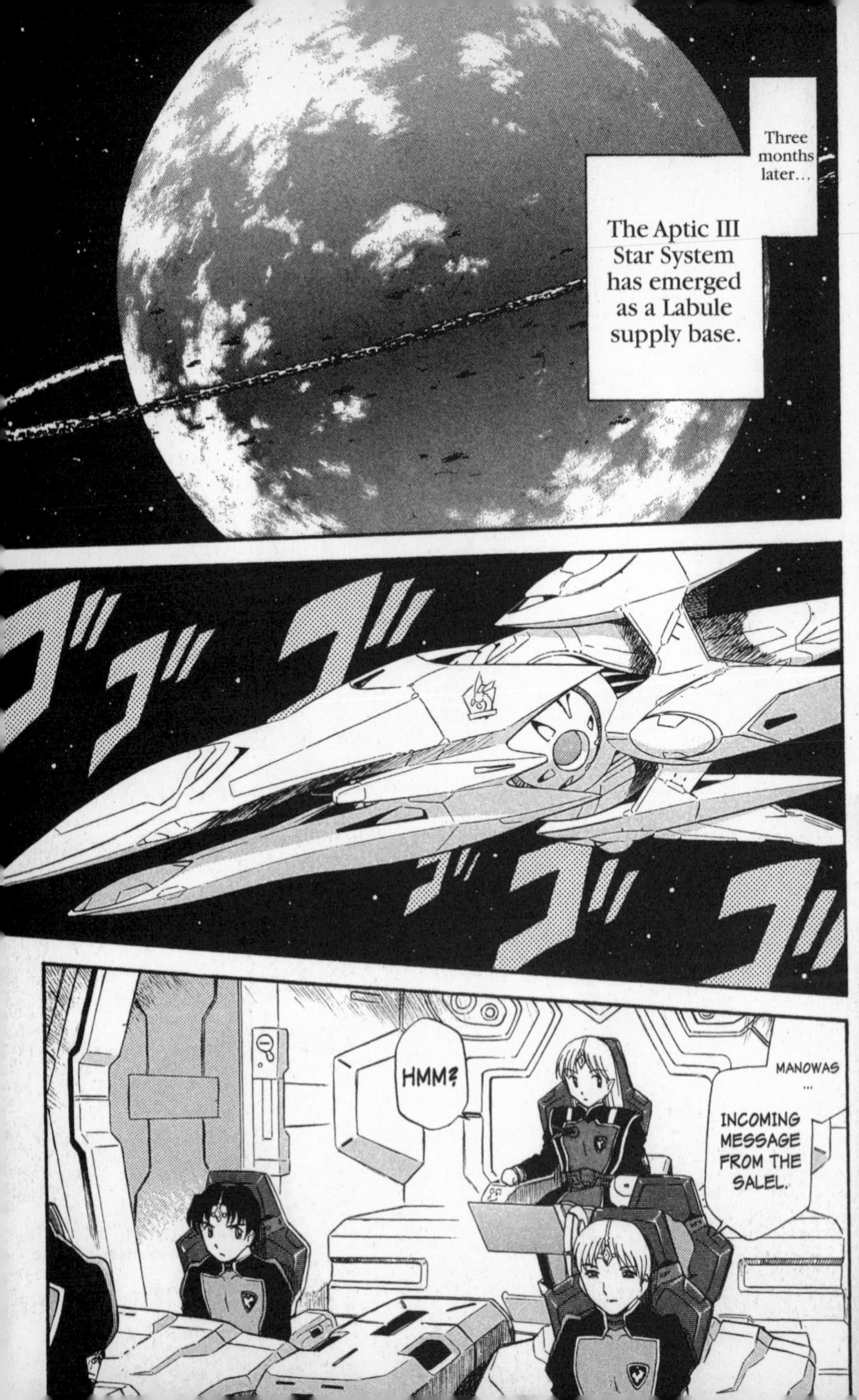
Three months later…
The Aptic III Star System has emerged as a Labule supply base.
ゴゴゴ
ゴゴゴ
MANOWAS…
INCOMING MESSAGE FROM THE SALEL.
HMM?

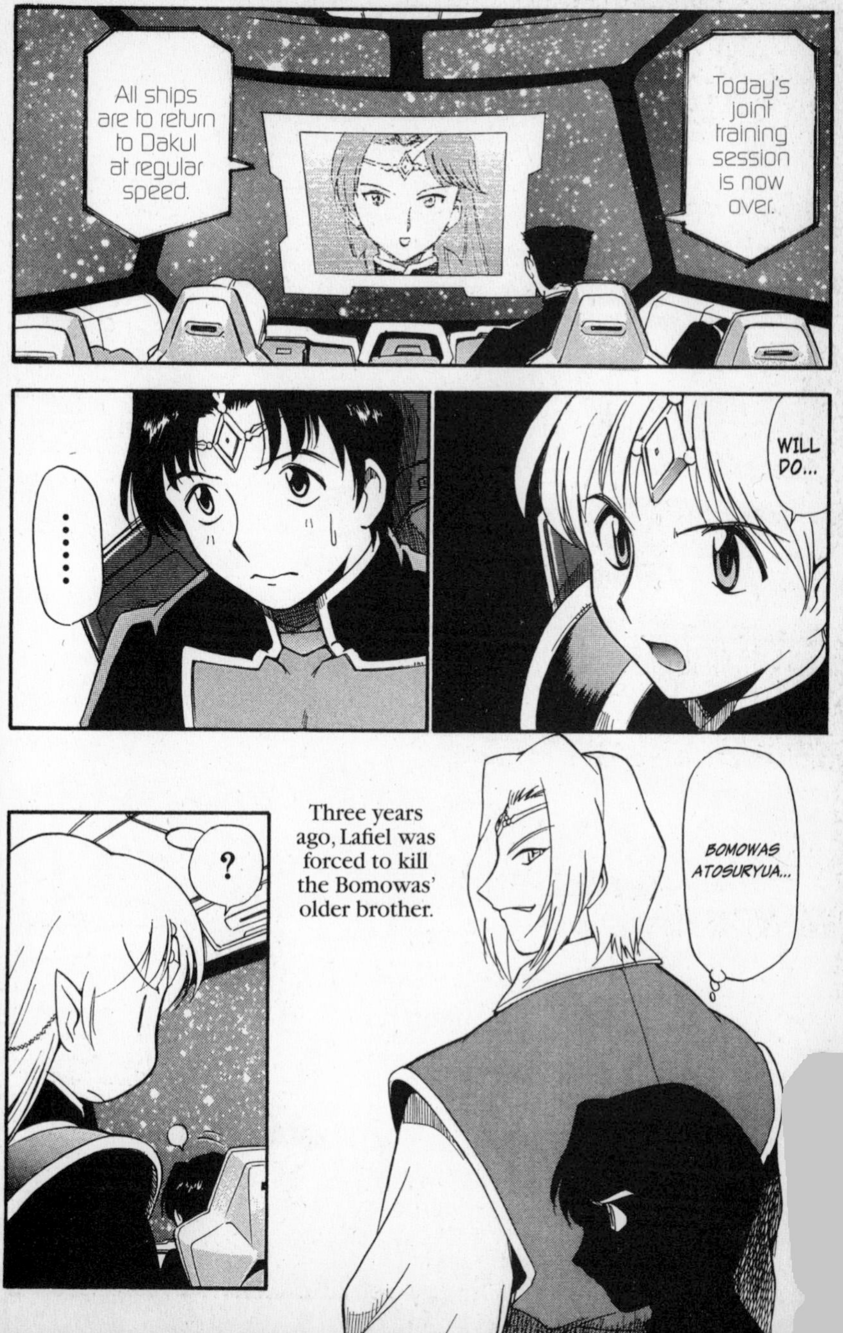
Today's joint training session is now over.
All ships are to return to Dakul at regular speed.
WILL DO...
......
BOMOWAS ATOSURYUA...
Three years ago, Lafiel was forced to kill the Bomowas' older brother.
?

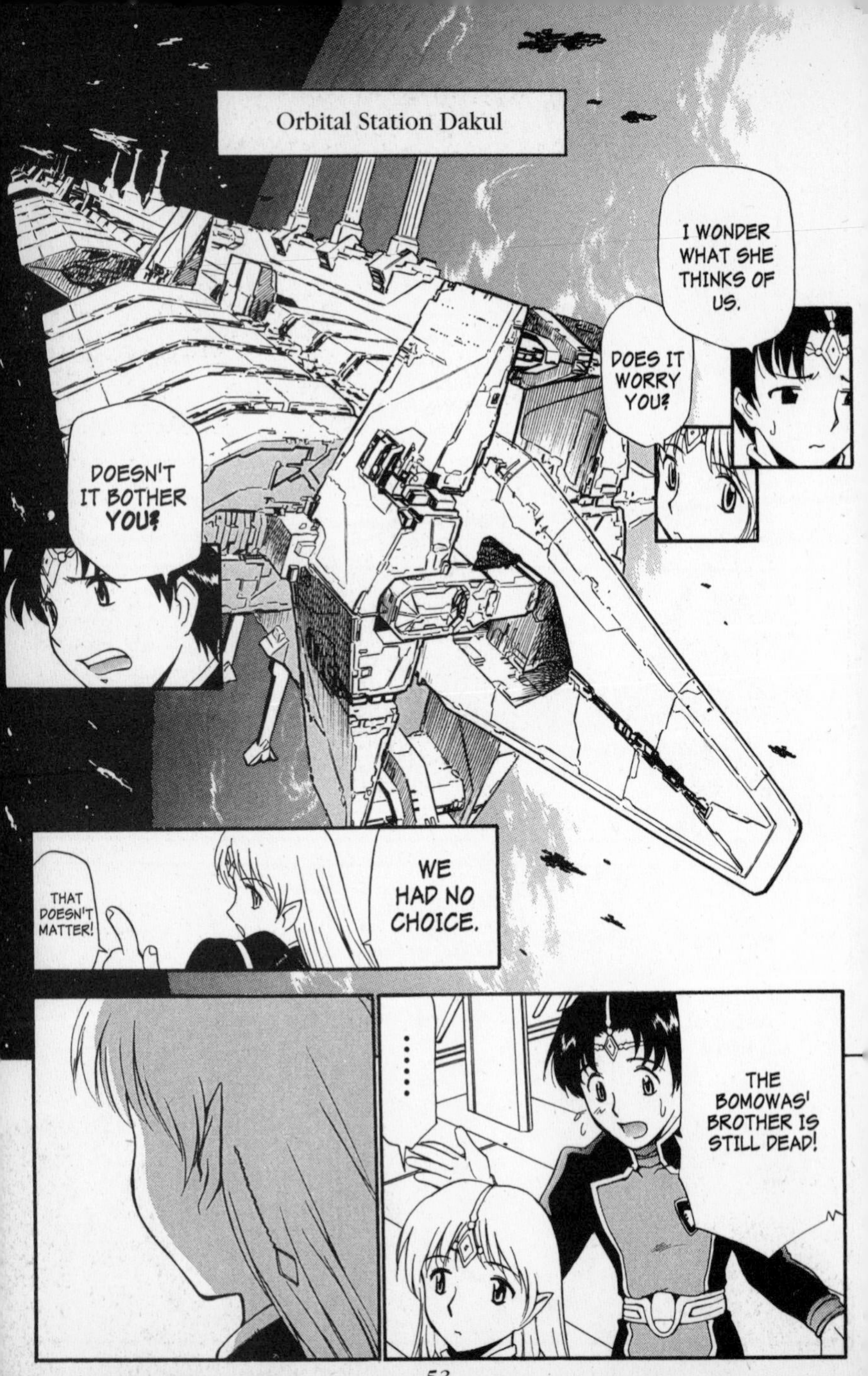
Orbital Station Dakul
I WONDER WHAT SHE THINKS OF US.
DOES IT WORRY YOU?
DOESN'T IT BOTHER YOU?
WE HAD NO CHOICE.
THAT DOESN'T MATTER!
THE BOMOWAS' BROTHER IS STILL DEAD!
......

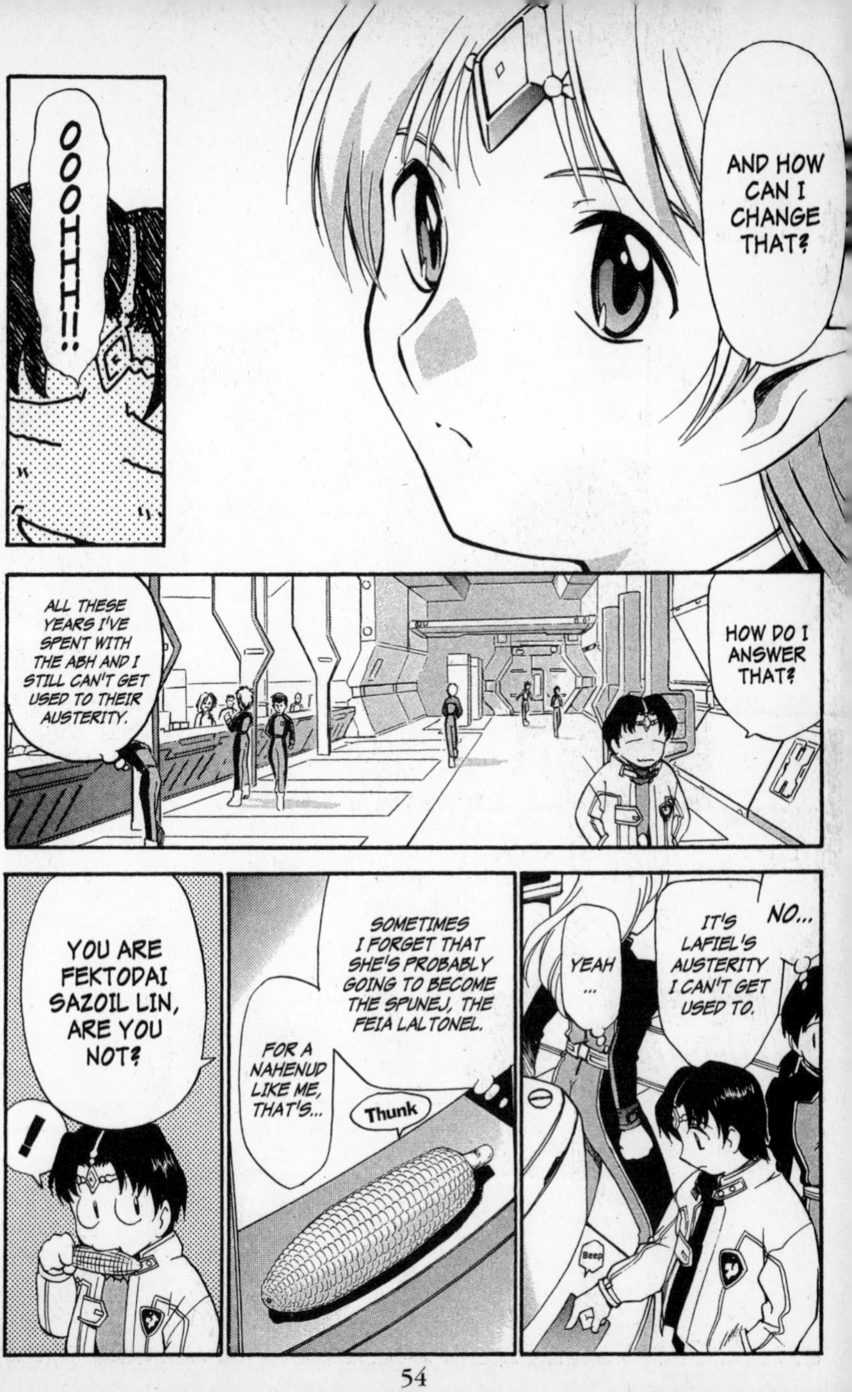
AND HOW CAN I CHANGE THAT?
OOOHHH!!
HOW DO I ANSWER THAT?
ALL THESE YEARS I'VE SPENT WITH THE ABH AND I STILL CAN'T GET USED TO THEIR AUSTERITY.
NO...
IT'S LAFIEL'S AUSTERITY I CAN'T GET USED TO.
YEAH ...
Beep
SOMETIMES I FORGET THAT SHE'S PROBABLY GOING TO BECOME THE SPUNEJ, THE FEIA LALTONEL.
FOR A NAHENUD LIKE ME, THAT'S...
Thunk
YOU ARE FEKTODAI SAZOIL LIN, ARE YOU NOT?
!

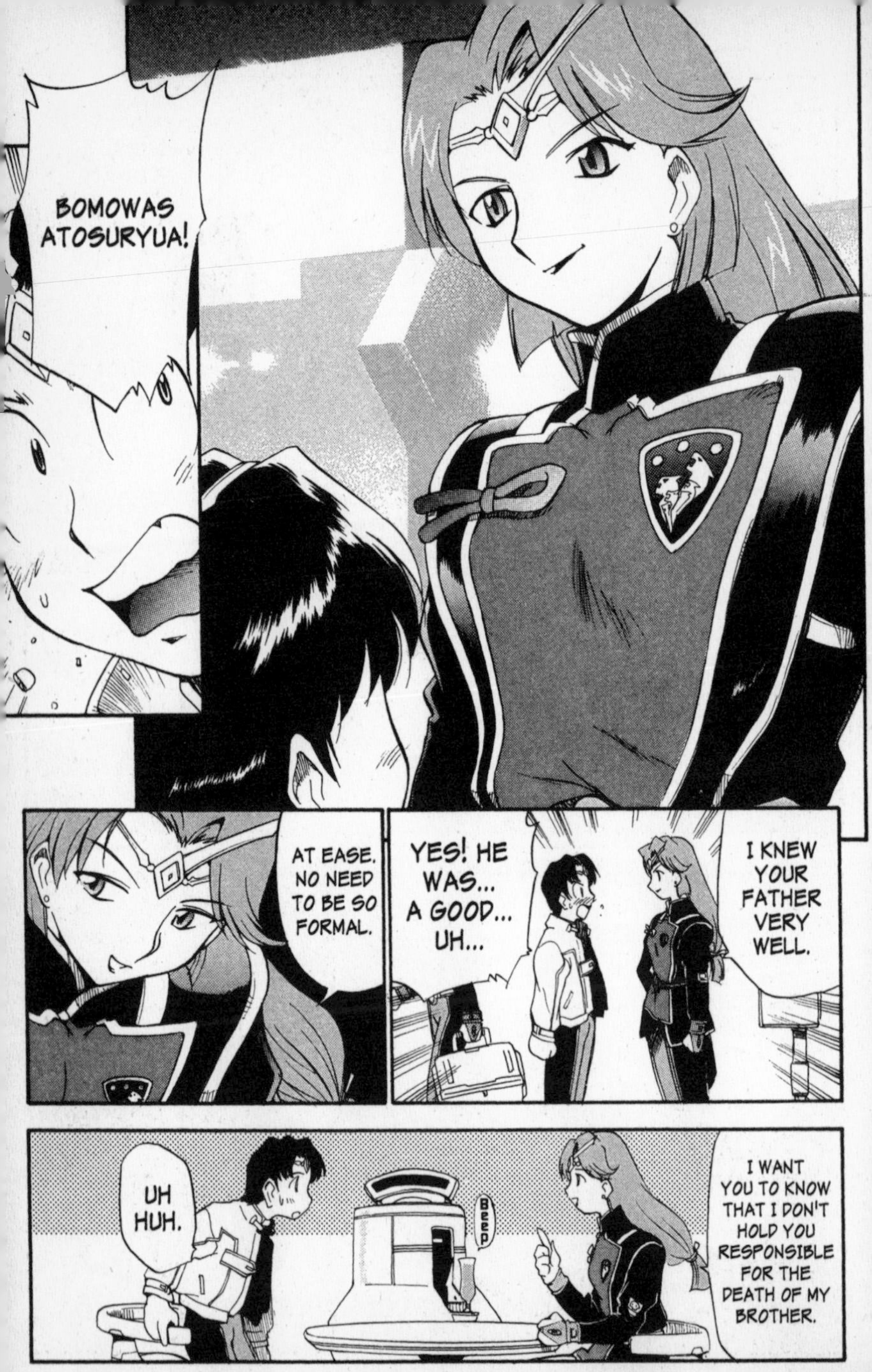
BOMOWAS ATOSURYUA!
I KNEW YOUR FATHER VERY WELL.
YES! HE WAS... A GOOD... UH...
AT EASE. NO NEED TO BE SO FORMAL.
I WANT YOU TO KNOW THAT I DON'T HOLD YOU RESPONSIBLE FOR THE DEATH OF MY BROTHER.
Beep
UH HUH.

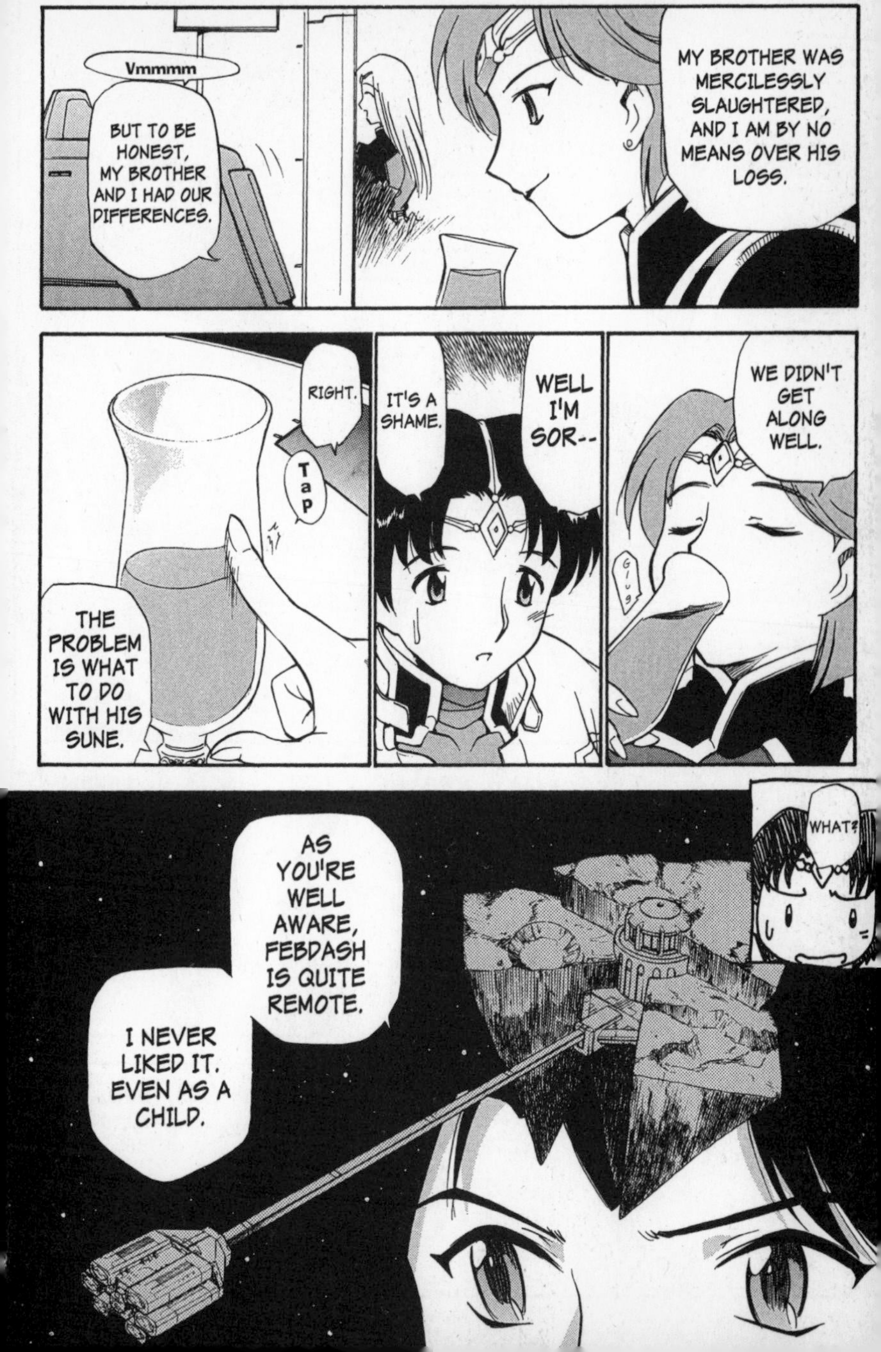
MY BROTHER WAS MERCILESSLY SLAUGHTERED, AND I AM BY NO MEANS OVER HIS LOSS.
Vmmmm
BUT TO BE HONEST, MY BROTHER AND I HAD OUR DIFFERENCES.
WE DIDN'T GET ALONG WELL.
Glug
WELL I'M SOR--
IT'S A SHAME.
RIGHT.
Tap
THE PROBLEM IS WHAT TO DO WITH HIS SUNE.
WHAT?
AS YOU'RE WELL AWARE, FEBDASH IS QUITE REMOTE.
I NEVER LIKED IT. EVEN AS A CHILD.

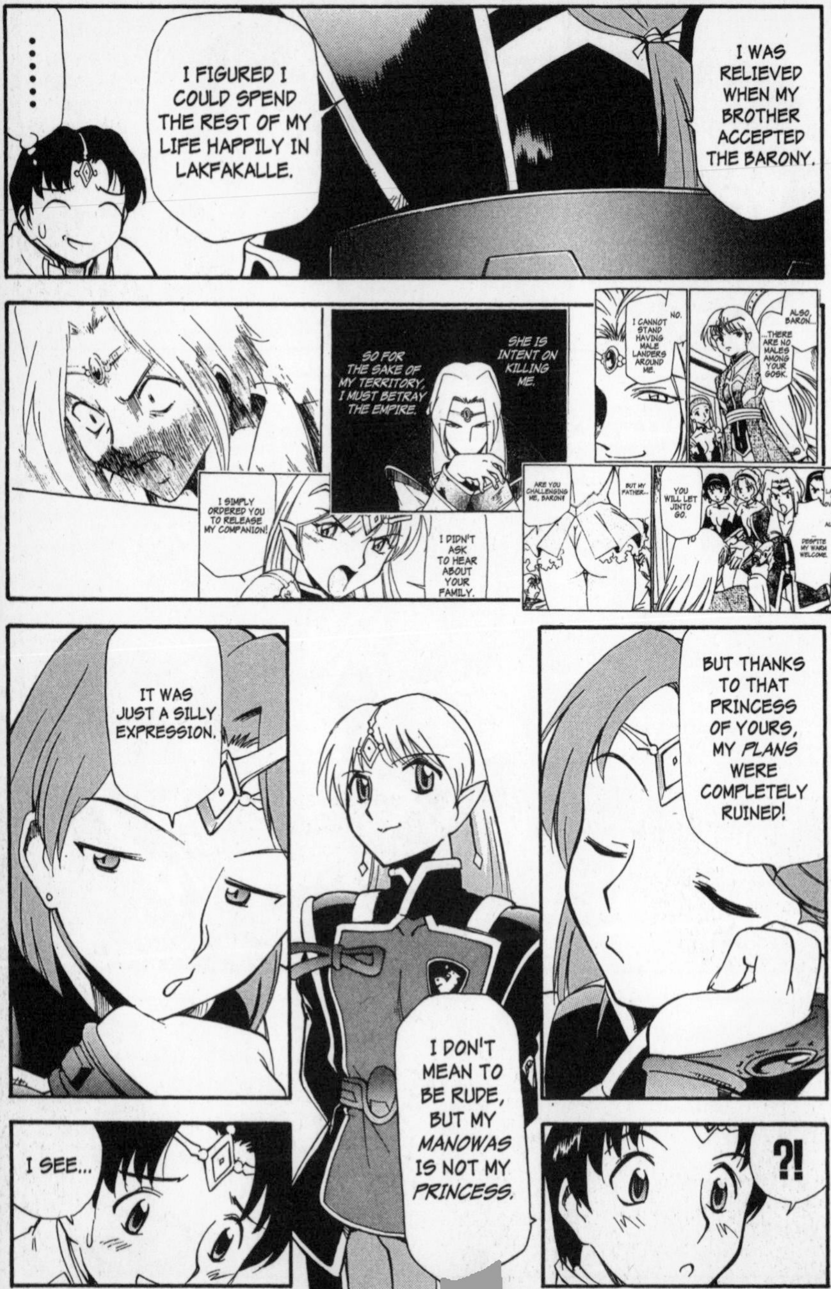
I WAS RELIEVED WHEN MY BROTHER ACCEPTED THE BARONY.
I FIGURED I COULD SPEND THE REST OF MY LIFE HAPPILY IN LAKFAKALLE.
......
ALSO, BARON...
...THERE ARE NO MALES AMONG YOUR GOSK.
NO.
I CANNOT STAND HAVING MALE LANDERS AROUND ME.
FEIA LALTONEL, YOU'RE OVERSTEPPING YOUR AUTHORITY...
DESPITE MY WARM WELCOME.
YOU WILL LET JINTO GO.
BUT MY FATHER...
ARE YOU CHALLENGING ME, BARON!
SHE IS INTENT ON KILLING ME.
SO FOR THE SAKE OF MY TERRITORY, I MUST BETRAY THE EMPIRE.
I DIDN'T ASK TO HEAR ABOUT YOUR FAMILY.
I SIMPLY ORDERED YOU TO RELEASE MY COMPANION!
BUT THANKS TO THAT PRINCESS OF YOURS, MY *PLANS* WERE COMPLETELY RUINED!
?!
I DON'T MEAN TO BE RUDE, BUT MY *MANOWAS* IS NOT MY *PRINCESS*.
IT WAS JUST A SILLY EXPRESSION.
I SEE...

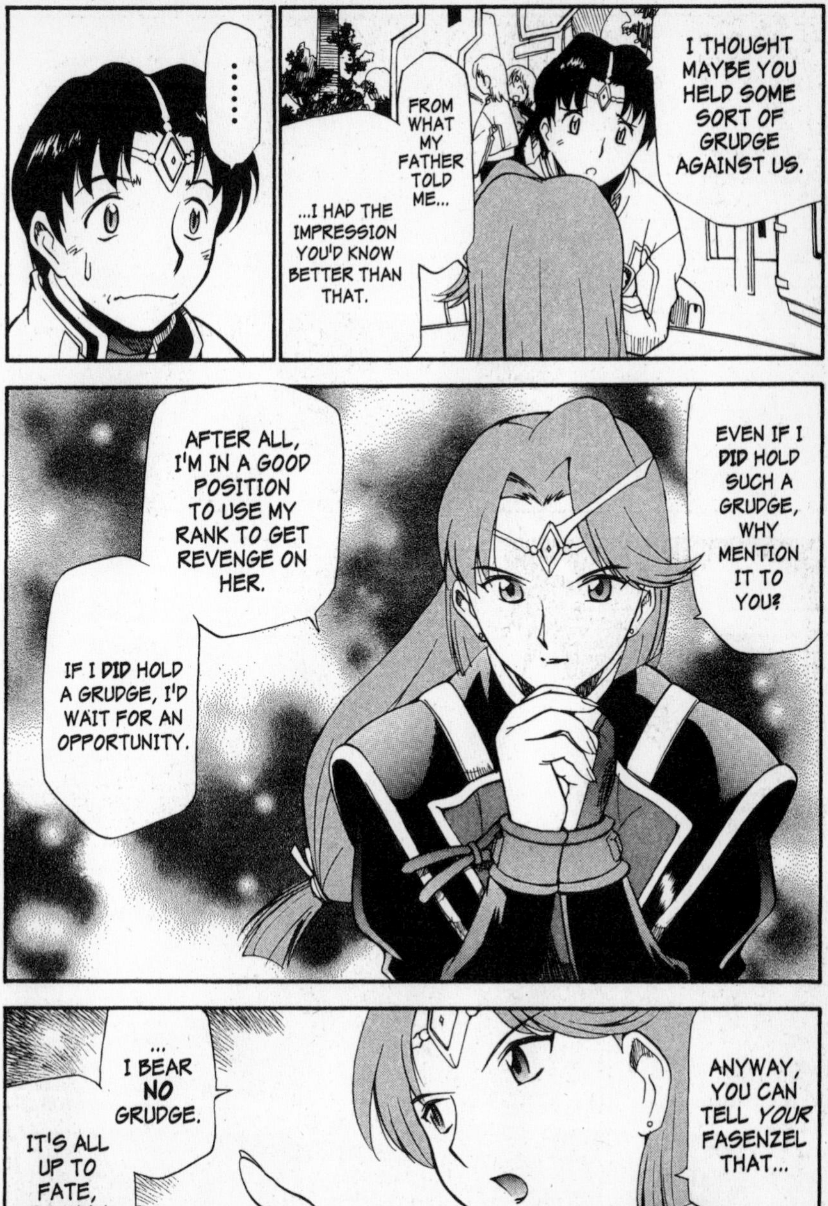
I THOUGHT MAYBE YOU HELD SOME SORT OF GRUDGE AGAINST US.
FROM WHAT MY FATHER TOLD ME...
...I HAD THE IMPRESSION YOU'D KNOW BETTER THAN THAT.
......
EVEN IF I **DID** HOLD SUCH A GRUDGE, WHY MENTION IT TO YOU?
AFTER ALL, I'M IN A GOOD POSITION TO USE MY RANK TO GET REVENGE ON HER.
IF I **DID** HOLD A GRUDGE, I'D WAIT FOR AN OPPORTUNITY.
ANYWAY, YOU CAN TELL *YOUR* FASENZEL THAT...
... I BEAR **NO** GRUDGE.
IT'S ALL UP TO FATE, SO WHY WORRY?

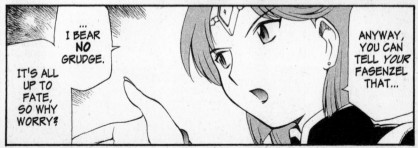

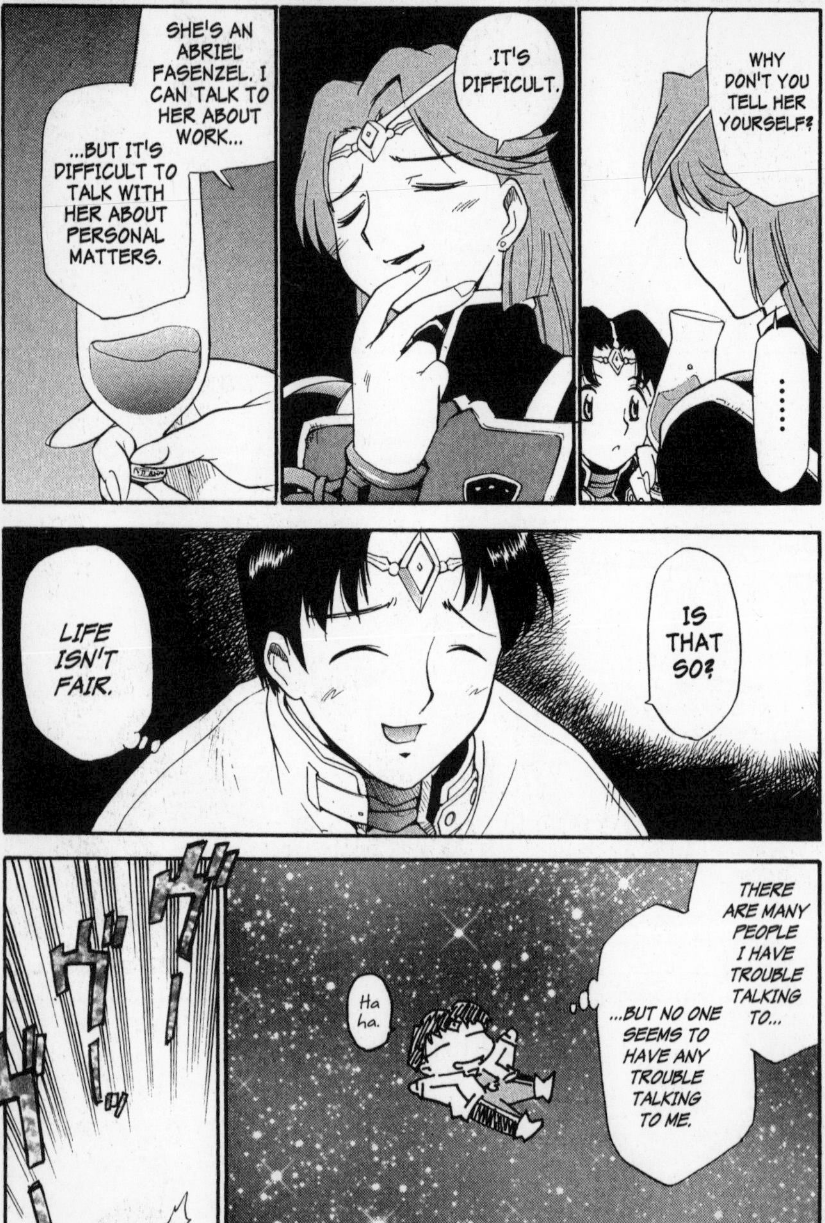
WHY DON'T YOU TELL HER YOURSELF?
......
IT'S DIFFICULT.
SHE'S AN ABRIEL FASENZEL. I CAN TALK TO HER ABOUT WORK...
...BUT IT'S DIFFICULT TO TALK WITH HER ABOUT PERSONAL MATTERS.
IS THAT SO?
LIFE ISN'T FAIR.
THERE ARE MANY PEOPLE I HAVE TROUBLE TALKING TO...
...BUT NO ONE SEEMS TO HAVE ANY TROUBLE TALKING TO ME.
Ha ha.

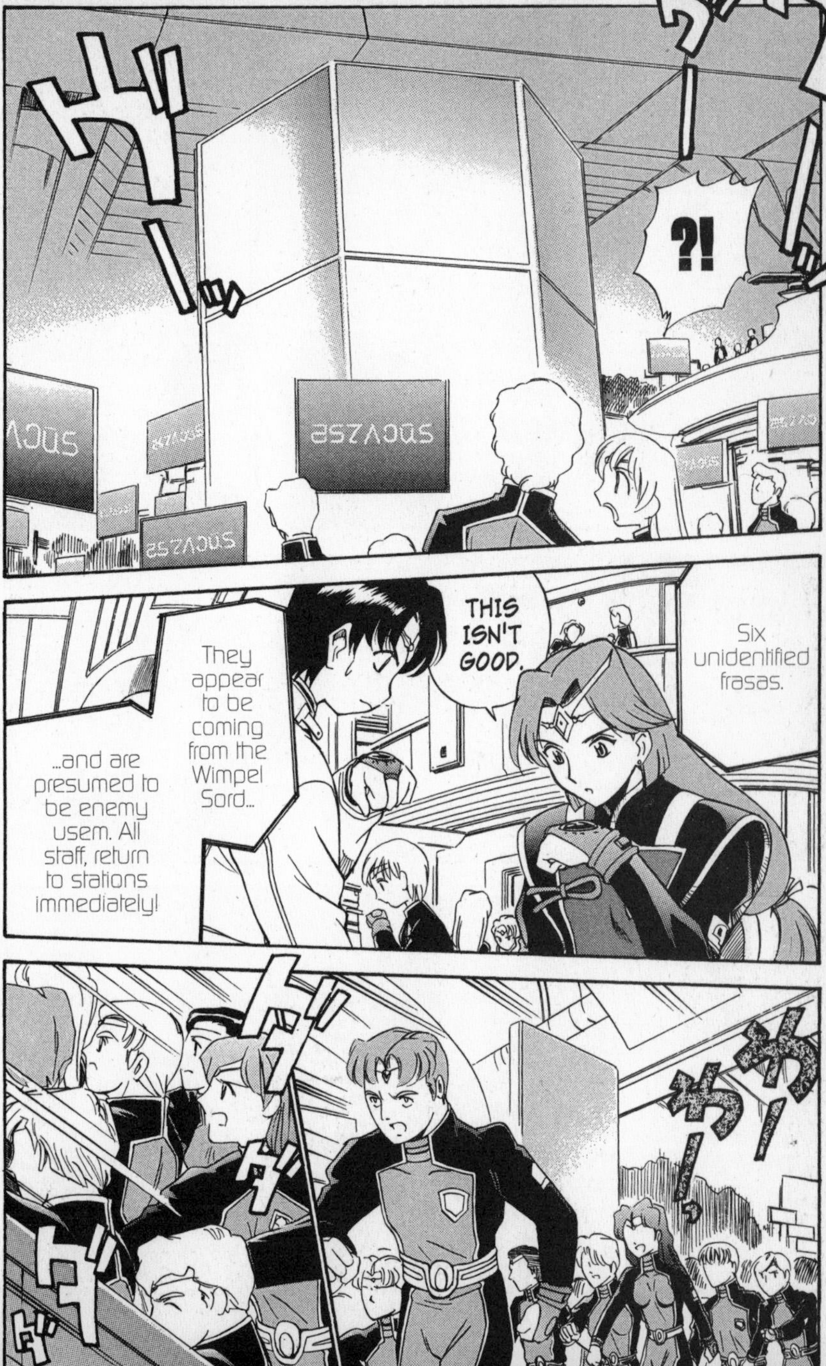
?!
Six unidentified frasas.
THIS ISN'T GOOD.
They appear to be coming from the Wimpel Sord...
...and are presumed to be enemy usem. All staff, return to stations immediately!

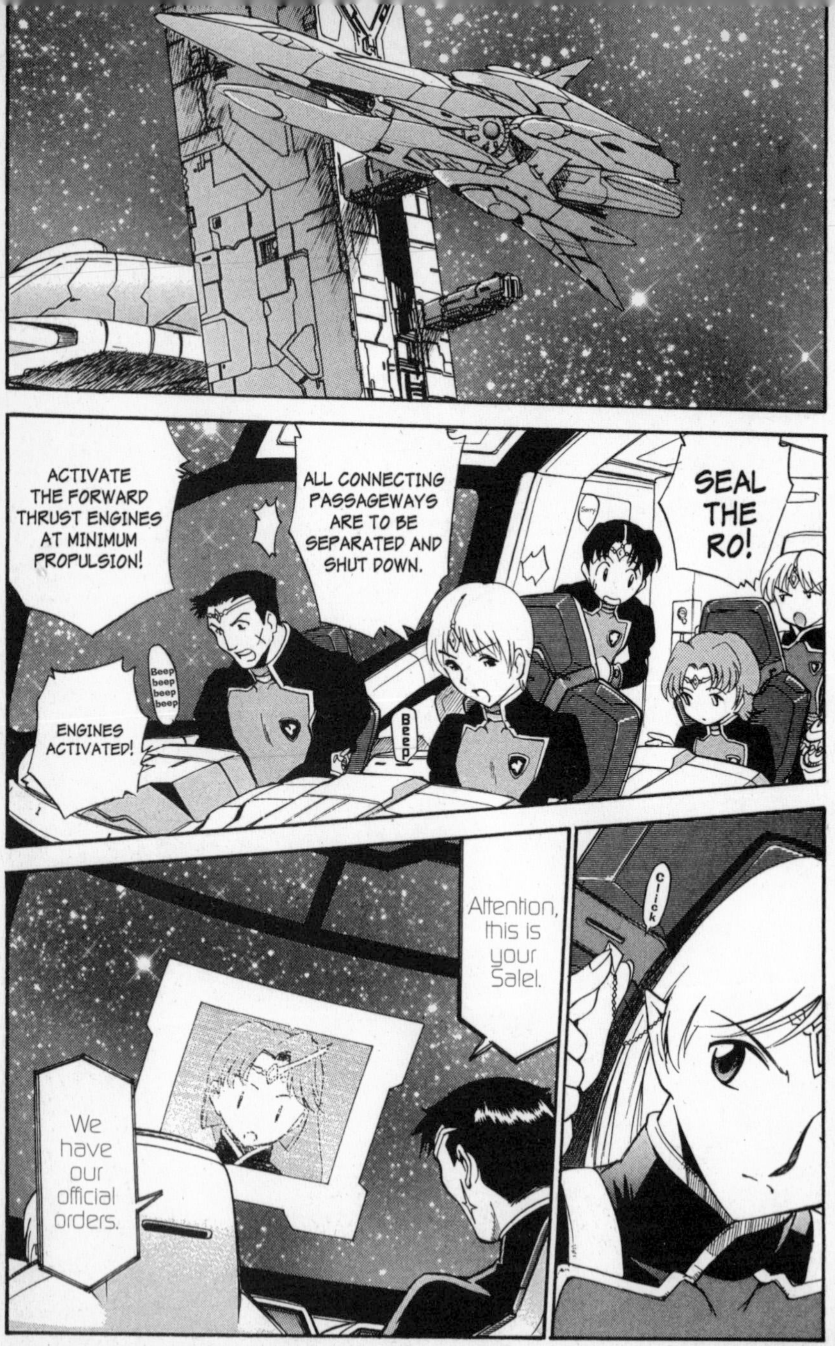
SEAL THE RO!
ALL CONNECTING PASSAGEWAYS ARE TO BE SEPARATED AND SHUT DOWN.
ACTIVATE THE FORWARD THRUST ENGINES AT MINIMUM PROPULSION!
Beep
Beep beep beep beep
ENGINES ACTIVATED!
Click
Attention, this is your Salel.
We have our official orders.

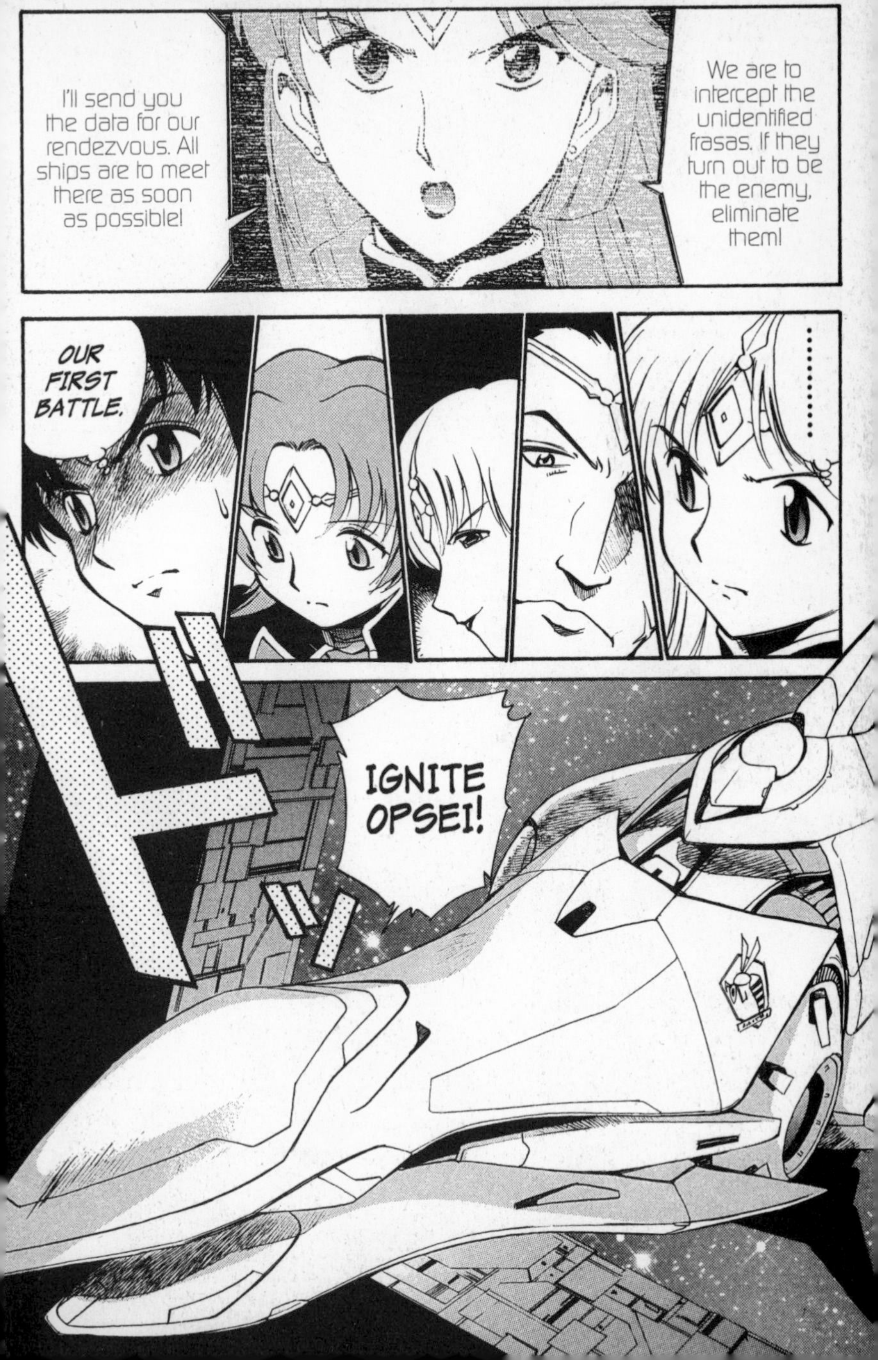
We are to intercept the unidentified frasas. If they turn out to be the enemy, eliminate them!
I'll send you the data for our rendezvous. All ships are to meet there as soon as possible!
......
OUR FIRST BATTLE.
IGNITE OPSEI!

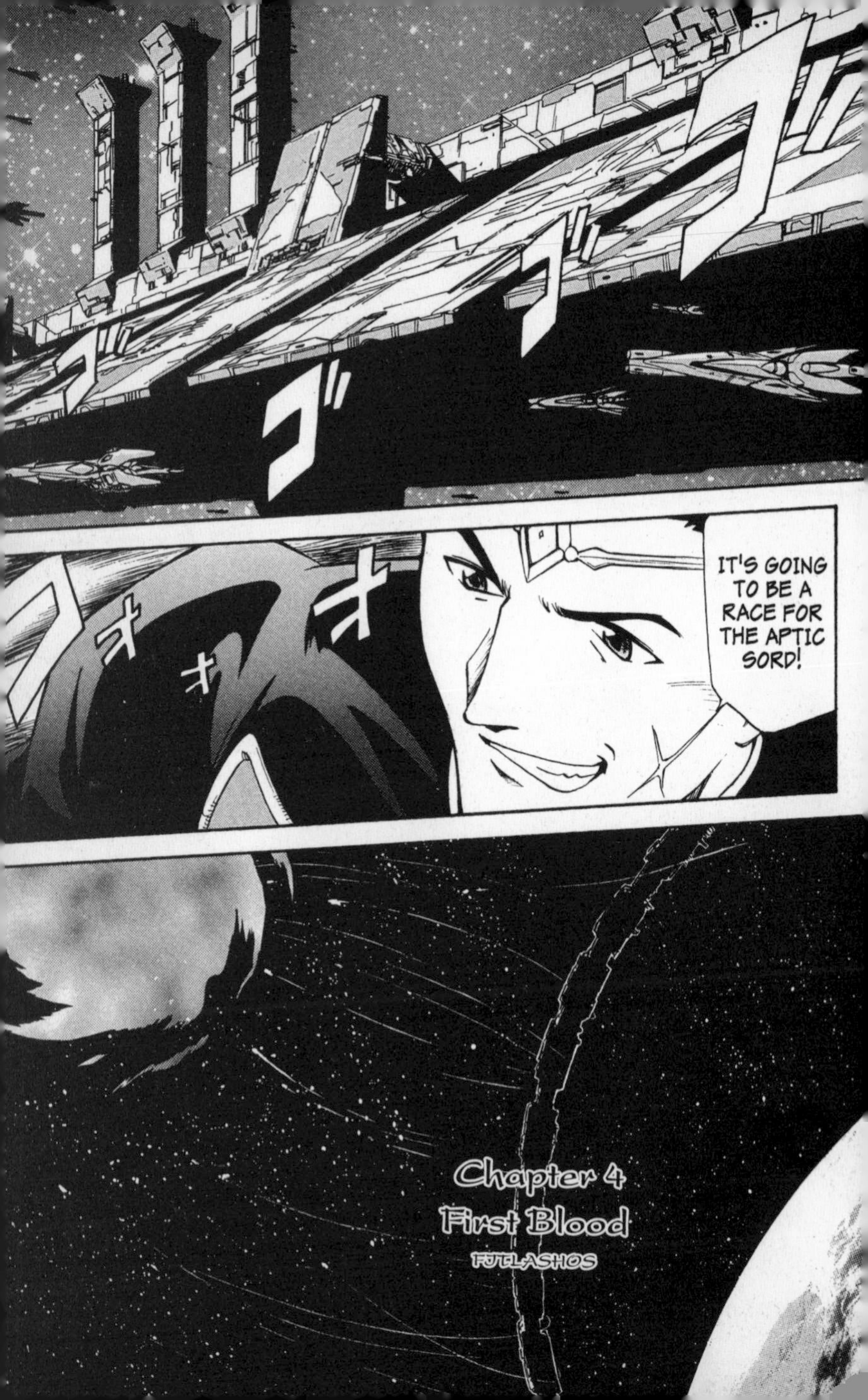
IT'S GOING TO BE A RACE FOR THE APTIC SORD!
Chapter 4
First Blood
FUTLASHOS

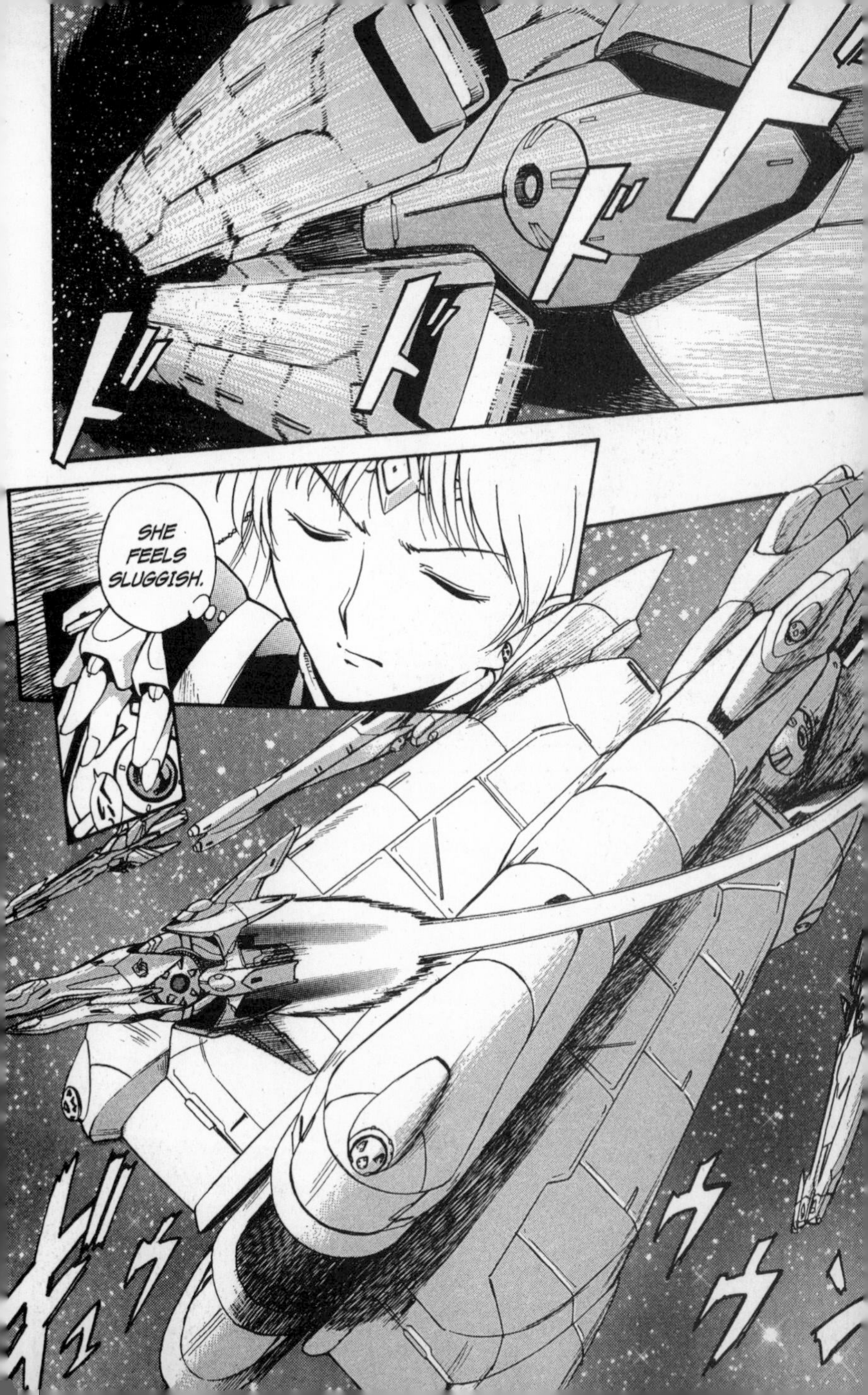
SHE FEELS SLUGGISH.

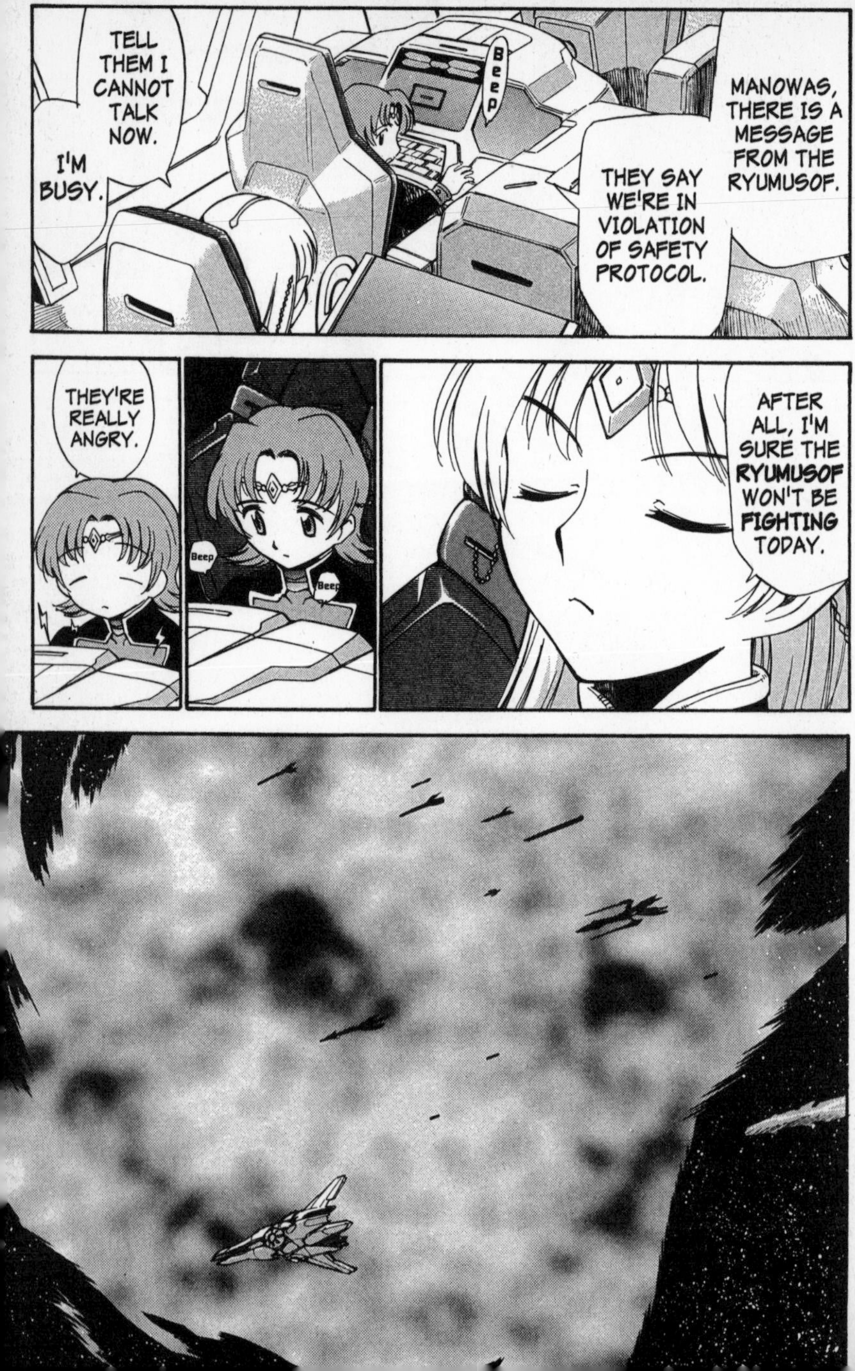
MANOWAS, THERE IS A MESSAGE FROM THE RYUMUSOF.
THEY SAY WE'RE IN VIOLATION OF SAFETY PROTOCOL.
Beep
TELL THEM I CANNOT TALK NOW.
I'M BUSY.
AFTER ALL, I'M SURE THE **RYUMUSOF** WON'T BE **FIGHTING** TODAY.
Beep
Beep
THEY'RE REALLY ANGRY.

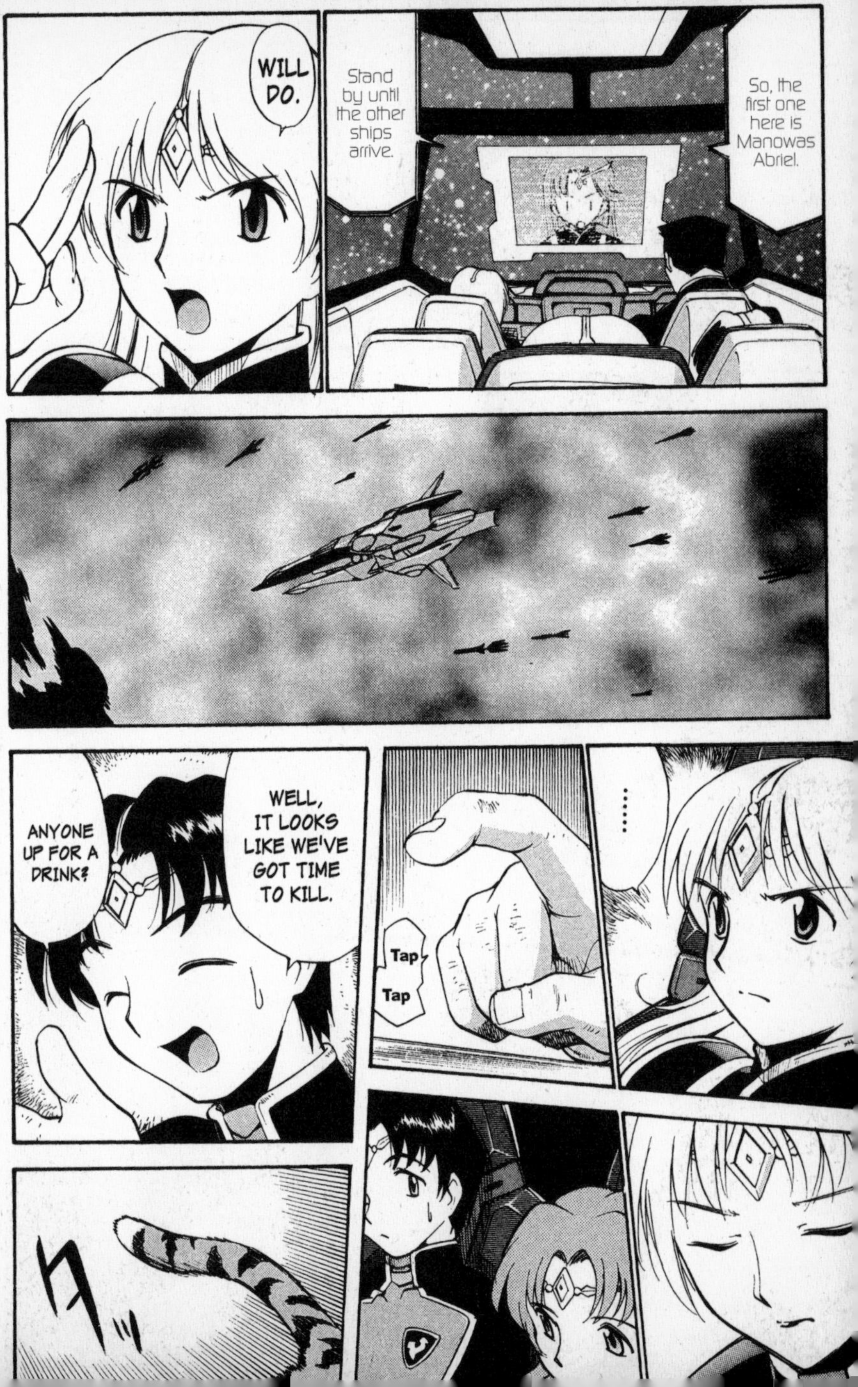
So, the first one here is Manowas Abriel.
Stand by until the other ships arrive.
WILL DO.
......
Tap
Tap
WELL, IT LOOKS LIKE WE'VE GOT TIME TO KILL.
ANYONE UP FOR A DRINK?

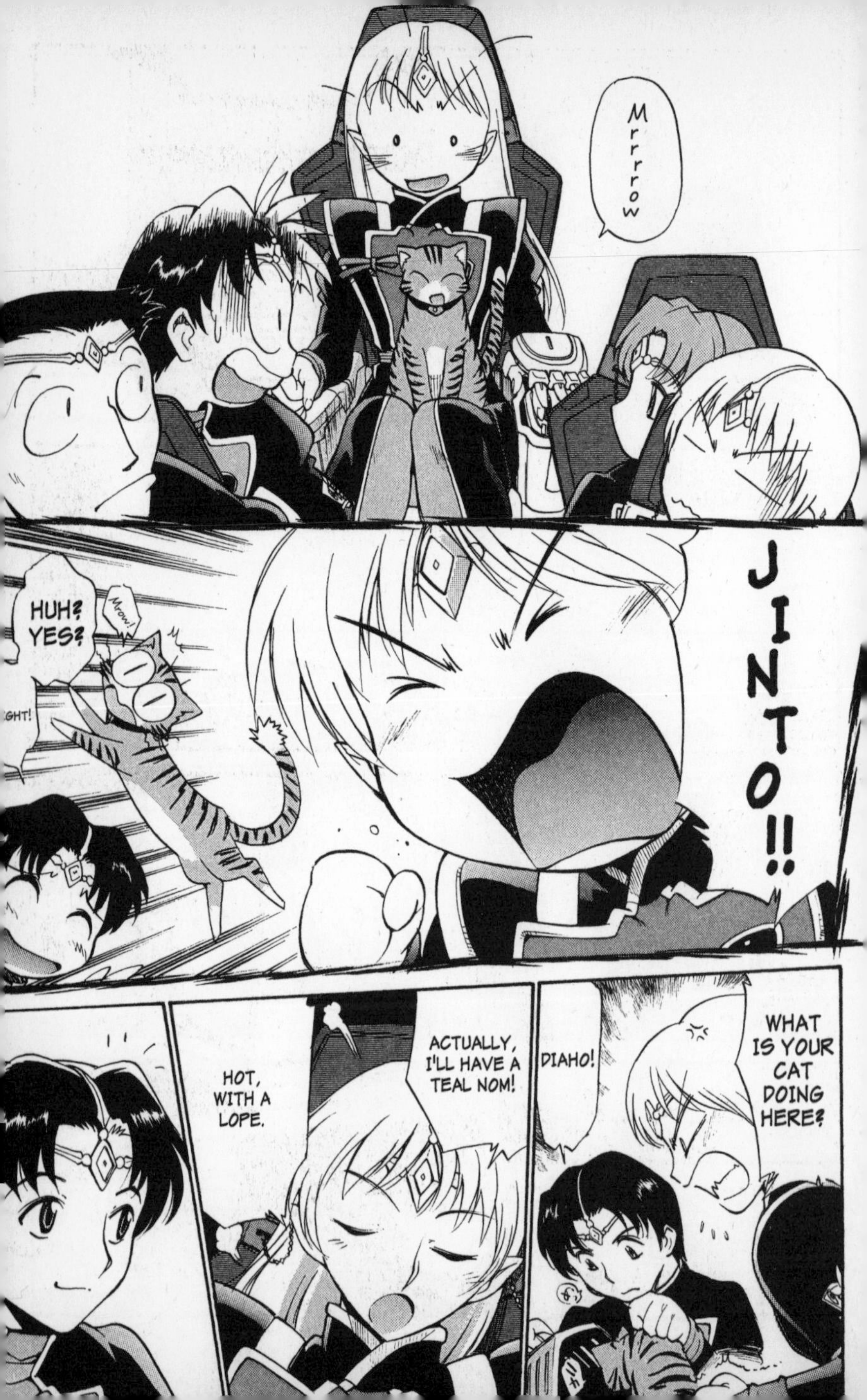
Mrrrow
JINTO!!
Mrow!
HUH? YES?
GHT!
WHAT IS YOUR CAT DOING HERE?
DIAHO!
ACTUALLY, I'LL HAVE A TEAL NOM!
HOT, WITH A LOPE.

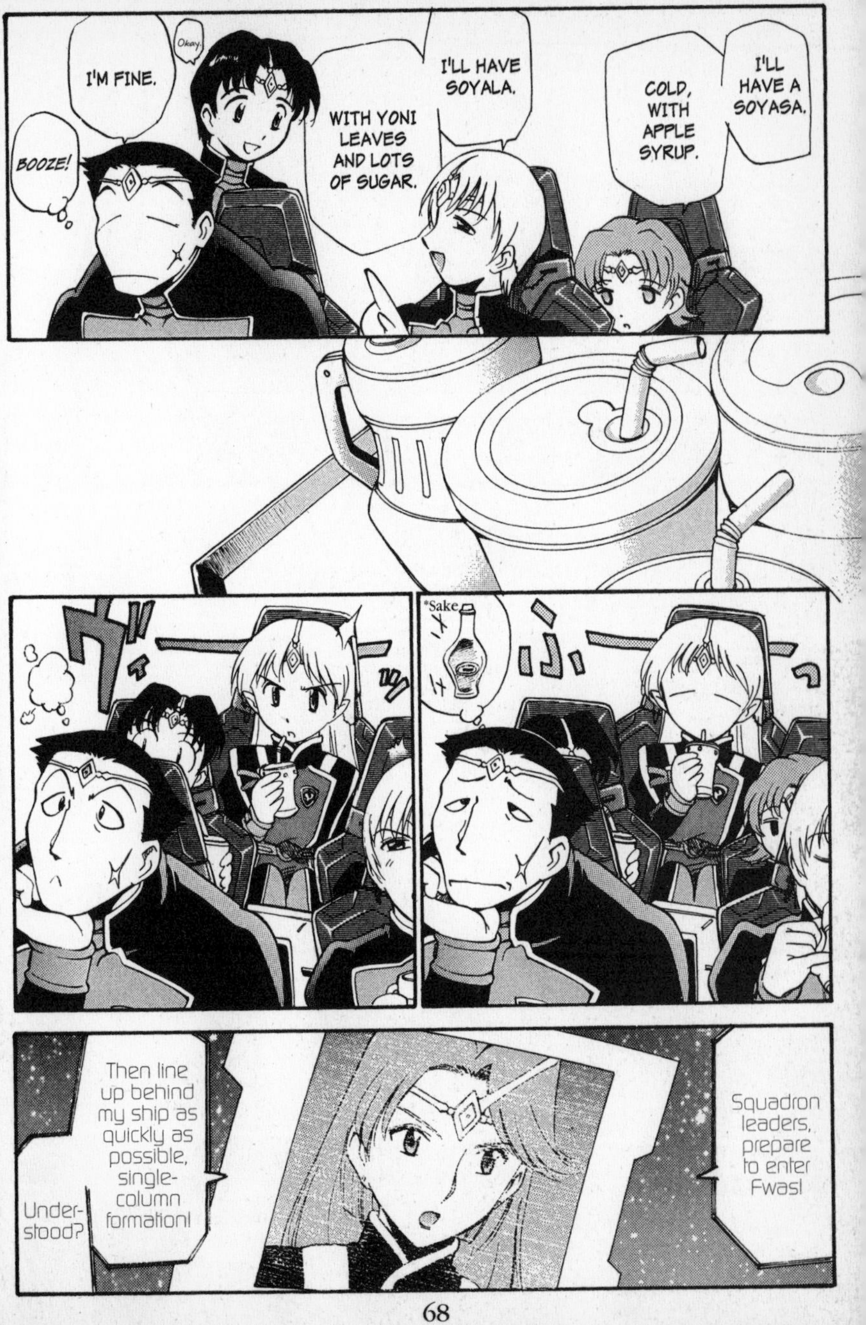
I'LL HAVE A SOYASA.
COLD, WITH APPLE SYRUP.
I'LL HAVE SOYALA.
WITH YONI LEAVES AND LOTS OF SUGAR.
Okay.
I'M FINE.
BOOZE!
*Sake
Squadron leaders, prepare to enter Fwas!
Then line up behind my ship as quickly as possible, single-column formation!
Under-stood?

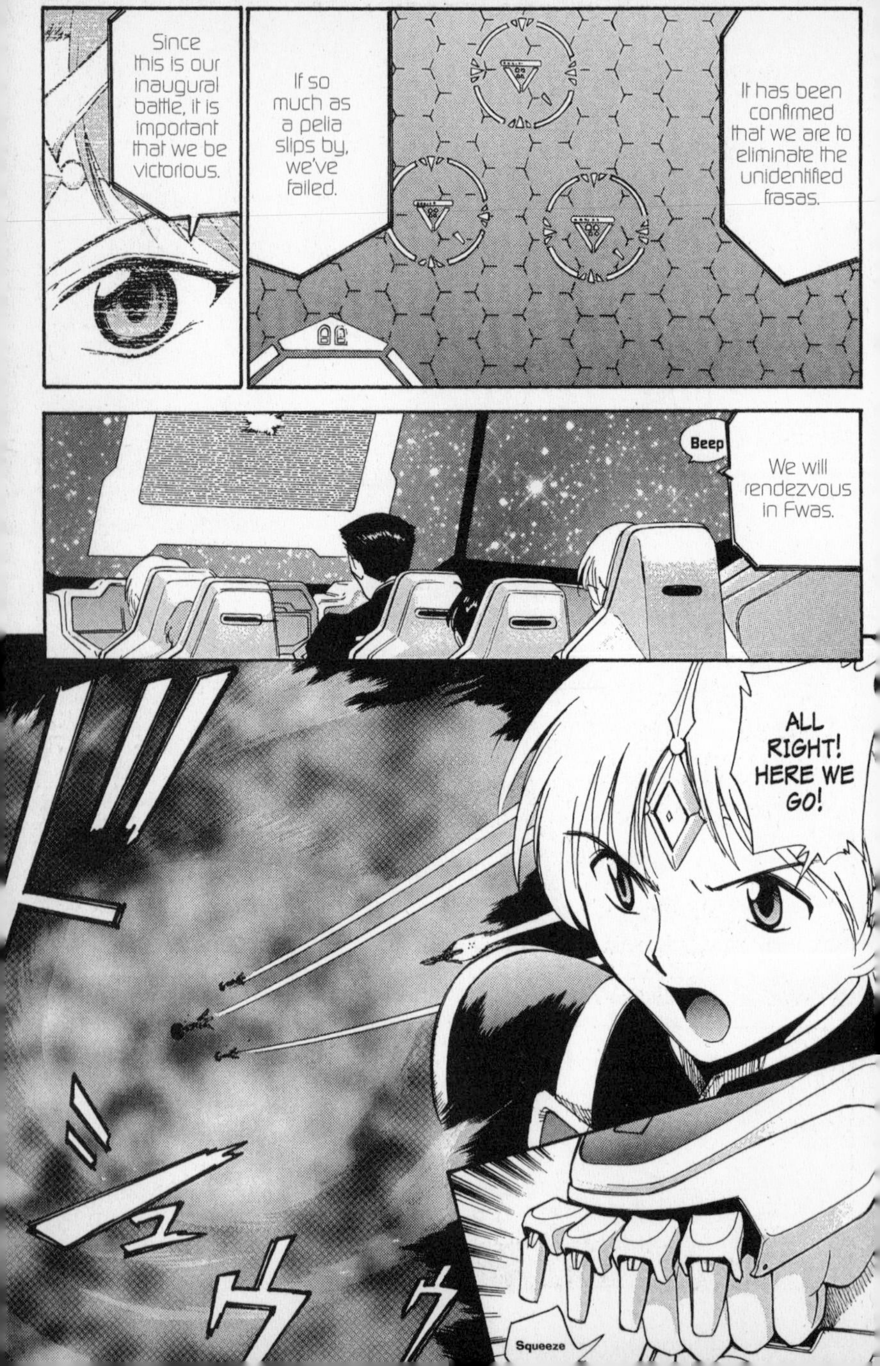
It has been confirmed that we are to eliminate the unidentified frasas.
If so much as a pelia slips by, we've failed.
Since this is our inaugural battle, it is important that we be victorious.
Beep
We will rendezvous in Fwas.
ALL RIGHT! HERE WE GO!
Squeeze

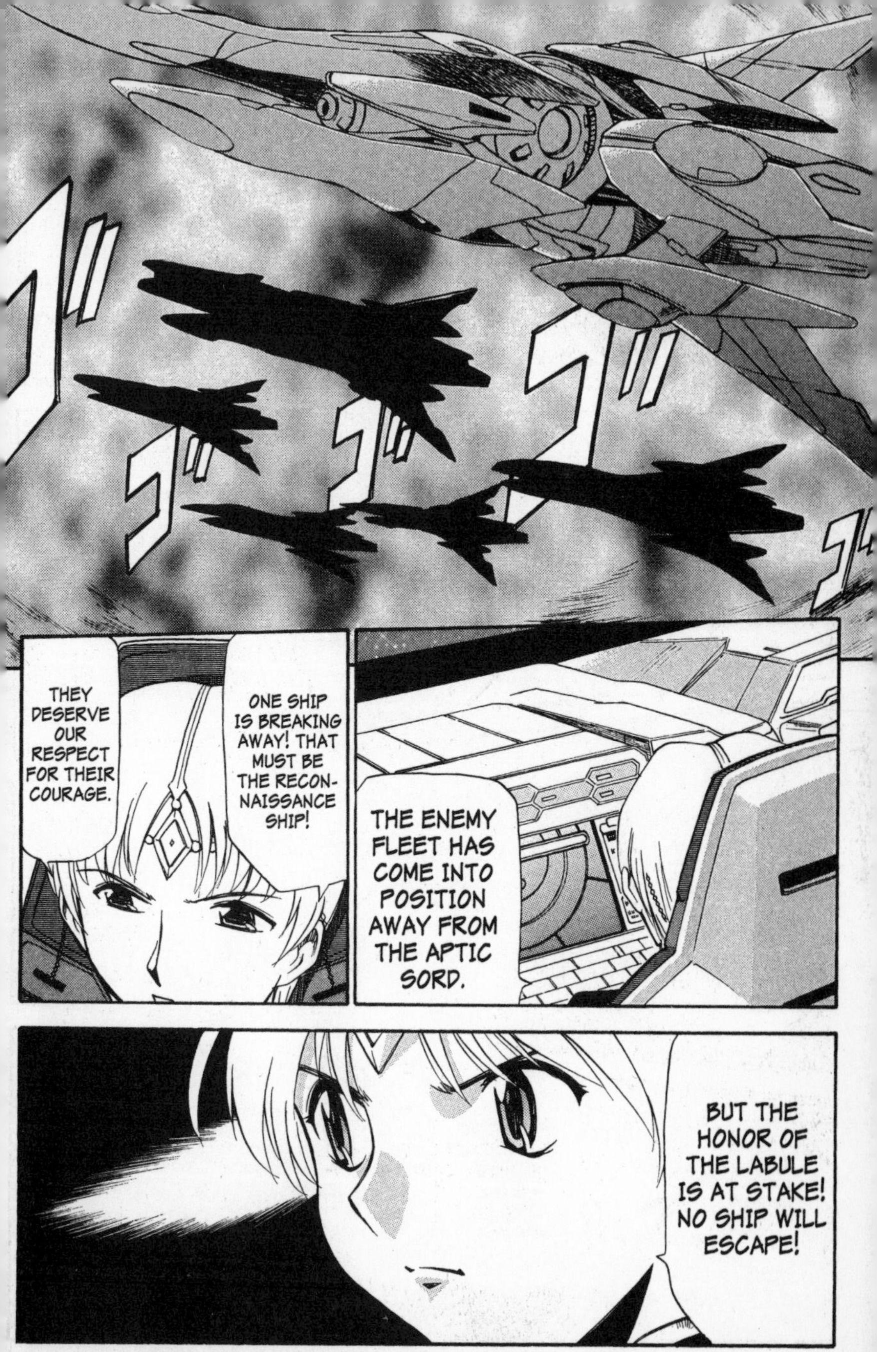
ゴ ゴ ゴ ゴ
THE ENEMY FLEET HAS COME INTO POSITION AWAY FROM THE APTIC SORD.
ONE SHIP IS BREAKING AWAY! THAT MUST BE THE RECON-NAISSANCE SHIP!
THEY DESERVE OUR RESPECT FOR THEIR COURAGE.
BUT THE HONOR OF THE LABULE IS AT STAKE! NO SHIP WILL ESCAPE!

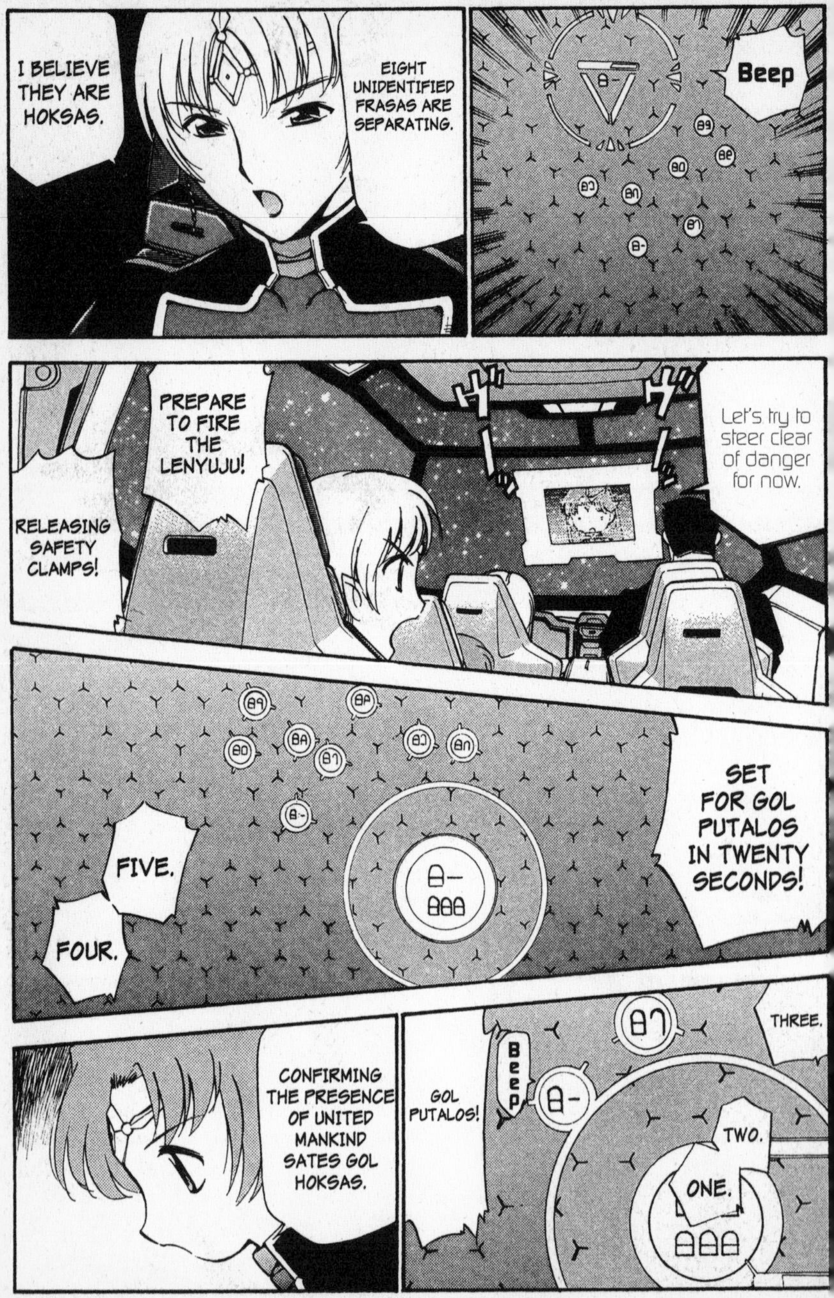
Beep
EIGHT UNIDENTIFIED FRASAS ARE SEPARATING.
I BELIEVE THEY ARE HOKSAS.
Let's try to steer clear of danger for now.
PREPARE TO FIRE THE LENYUJU!
RELEASING SAFETY CLAMPS!
SET FOR GOL PUTALOS IN TWENTY SECONDS!
FIVE.
FOUR.
THREE.
Beep
GOL PUTALOS!
TWO.
ONE.
CONFIRMING THE PRESENCE OF UNITED MANKIND SATES GOL HOKSAS.

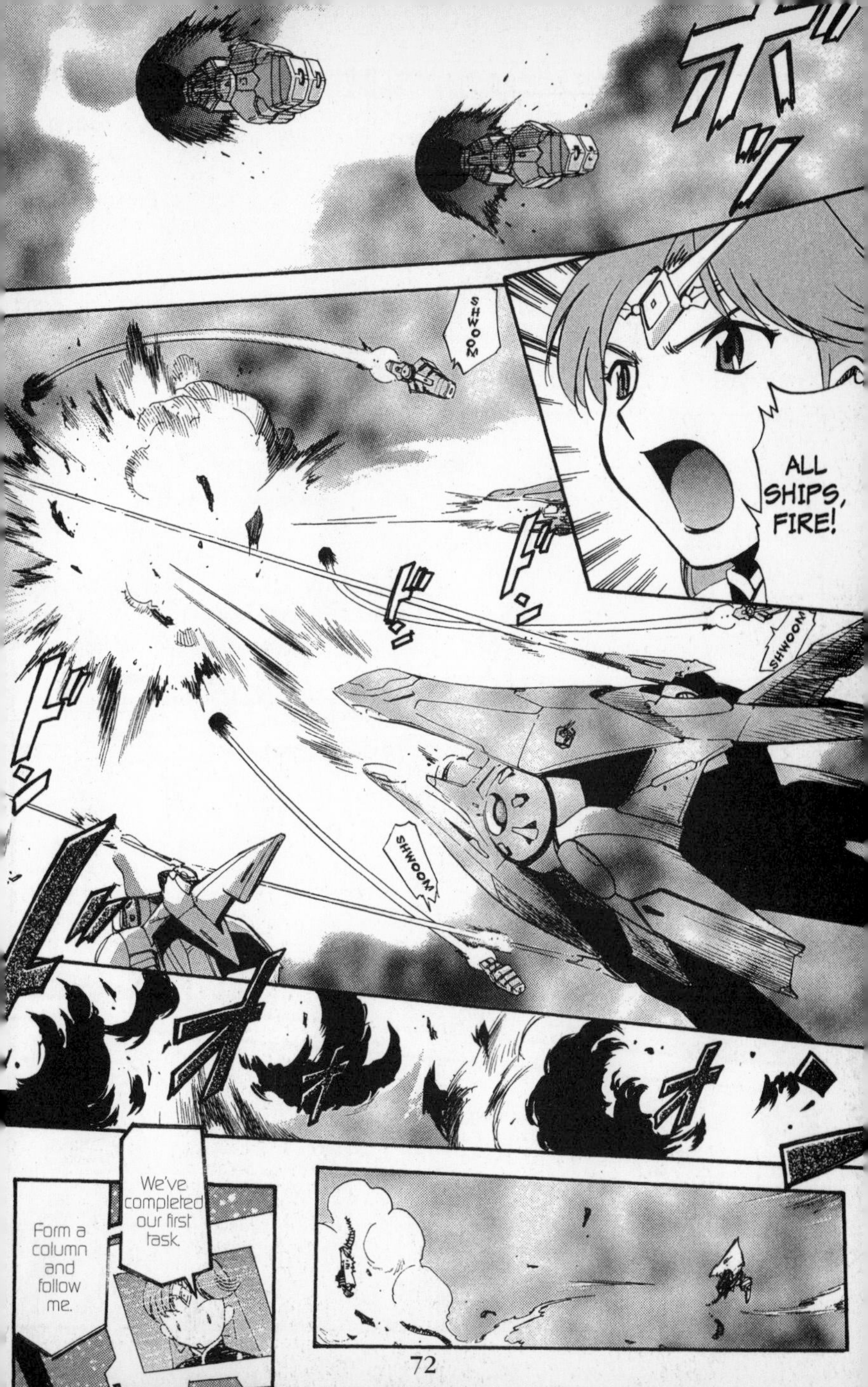
ALL SHIPS, FIRE!
SHWOOM
SHWOOM
SHWOOM
We've completed our first task.
Form a column and follow me.

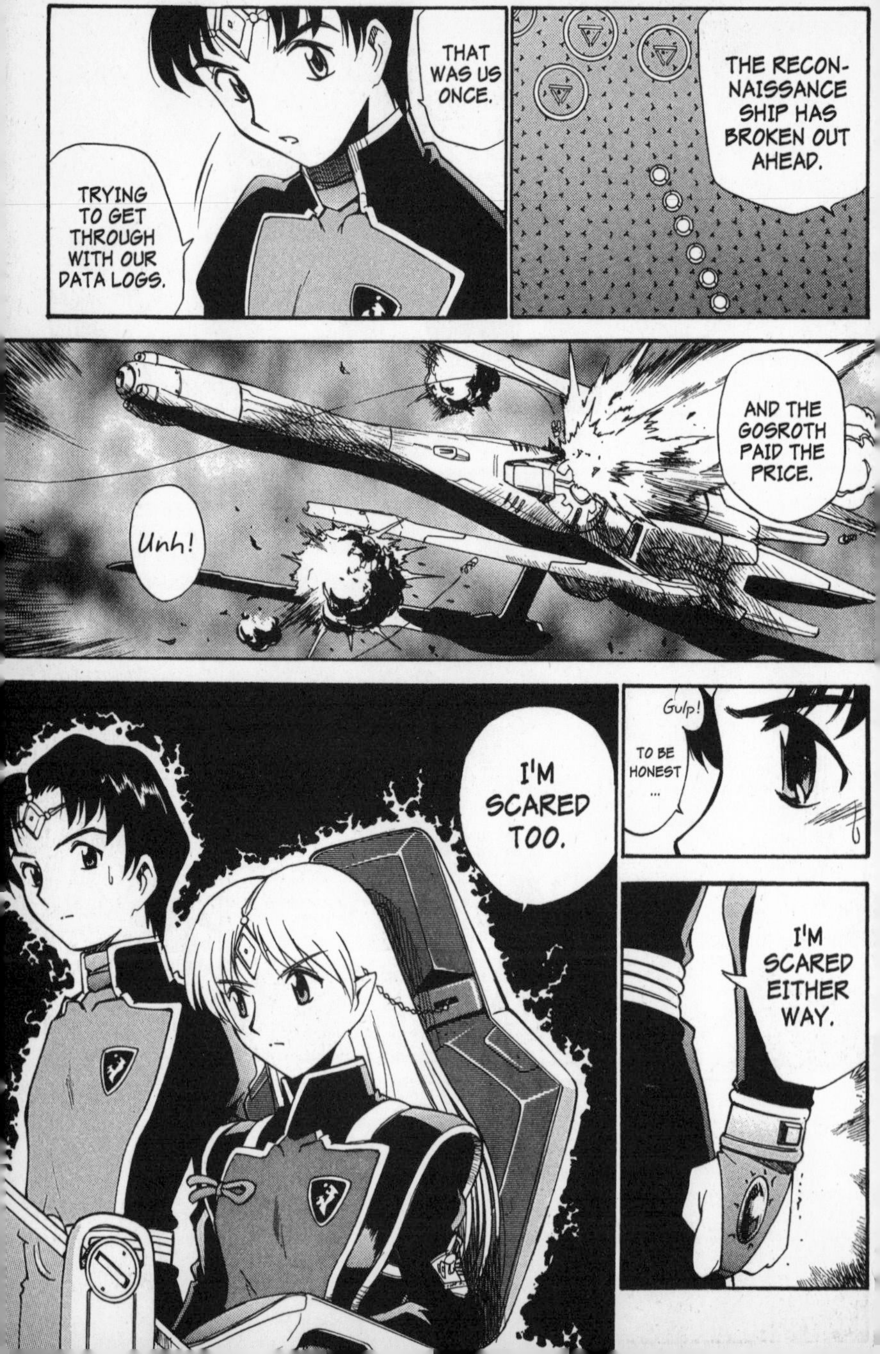
THE RECONNAISSANCE SHIP HAS BROKEN OUT AHEAD.
THAT WAS US ONCE.
TRYING TO GET THROUGH WITH OUR DATA LOGS.
AND THE GOSROTH PAID THE PRICE.
Unh!
Gulp!
TO BE HONEST ...
I'M SCARED EITHER WAY.
I'M SCARED TOO.

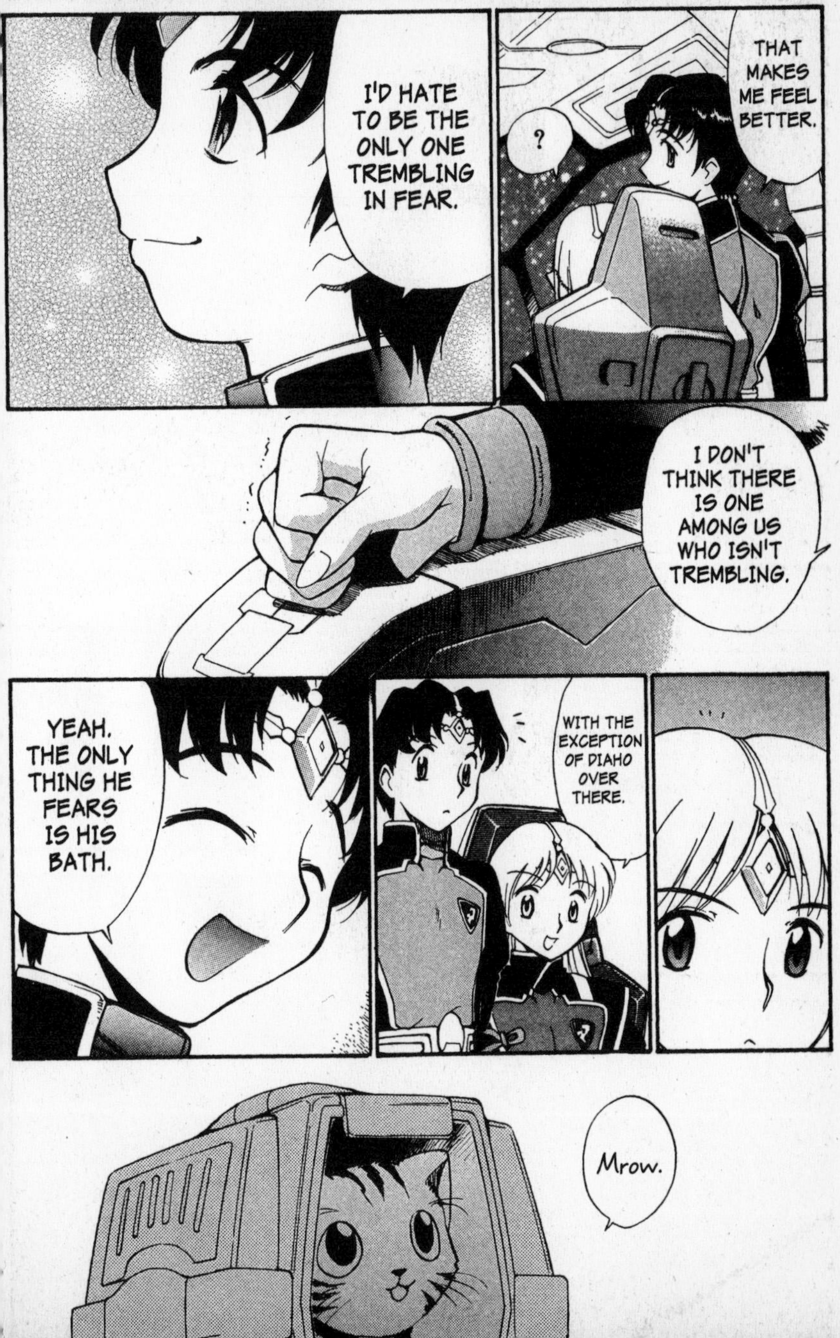
THAT MAKES ME FEEL BETTER.
?
I'D HATE TO BE THE ONLY ONE TREMBLING IN FEAR.
I DON'T THINK THERE IS ONE AMONG US WHO ISN'T TREMBLING.
WITH THE EXCEPTION OF DIAHO OVER THERE.
YEAH. THE ONLY THING HE FEARS IS HIS BATH.
Mrow.

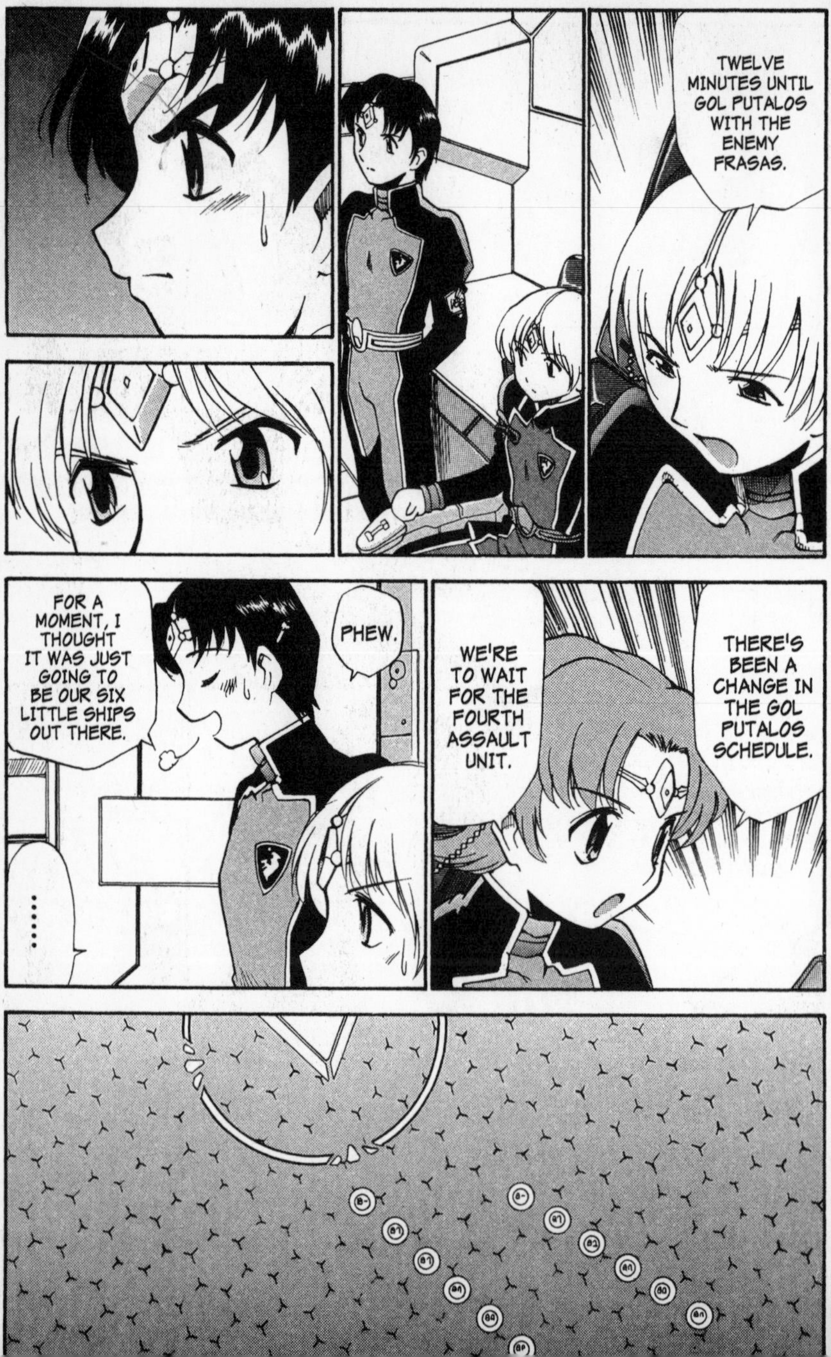

TWELVE MINUTES UNTIL GOL PUTALOS WITH THE ENEMY FRASAS.
THERE'S BEEN A CHANGE IN THE GOL PUTALOS SCHEDULE.
WE'RE TO WAIT FOR THE FOURTH ASSAULT UNIT.
PHEW.
FOR A MOMENT, I THOUGHT IT WAS JUST GOING TO BE OUR SIX LITTLE SHIPS OUT THERE.
......

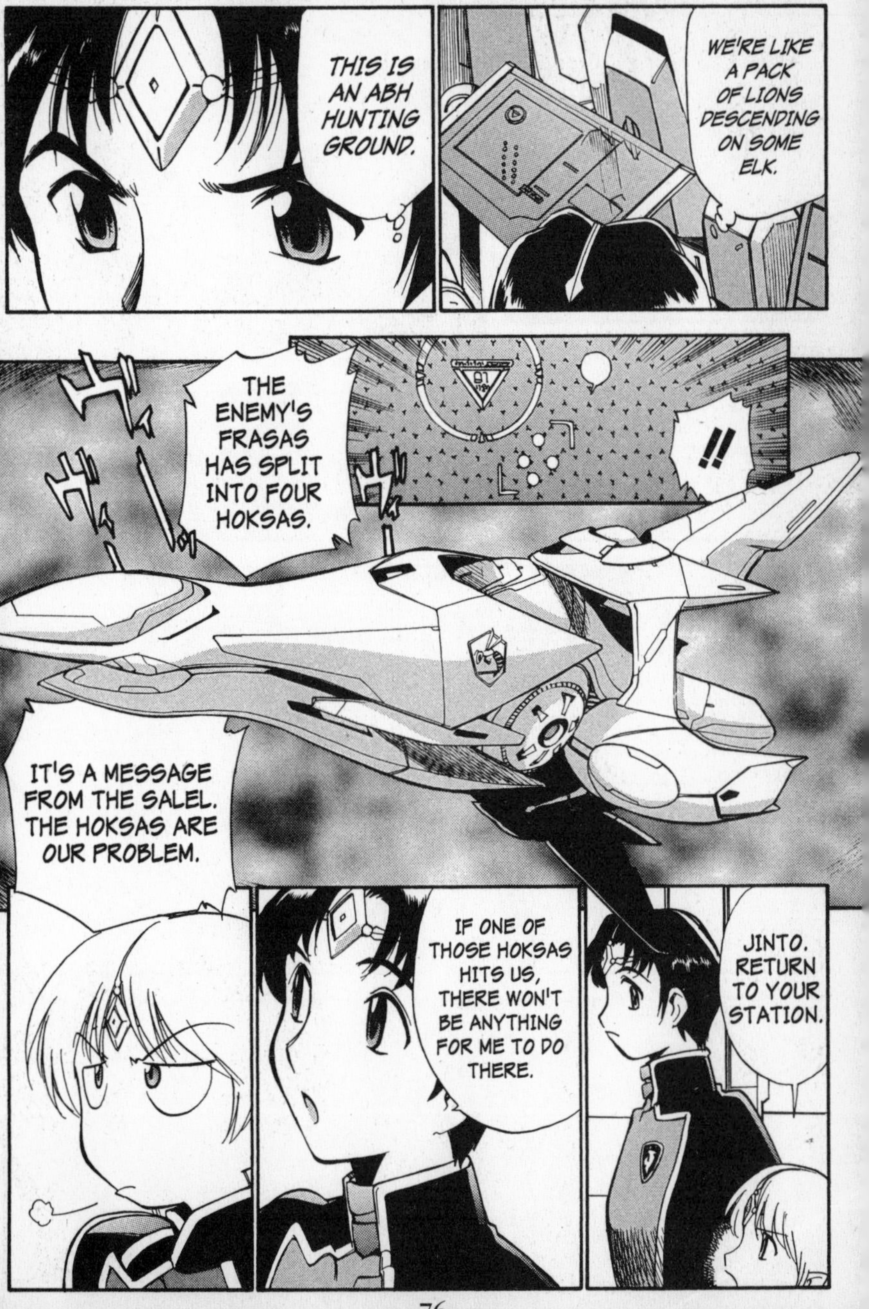
WE'RE LIKE A PACK OF LIONS DESCENDING ON SOME ELK.
THIS IS AN ABH HUNTING GROUND.
!!
THE ENEMY'S FRASAS HAS SPLIT INTO FOUR HOKSAS.
IT'S A MESSAGE FROM THE SALEL. THE HOKSAS ARE OUR PROBLEM.
JINTO. RETURN TO YOUR STATION.
IF ONE OF THOSE HOKSAS HITS US, THERE WON'T BE ANYTHING FOR ME TO DO THERE.

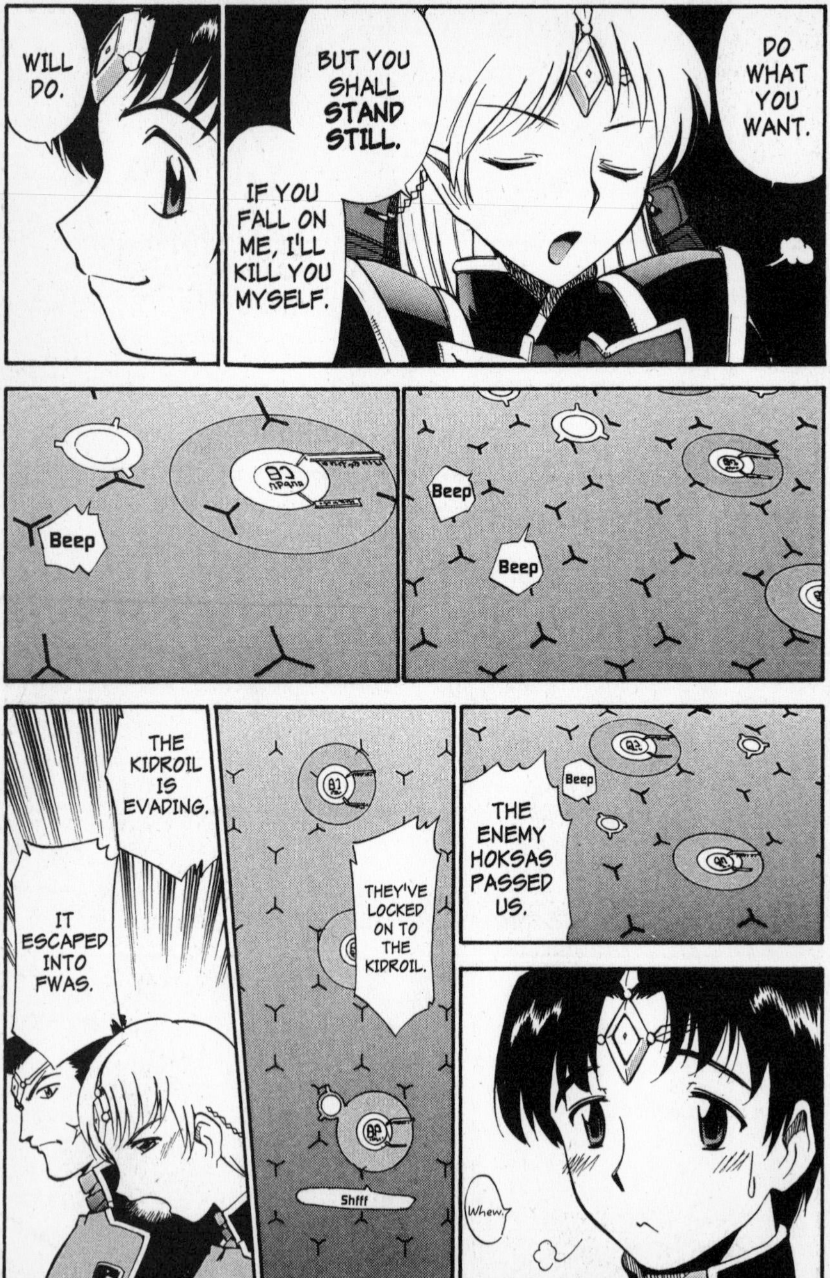
DO WHAT YOU WANT.
BUT YOU SHALL **STAND STILL.**
IF YOU FALL ON ME, I'LL KILL YOU MYSELF.
WILL DO.
Beep
Beep
Beep
Beep
THE ENEMY HOKSAS PASSED US.
Whew.
THEY'VE LOCKED ON TO THE KIDROIL.
Shfff
THE KIDROIL IS EVADING.
IT ESCAPED INTO FWAS.

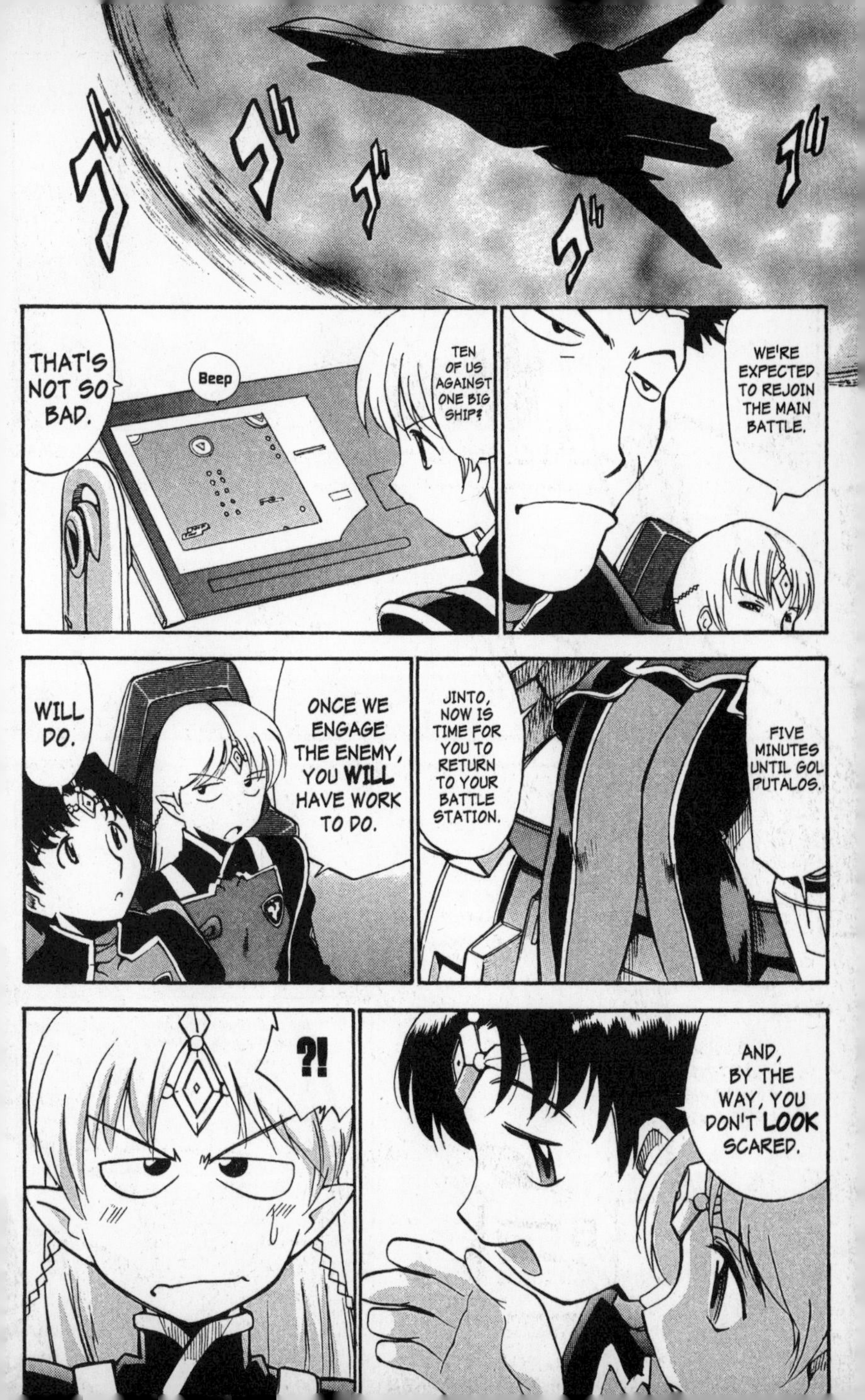
WE'RE EXPECTED TO REJOIN THE MAIN BATTLE.
TEN OF US AGAINST ONE BIG SHIP?
Beep
THAT'S NOT SO BAD.
FIVE MINUTES UNTIL GOL PUTALOS.
JINTO, NOW IS TIME FOR YOU TO RETURN TO YOUR BATTLE STATION.
ONCE WE ENGAGE THE ENEMY, YOU **WILL** HAVE WORK TO DO.
WILL DO.
AND, BY THE WAY, YOU DON'T **LOOK** SCARED.
?!

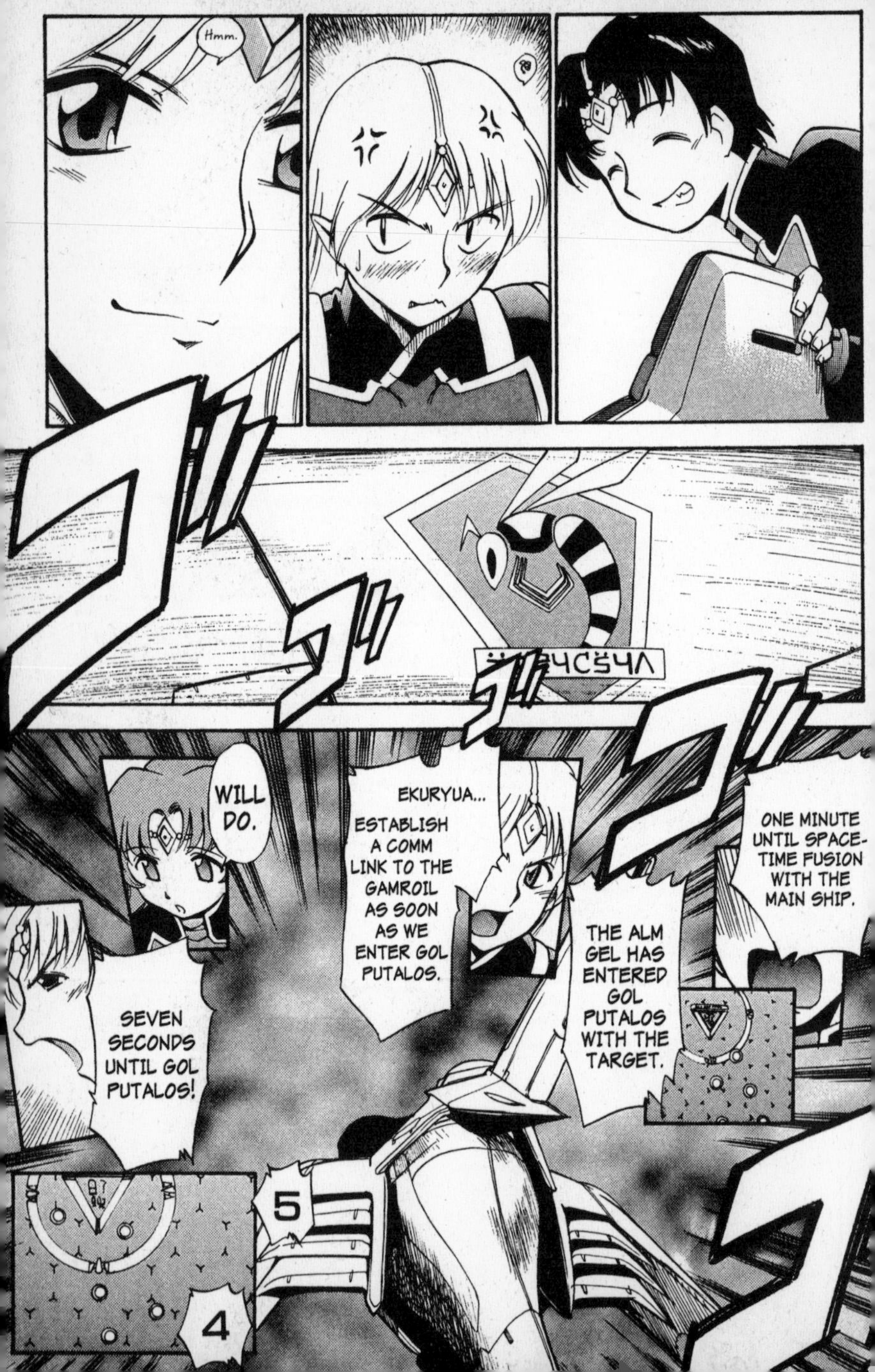
Hmm.
ONE MINUTE UNTIL SPACE-TIME FUSION WITH THE MAIN SHIP.
THE ALM GEL HAS ENTERED GOL PUTALOS WITH THE TARGET.
EKURYUA... ESTABLISH A COMM LINK TO THE GAMROIL AS SOON AS WE ENTER GOL PUTALOS.
WILL DO.
SEVEN SECONDS UNTIL GOL PUTALOS!
5
4

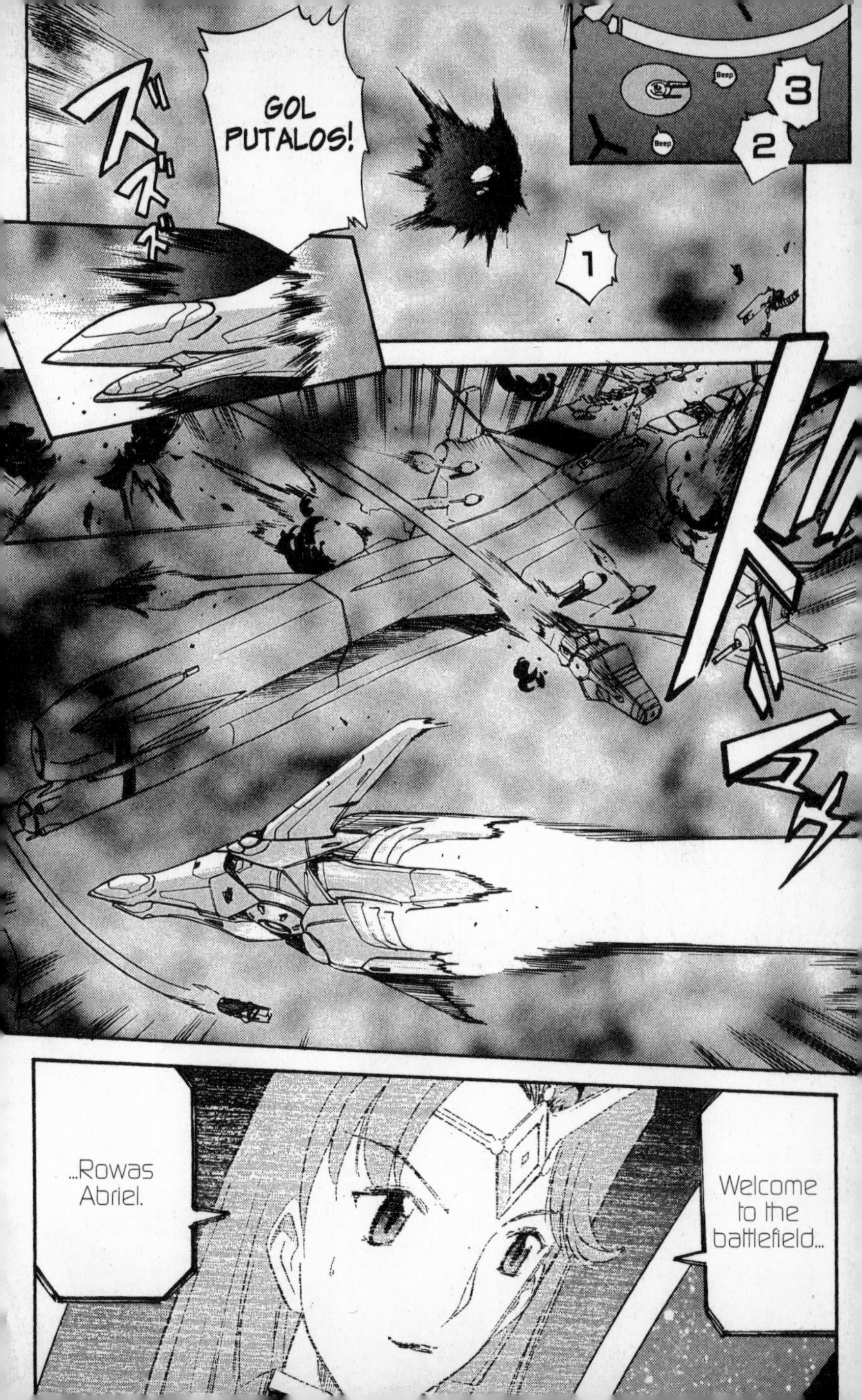
3
Beep
2
Beep
GOL PUTALOS!
1
Welcome to the battlefield...
...Rowas Abriel.

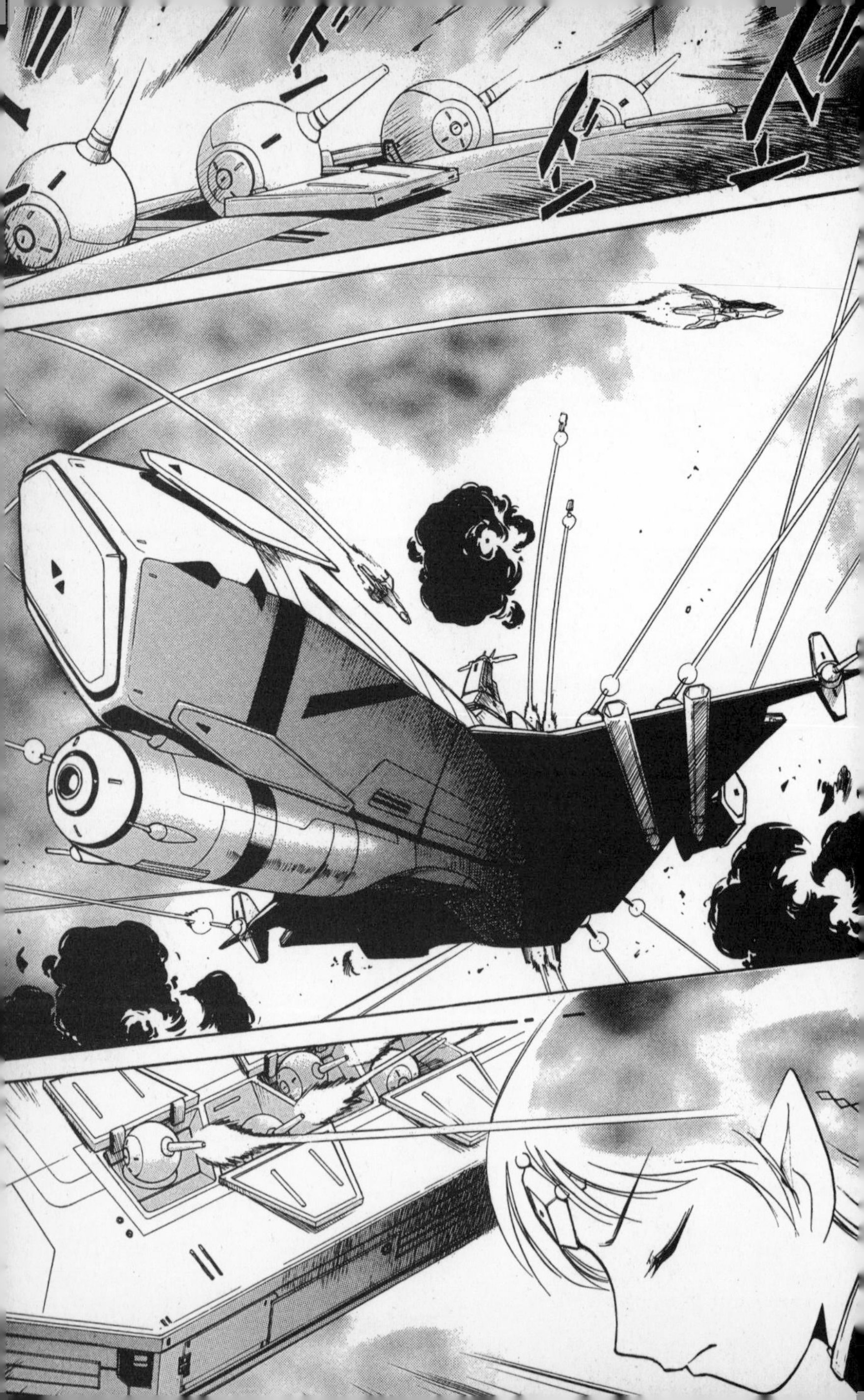
ドン
ドン
ドン

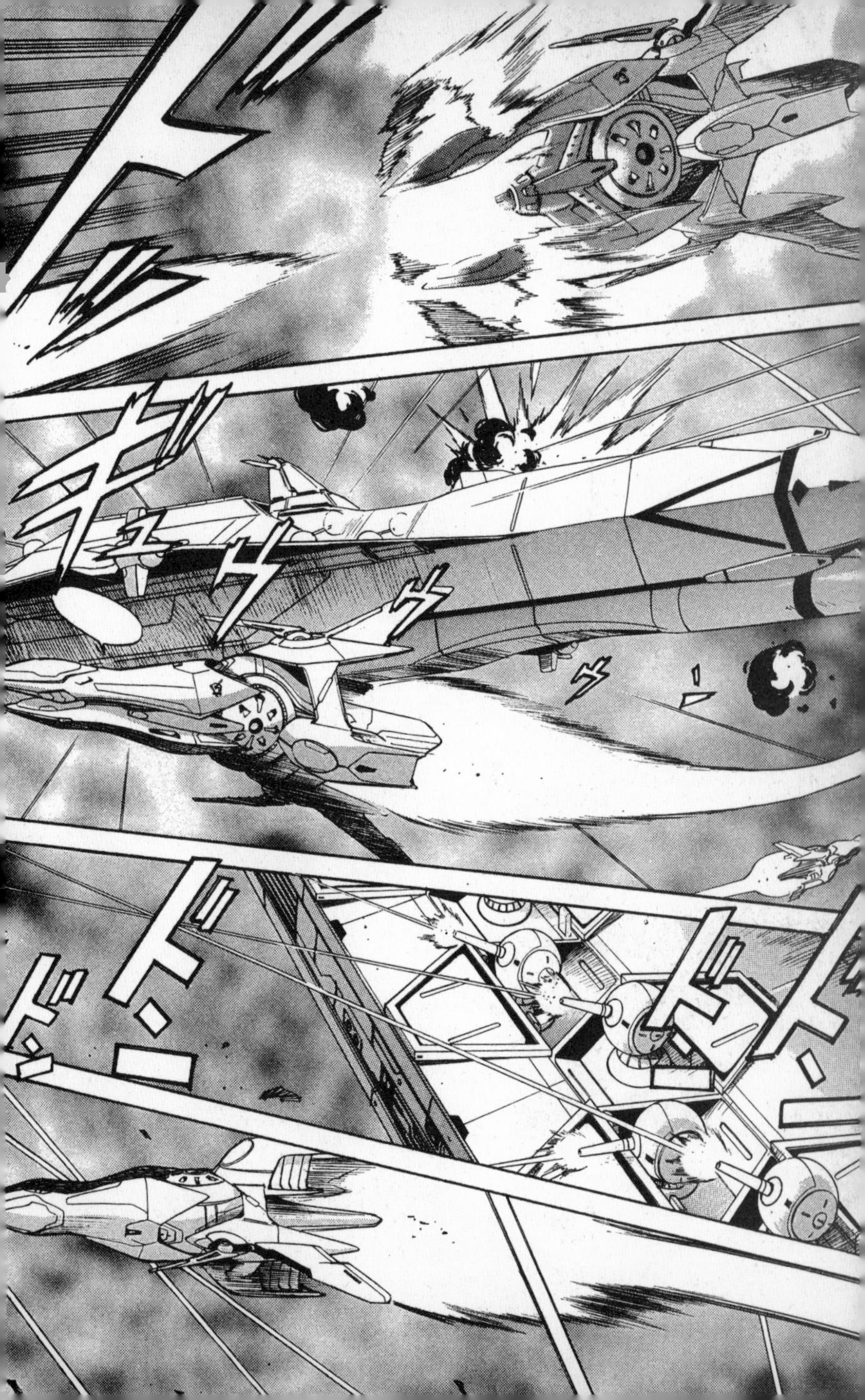
ギュゥゥ
ドドッ
ドドッ

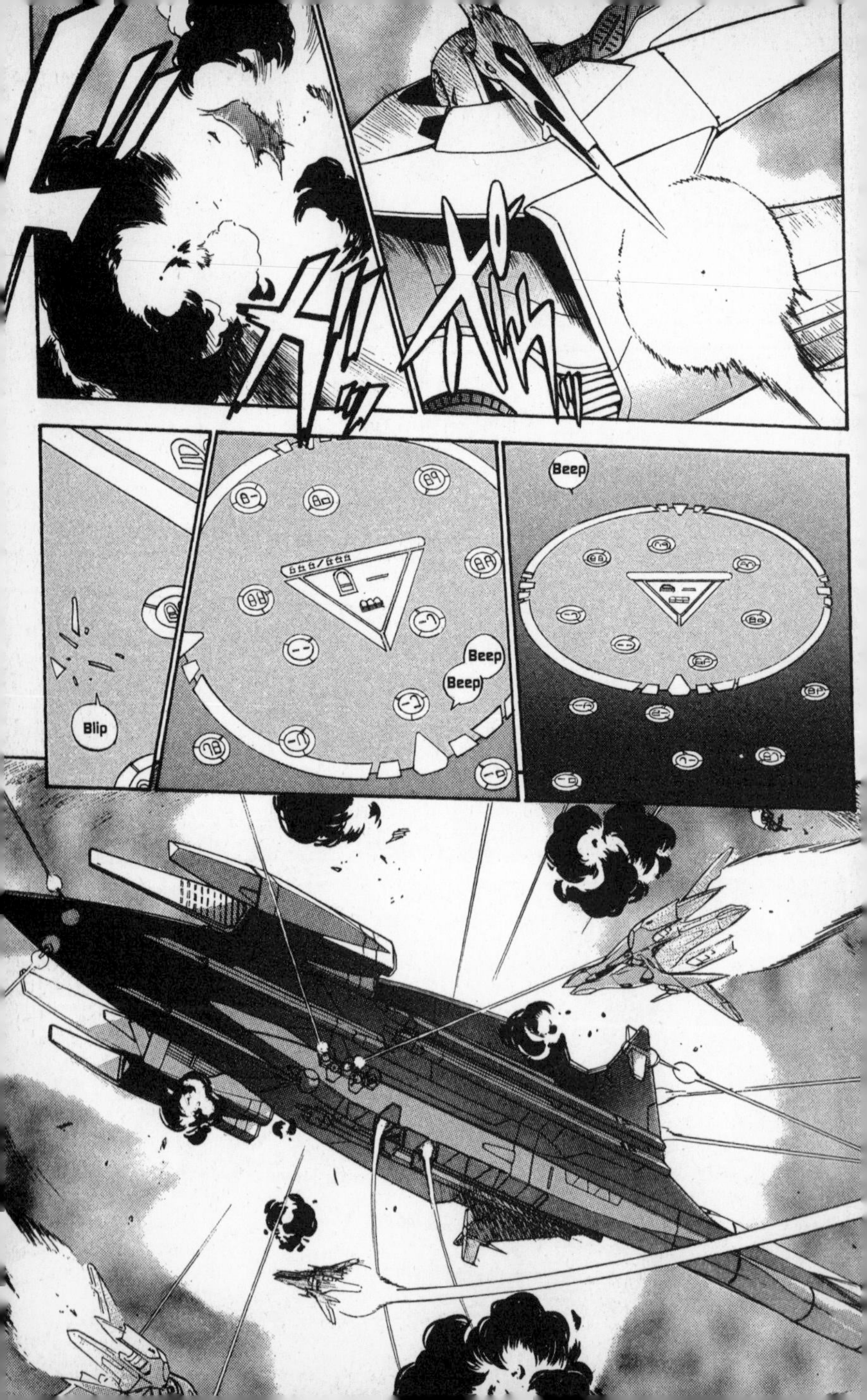
Beep
Beep
Beep
Blip

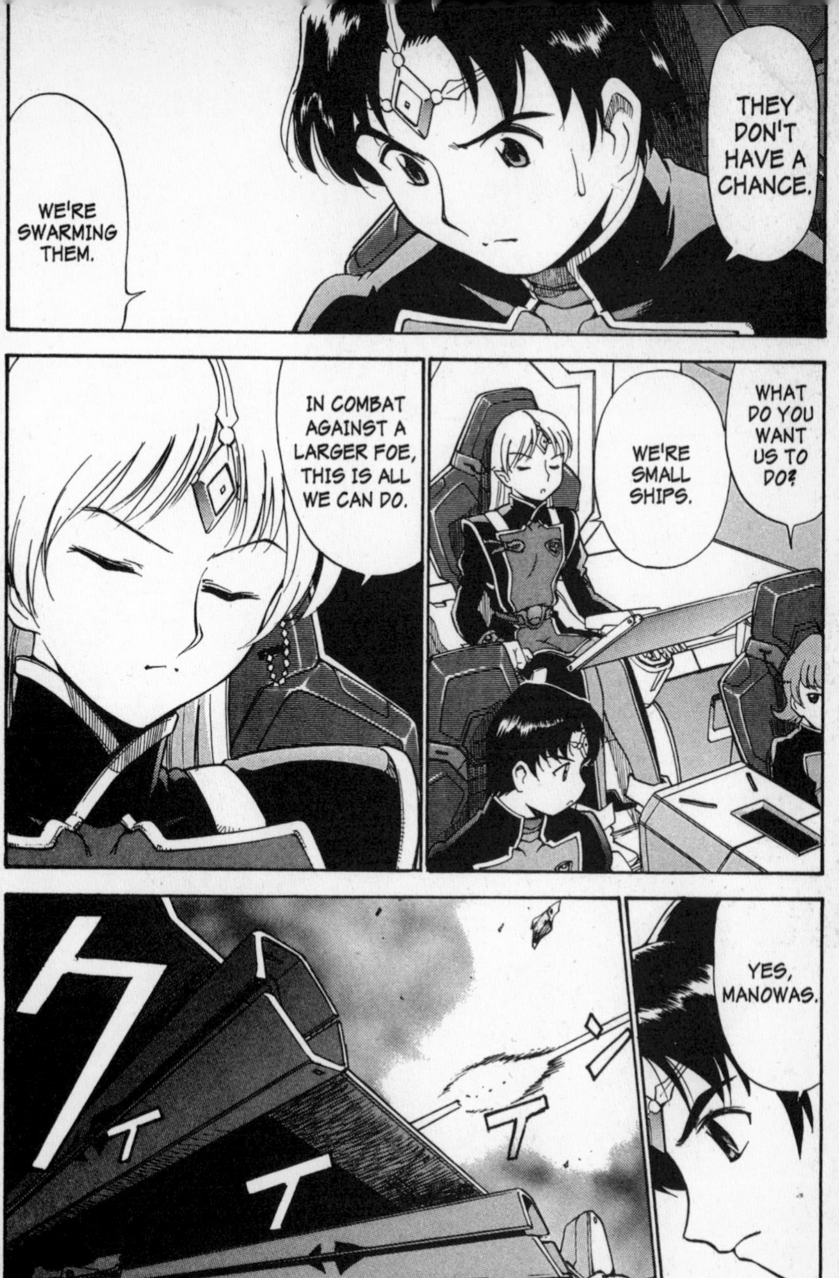
THEY DON'T HAVE A CHANCE.
WE'RE SWARMING THEM.
WHAT DO YOU WANT US TO DO?
WE'RE SMALL SHIPS.
IN COMBAT AGAINST A LARGER FOE, THIS IS ALL WE CAN DO.
YES, MANOWAS.

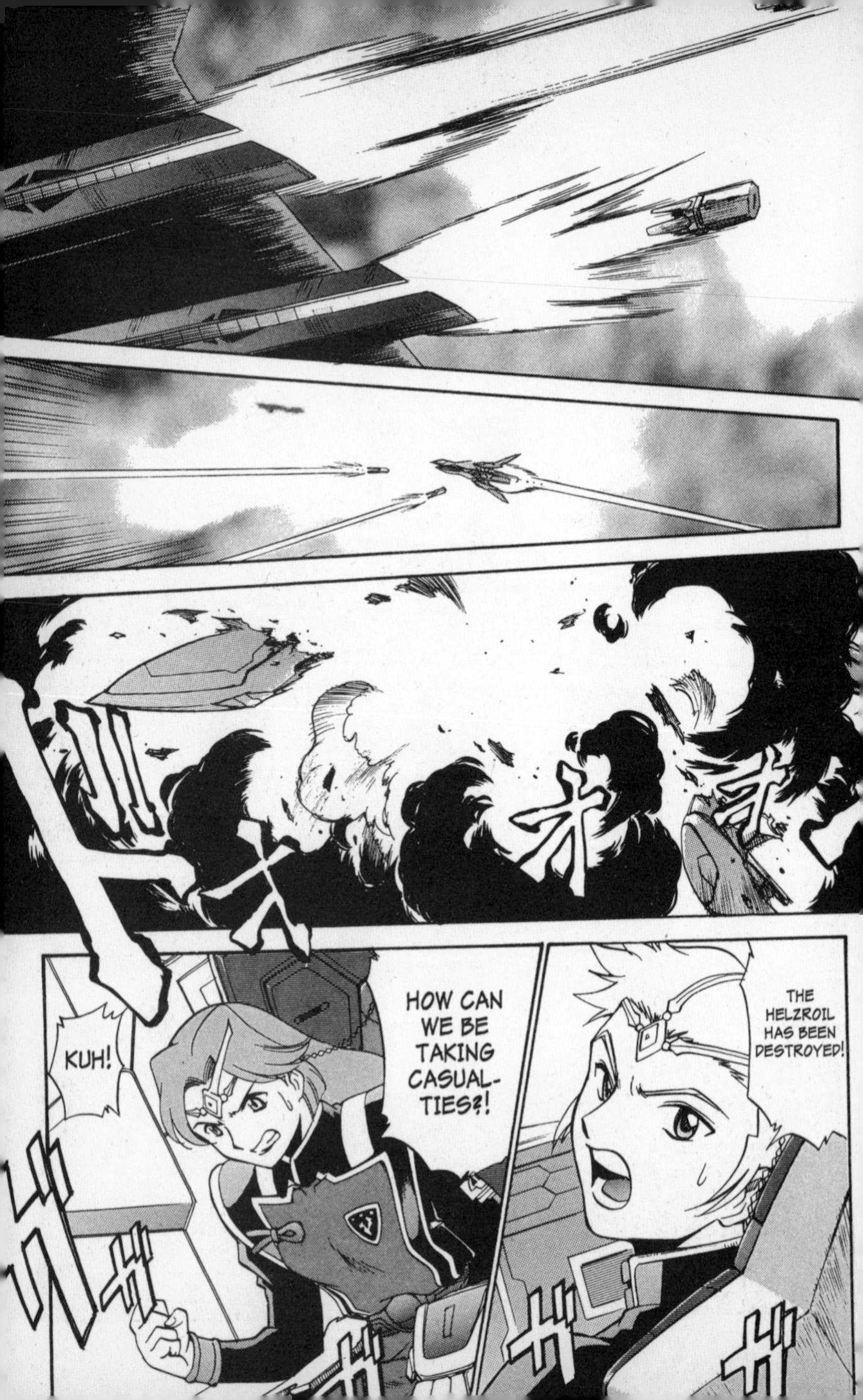
THE HELZROIL HAS BEEN DESTROYED!
HOW CAN WE BE TAKING CASUAL-TIES?!
KUH!

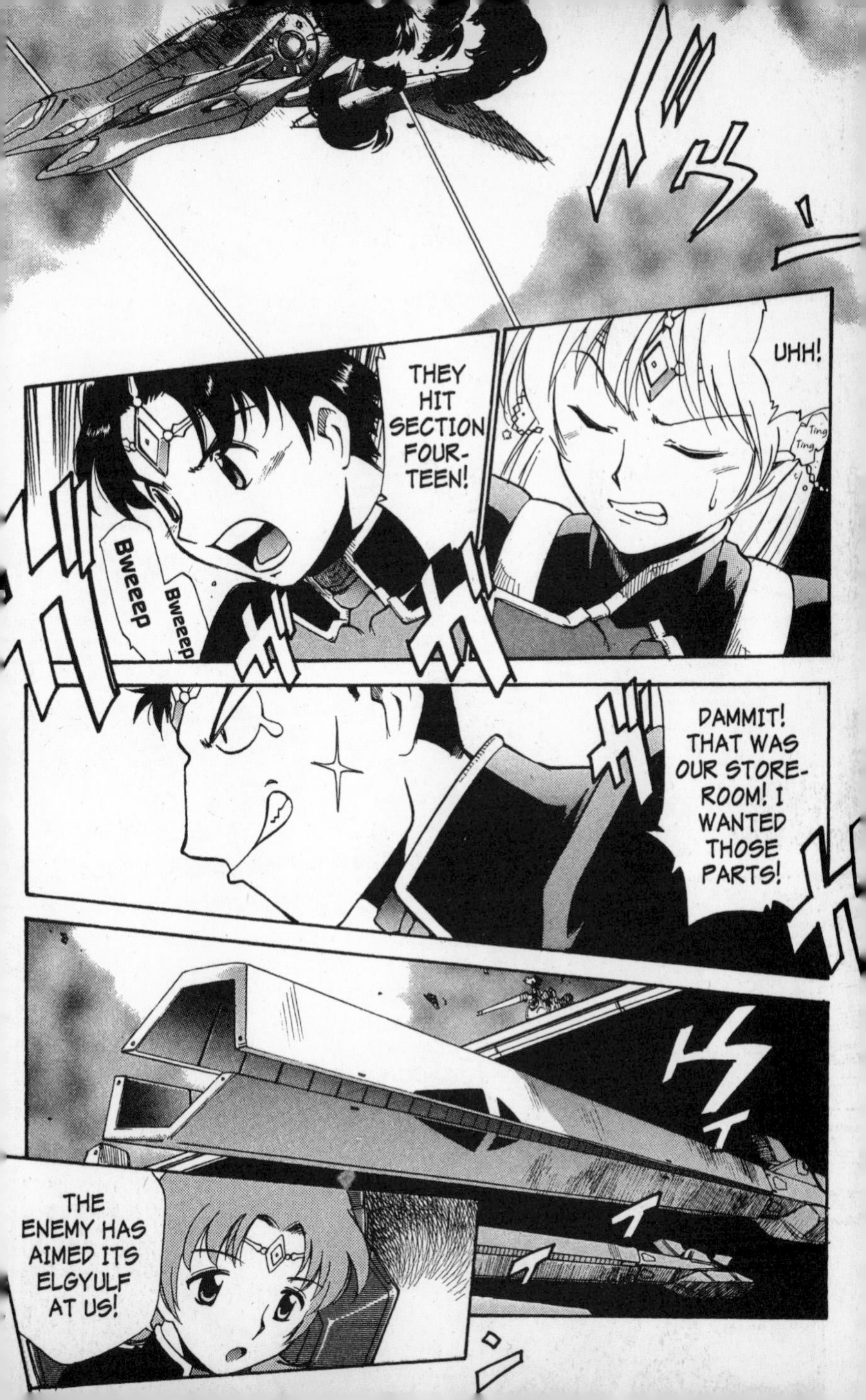
UHH!
Ting
Ting
THEY HIT SECTION FOURTEEN!
Bweeep
Bweeep
DAMMIT! THAT WAS OUR STOREROOM! I WANTED THOSE PARTS!
THE ENEMY HAS AIMED ITS ELGYULF AT US!

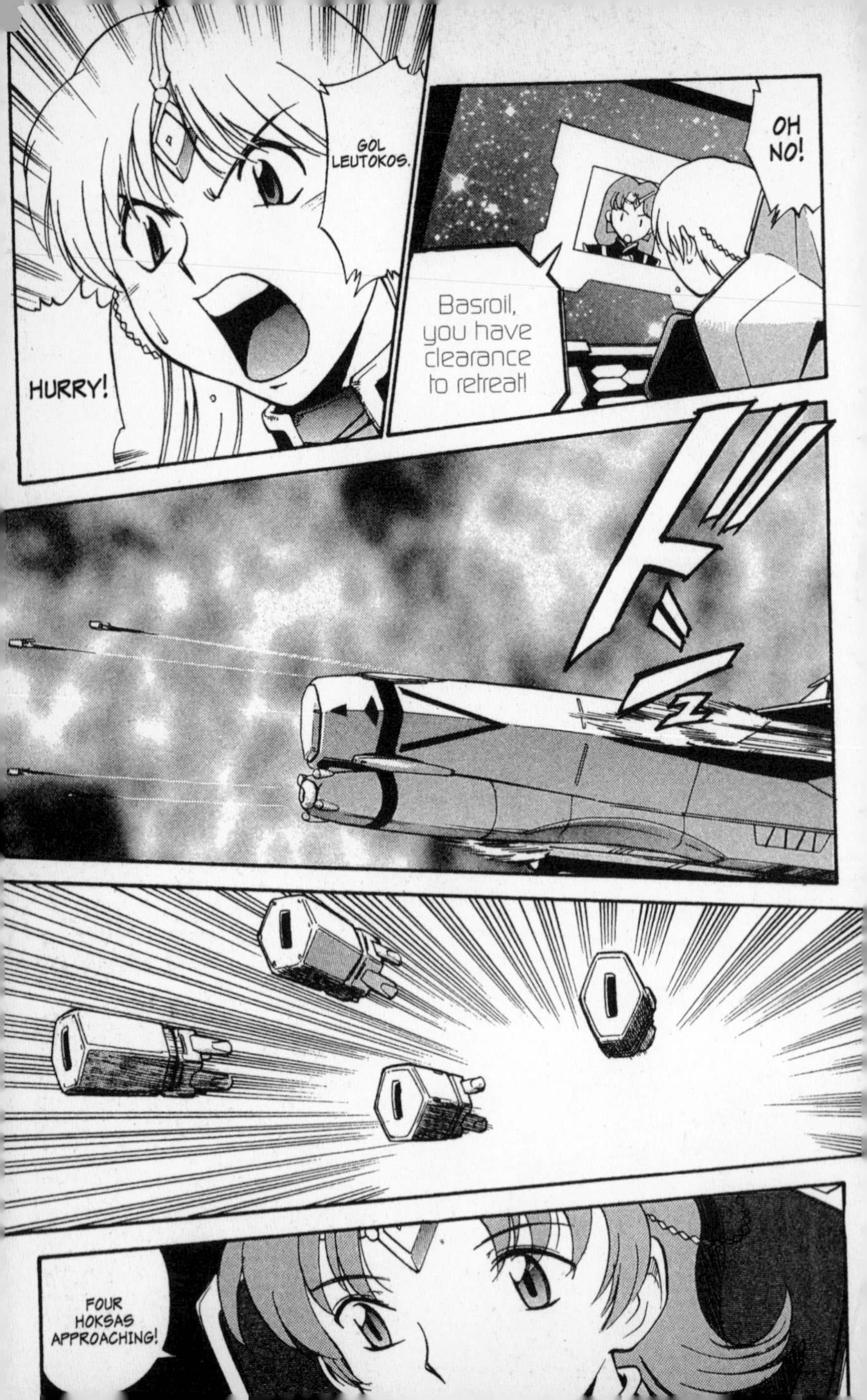
OH NO!
Basroil, you have clearance to retreat!
GOL LEUTOKOS.
HURRY!
FOUR HOKSAS APPROACHING!

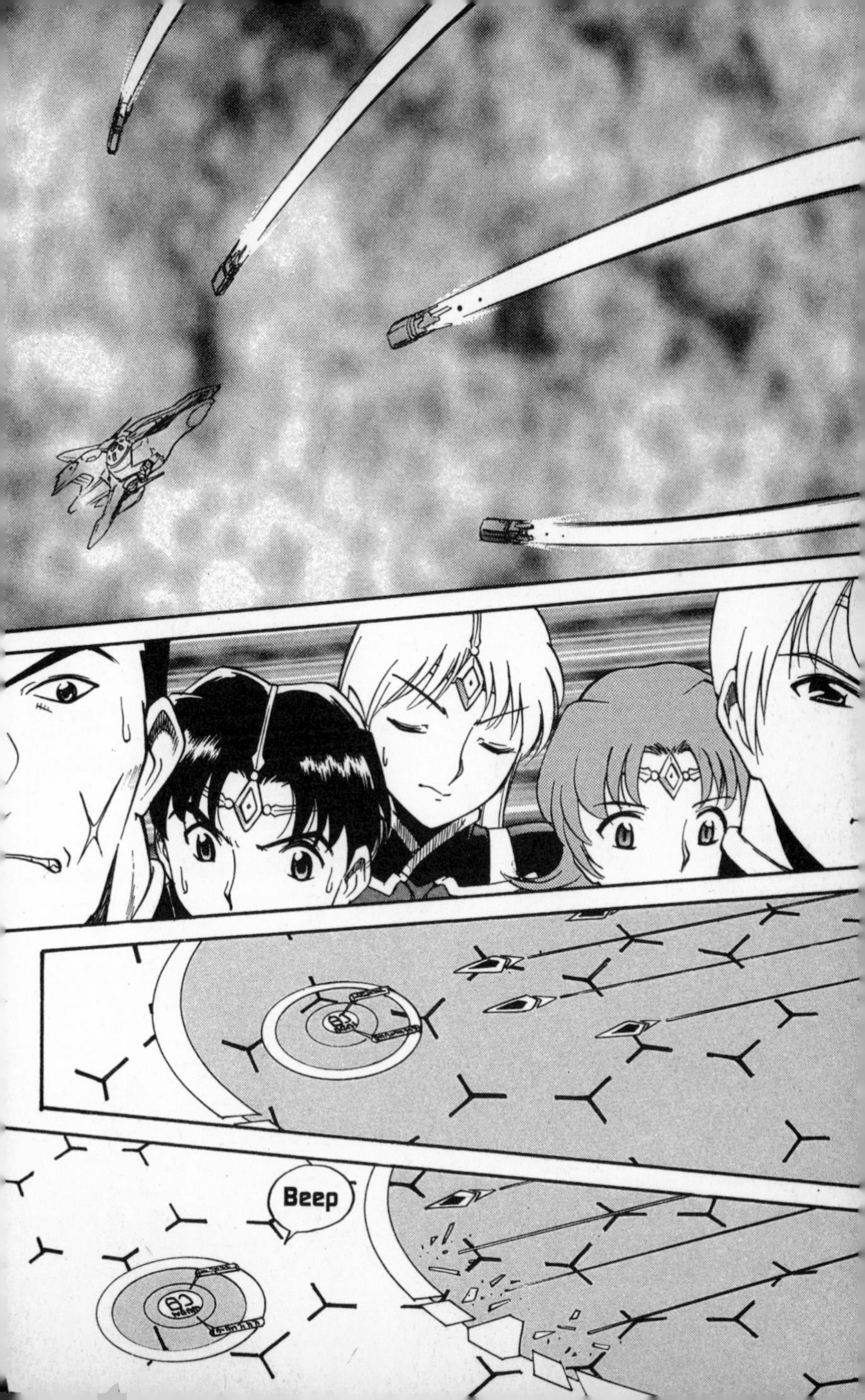
Beep

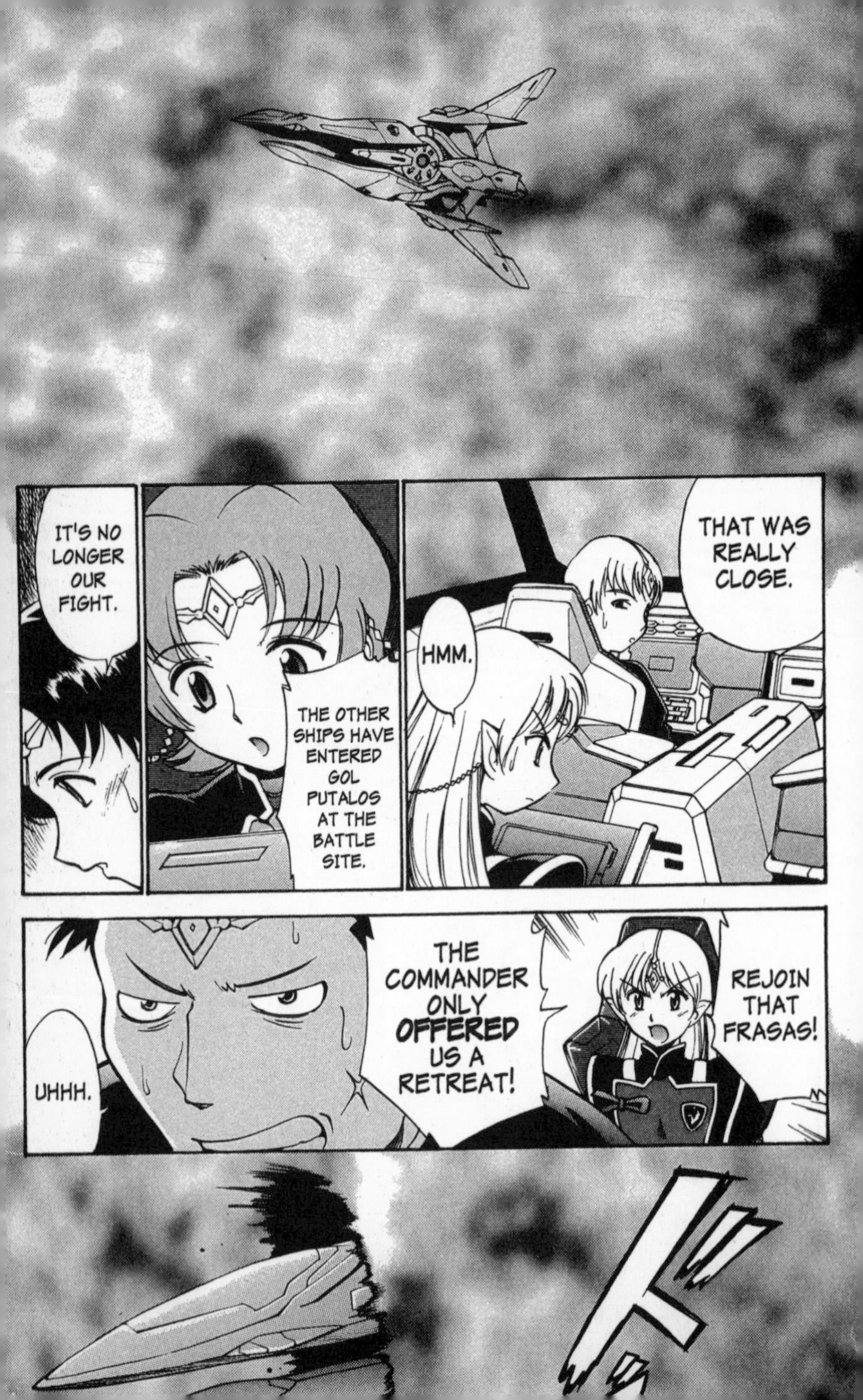

THAT WAS REALLY CLOSE.
HMM.
THE OTHER SHIPS HAVE ENTERED GOL PUTALOS AT THE BATTLE SITE.
IT'S NO LONGER OUR FIGHT.
REJOIN THAT FRASAS!
THE COMMANDER ONLY **OFFERED** US A RETREAT!
UHHH.
ド

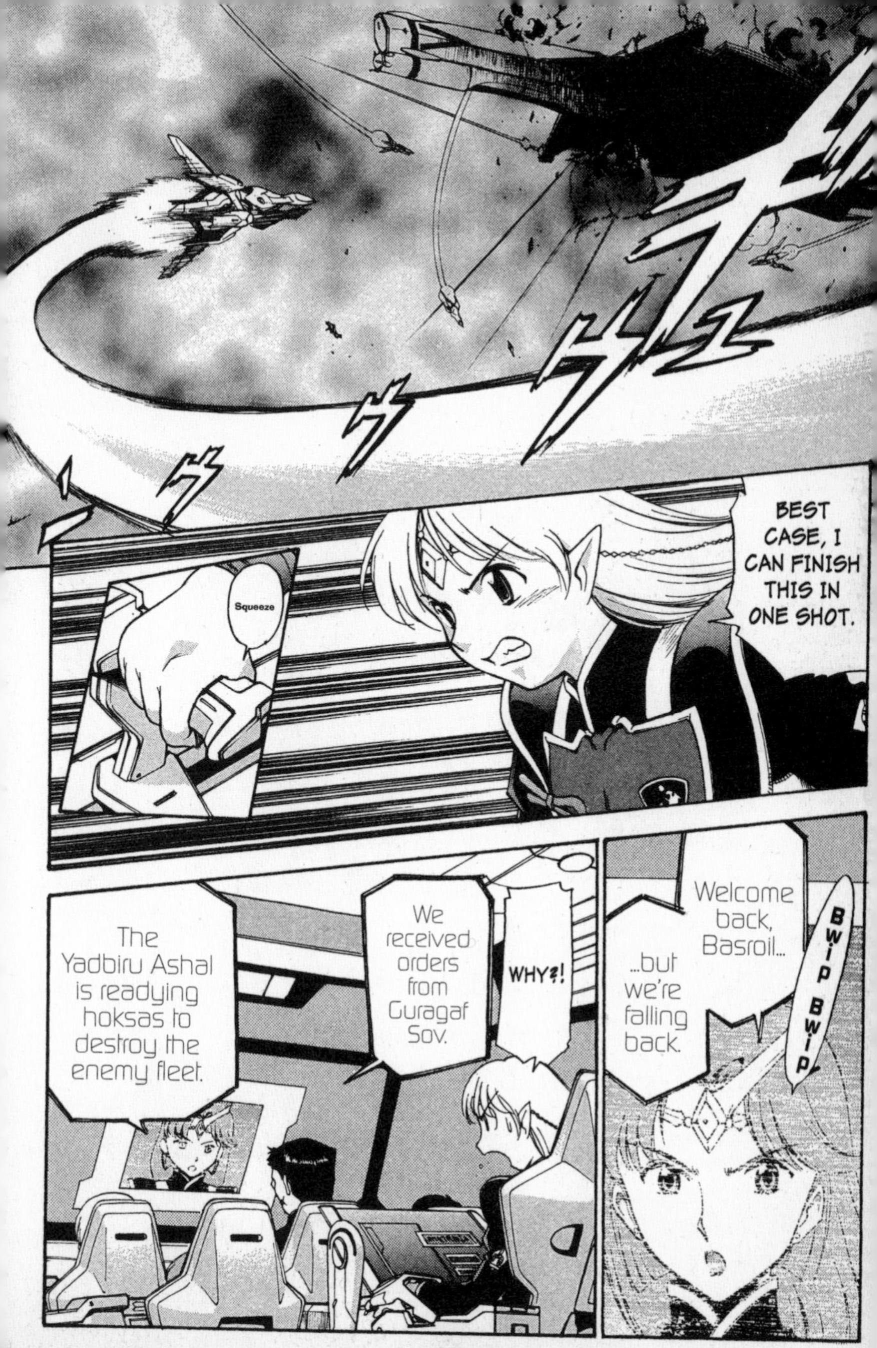
BEST CASE, I CAN FINISH THIS IN ONE SHOT.
Squeeze
Welcome back, Basroil...
BWIP BWIP
...but we're falling back.
WHY?!
We received orders from Guragaf Sov.
The Yadbiru Ashal is readying hoksas to destroy the enemy fleet.

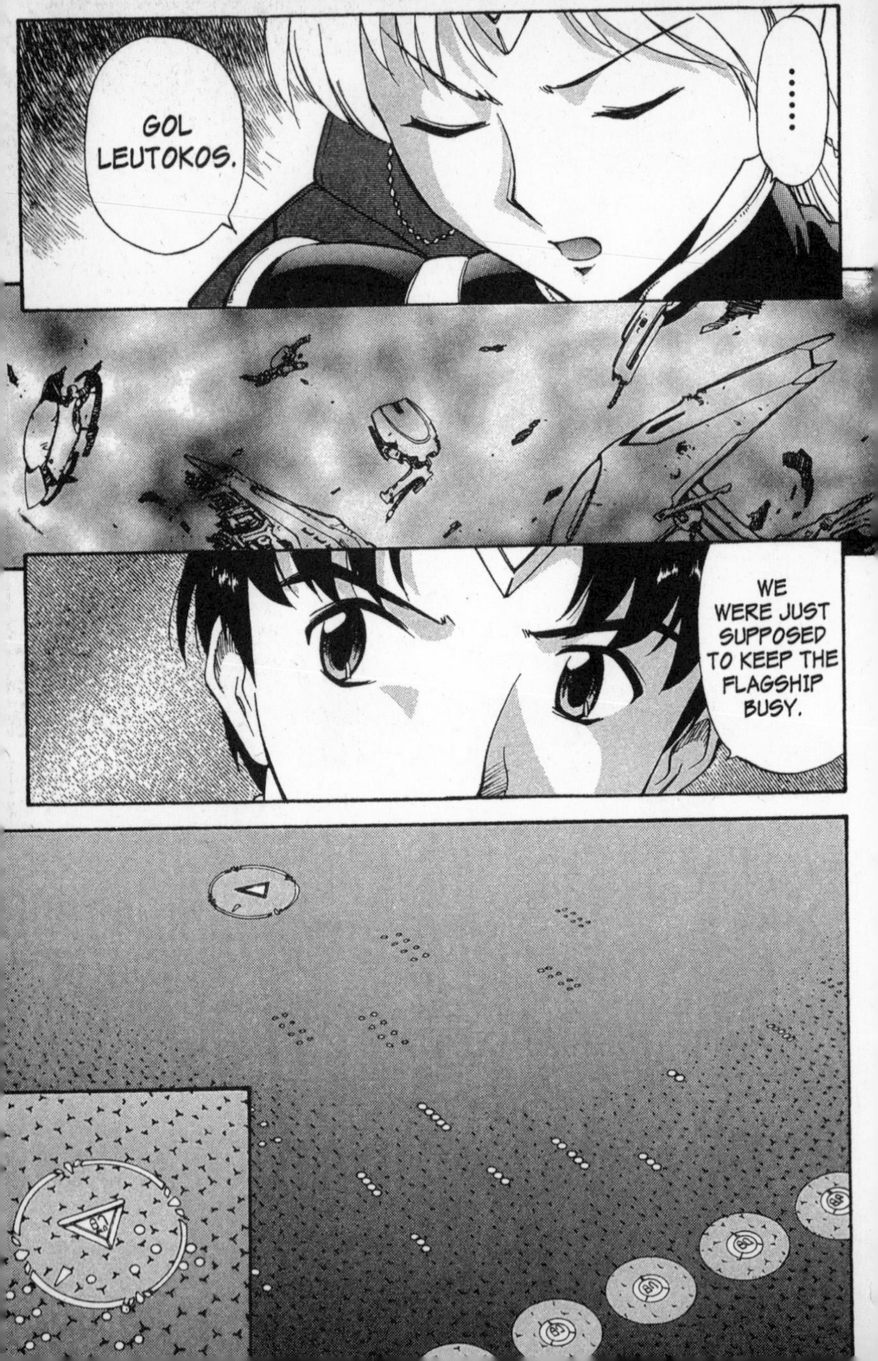
......
GOL LEUTOKOS.
WE WERE JUST SUPPOSED TO KEEP THE FLAGSHIP BUSY.

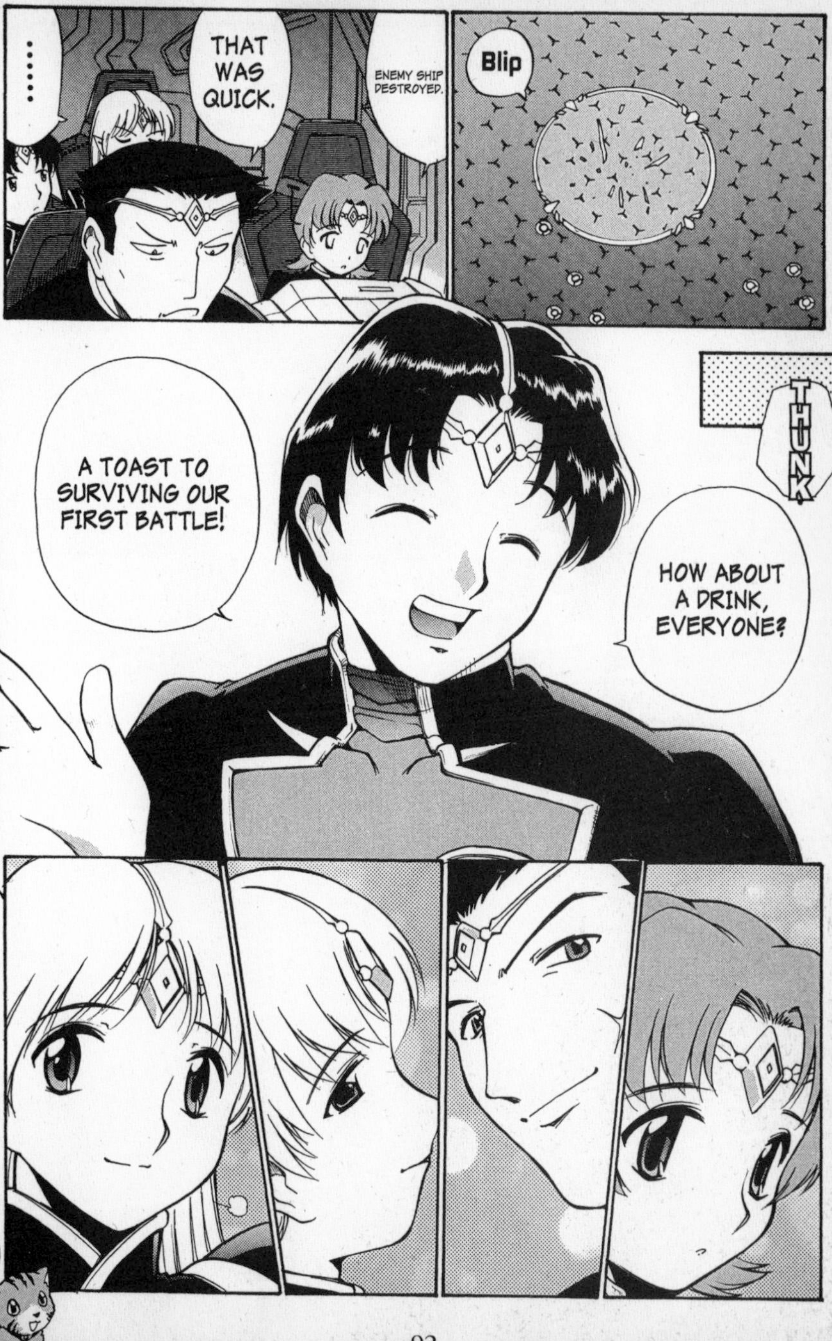
Blip
ENEMY SHIP DESTROYED.
THAT WAS QUICK.
......
THUNK
HOW ABOUT A DRINK, EVERYONE?
A TOAST TO SURVIVING OUR FIRST BATTLE!

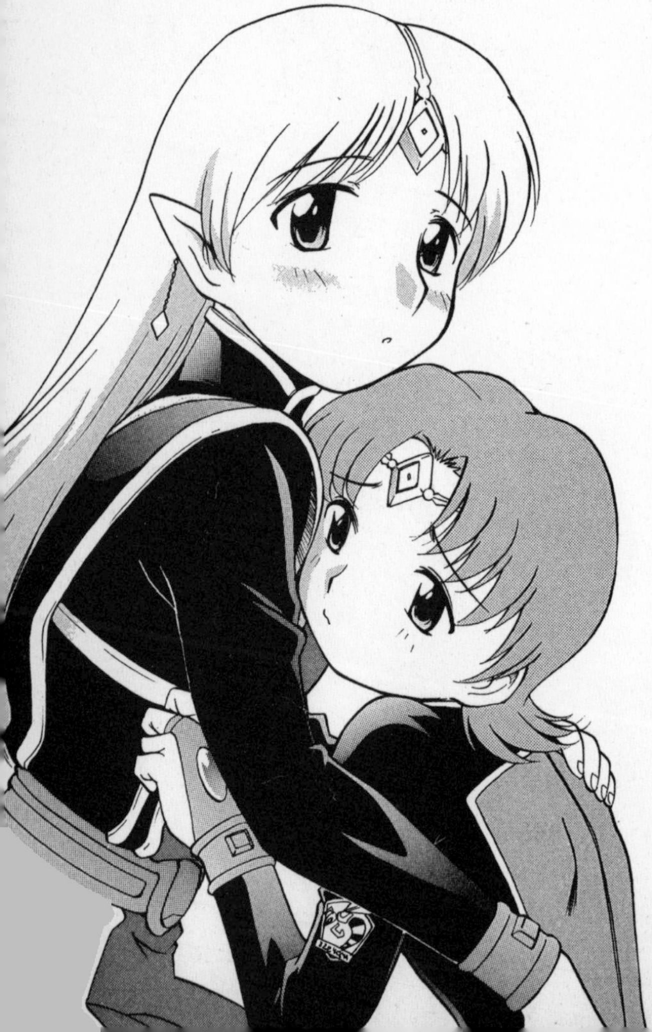

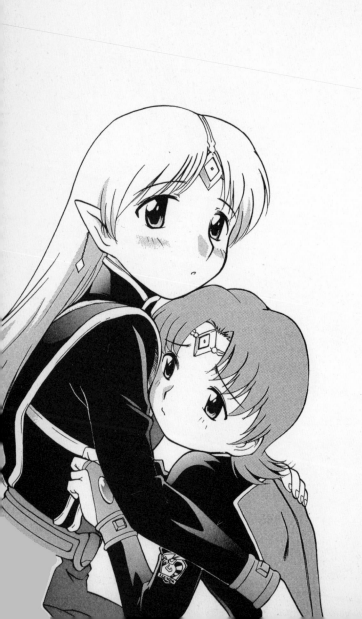

Chapter 5
Spectacular Insanity

LAFEK GUNANA

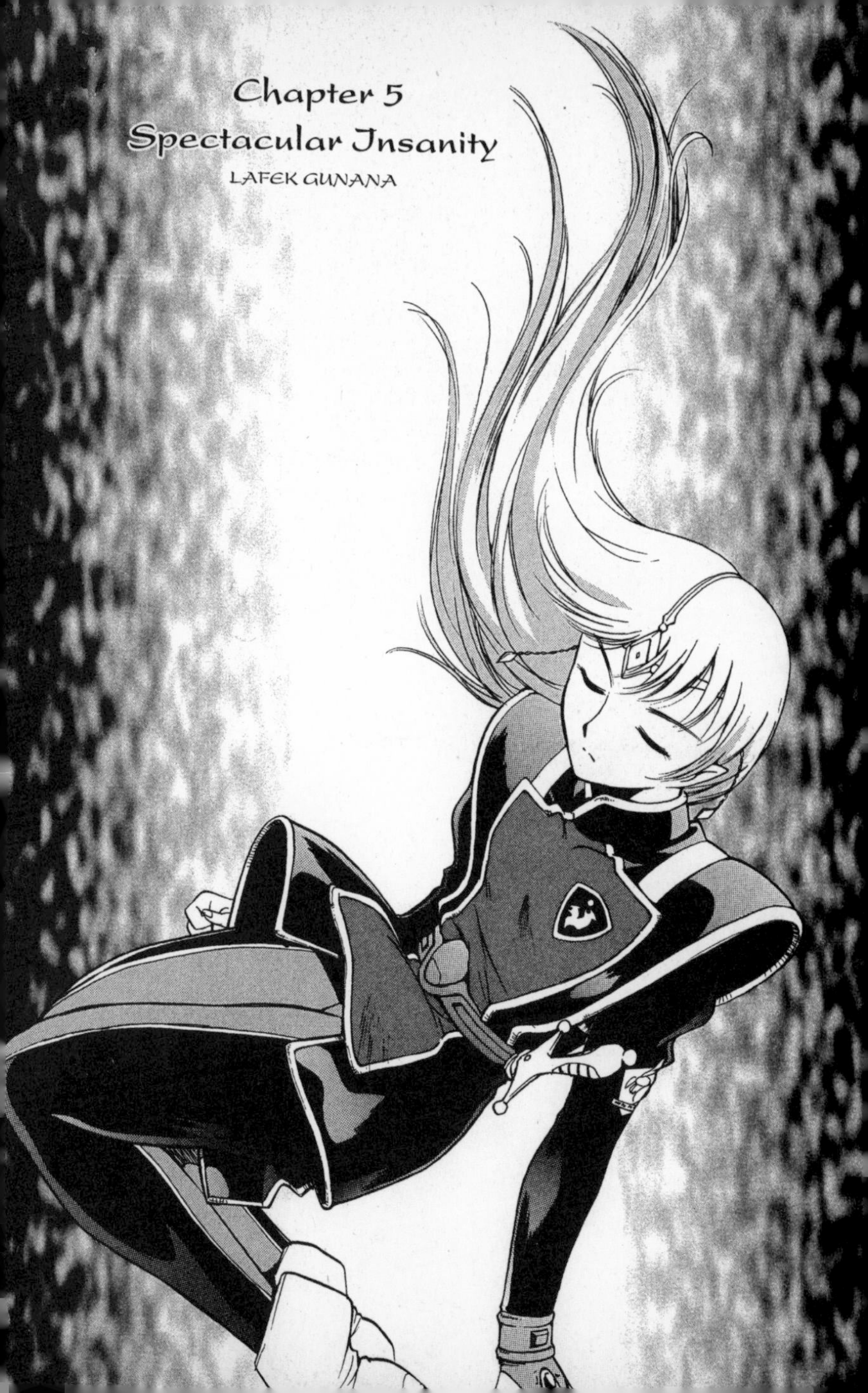

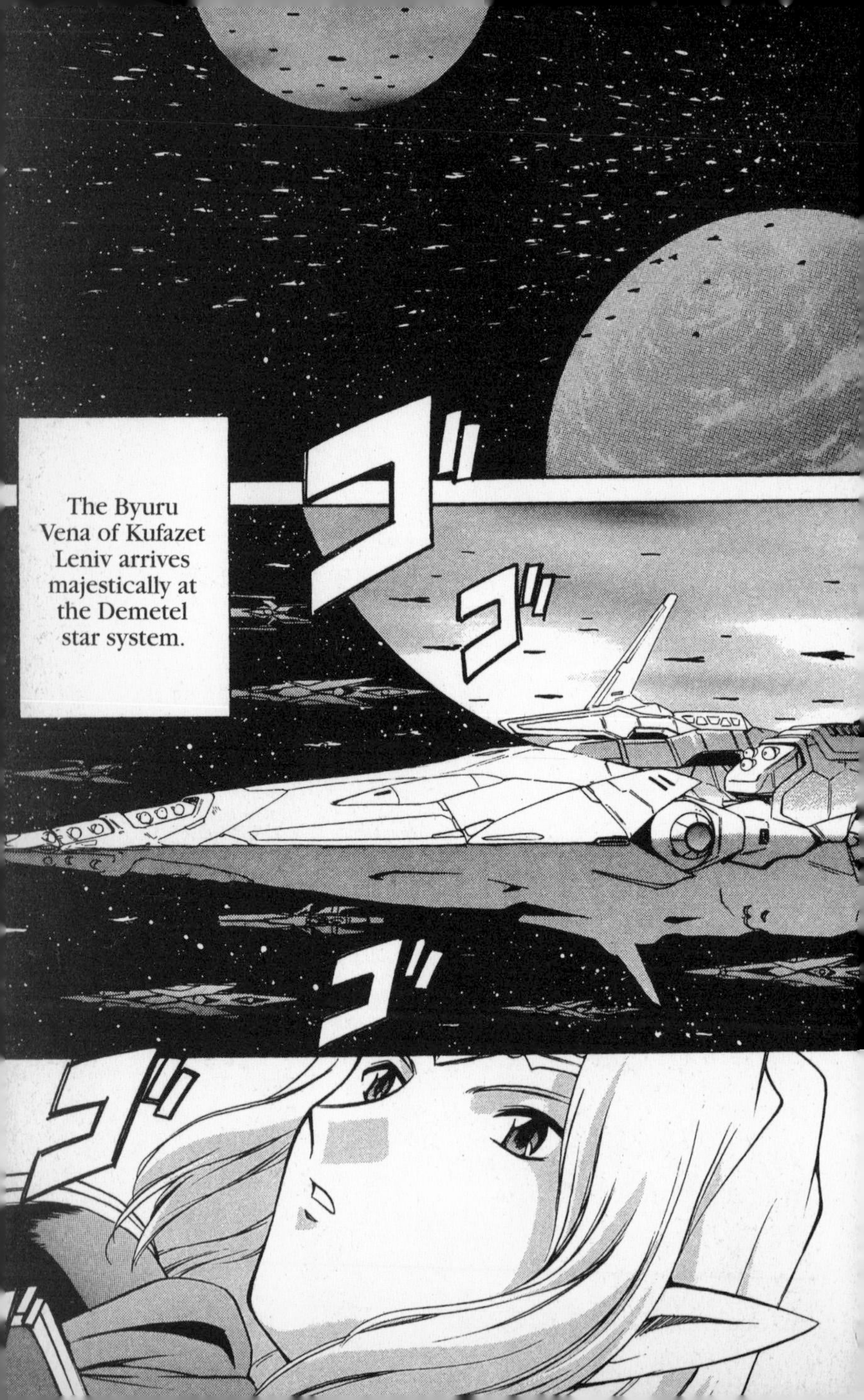
The Byuru Vena of Kufazet Leniv arrives majestically at the Demetel star system.
ゴ
ゴ
ゴ
ゴ

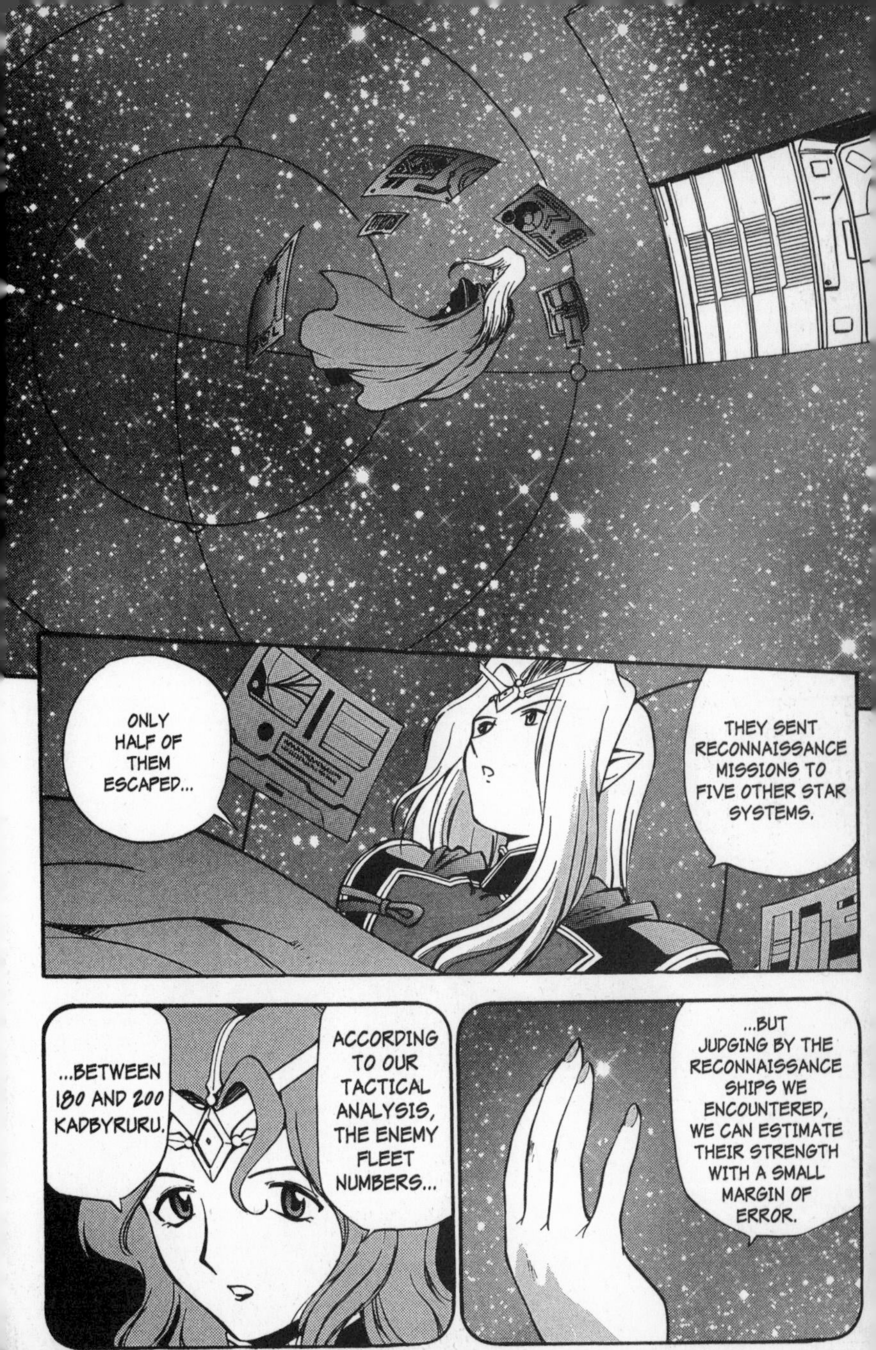
THEY SENT RECONNAISSANCE MISSIONS TO FIVE OTHER STAR SYSTEMS.
ONLY HALF OF THEM ESCAPED...
...BUT JUDGING BY THE RECONNAISSANCE SHIPS WE ENCOUNTERED, WE CAN ESTIMATE THEIR STRENGTH WITH A SMALL MARGIN OF ERROR.
ACCORDING TO OUR TACTICAL ANALYSIS, THE ENEMY FLEET NUMBERS...
...BETWEEN 180 AND 200 KADBYRURU.

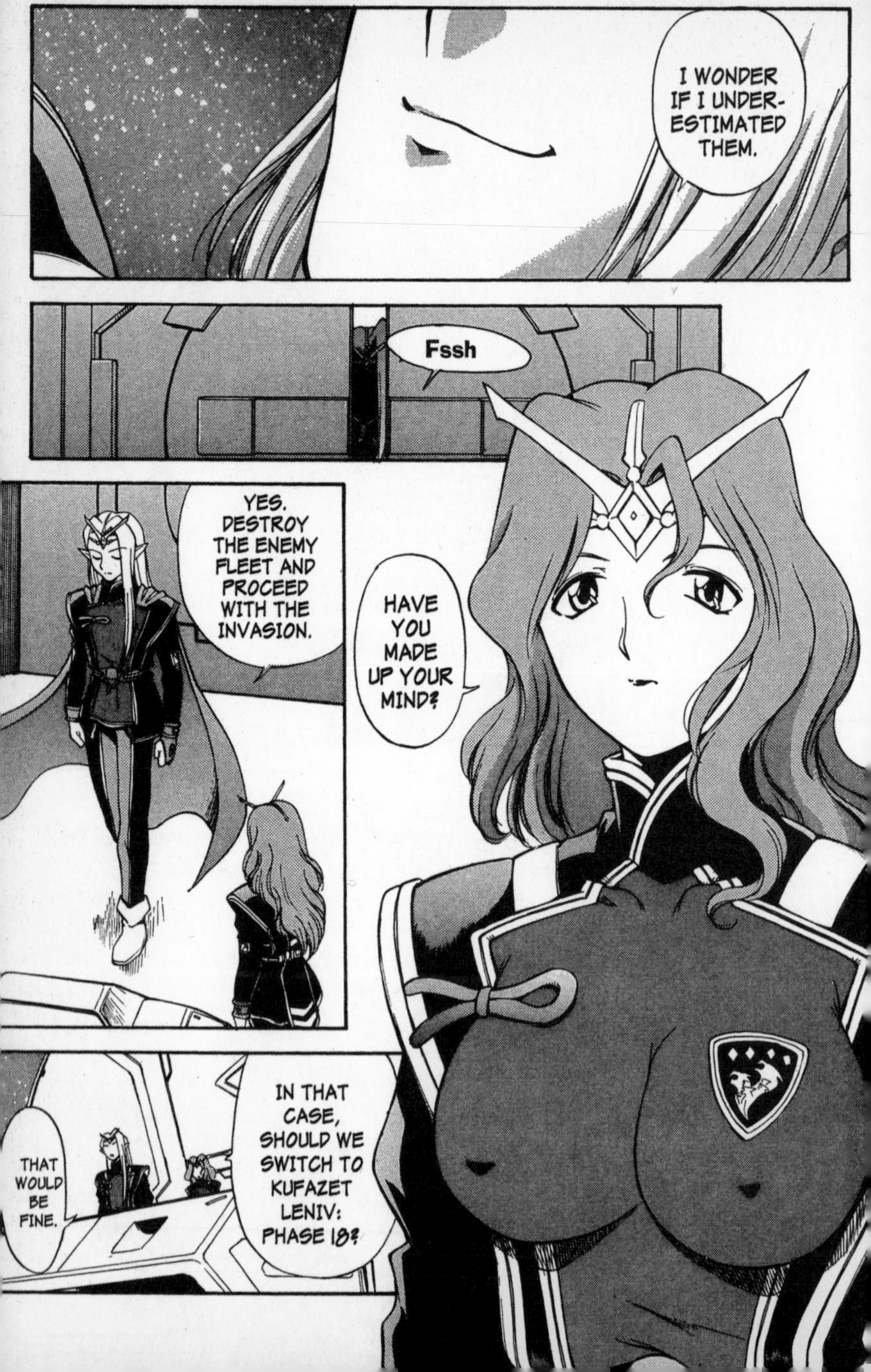
I WONDER IF I UNDER-ESTIMATED THEM.
HAVE YOU MADE UP YOUR MIND?
Fssh
YES. DESTROY THE ENEMY FLEET AND PROCEED WITH THE INVASION.
IN THAT CASE, SHOULD WE SWITCH TO KUFAZET LENIV: PHASE 18?
THAT WOULD BE FINE.

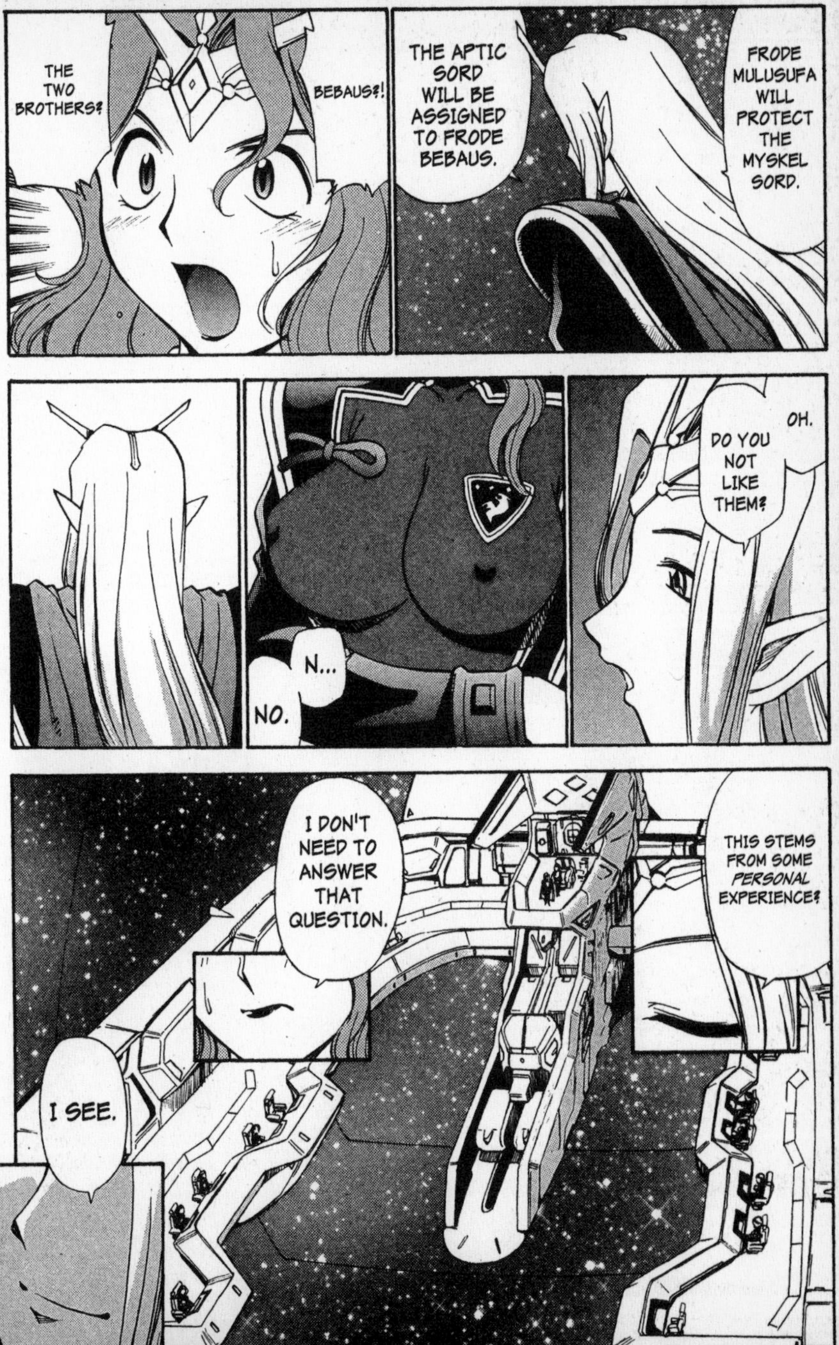
FRODE MULUSUFA WILL PROTECT THE MYSKEL SORD.
THE APTIC SORD WILL BE ASSIGNED TO FRODE BEBAUS.
BEBAUS?!
THE TWO BROTHERS?
OH.
DO YOU NOT LIKE THEM?
N...
NO.
THIS STEMS FROM SOME *PERSONAL* EXPERIENCE?
I DON'T NEED TO ANSWER THAT QUESTION.
I SEE.

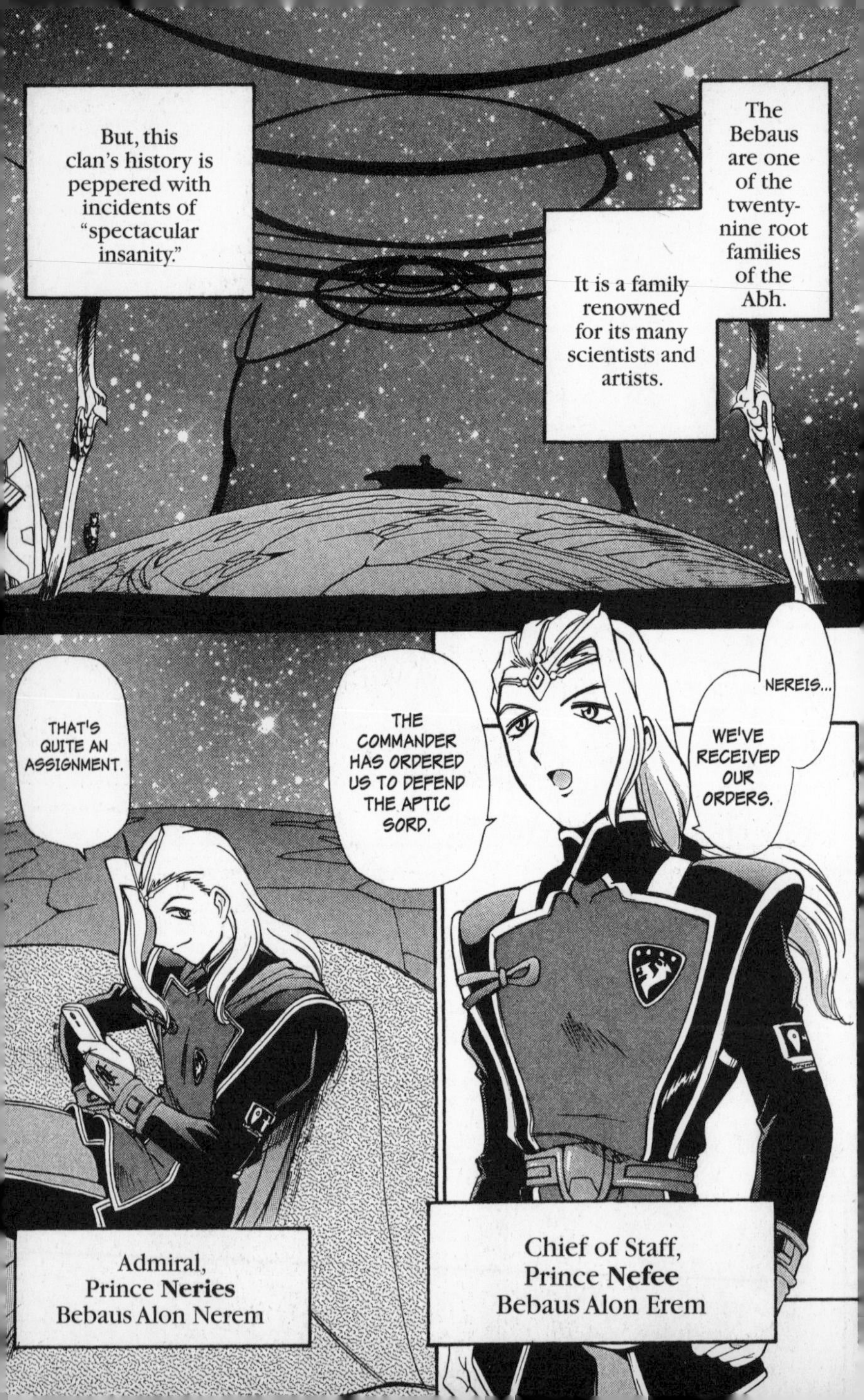
The Bebaus are one of the twenty-nine root families of the Abh.
It is a family renowned for its many scientists and artists.
But, this clan's history is peppered with incidents of "spectacular insanity."
NEREIS...
WE'VE RECEIVED OUR ORDERS.
THE COMMANDER HAS ORDERED US TO DEFEND THE APTIC SORD.
Chief of Staff, Prince **Nefee** Bebaus Alon Erem
THAT'S QUITE AN ASSIGNMENT.
Admiral, Prince **Neries** Bebaus Alon Nerem

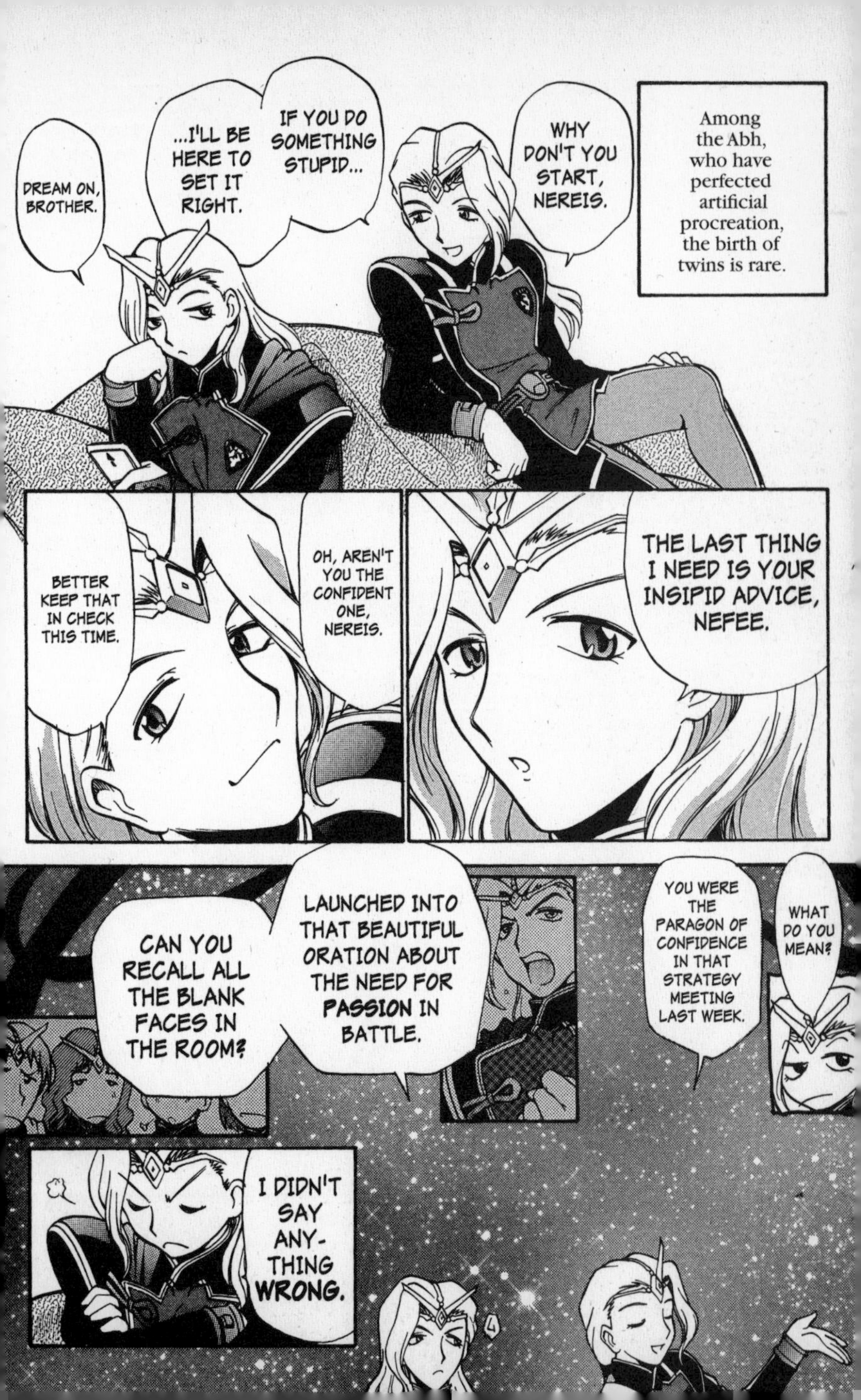
Among the Abh, who have perfected artificial procreation, the birth of twins is rare.
WHY DON'T YOU START, NEREIS.
IF YOU DO SOMETHING STUPID...
...I'LL BE HERE TO SET IT RIGHT.
DREAM ON, BROTHER.
THE LAST THING I NEED IS YOUR INSIPID ADVICE, NEFEE.
OH, AREN'T YOU THE CONFIDENT ONE, NEREIS.
BETTER KEEP THAT IN CHECK THIS TIME.
WHAT DO YOU MEAN?
YOU WERE THE PARAGON OF CONFIDENCE IN THAT STRATEGY MEETING LAST WEEK.
LAUNCHED INTO THAT BEAUTIFUL ORATION ABOUT THE NEED FOR **PASSION** IN BATTLE.
CAN YOU RECALL ALL THE BLANK FACES IN THE ROOM?
I DIDN'T SAY ANY-THING **WRONG.**

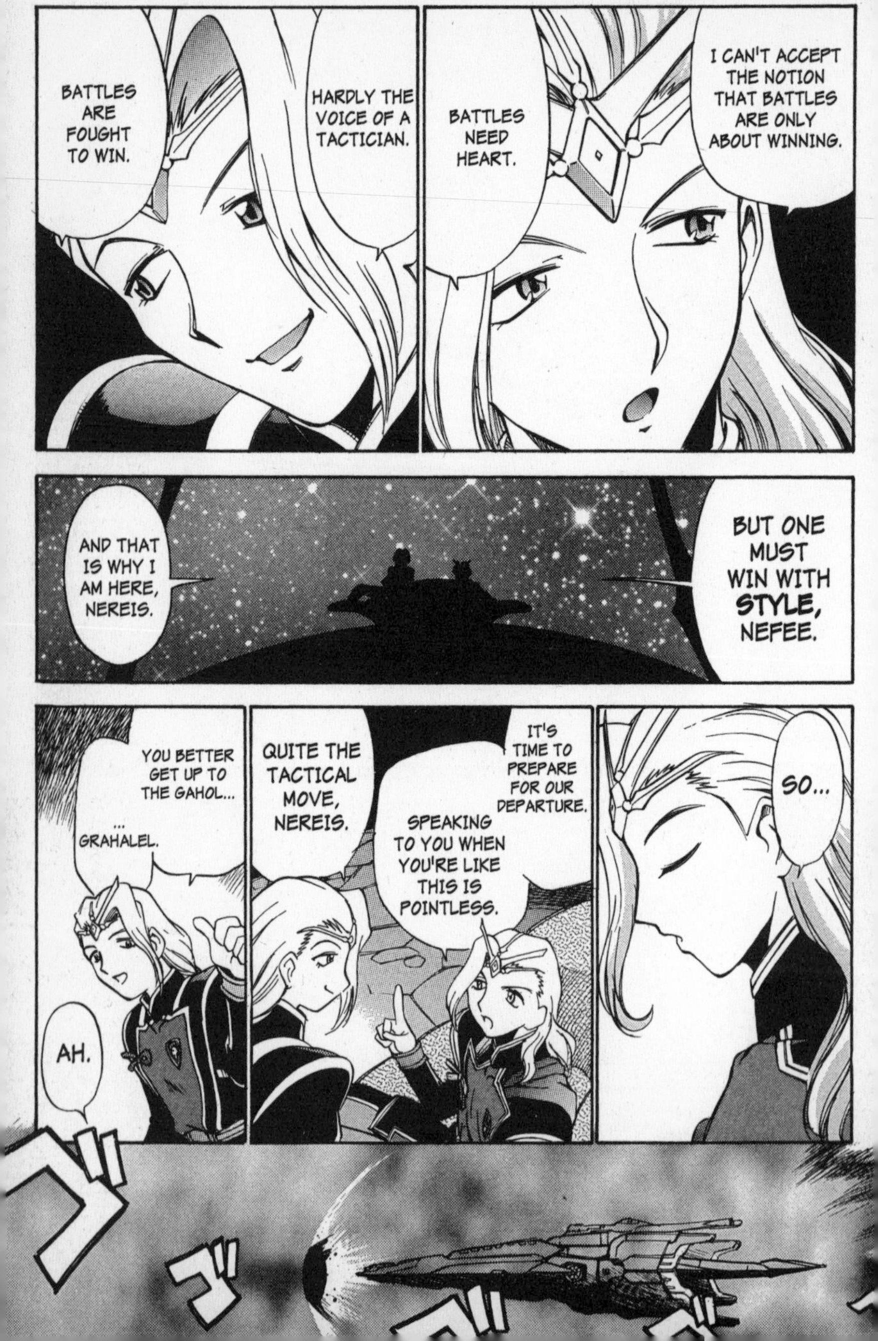
I CAN'T ACCEPT THE NOTION THAT BATTLES ARE ONLY ABOUT WINNING.
BATTLES NEED HEART.
HARDLY THE VOICE OF A TACTICIAN.
BATTLES ARE FOUGHT TO WIN.
BUT ONE MUST WIN WITH STYLE, NEFEE.
AND THAT IS WHY I AM HERE, NEREIS.
SO...
IT'S TIME TO PREPARE FOR OUR DEPARTURE.
SPEAKING TO YOU WHEN YOU'RE LIKE THIS IS POINTLESS.
QUITE THE TACTICAL MOVE, NEREIS.
YOU BETTER GET UP TO THE GAHOL...
... GRAHALEL.
AH.

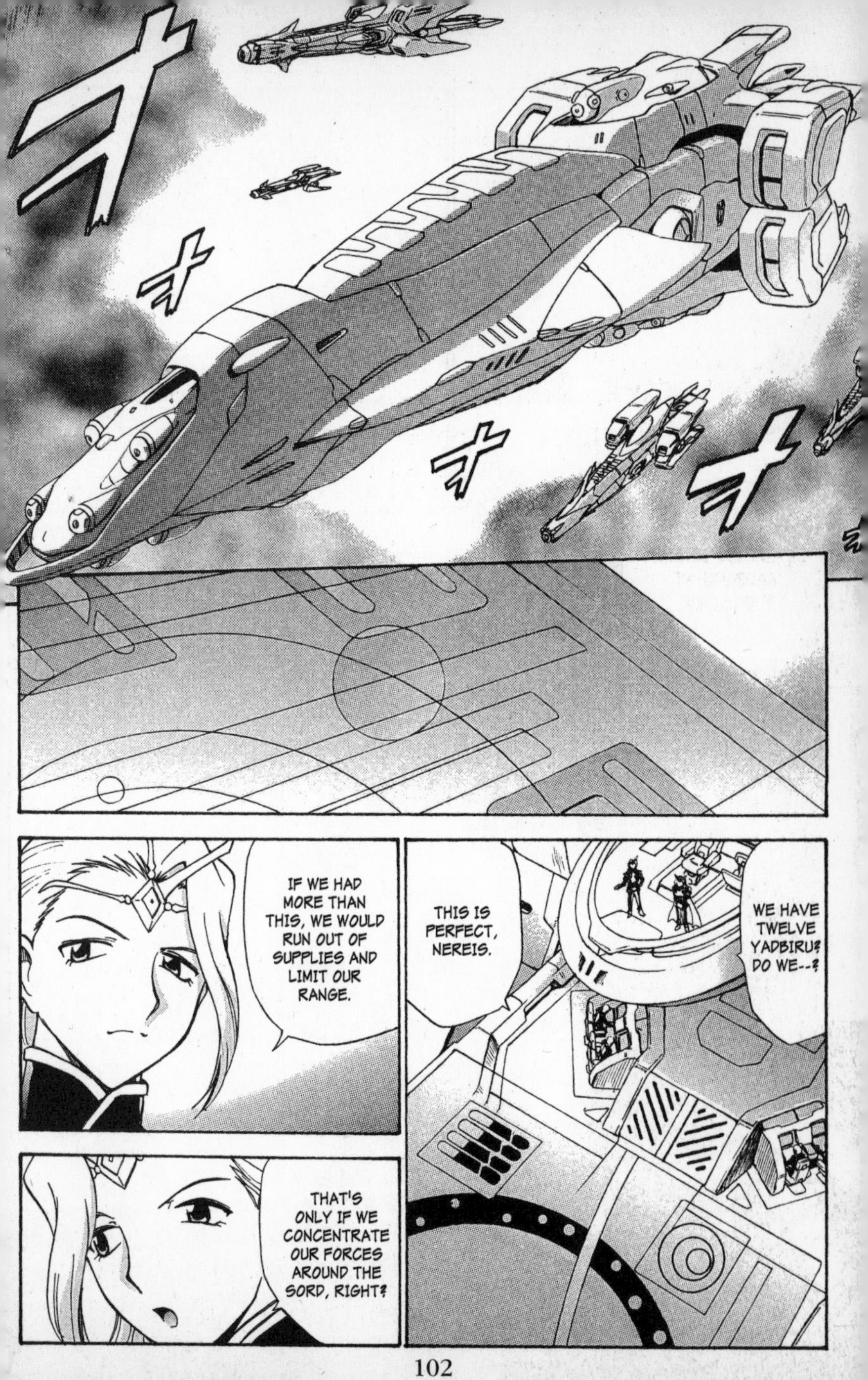
WE HAVE TWELVE YADBIRU? DO WE--?
THIS IS PERFECT, NEREIS.
IF WE HAD MORE THAN THIS, WE WOULD RUN OUT OF SUPPLIES AND LIMIT OUR RANGE.
THAT'S ONLY IF WE CONCENTRATE OUR FORCES AROUND THE SORD, RIGHT?

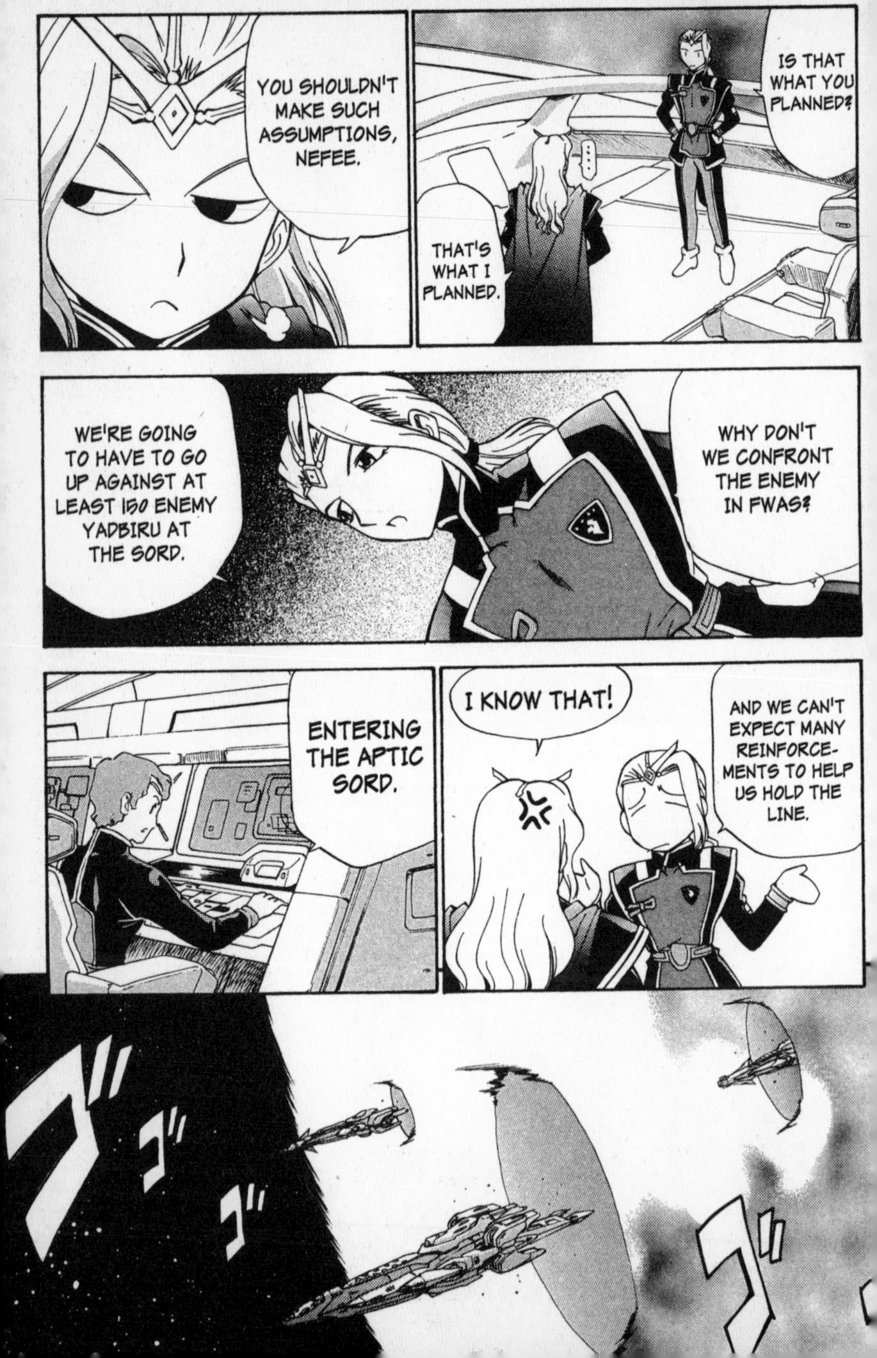
IS THAT WHAT YOU PLANNED?
....
THAT'S WHAT I PLANNED.
YOU SHOULDN'T MAKE SUCH ASSUMPTIONS, NEFEE.
WHY DON'T WE CONFRONT THE ENEMY IN FWAS?
WE'RE GOING TO HAVE TO GO UP AGAINST AT LEAST 150 ENEMY YADBIRU AT THE SORD.
AND WE CAN'T EXPECT MANY REINFORCEMENTS TO HELP US HOLD THE LINE.
I KNOW THAT!
ENTERING THE APTIC SORD.
ゴ
ゴ
ゴ
ゴ
ゴ

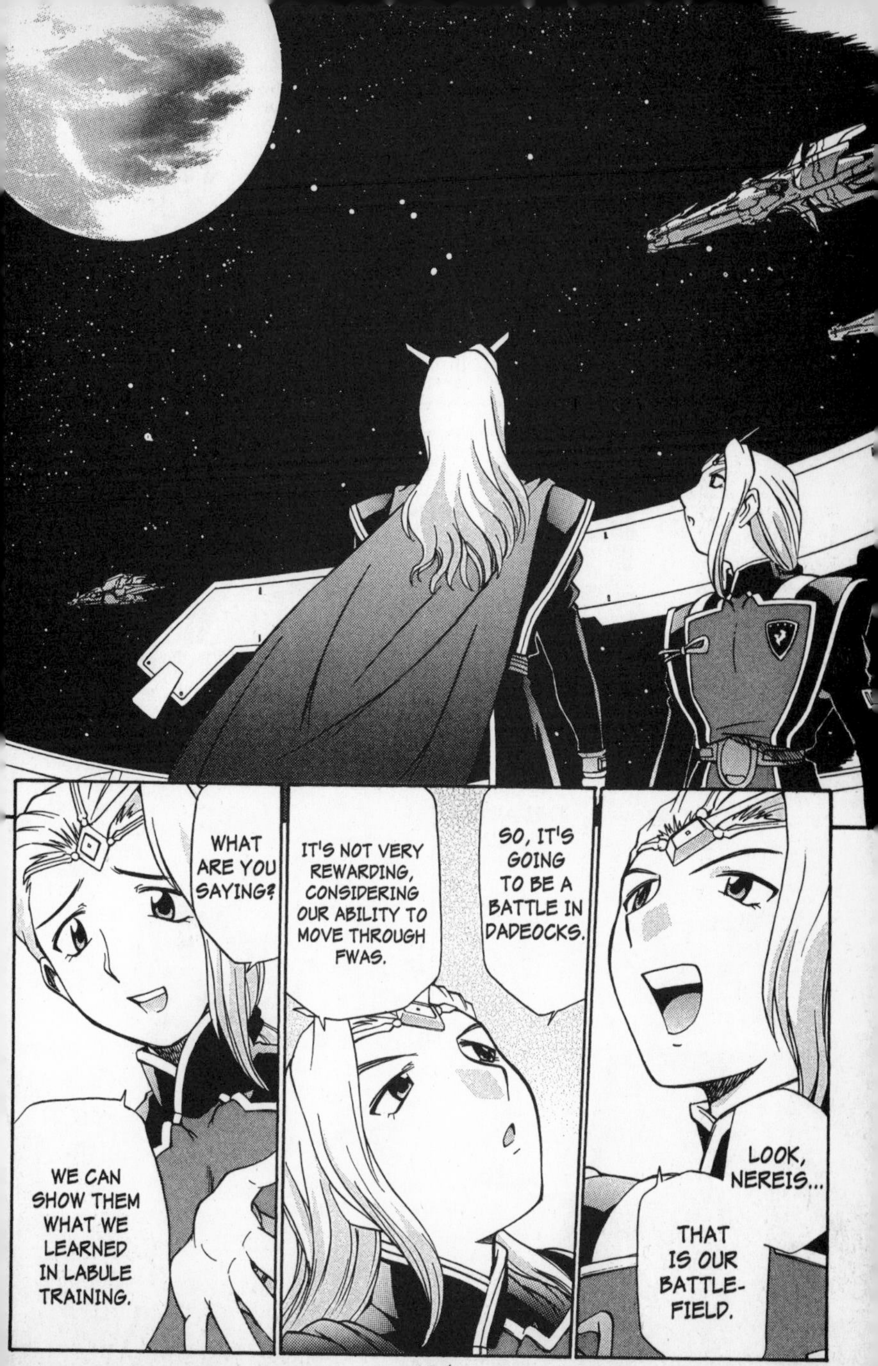
LOOK, NEREIS...
THAT IS OUR BATTLE-FIELD.
SO, IT'S GOING TO BE A BATTLE IN DADEOCKS.
IT'S NOT VERY REWARDING, CONSIDERING OUR ABILITY TO MOVE THROUGH FWAS.
WHAT ARE YOU SAYING?
WE CAN SHOW THEM WHAT WE LEARNED IN LABULE TRAINING.

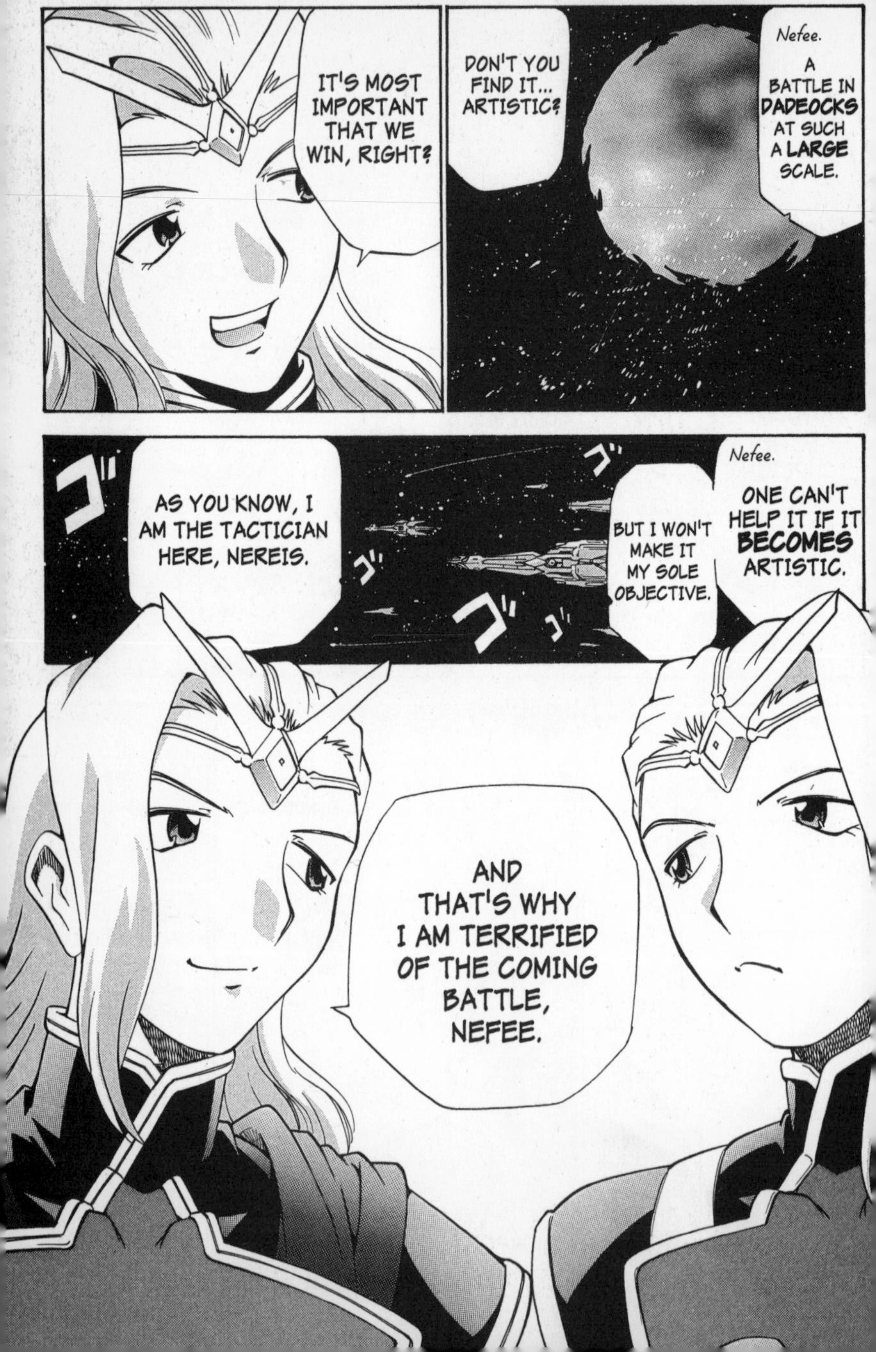
Nefee.
A BATTLE IN **DADEOCKS** AT SUCH A **LARGE** SCALE.
DON'T YOU FIND IT... ARTISTIC?
IT'S MOST IMPORTANT THAT WE WIN, RIGHT?
Nefee.
ONE CAN'T HELP IT IF IT **BECOMES** ARTISTIC.
BUT I WON'T MAKE IT MY SOLE OBJECTIVE.
ゴ
AS YOU KNOW, I AM THE TACTICIAN HERE, NEREIS.
AND THAT'S WHY I AM TERRIFIED OF THE COMING BATTLE, NEFEE.

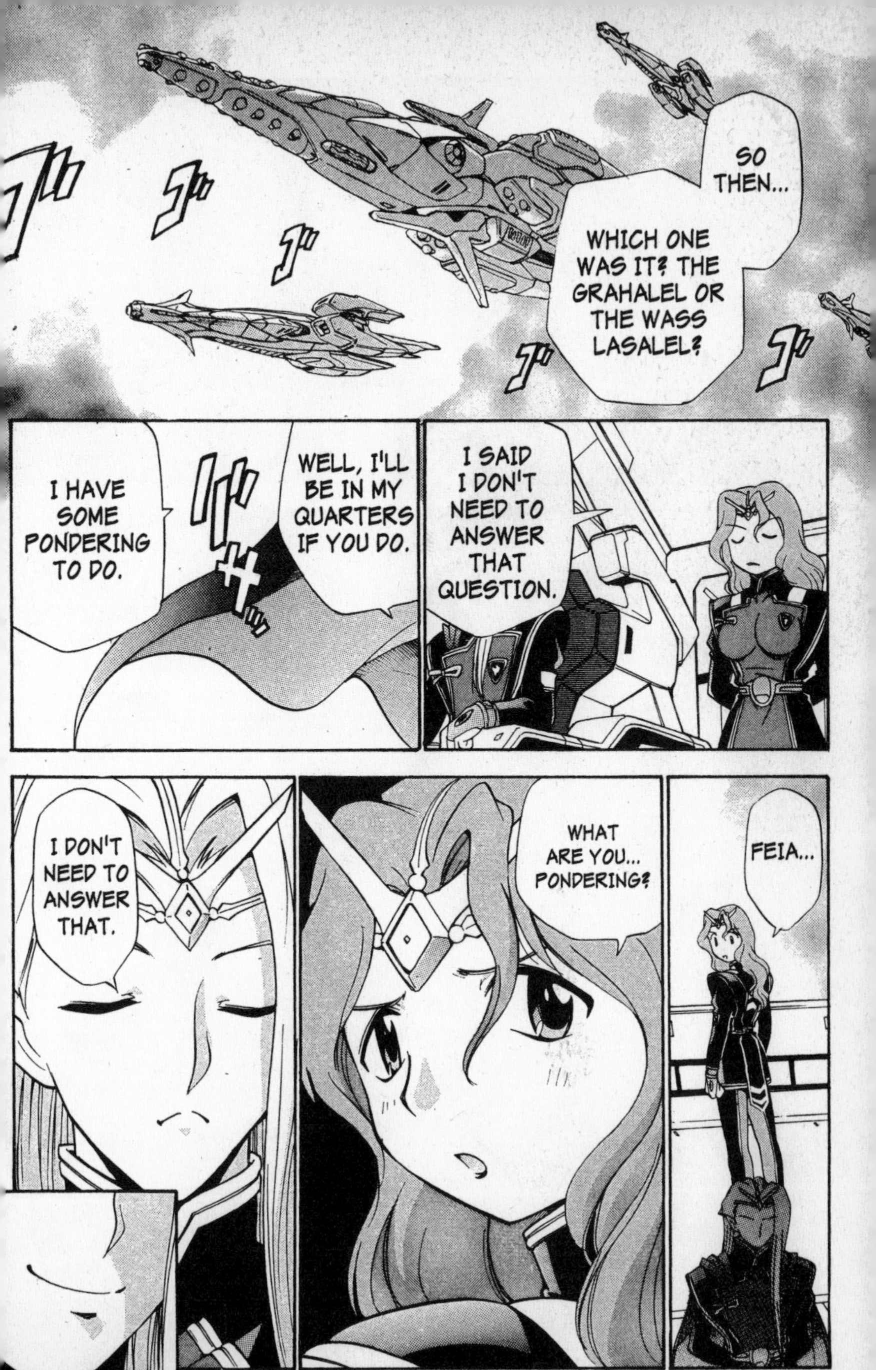
SO THEN...
WHICH ONE WAS IT? THE GRAHALEL OR THE WASS LASALEL?
I SAID I DON'T NEED TO ANSWER THAT QUESTION.
WELL, I'LL BE IN MY QUARTERS IF YOU DO.
I HAVE SOME PONDERING TO DO.
FEIA...
WHAT ARE YOU... PONDERING?
I DON'T NEED TO ANSWER THAT.

Chapter 6
Remembrance Dinner

GYUK LOBROT

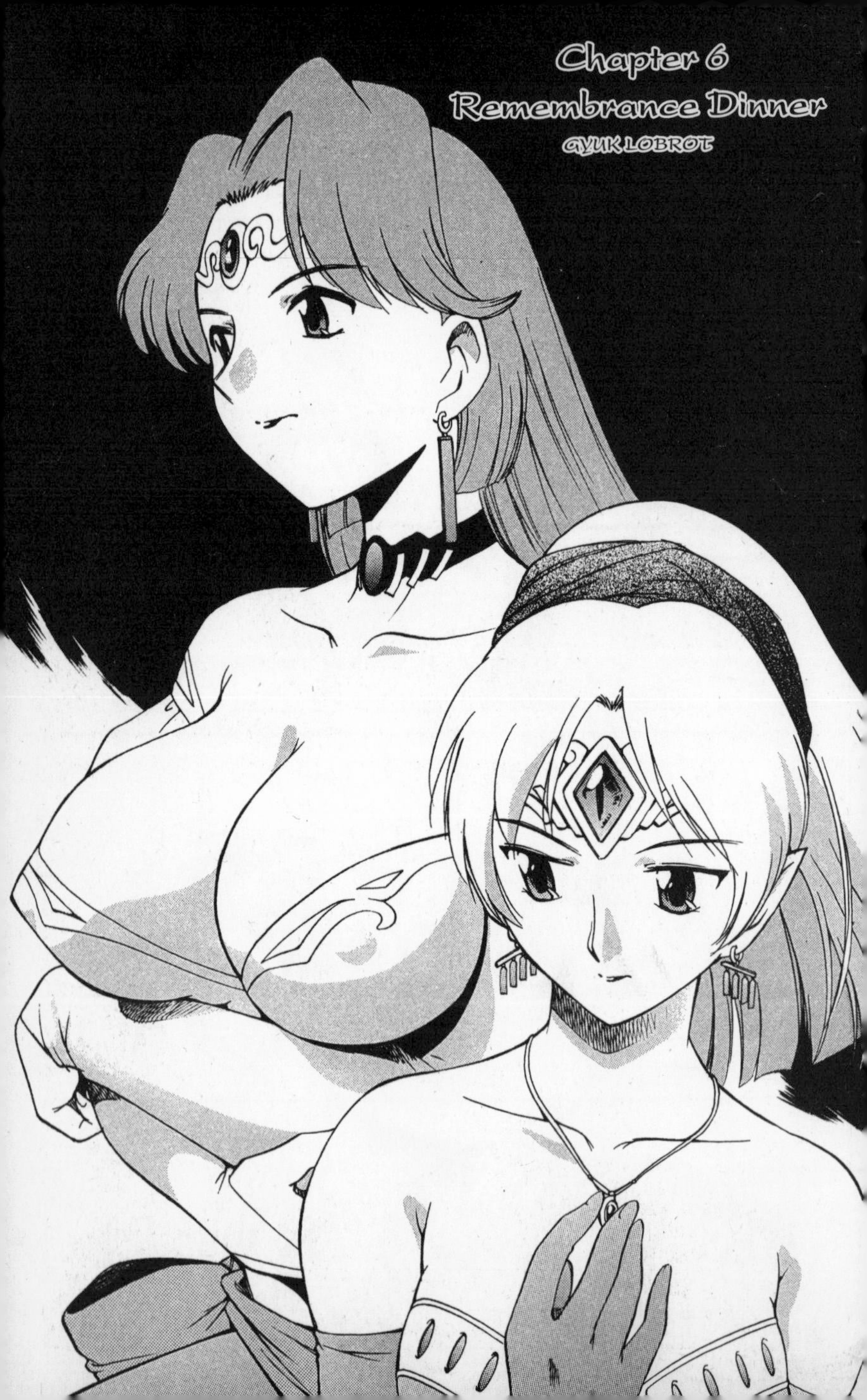

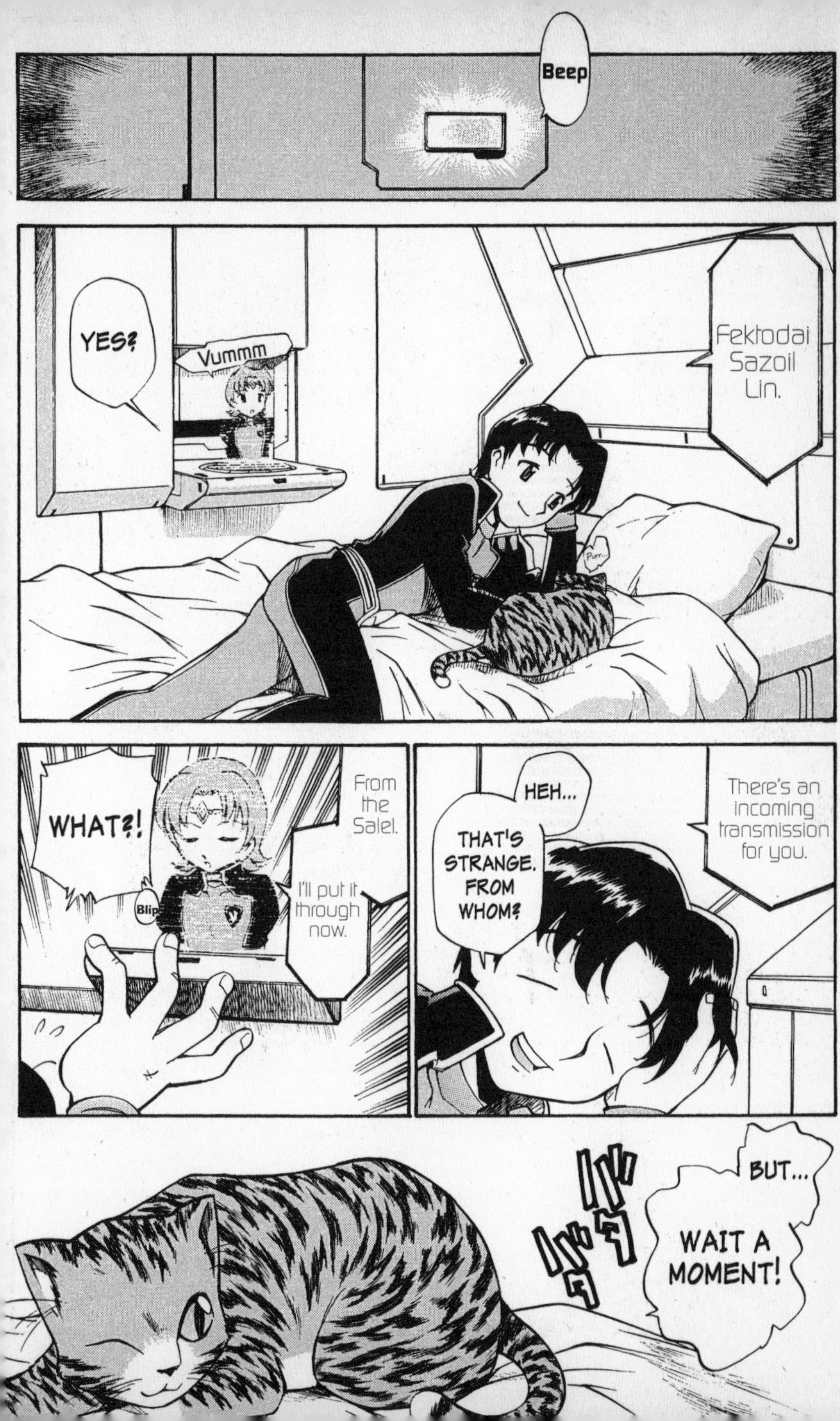
Beep
Fektodai Sazoil Lin.
YES?
Vummm
Purr...
There's an incoming transmission for you.
HEH...
THAT'S STRANGE. FROM WHOM?
From the Salel.
I'll put it through now.
Blip
WHAT?!
BUT...
WAIT A MOMENT!

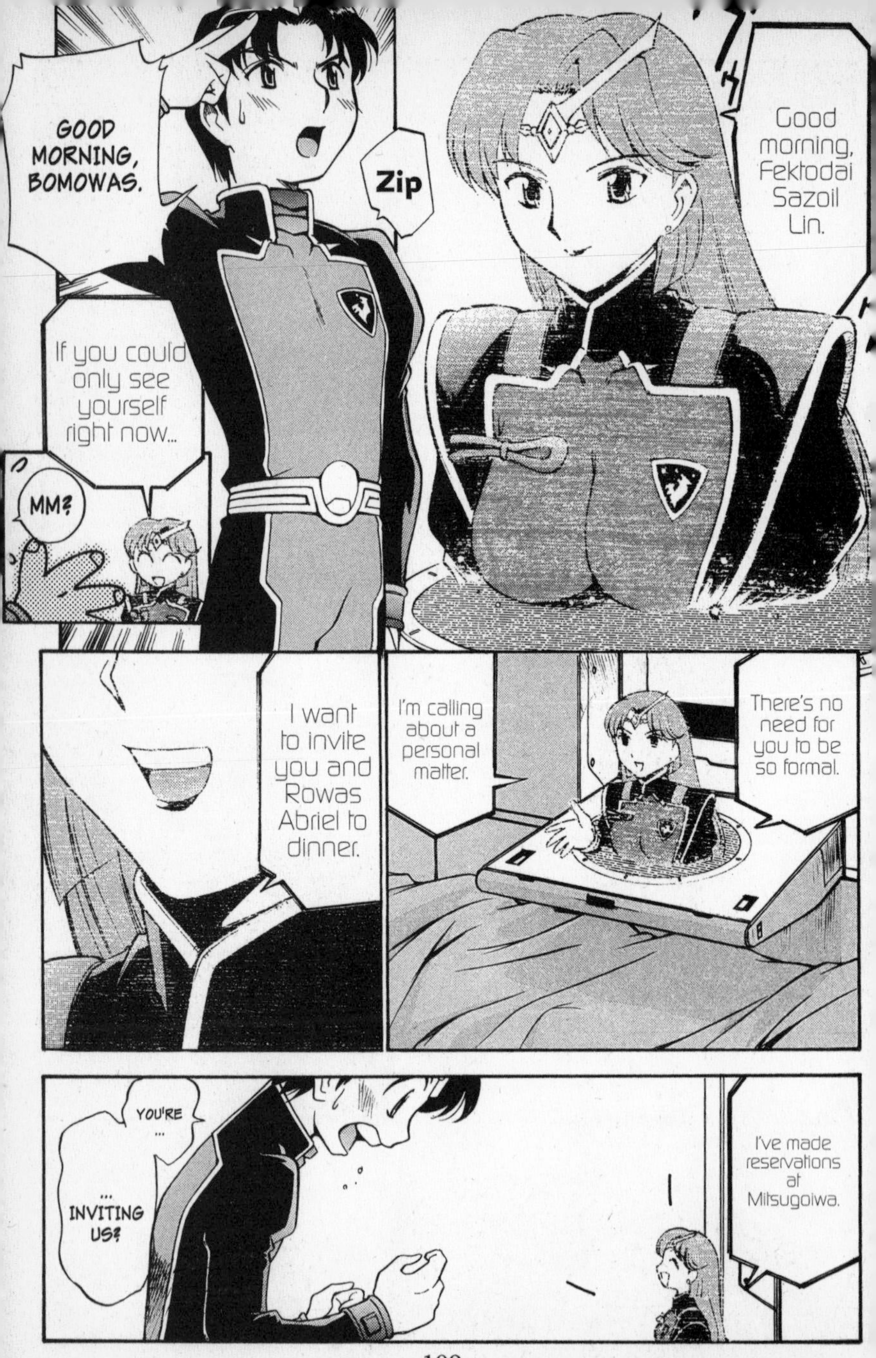
Good morning, Fektodai Sazoil Lin.
Zip
GOOD MORNING, BOMOWAS.
If you could only see yourself right now...
MM?
There's no need for you to be so formal.
I'm calling about a personal matter.
I want to invite you and Rowas Abriel to dinner.
I've made reservations at Mitsugoiwa.
YOU'RE ...
... INVITING US?

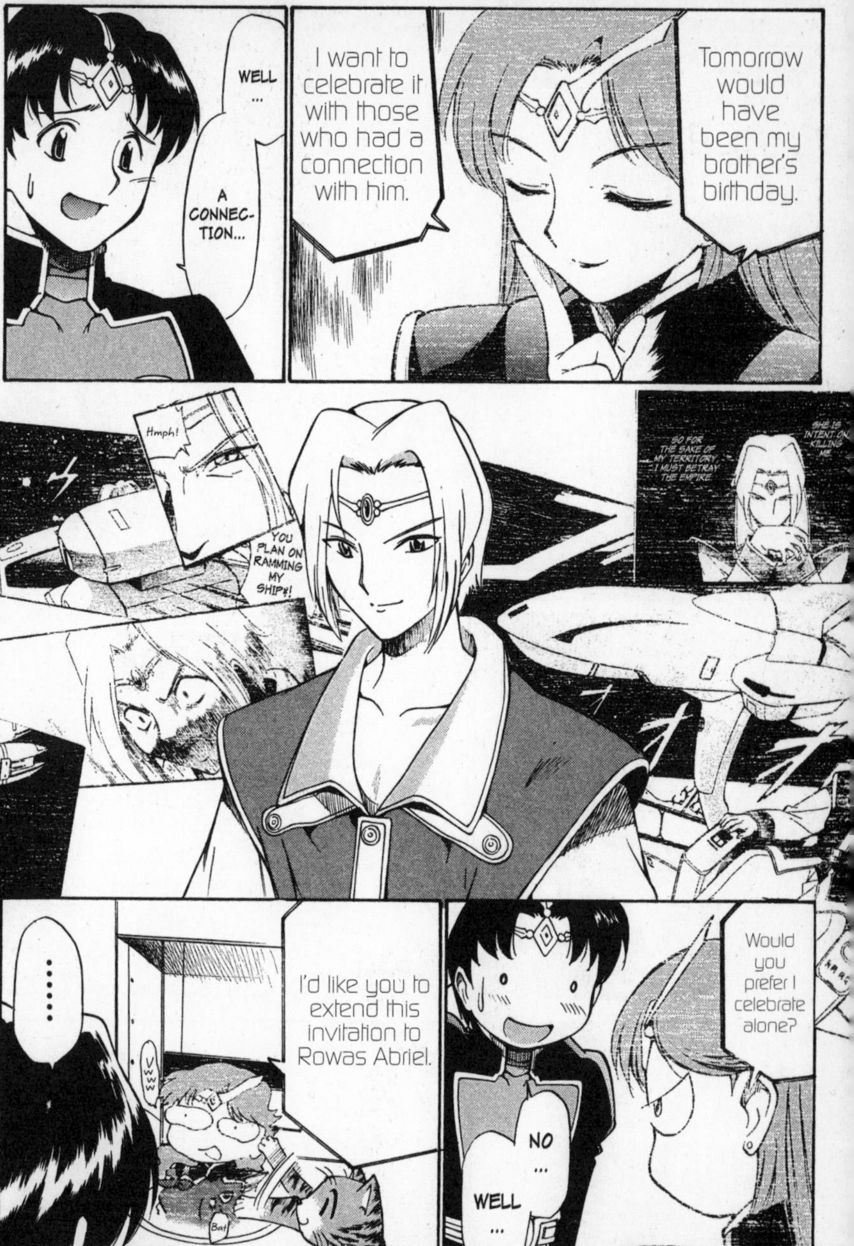
Tomorrow would have been my brother's birthday.
I want to celebrate it with those who had a connection with him.
WELL ...
A CONNECTION...
SHE IS INTENT ON KILLING ME.
SO FOR THE SAKE OF MY TERRITORY, I MUST BETRAY THE EMPIRE.
Hmph!
YOU PLAN ON RAMMING MY SHIP?!
Would you prefer I celebrate alone?
NO ... WELL ...
I'd like you to extend this invitation to Rowas Abriel.
......

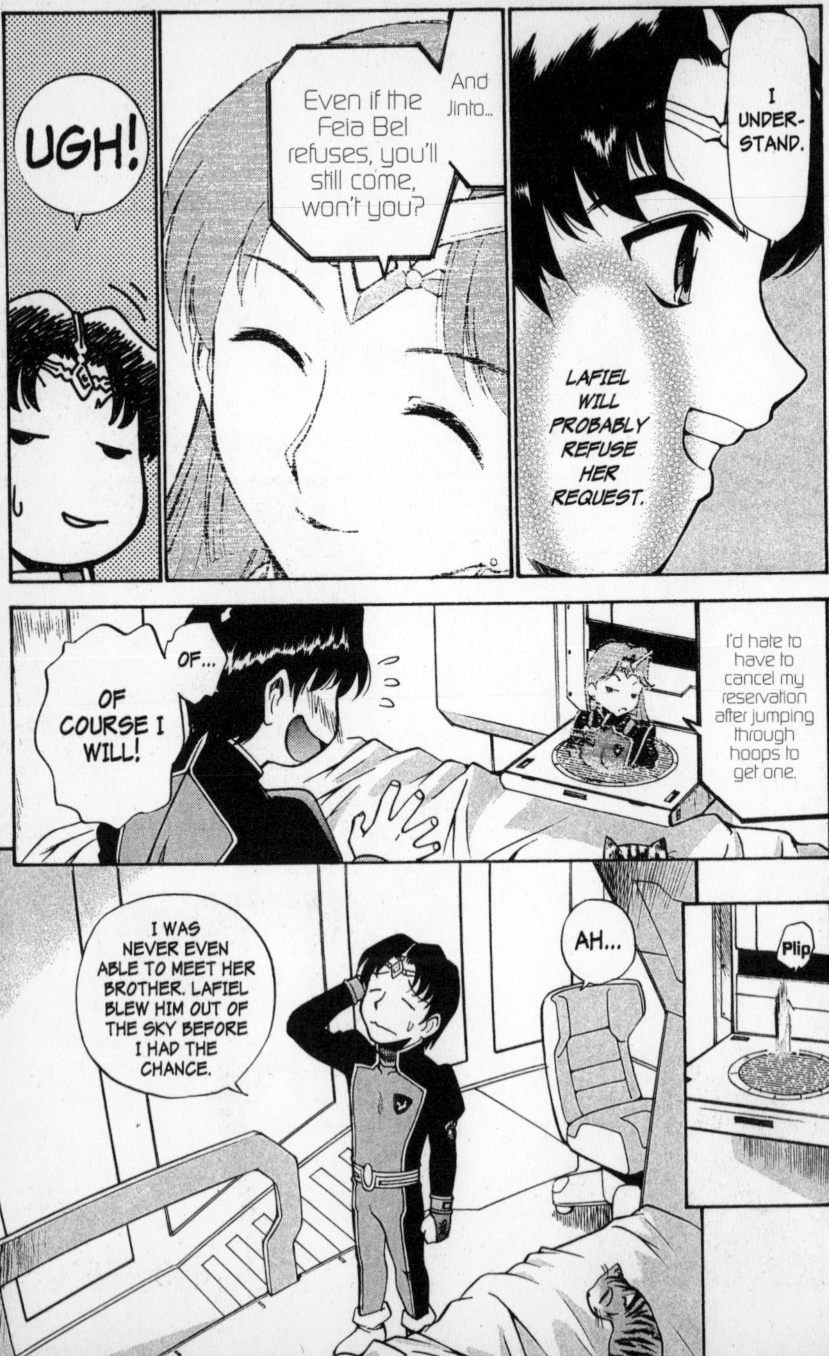
I UNDER-STAND.
LAFIEL WILL PROBABLY REFUSE HER REQUEST.
And Jinto...
Even if the Feia Bel refuses, you'll still come, won't you?
UGH!
I'd hate to have to cancel my reservation after jumping through hoops to get one.
OF...
OF COURSE I WILL!
Plip
AH...
I WAS NEVER EVEN ABLE TO MEET HER BROTHER. LAFIEL BLEW HIM OUT OF THE SKY BEFORE I HAD THE CHANCE.

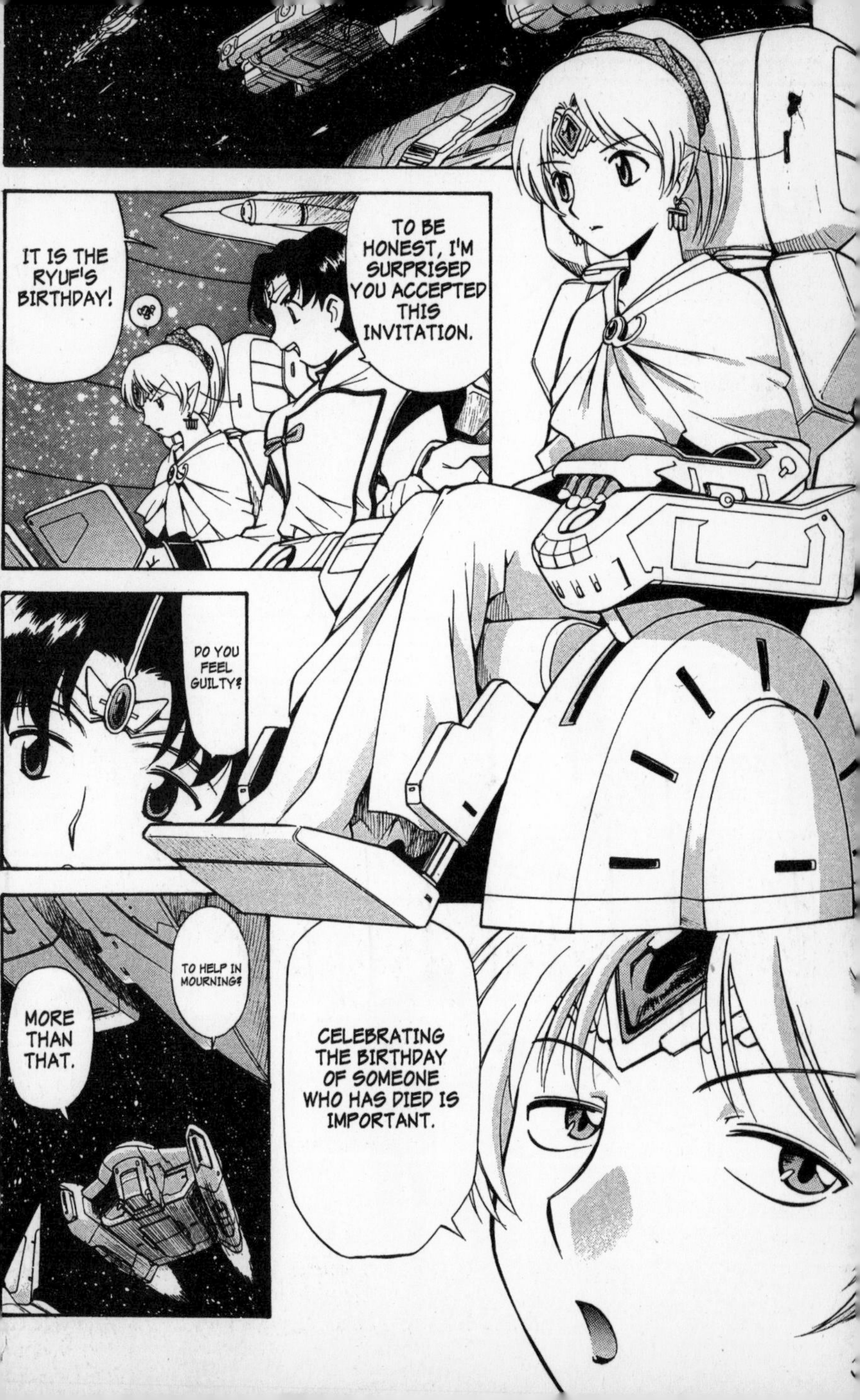
TO BE HONEST, I'M SURPRISED YOU ACCEPTED THIS INVITATION.
IT IS THE RYUF'S BIRTHDAY!
DO YOU FEEL GUILTY?
CELEBRATING THE BIRTHDAY OF SOMEONE WHO HAS DIED IS IMPORTANT.
TO HELP IN MOURNING?
MORE THAN THAT.

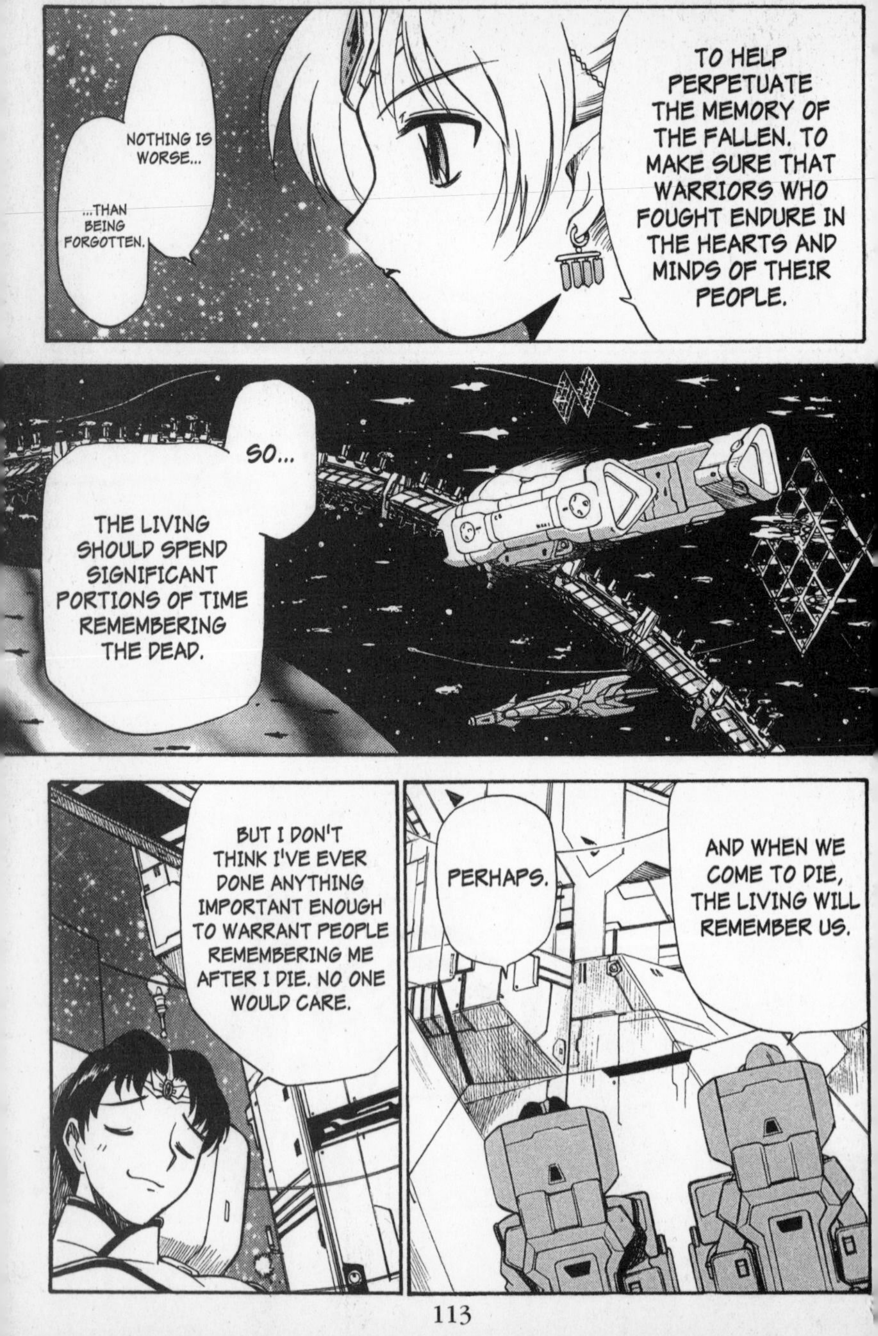
TO HELP PERPETUATE THE MEMORY OF THE FALLEN. TO MAKE SURE THAT WARRIORS WHO FOUGHT ENDURE IN THE HEARTS AND MINDS OF THEIR PEOPLE.
NOTHING IS WORSE...
...THAN BEING FORGOTTEN.
SO...
THE LIVING SHOULD SPEND SIGNIFICANT PORTIONS OF TIME REMEMBERING THE DEAD.
AND WHEN WE COME TO DIE, THE LIVING WILL REMEMBER US.
PERHAPS.
BUT I DON'T THINK I'VE EVER DONE ANYTHING IMPORTANT ENOUGH TO WARRANT PEOPLE REMEMBERING ME AFTER I DIE. NO ONE WOULD CARE.

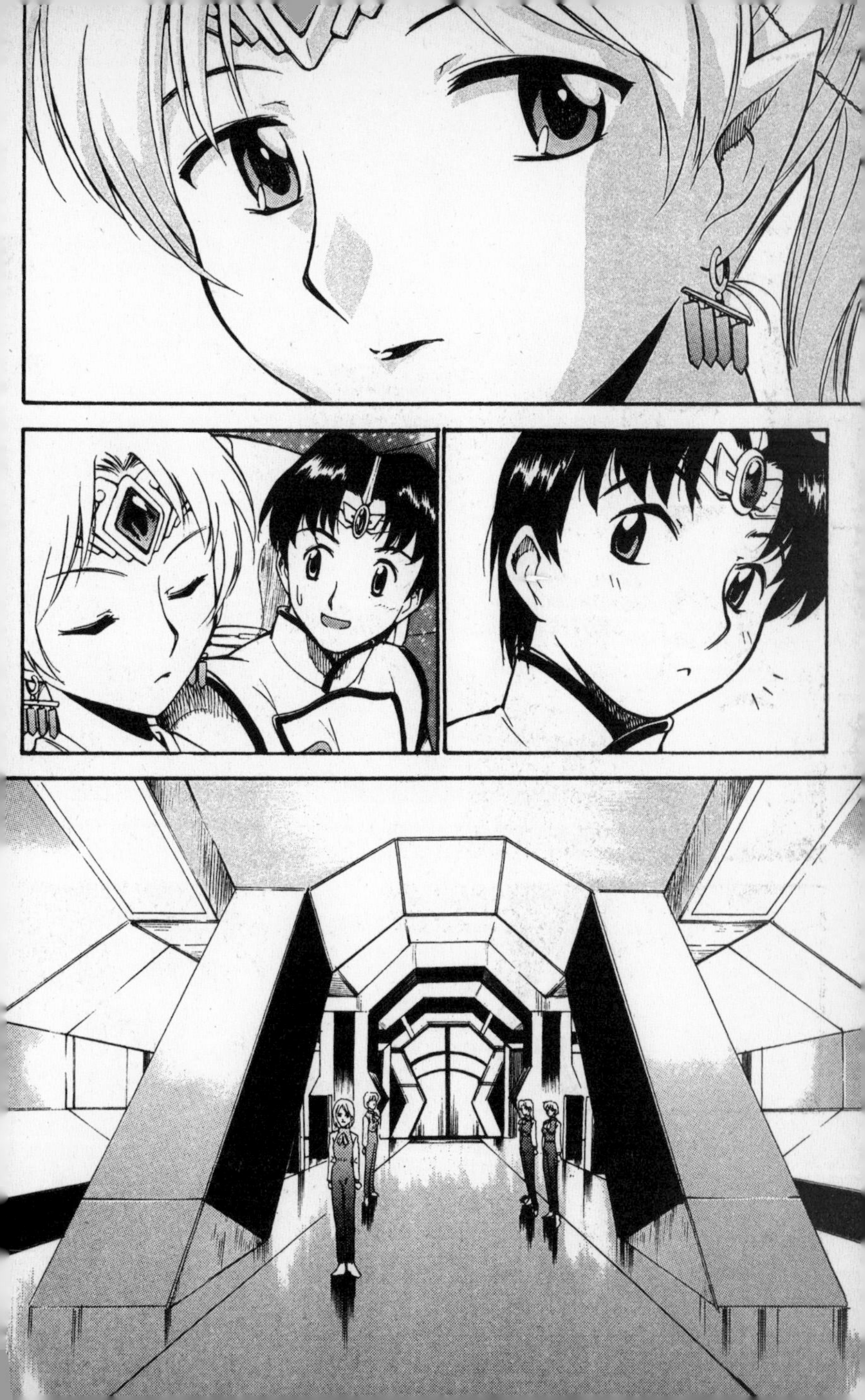

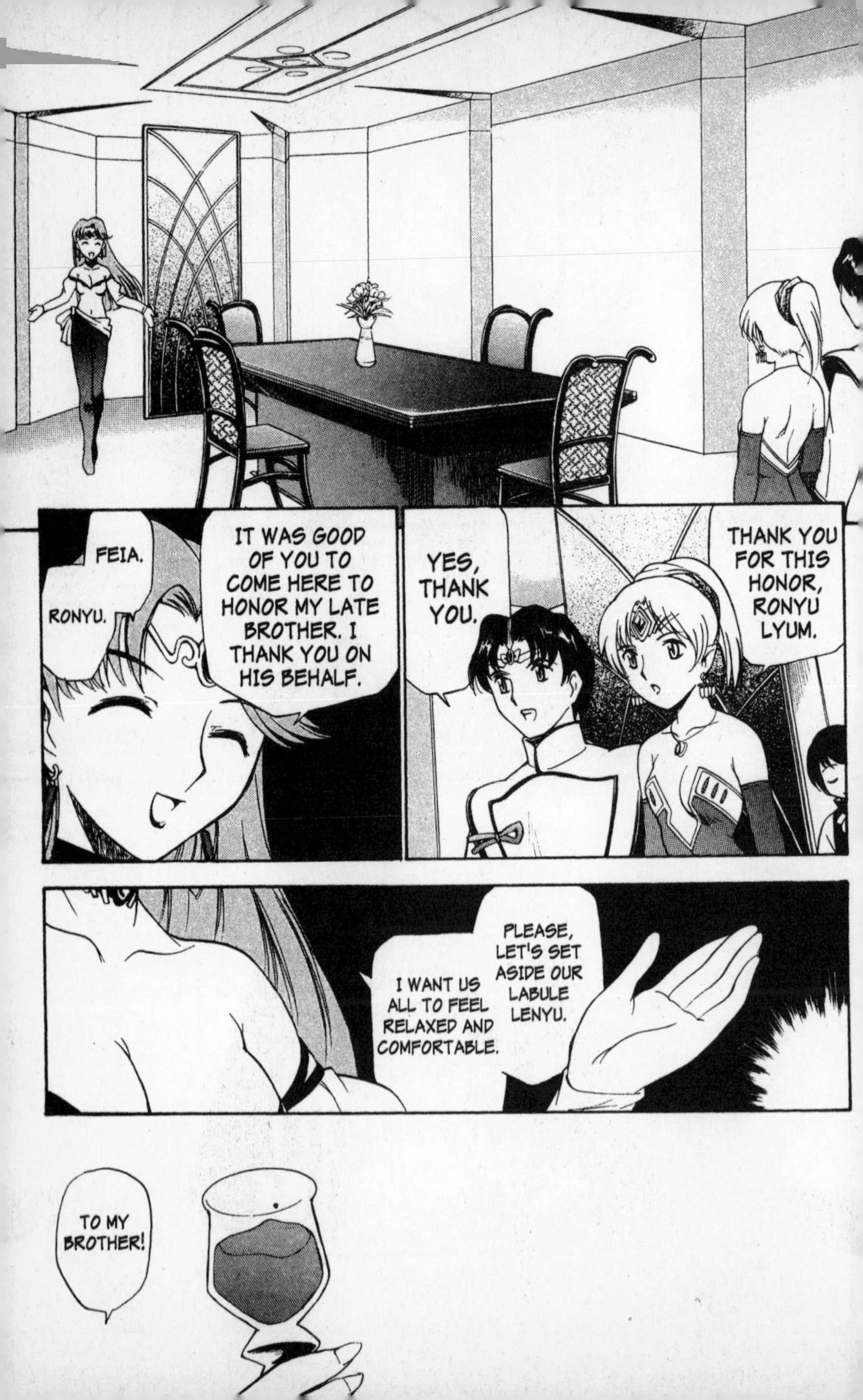
THANK YOU FOR THIS HONOR, RONYU LYUM.
YES, THANK YOU.
IT WAS GOOD OF YOU TO COME HERE TO HONOR MY LATE BROTHER. I THANK YOU ON HIS BEHALF.
FEIA.
RONYU.
PLEASE, LET'S SET ASIDE OUR LABULE LENYU.
I WANT US ALL TO FEEL RELAXED AND COMFORTABLE.
TO MY BROTHER!

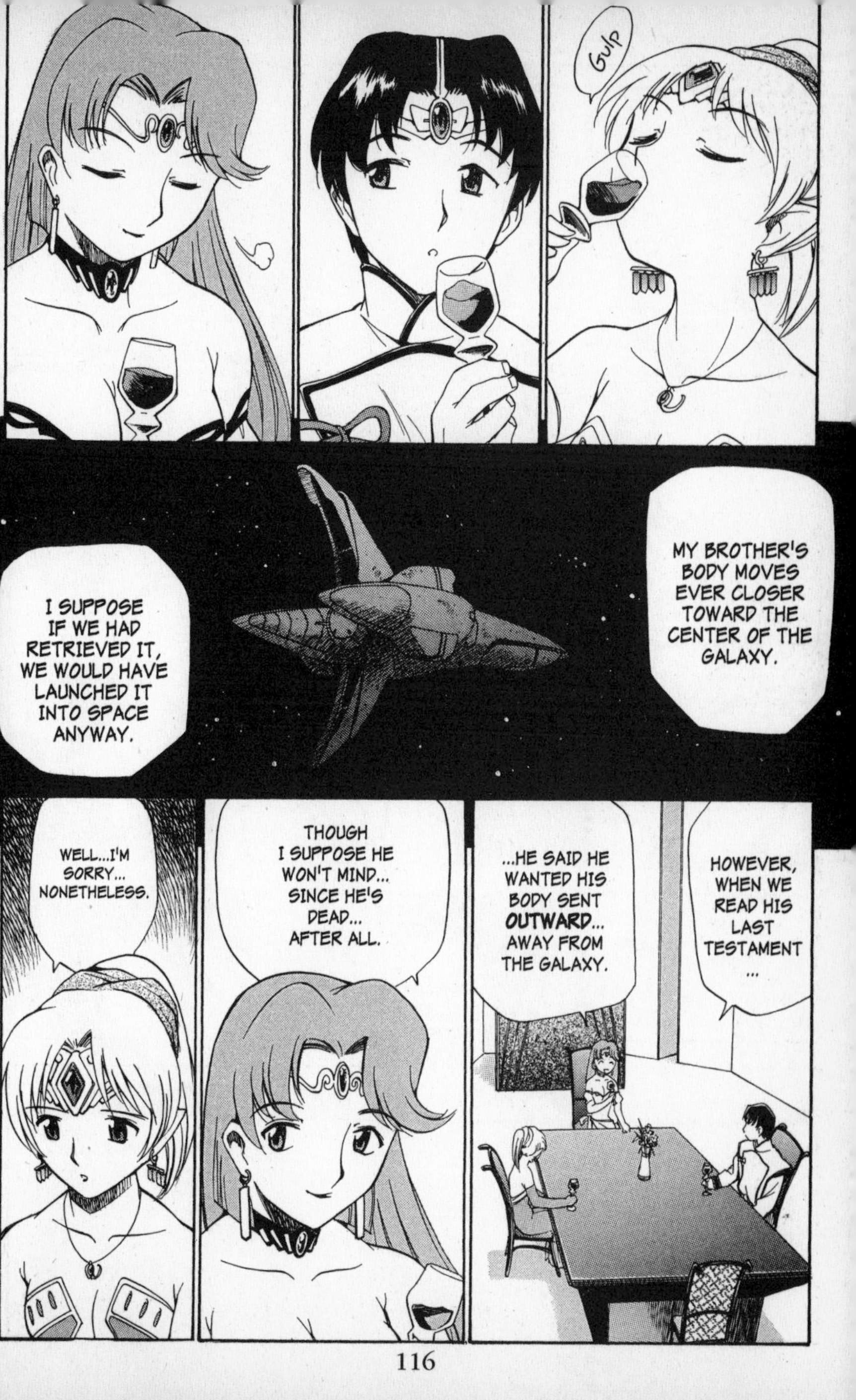
Gulp
MY BROTHER'S BODY MOVES EVER CLOSER TOWARD THE CENTER OF THE GALAXY.
I SUPPOSE IF WE HAD RETRIEVED IT, WE WOULD HAVE LAUNCHED IT INTO SPACE ANYWAY.
HOWEVER, WHEN WE READ HIS LAST TESTAMENT ...
...HE SAID HE WANTED HIS BODY SENT **OUTWARD**... AWAY FROM THE GALAXY.
THOUGH I SUPPOSE HE WON'T MIND... SINCE HE'S DEAD... AFTER ALL.
WELL...I'M SORRY... NONETHELESS.

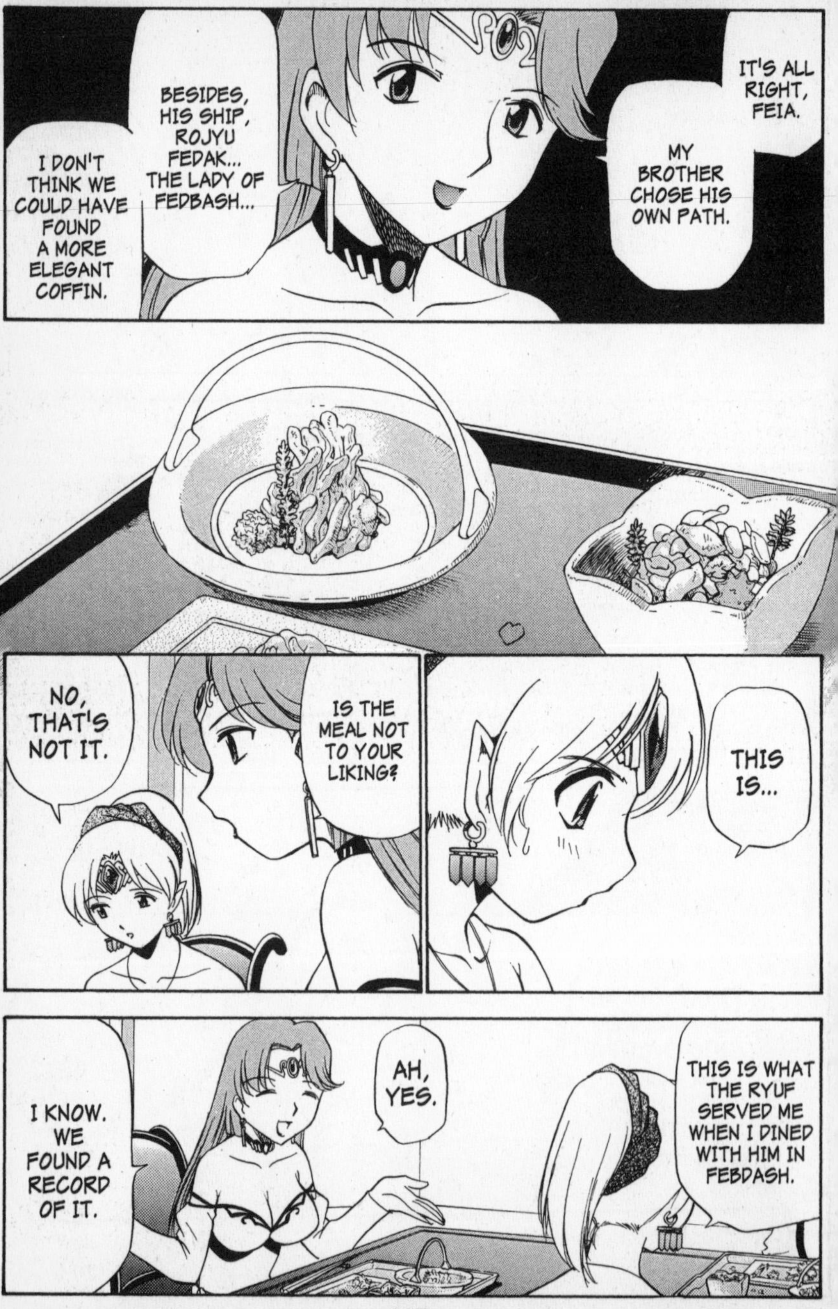
IT'S ALL RIGHT, FEIA.
MY BROTHER CHOSE HIS OWN PATH.
BESIDES, HIS SHIP, ROJYU FEDAK... THE LADY OF FEDBASH...
I DON'T THINK WE COULD HAVE FOUND A MORE ELEGANT COFFIN.
THIS IS...
IS THE MEAL NOT TO YOUR LIKING?
NO, THAT'S NOT IT.
THIS IS WHAT THE RYUF SERVED ME WHEN I DINED WITH HIM IN FEBDASH.
AH, YES.
I KNOW. WE FOUND A RECORD OF IT.

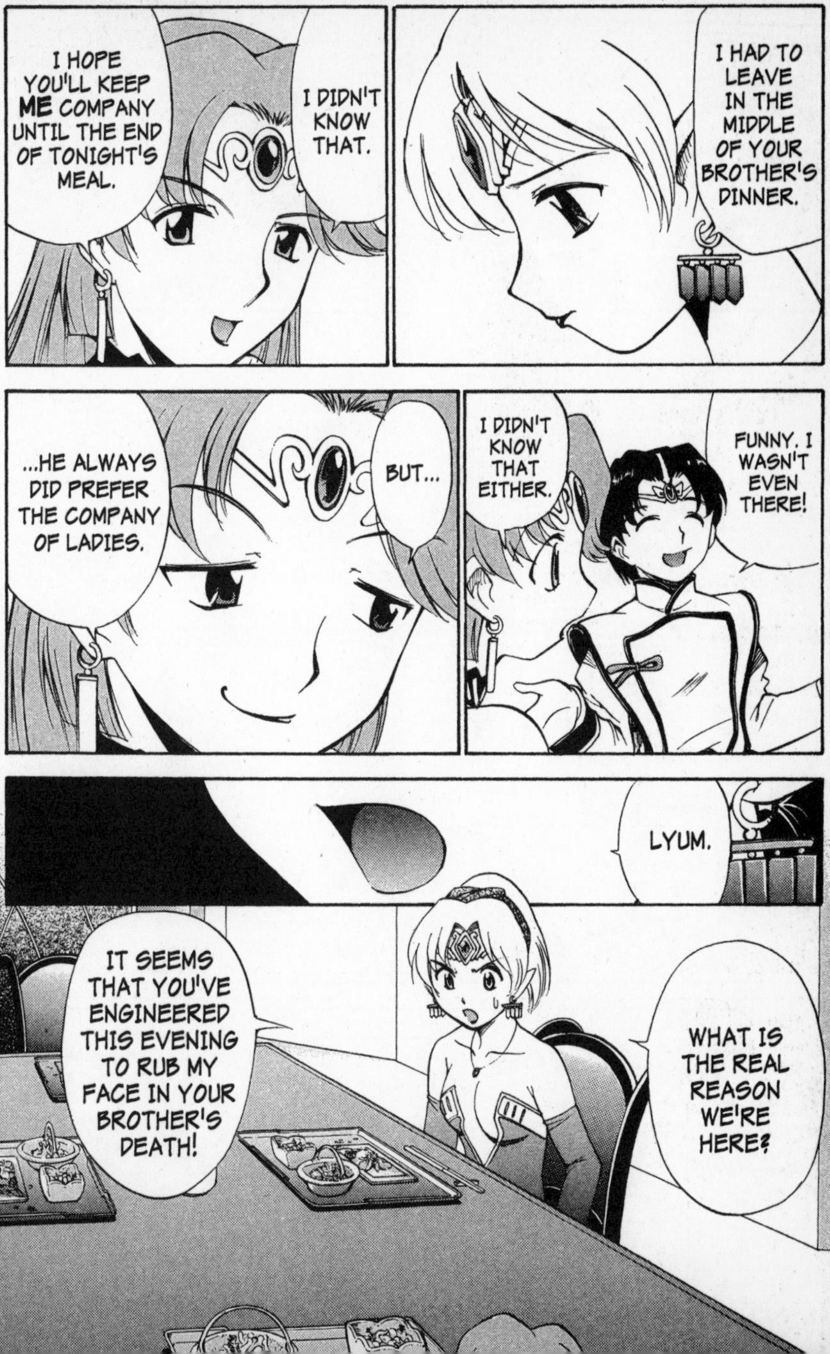
I HAD TO LEAVE IN THE MIDDLE OF YOUR BROTHER'S DINNER.
I DIDN'T KNOW THAT.
I HOPE YOU'LL KEEP **ME** COMPANY UNTIL THE END OF TONIGHT'S MEAL.
FUNNY. I WASN'T EVEN THERE!
I DIDN'T KNOW THAT EITHER.
BUT...
...HE ALWAYS DID PREFER THE COMPANY OF LADIES.
LYUM.
WHAT IS THE REAL REASON WE'RE HERE?
IT SEEMS THAT YOU'VE ENGINEERED THIS EVENING TO RUB MY FACE IN YOUR BROTHER'S DEATH!

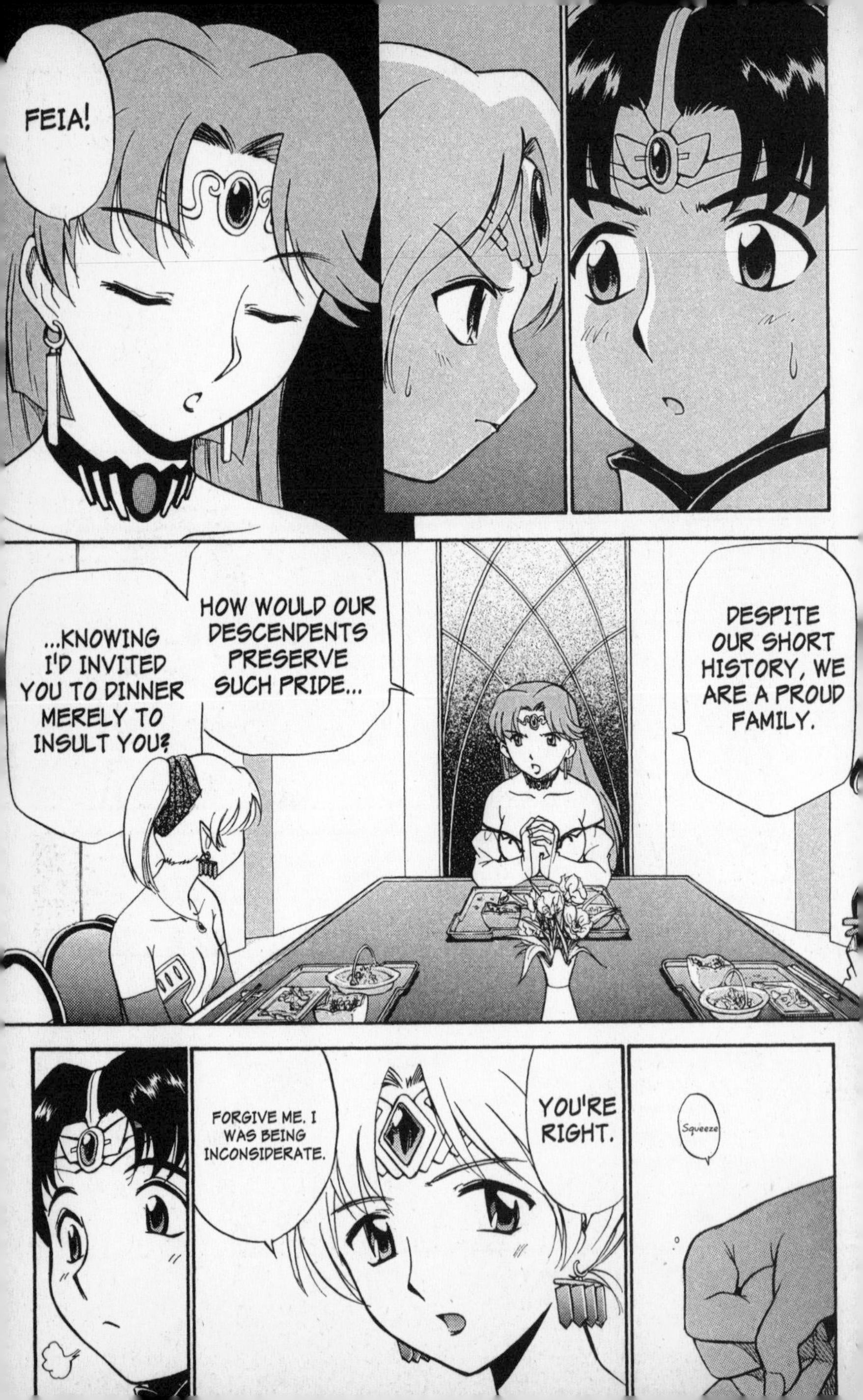
FEIA!
DESPITE OUR SHORT HISTORY, WE ARE A PROUD FAMILY.
HOW WOULD OUR DESCENDENTS PRESERVE SUCH PRIDE...
...KNOWING I'D INVITED YOU TO DINNER MERELY TO INSULT YOU?
Squeeze
YOU'RE RIGHT.
FORGIVE ME. I WAS BEING INCONSIDERATE.

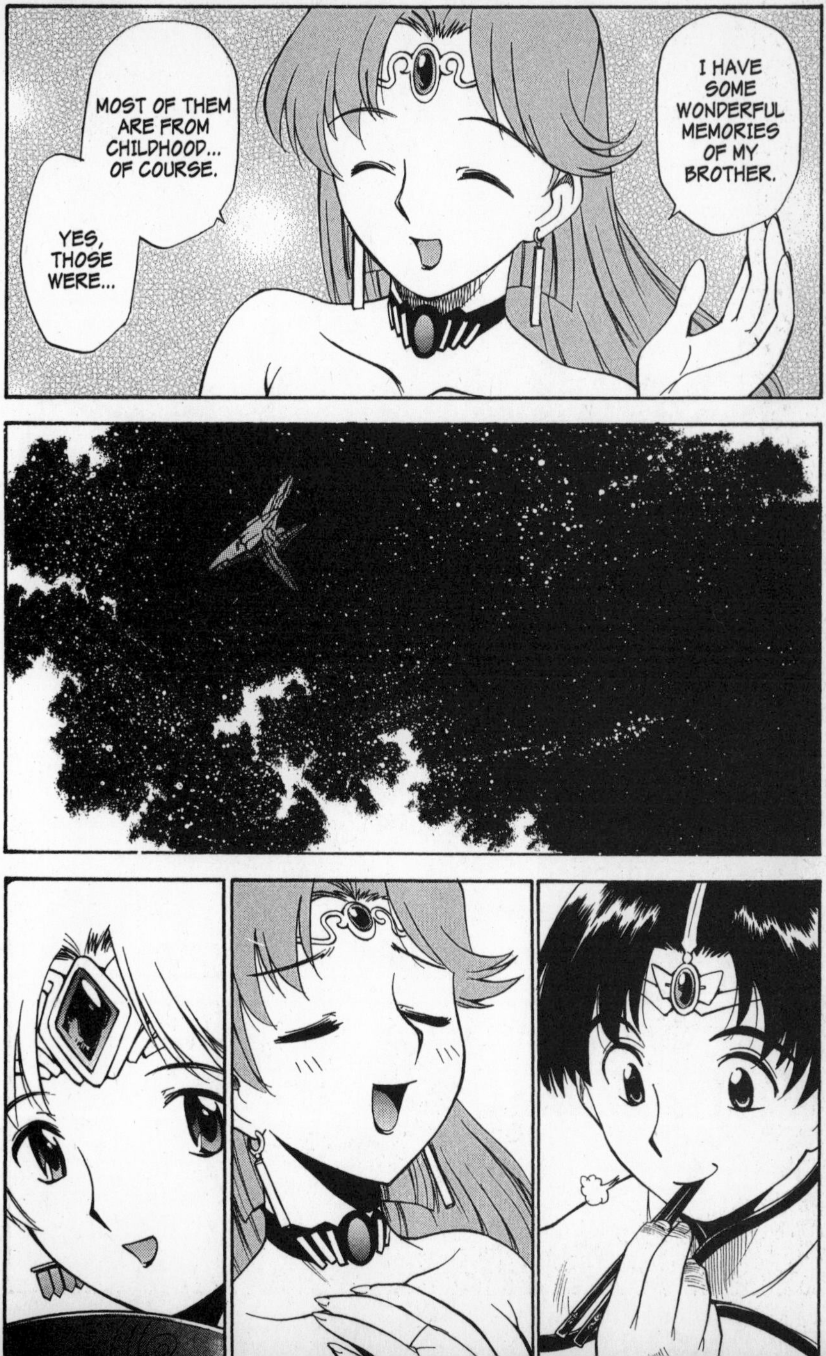
I HAVE SOME WONDERFUL MEMORIES OF MY BROTHER.
MOST OF THEM ARE FROM CHILDHOOD... OF COURSE.
YES, THOSE WERE...

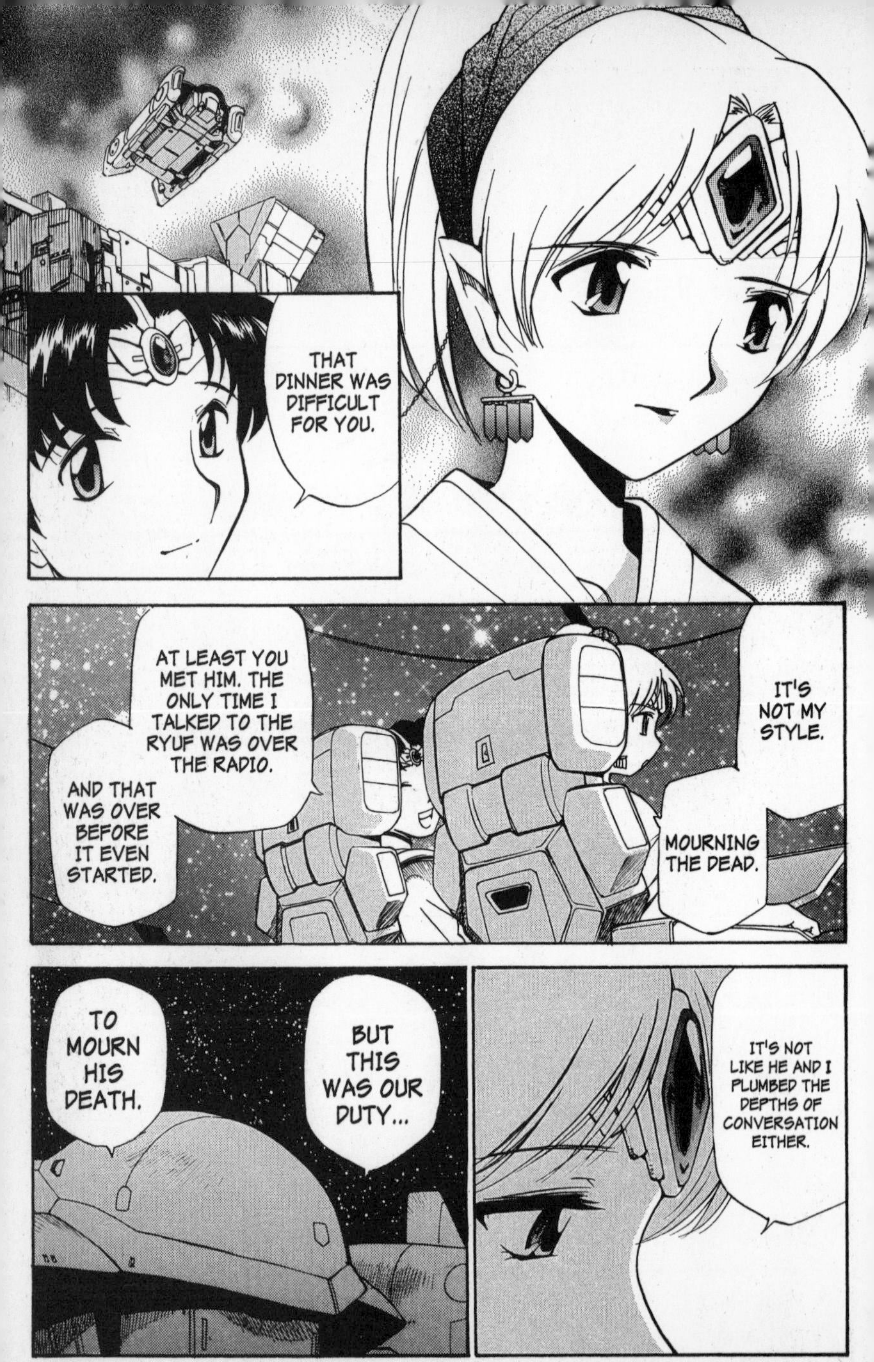
THAT DINNER WAS DIFFICULT FOR YOU.
IT'S NOT MY STYLE.
MOURNING THE DEAD.
AT LEAST YOU MET HIM. THE ONLY TIME I TALKED TO THE RYUF WAS OVER THE RADIO.
AND THAT WAS OVER BEFORE IT EVEN STARTED.
IT'S NOT LIKE HE AND I PLUMBED THE DEPTHS OF CONVERSATION EITHER.
BUT THIS WAS OUR DUTY...
TO MOURN HIS DEATH.

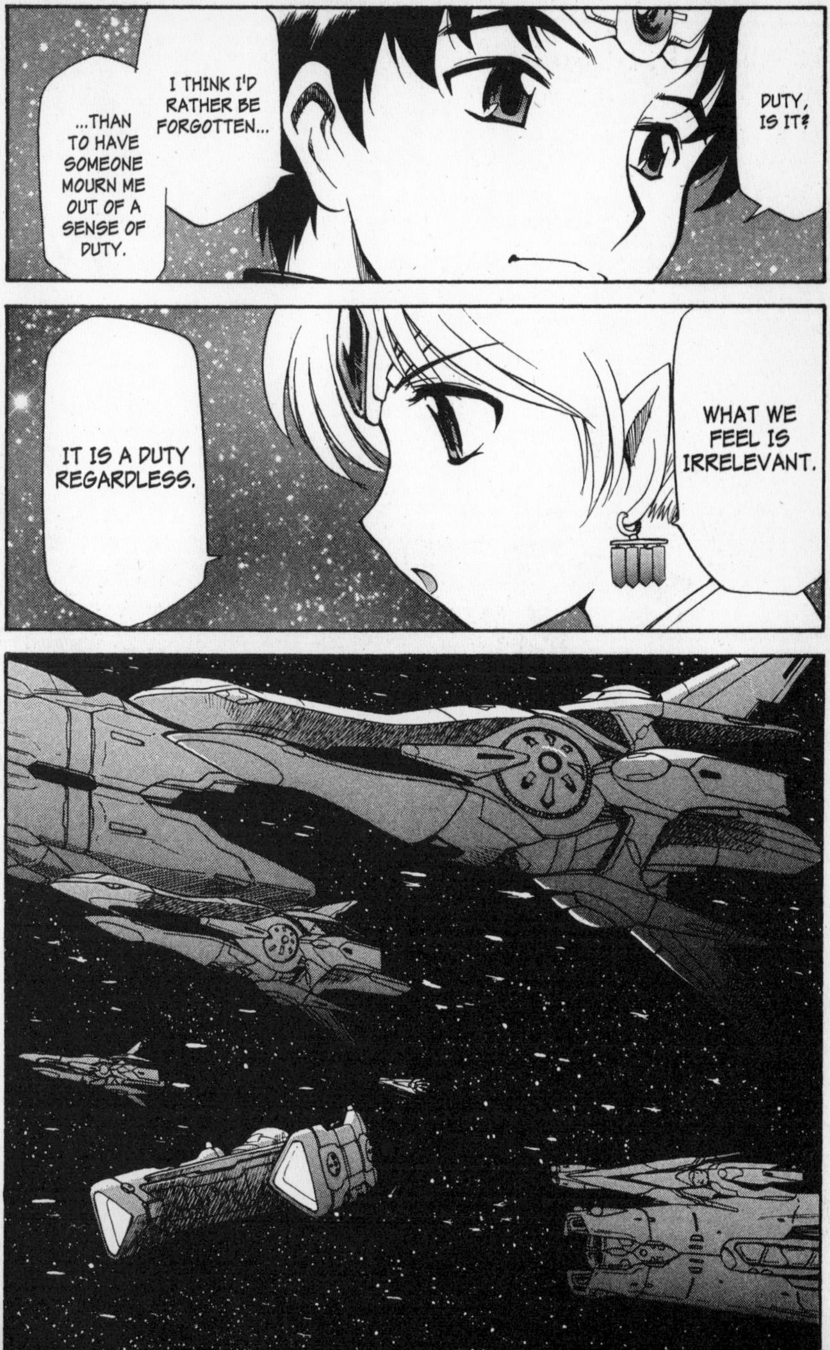
DUTY, IS IT?
I THINK I'D RATHER BE FORGOTTEN...
...THAN TO HAVE SOMEONE MOURN ME OUT OF A SENSE OF DUTY.
WHAT WE FEEL IS IRRELEVANT.
IT IS A DUTY REGARDLESS.

Chapter 7
Battlefield at the Aptic Gate

LAJSHAKAL WEK SODAL APTJCAL

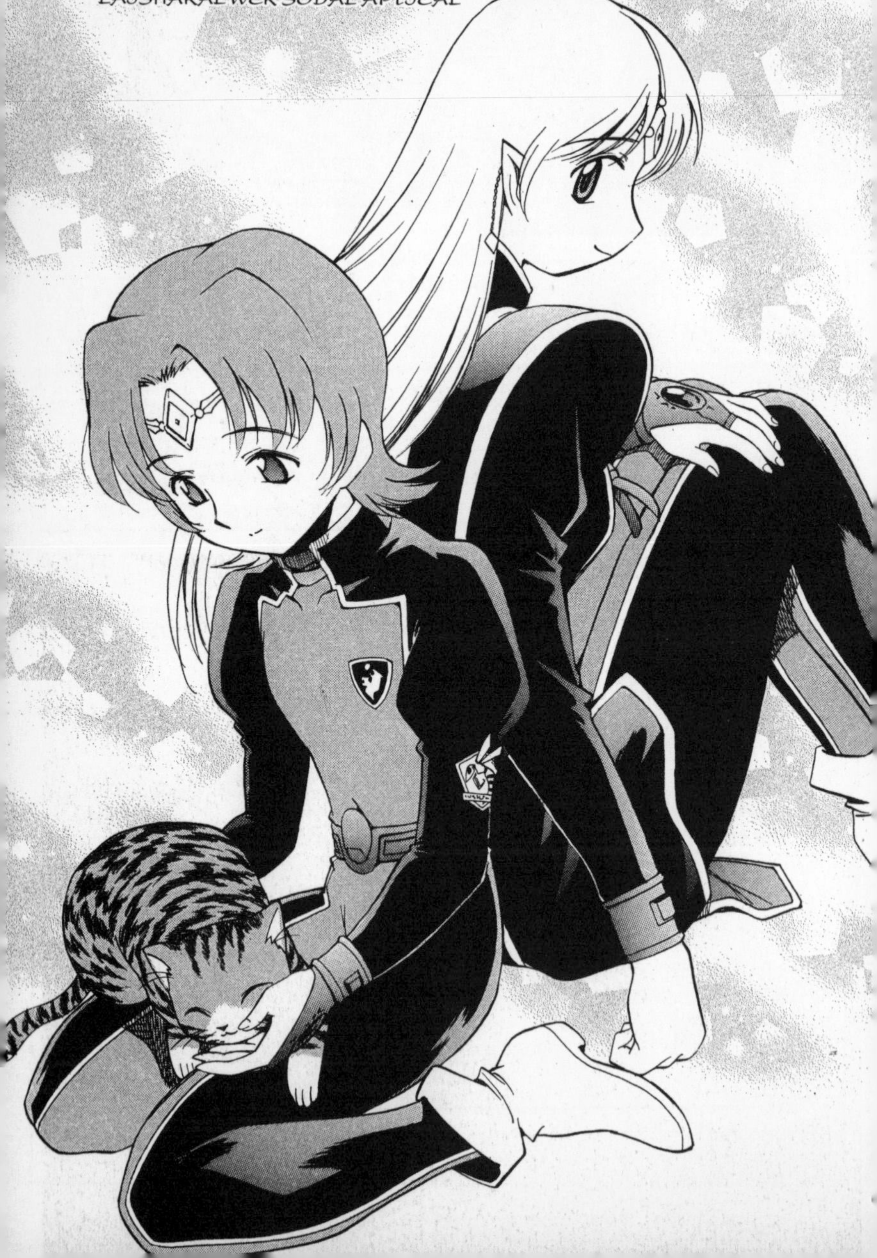

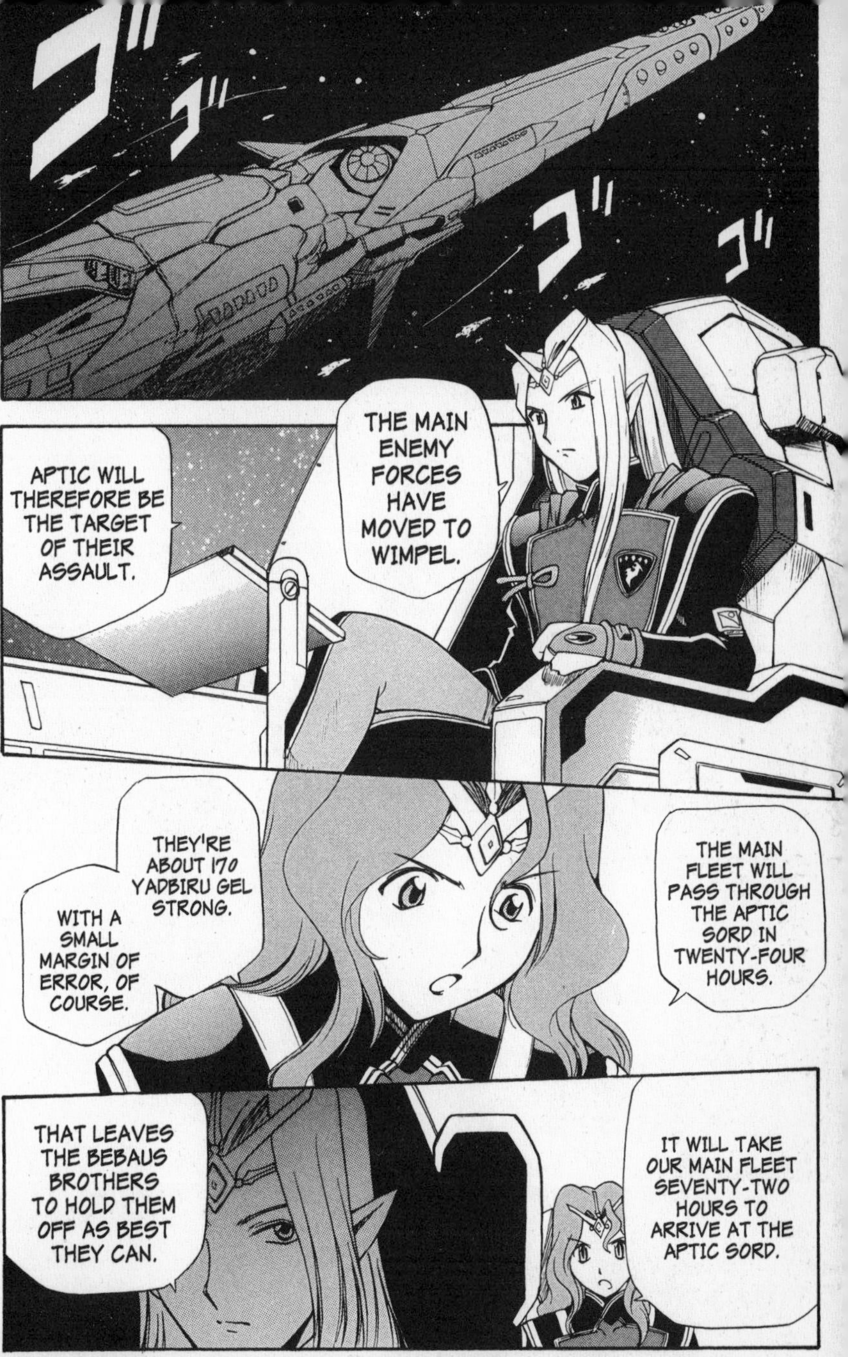
ゴ
ゴ
ゴ
ゴ
THE MAIN ENEMY FORCES HAVE MOVED TO WIMPEL.
APTIC WILL THEREFORE BE THE TARGET OF THEIR ASSAULT.
THE MAIN FLEET WILL PASS THROUGH THE APTIC SORD IN TWENTY-FOUR HOURS.
THEY'RE ABOUT 170 YADBIRU GEL STRONG.
WITH A SMALL MARGIN OF ERROR, OF COURSE.
IT WILL TAKE OUR MAIN FLEET SEVENTY-TWO HOURS TO ARRIVE AT THE APTIC SORD.
THAT LEAVES THE BEBAUS BROTHERS TO HOLD THEM OFF AS BEST THEY CAN.

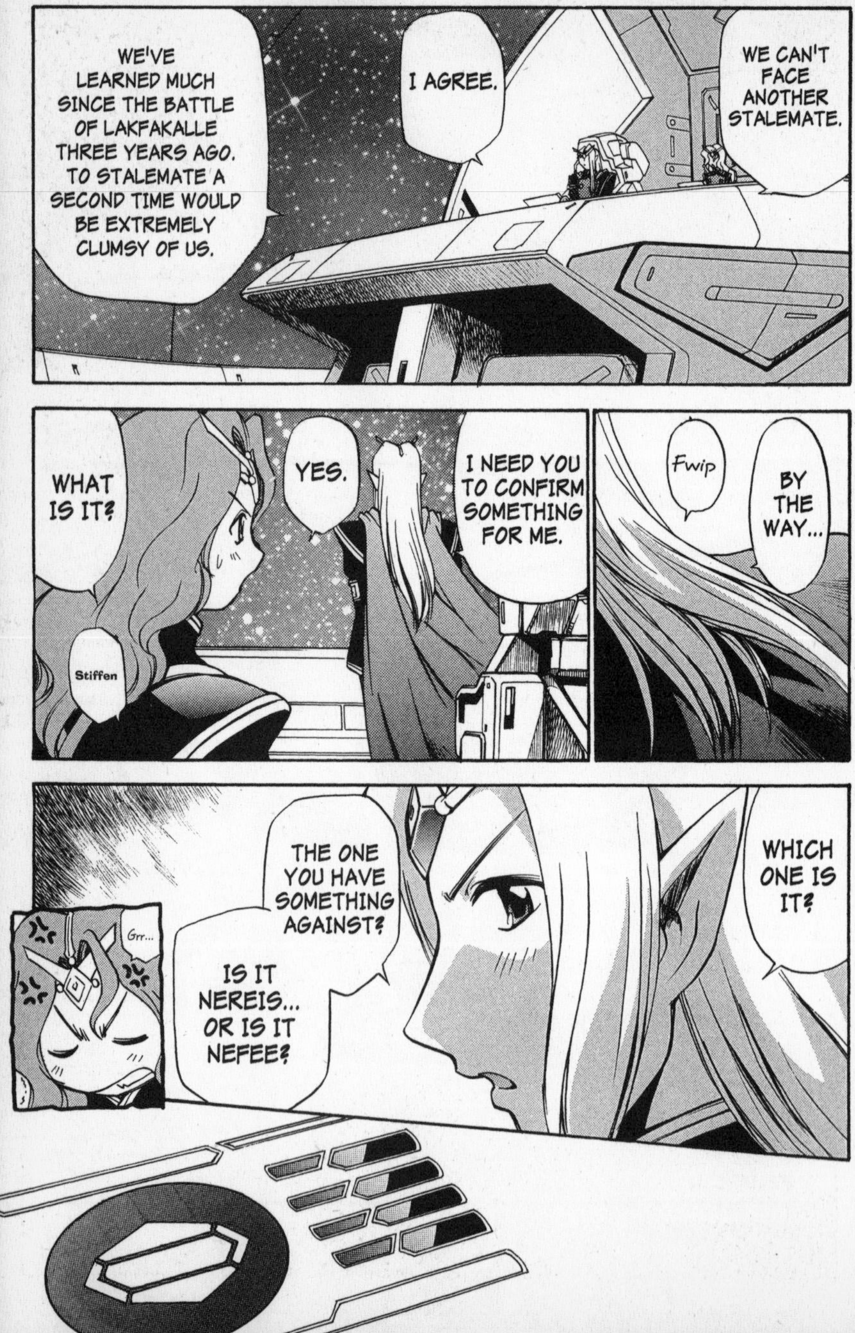
WE CAN'T FACE ANOTHER STALEMATE.
I AGREE.
WE'VE LEARNED MUCH SINCE THE BATTLE OF LAKFAKALLE THREE YEARS AGO. TO STALEMATE A SECOND TIME WOULD BE EXTREMELY CLUMSY OF US.
BY THE WAY...
Fwip
I NEED YOU TO CONFIRM SOMETHING FOR ME.
YES.
WHAT IS IT?
Stiffen
WHICH ONE IS IT?
THE ONE YOU HAVE SOMETHING AGAINST?
IS IT NEREIS... OR IS IT NEFEE?
Grr...

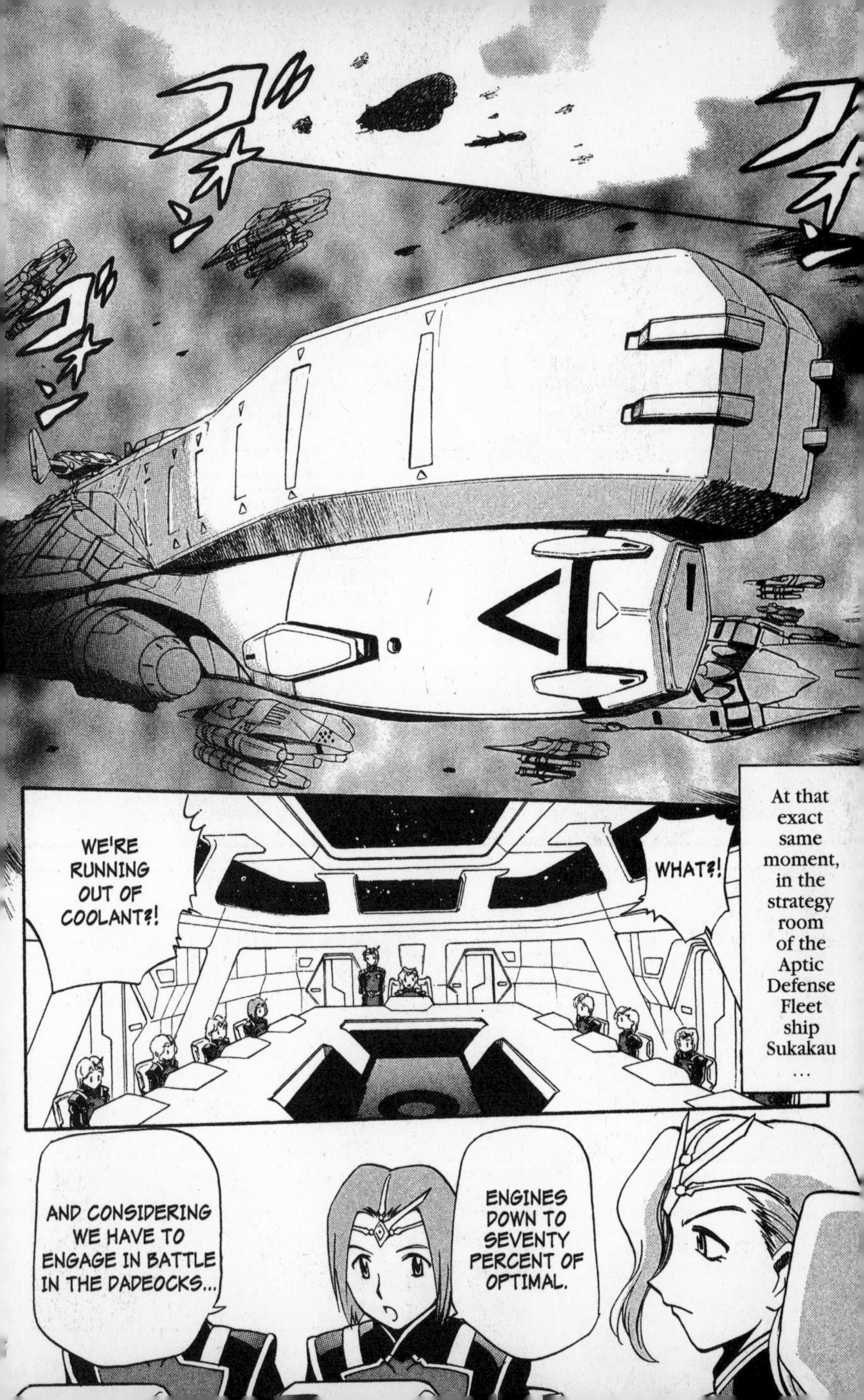
At that exact same moment, in the strategy room of the Aptic Defense Fleet ship Sukakau . . .
WHAT?!
WE'RE RUNNING OUT OF COOLANT?!
ENGINES DOWN TO SEVENTY PERCENT OF OPTIMAL.
AND CONSIDERING WE HAVE TO ENGAGE IN BATTLE IN THE DADEOCKS...

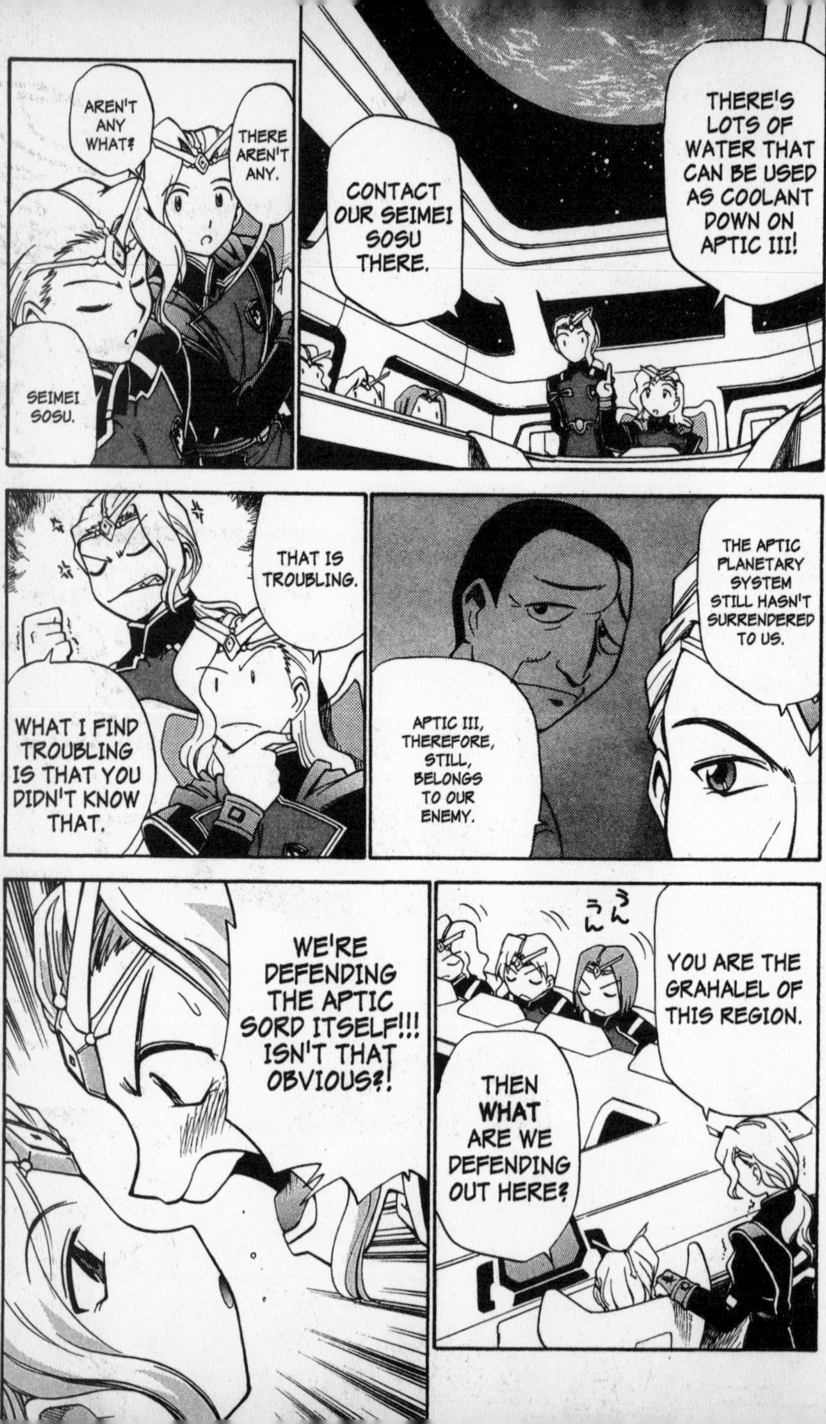

THERE'S LOTS OF WATER THAT CAN BE USED AS COOLANT DOWN ON APTIC III!
CONTACT OUR SEIMEI SOSU THERE.
THERE AREN'T ANY.
AREN'T ANY WHAT?
SEIMEI SOSU.
THE APTIC PLANETARY SYSTEM STILL HASN'T SURRENDERED TO US.
APTIC III, THEREFORE, STILL, BELONGS TO OUR ENEMY.
THAT IS TROUBLING.
WHAT I FIND TROUBLING IS THAT YOU DIDN'T KNOW THAT.
うんうん
YOU ARE THE GRAHALEL OF THIS REGION.
THEN WHAT ARE WE DEFENDING OUT HERE?
WE'RE DEFENDING THE APTIC SORD ITSELF!!! ISN'T THAT OBVIOUS?!

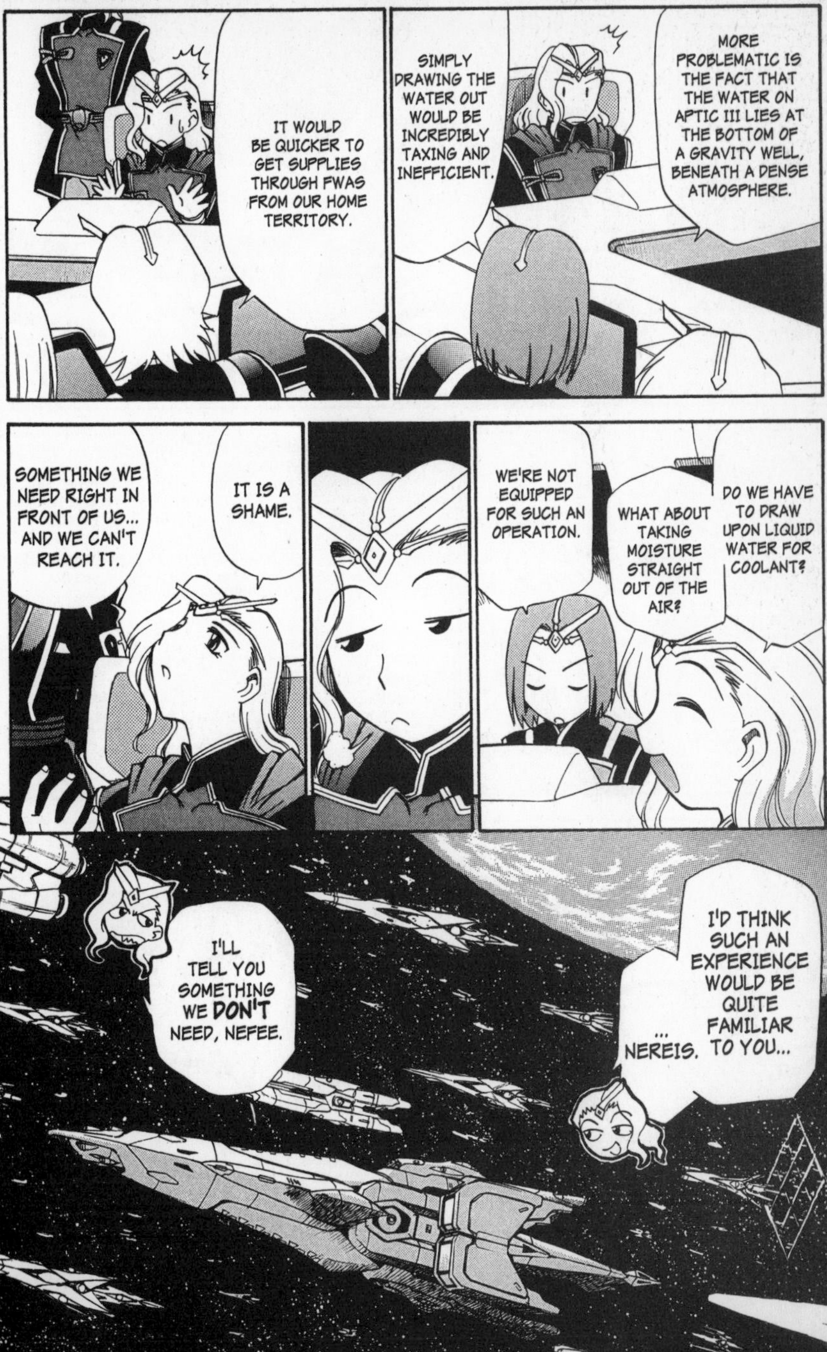
MORE PROBLEMATIC IS THE FACT THAT THE WATER ON APTIC III LIES AT THE BOTTOM OF A GRAVITY WELL, BENEATH A DENSE ATMOSPHERE.
SIMPLY DRAWING THE WATER OUT WOULD BE INCREDIBLY TAXING AND INEFFICIENT.
IT WOULD BE QUICKER TO GET SUPPLIES THROUGH FWAS FROM OUR HOME TERRITORY.
DO WE HAVE TO DRAW UPON LIQUID WATER FOR COOLANT?
WHAT ABOUT TAKING MOISTURE STRAIGHT OUT OF THE AIR?
WE'RE NOT EQUIPPED FOR SUCH AN OPERATION.
IT IS A SHAME.
SOMETHING WE NEED RIGHT IN FRONT OF US... AND WE CAN'T REACH IT.
I'D THINK SUCH AN EXPERIENCE WOULD BE QUITE FAMILIAR TO YOU...
...NEREIS.
I'LL TELL YOU SOMETHING WE DON'T NEED, NEFEE.

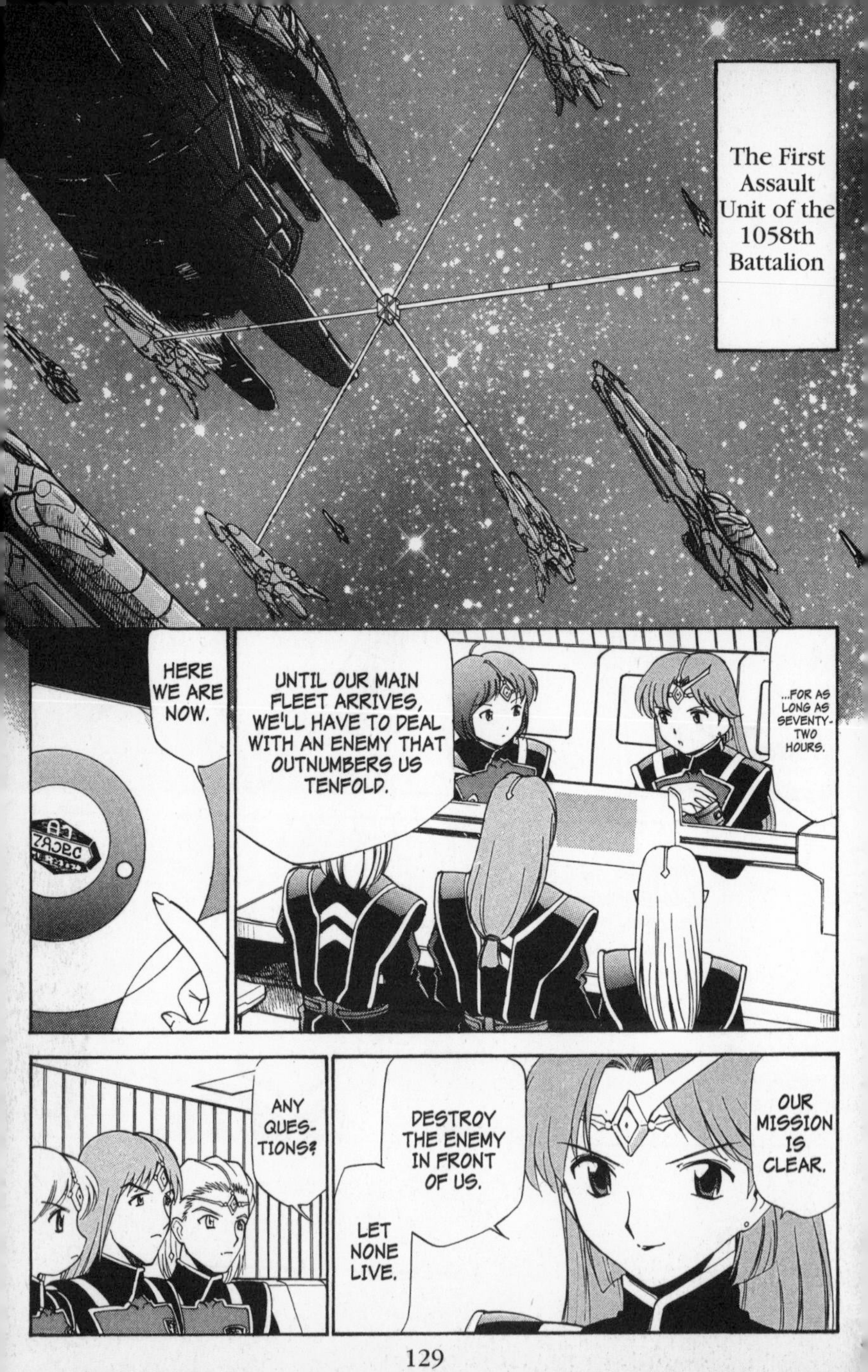
The First Assault Unit of the 1058th Battalion
UNTIL OUR MAIN FLEET ARRIVES, WE'LL HAVE TO DEAL WITH AN ENEMY THAT OUTNUMBERS US TENFOLD.
...FOR AS LONG AS SEVENTY-TWO HOURS.
HERE WE ARE NOW.
OUR MISSION IS CLEAR.
DESTROY THE ENEMY IN FRONT OF US.
LET NONE LIVE.
ANY QUESTIONS?

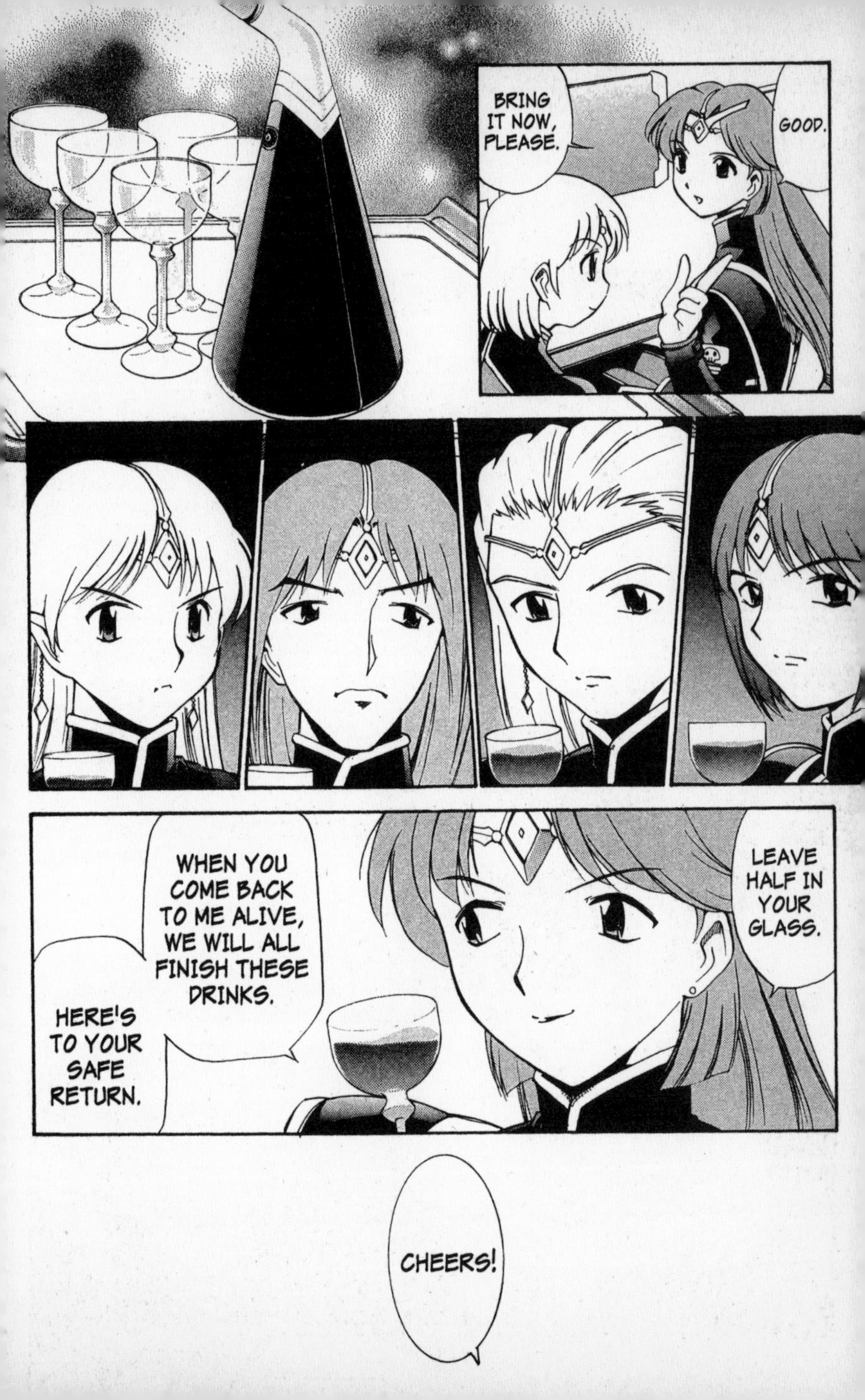
GOOD.
BRING IT NOW, PLEASE.
LEAVE HALF IN YOUR GLASS.
WHEN YOU COME BACK TO ME ALIVE, WE WILL ALL FINISH THESE DRINKS.
HERE'S TO YOUR SAFE RETURN.
CHEERS!

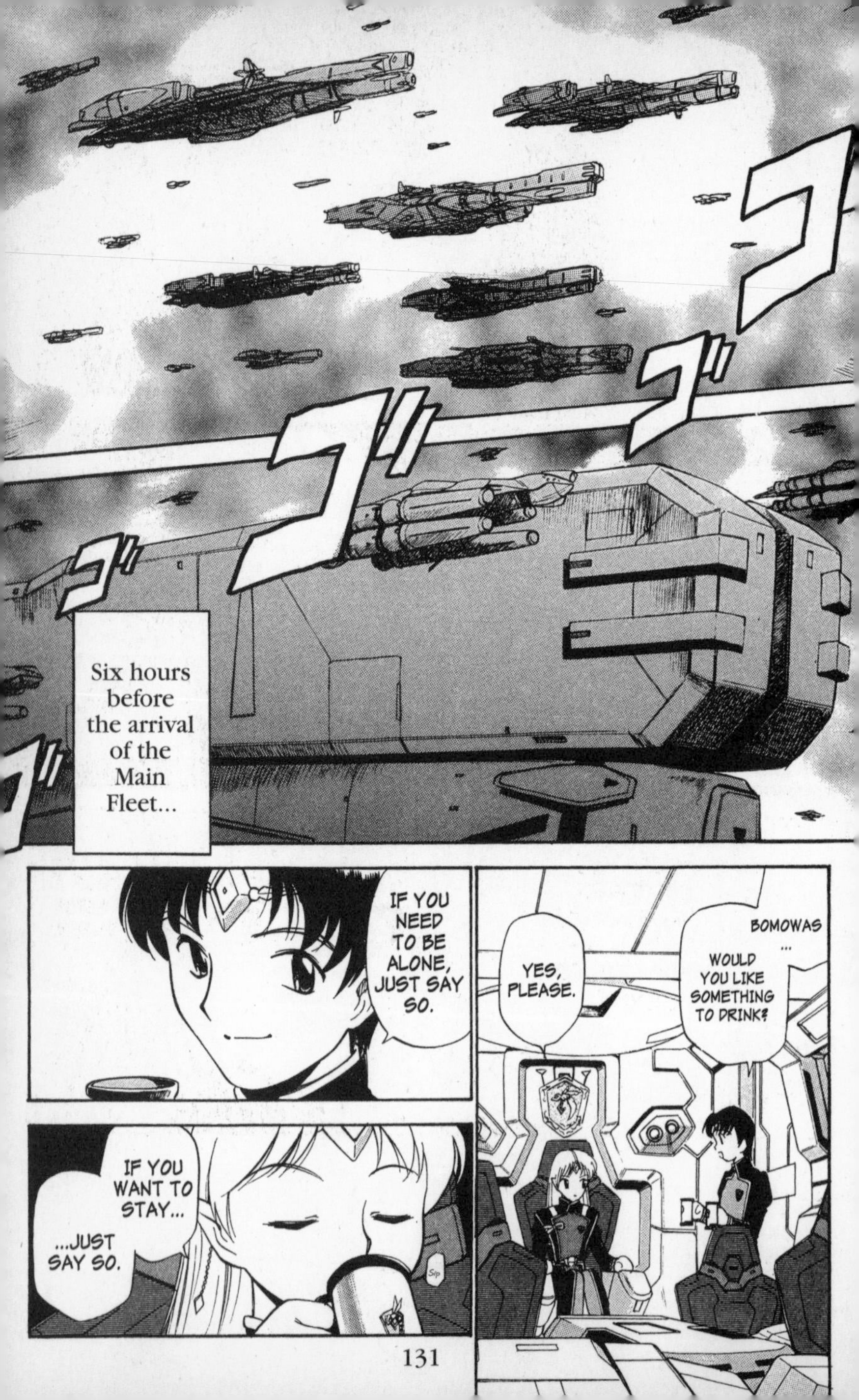
ゴゴゴゴゴ
Six hours before the arrival of the Main Fleet...
BOMOWAS...
WOULD YOU LIKE SOMETHING TO DRINK?
YES, PLEASE.
IF YOU NEED TO BE ALONE, JUST SAY SO.
IF YOU WANT TO STAY...
...JUST SAY SO.
Sip

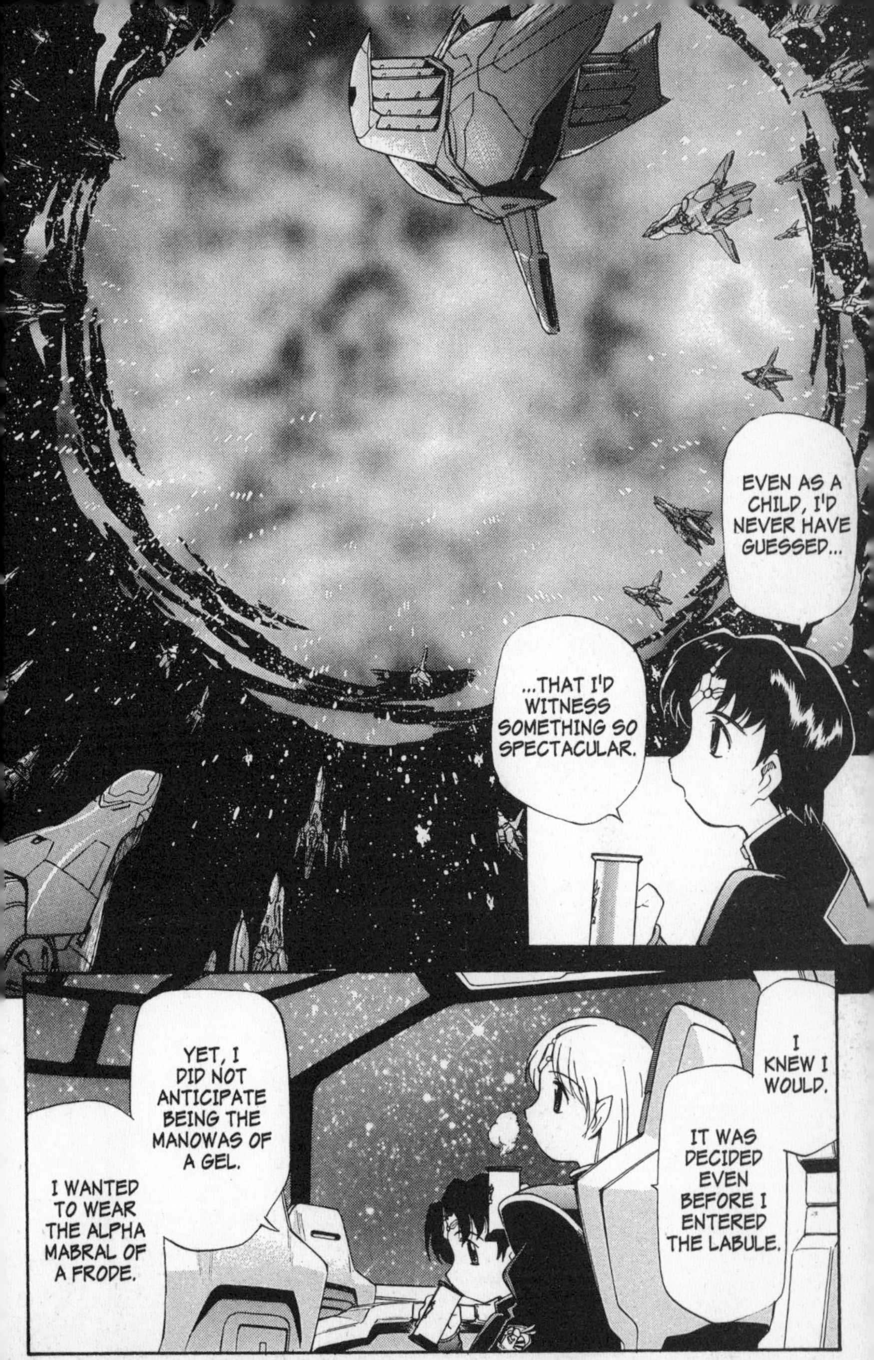
EVEN AS A CHILD, I'D NEVER HAVE GUESSED...
...THAT I'D WITNESS SOMETHING SO SPECTACULAR.
I KNEW I WOULD.
IT WAS DECIDED EVEN BEFORE I ENTERED THE LABULE.
YET, I DID NOT ANTICIPATE BEING THE MANOWAS OF A GEL.
I WANTED TO WEAR THE ALPHA MABRAL OF A FRODE.

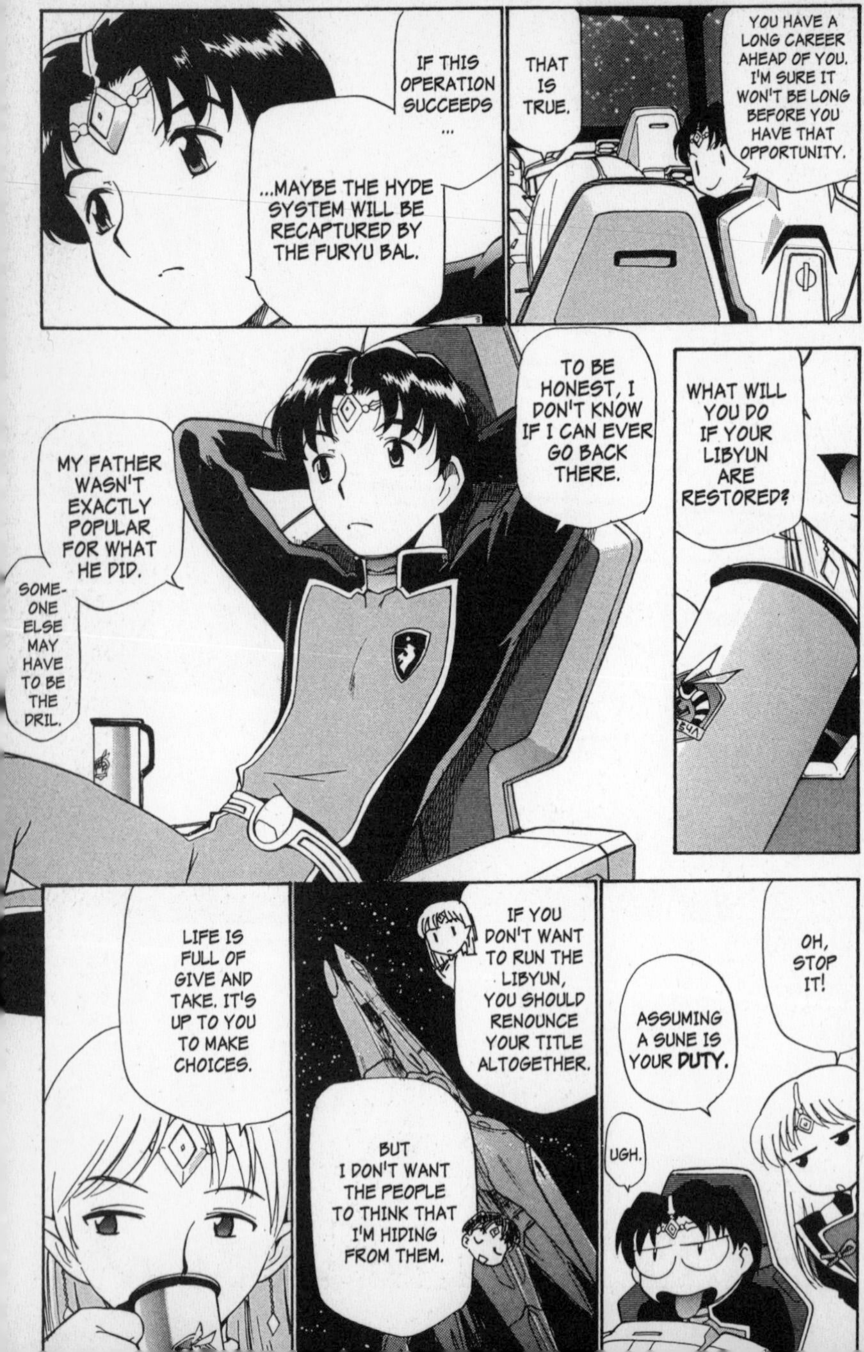
YOU HAVE A LONG CAREER AHEAD OF YOU. I'M SURE IT WON'T BE LONG BEFORE YOU HAVE THAT OPPORTUNITY.
THAT IS TRUE.
IF THIS OPERATION SUCCEEDS ...
...MAYBE THE HYDE SYSTEM WILL BE RECAPTURED BY THE FURYU BAL.
WHAT WILL YOU DO IF YOUR LIBYUN ARE RESTORED?
TO BE HONEST, I DON'T KNOW IF I CAN EVER GO BACK THERE.
MY FATHER WASN'T EXACTLY POPULAR FOR WHAT HE DID.
SOME-ONE ELSE MAY HAVE TO BE THE DRIL.
OH, STOP IT!
ASSUMING A SUNE IS YOUR **DUTY.**
UGH.
IF YOU DON'T WANT TO RUN THE LIBYUN, YOU SHOULD RENOUNCE YOUR TITLE ALTOGETHER.
BUT I DON'T WANT THE PEOPLE TO THINK THAT I'M HIDING FROM THEM.
LIFE IS FULL OF GIVE AND TAKE. IT'S UP TO YOU TO MAKE CHOICES.

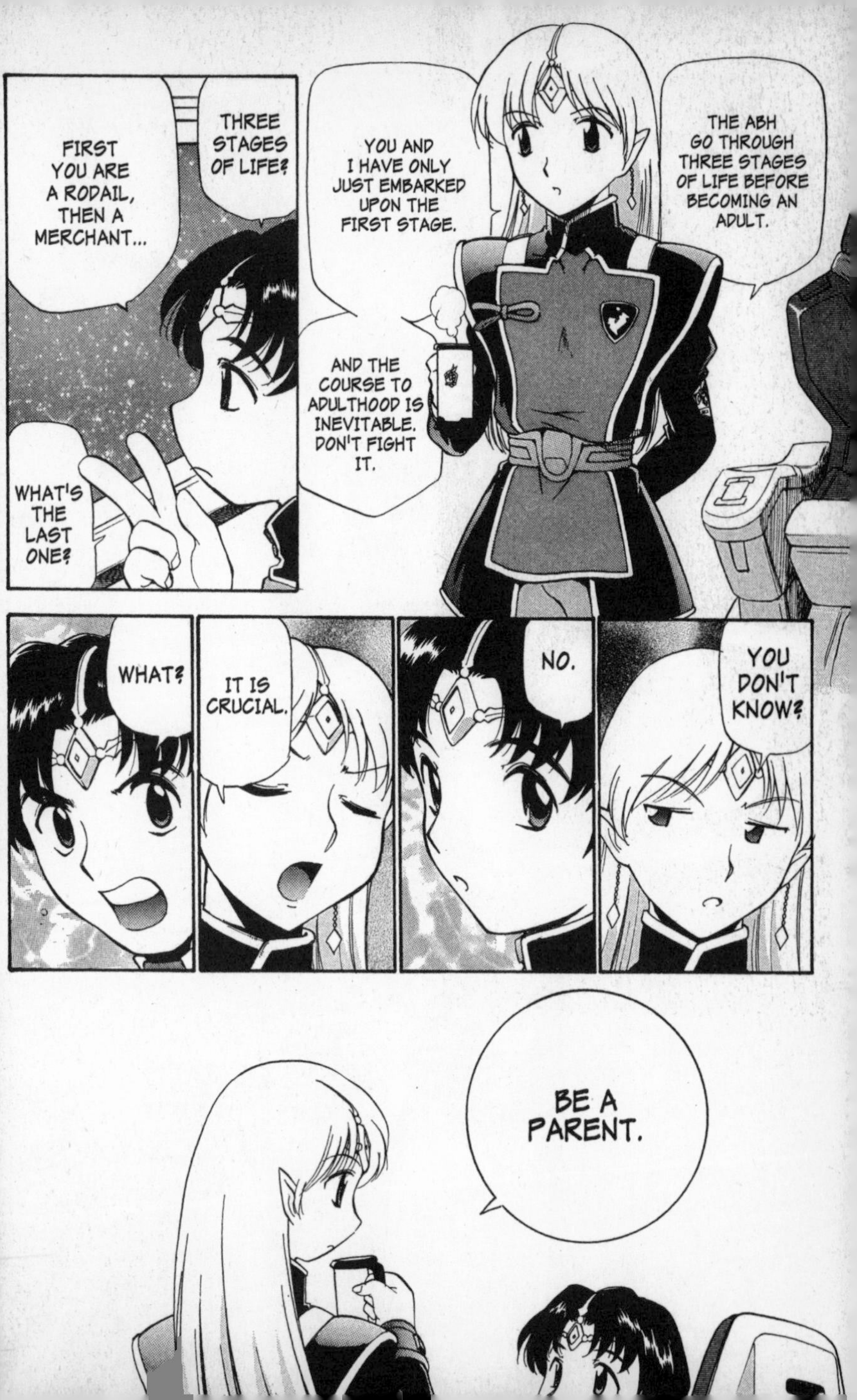
THE ABH GO THROUGH THREE STAGES OF LIFE BEFORE BECOMING AN ADULT.
YOU AND I HAVE ONLY JUST EMBARKED UPON THE FIRST STAGE.
AND THE COURSE TO ADULTHOOD IS INEVITABLE. DON'T FIGHT IT.
THREE STAGES OF LIFE?
FIRST YOU ARE A RODAIL, THEN A MERCHANT...
WHAT'S THE LAST ONE?
YOU DON'T KNOW?
NO.
IT IS CRUCIAL.
WHAT?
BE A PARENT.

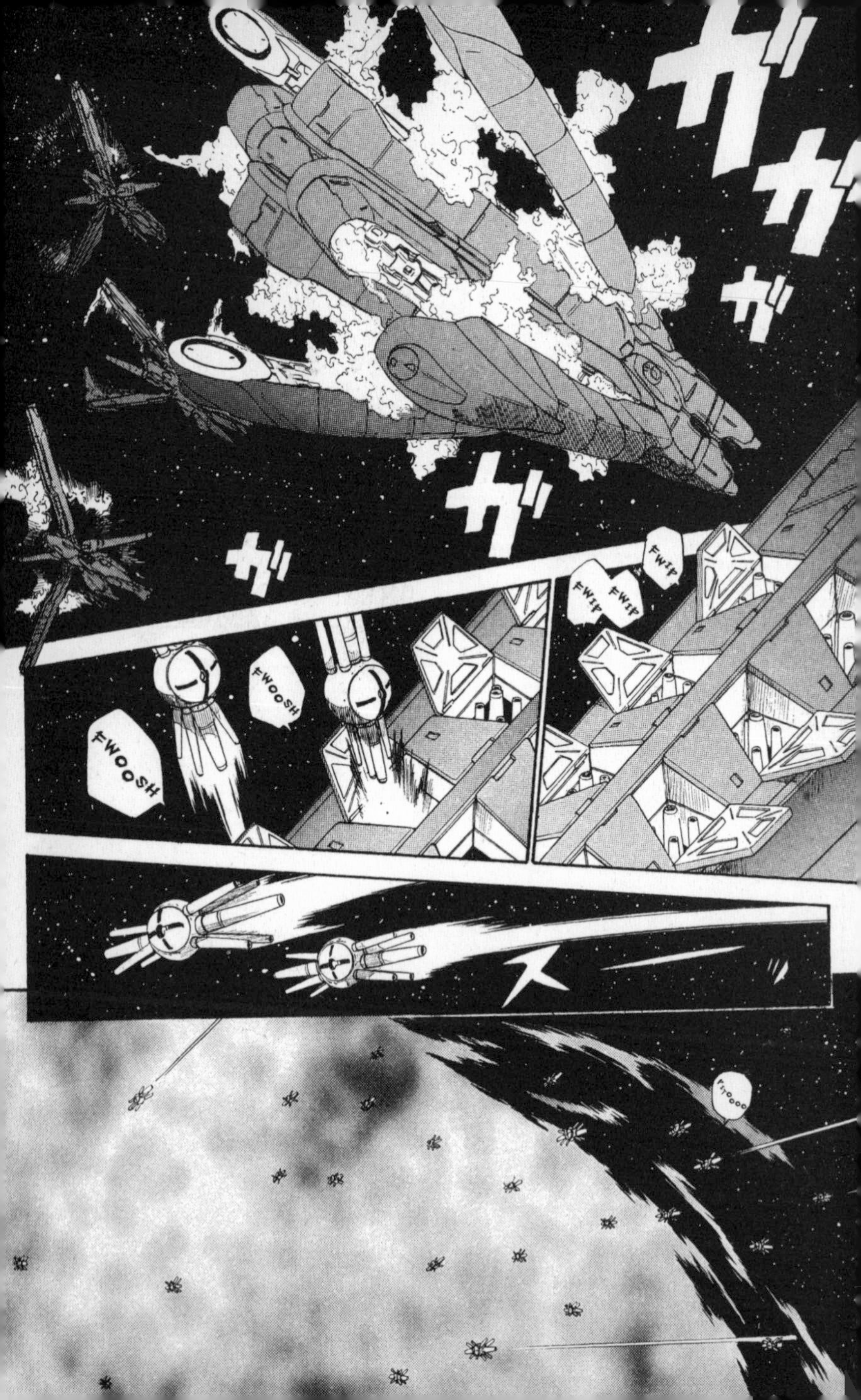
ガガガ
ガ
ガ
ガ
FWIP
FWIP
FWIP
FWOOSH
FWOOSH
ス
FTOOOO

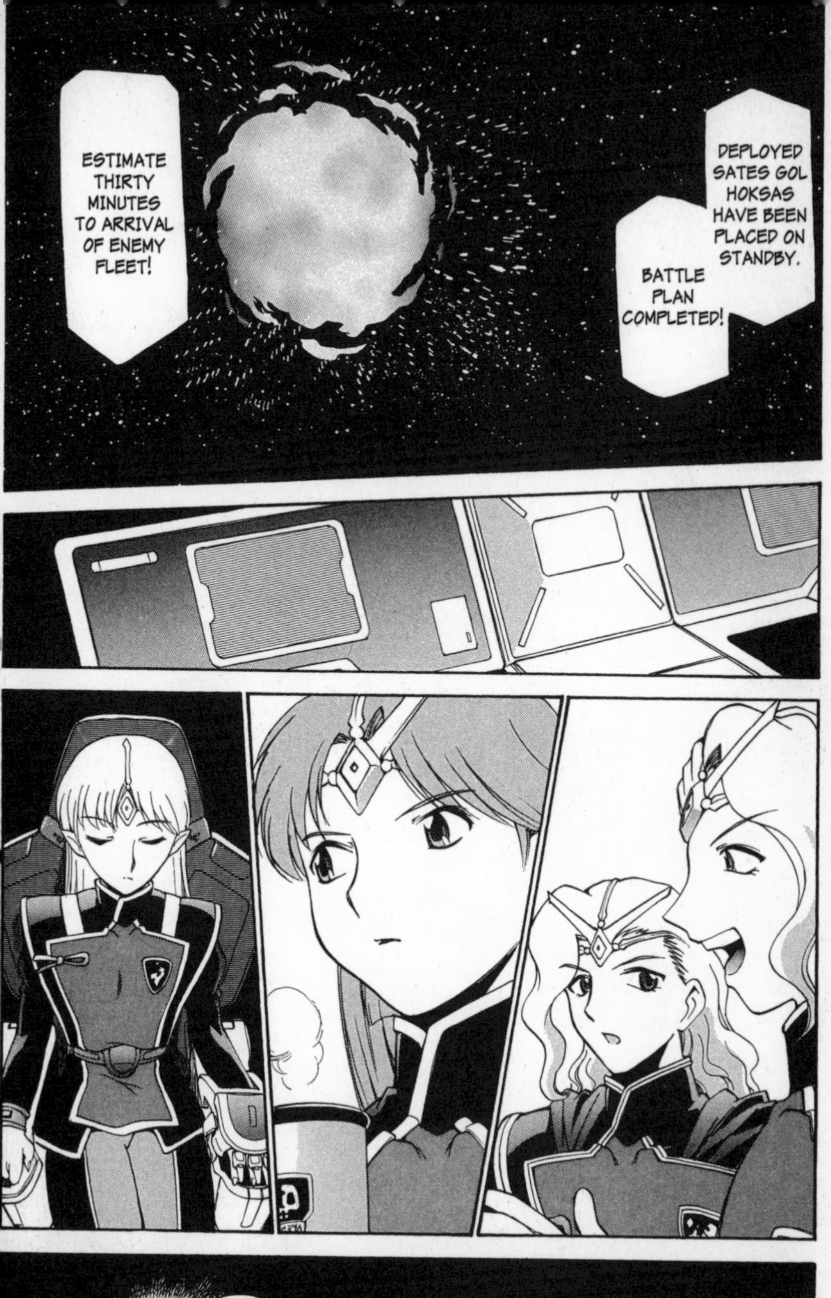
DEPLOYED SATES GOL HOKSAS HAVE BEEN PLACED ON STANDBY.
BATTLE PLAN COMPLETED!
ESTIMATE THIRTY MINUTES TO ARRIVAL OF ENEMY FLEET!
FSSH

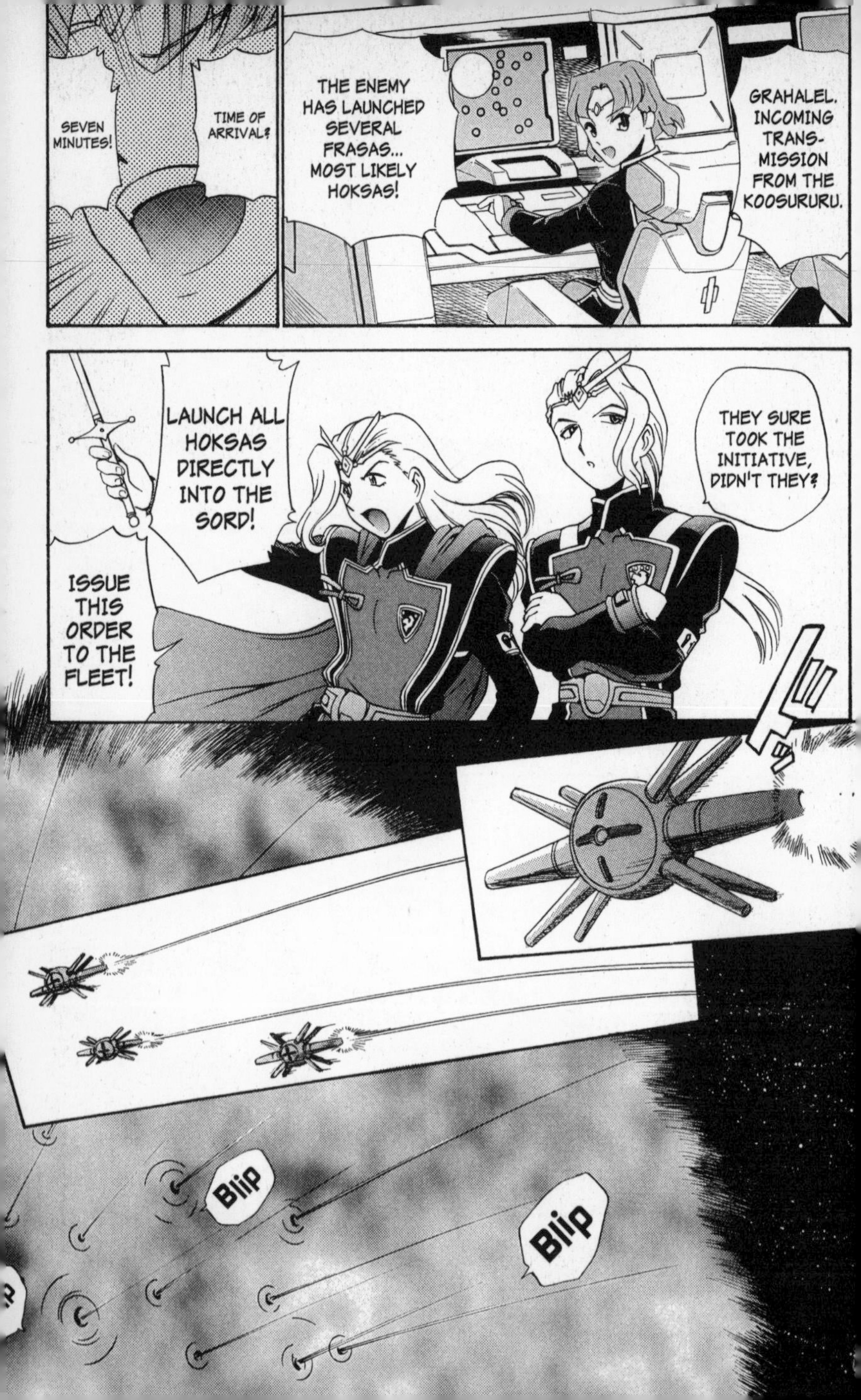
GRAHALEL. INCOMING TRANS-MISSION FROM THE KOOSURURU.
THE ENEMY HAS LAUNCHED SEVERAL FRASAS... MOST LIKELY HOKSAS!
TIME OF ARRIVAL?
SEVEN MINUTES!
THEY SURE TOOK THE INITIATIVE, DIDN'T THEY?
LAUNCH ALL HOKSAS DIRECTLY INTO THE SORD!
ISSUE THIS ORDER TO THE FLEET!
Blip
Blip

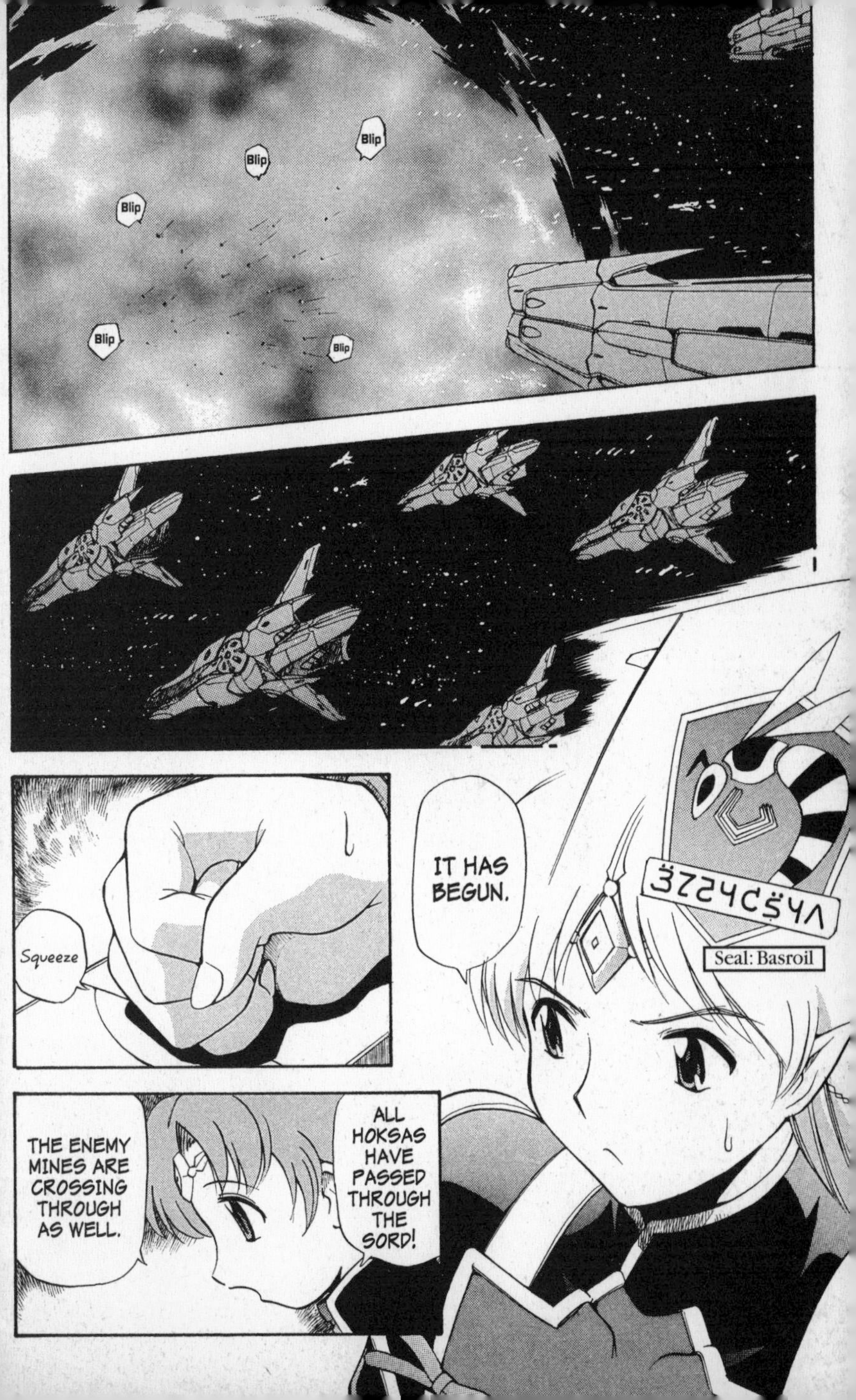
Blip
Blip
Blip
Blip
Blip
IT HAS BEGUN.
Seal: Basroil
Squeeze
ALL HOKSAS HAVE PASSED THROUGH THE SORD!
THE ENEMY MINES ARE CROSSING THROUGH AS WELL.

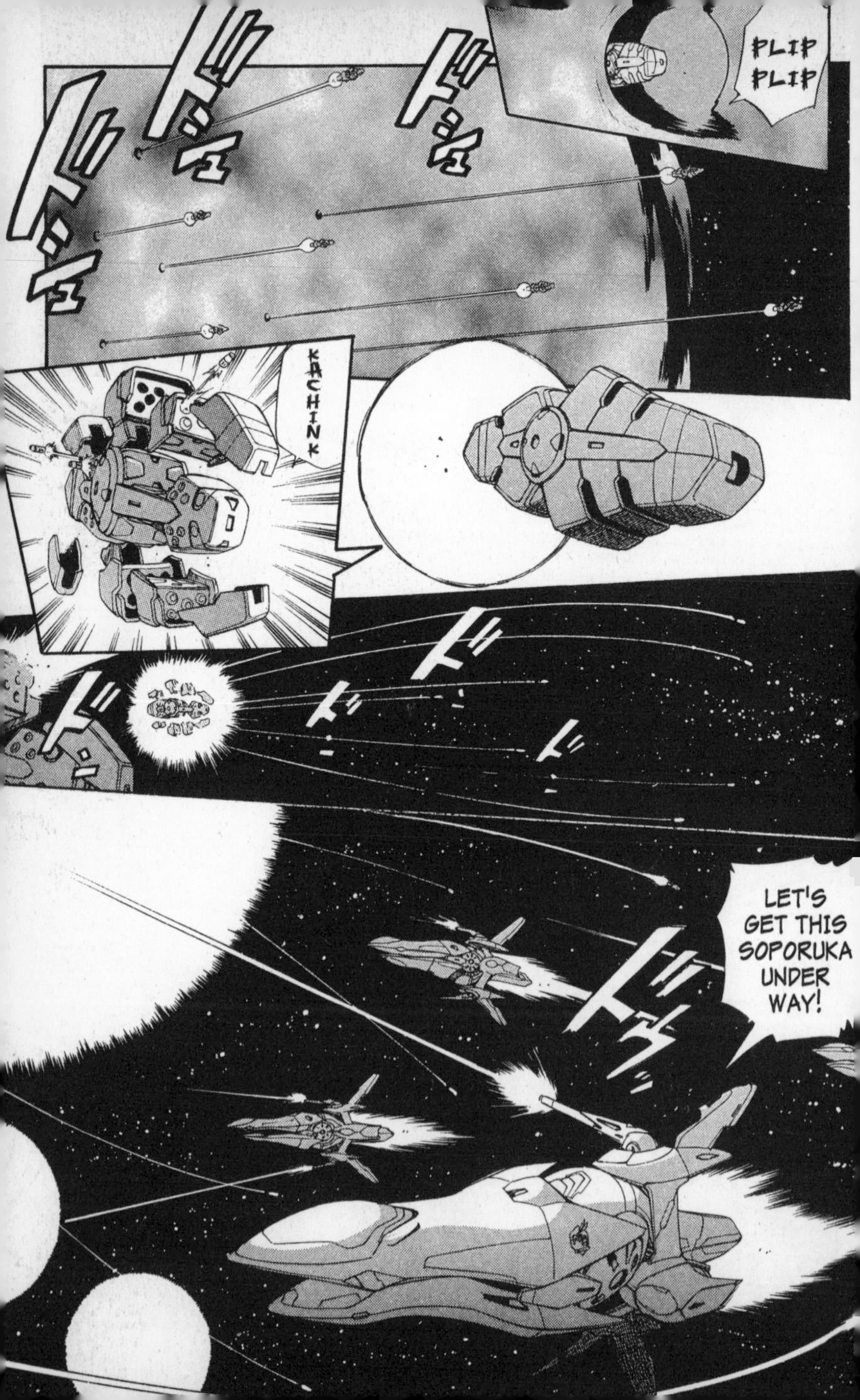
PLIP
PLIP
KACHINK
LET'S GET THIS SOPORUKA UNDER WAY!

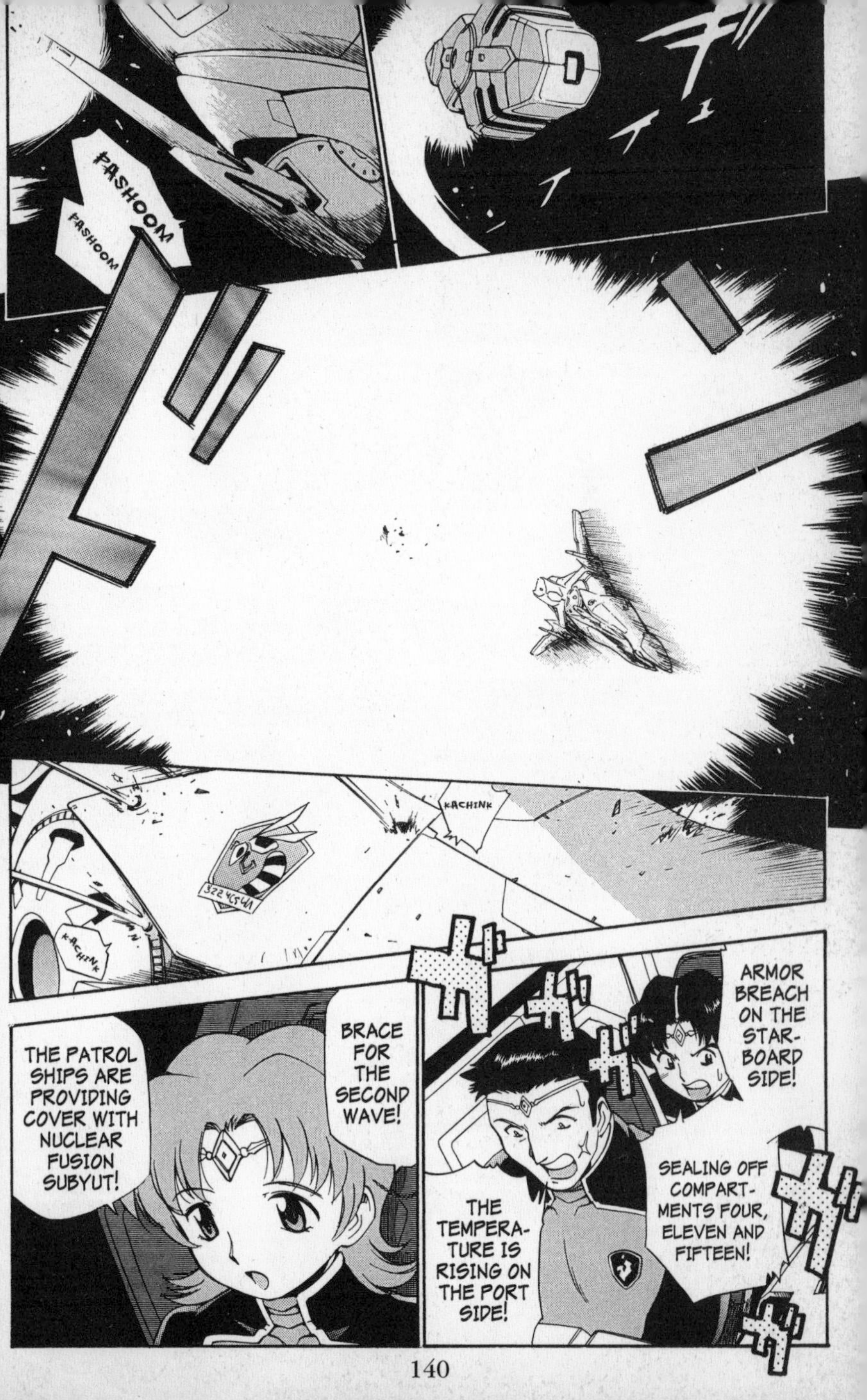
PASHOOM
PASHOOM
KACHINK
KACHINK
ARMOR BREACH ON THE STAR-BOARD SIDE!
SEALING OFF COMPART-MENTS FOUR, ELEVEN AND FIFTEEN!
THE TEMPERA-TURE IS RISING ON THE PORT SIDE!
BRACE FOR THE SECOND WAVE!
THE PATROL SHIPS ARE PROVIDING COVER WITH NUCLEAR FUSION SUBYUT!

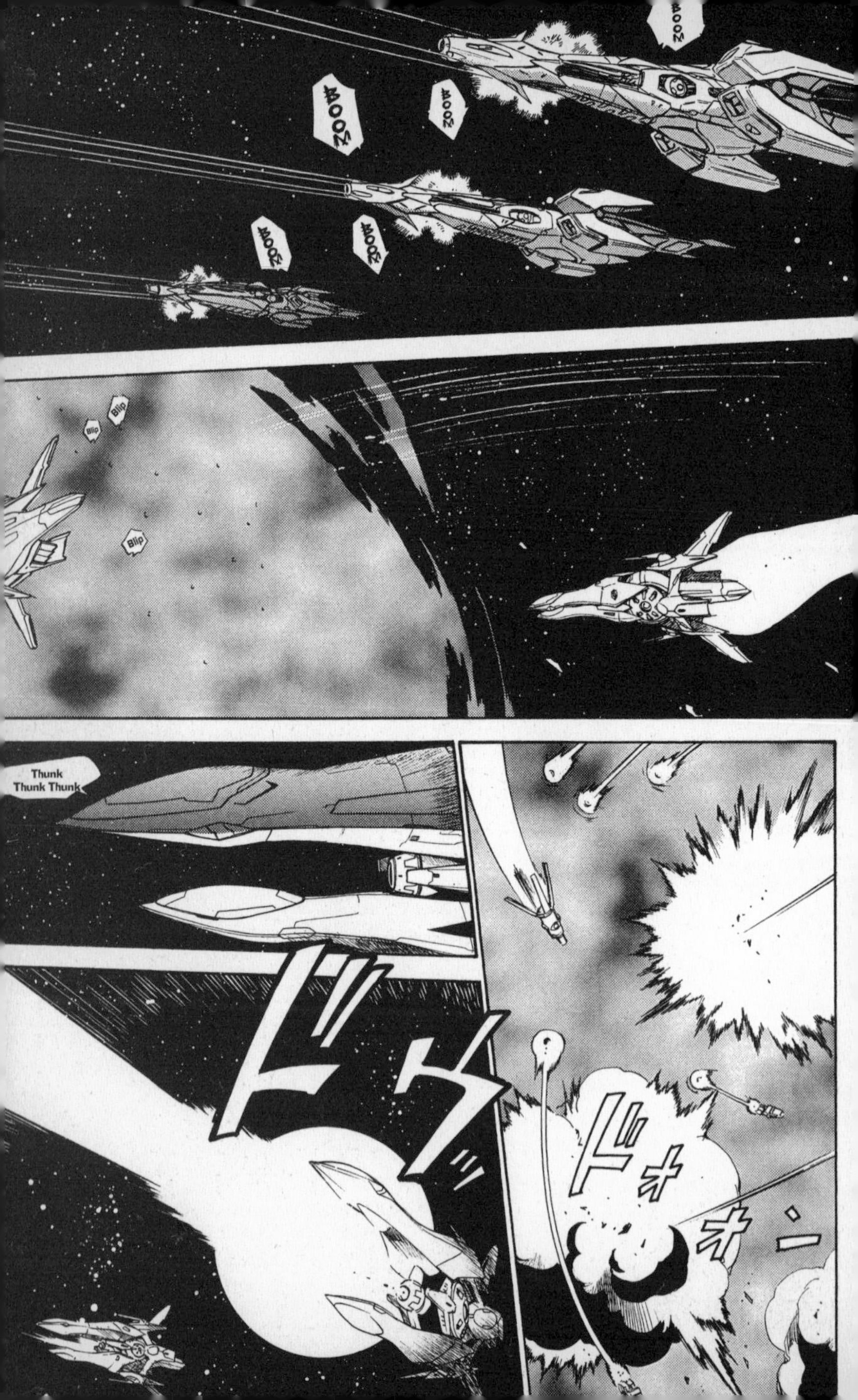

BOOM
BOOM
BOOM
BOOM
BOOM
Blip
Blip
Blip
ドォオー
Thunk Thunk Thunk
ドゥ

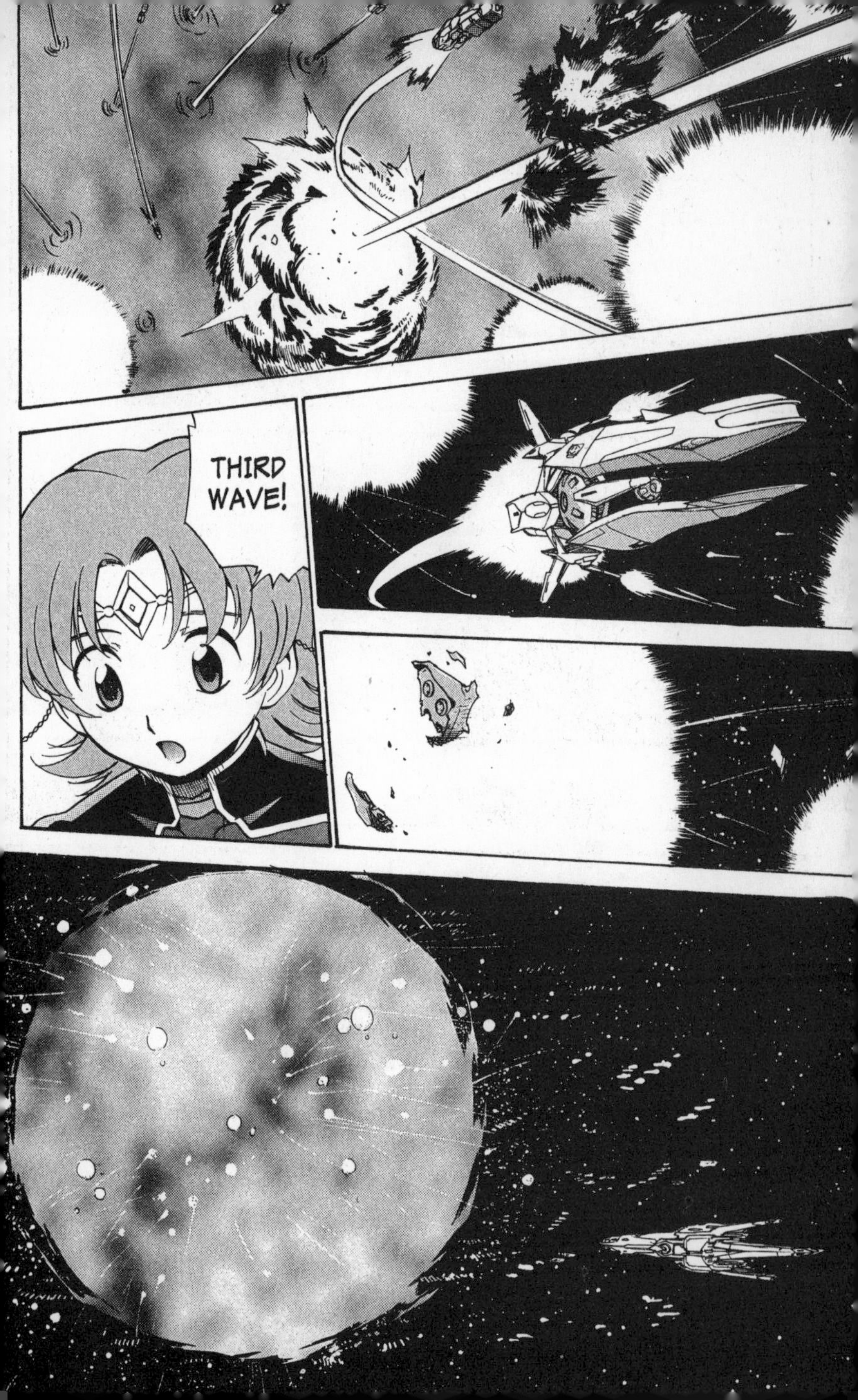
THIRD WAVE!

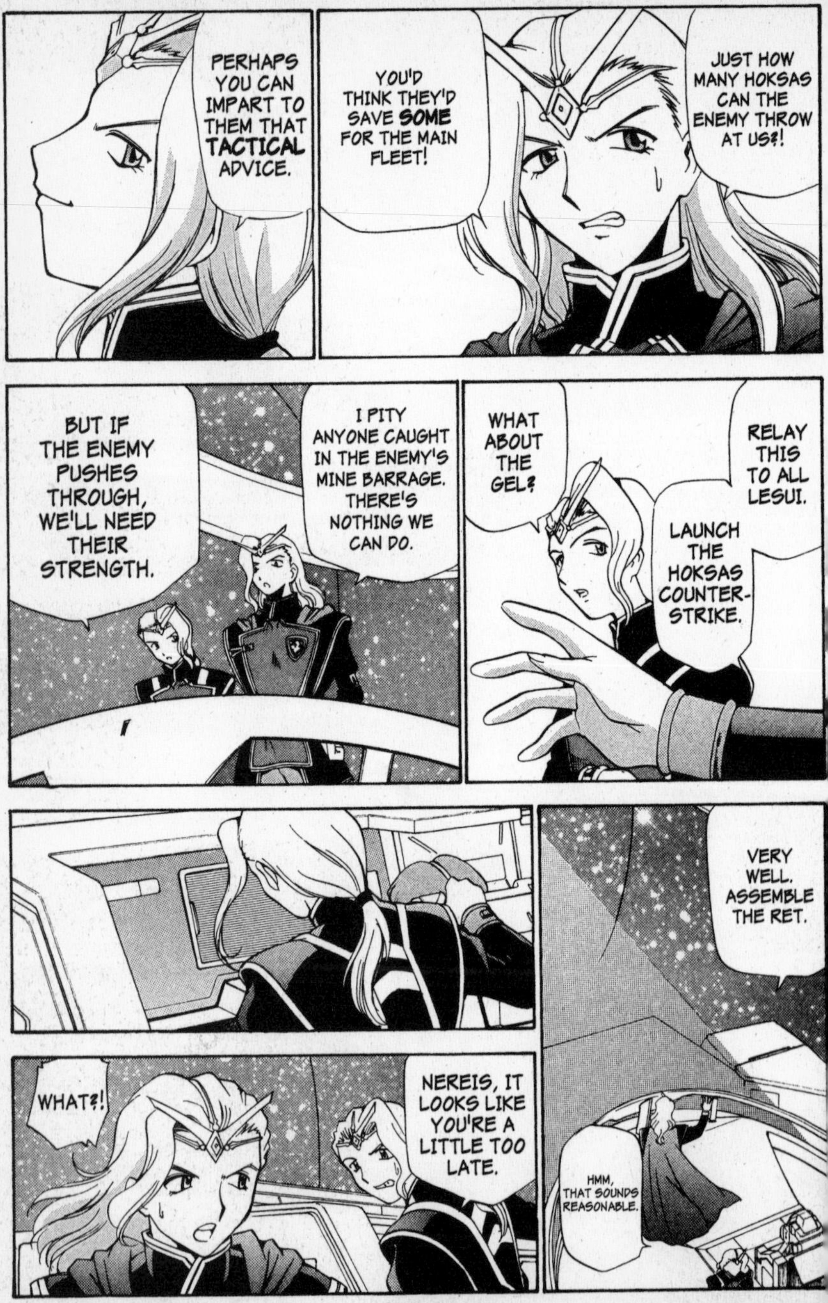
JUST HOW MANY HOKSAS CAN THE ENEMY THROW AT US?!
YOU'D THINK THEY'D SAVE **SOME** FOR THE MAIN FLEET!
PERHAPS YOU CAN IMPART TO THEM THAT **TACTICAL** ADVICE.
RELAY THIS TO ALL LESUI.
LAUNCH THE HOKSAS COUNTER-STRIKE.
WHAT ABOUT THE GEL?
I PITY ANYONE CAUGHT IN THE ENEMY'S MINE BARRAGE. THERE'S NOTHING WE CAN DO.
BUT IF THE ENEMY PUSHES THROUGH, WE'LL NEED THEIR STRENGTH.
VERY WELL. ASSEMBLE THE RET.
HMM, THAT SOUNDS REASONABLE.
NEREIS, IT LOOKS LIKE YOU'RE A LITTLE TOO LATE.
WHAT?!

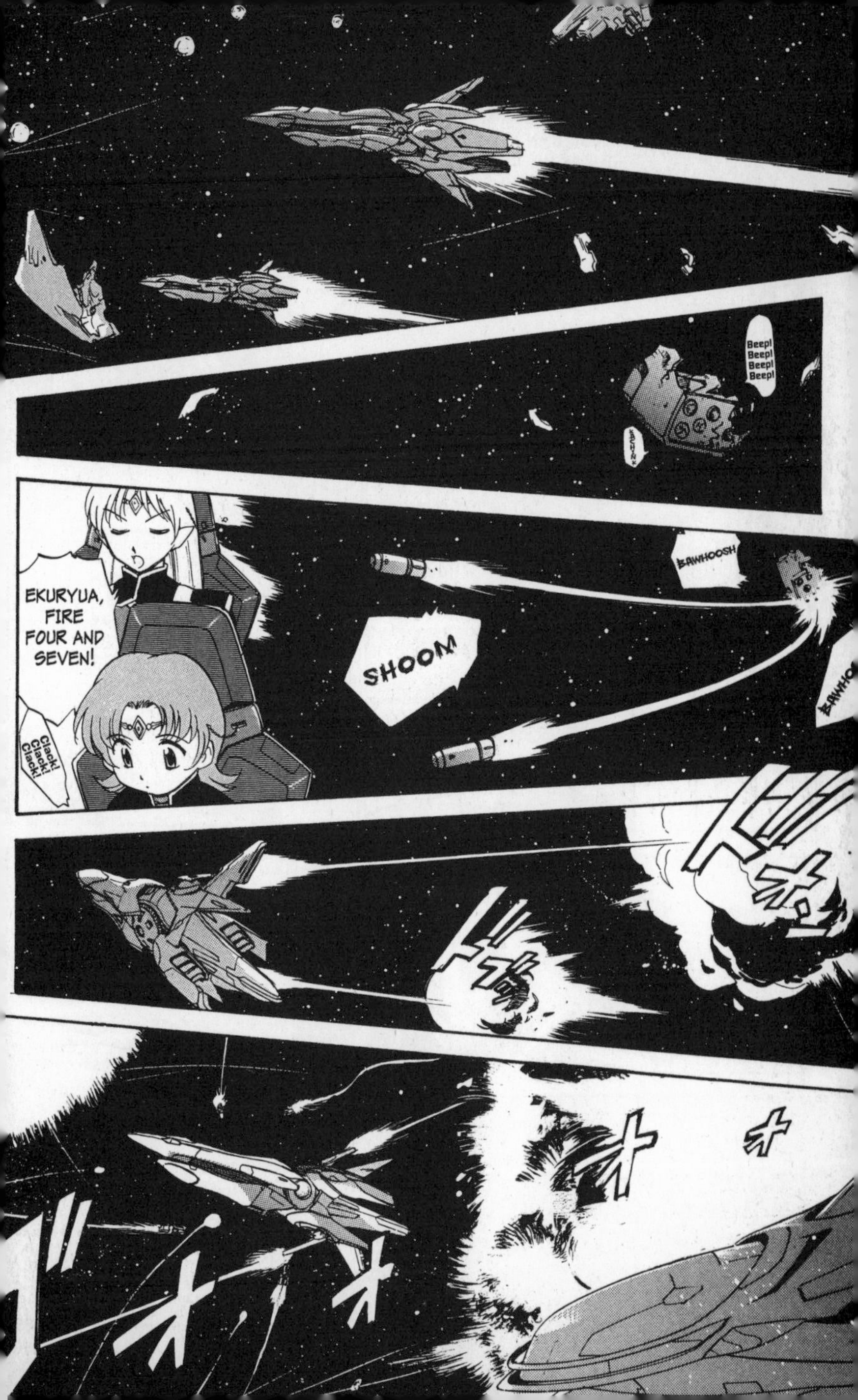
Beep! Beep! Beep! Beep!
KACHINK
BAWHOOSH
SHOOM
EKURYUA, FIRE FOUR AND SEVEN!
Clack! Clack! Clack!

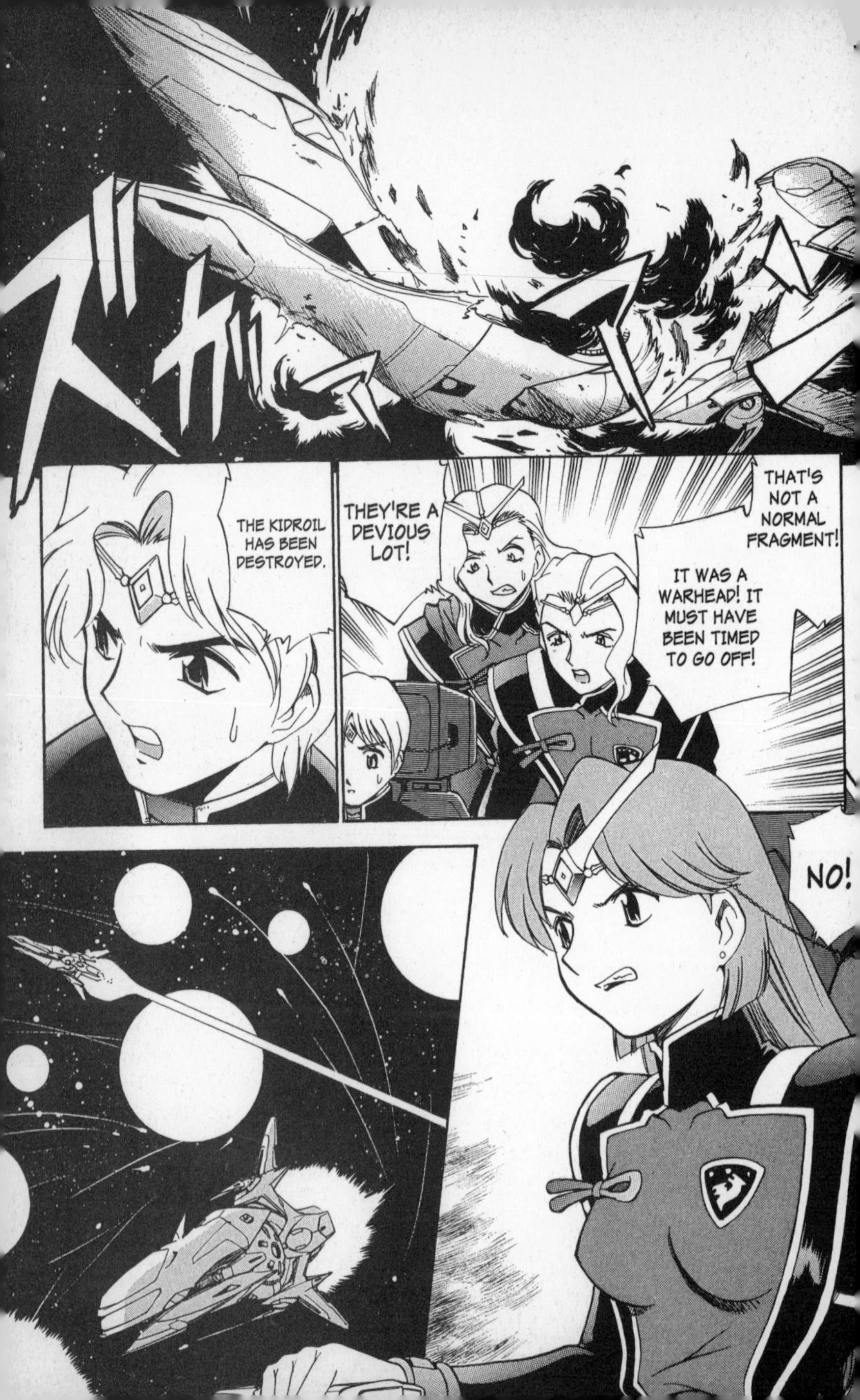
THAT'S NOT A NORMAL FRAGMENT!
IT WAS A WARHEAD! IT MUST HAVE BEEN TIMED TO GO OFF!
THEY'RE A DEVIOUS LOT!
THE KIDROIL HAS BEEN DESTROYED.
NO!

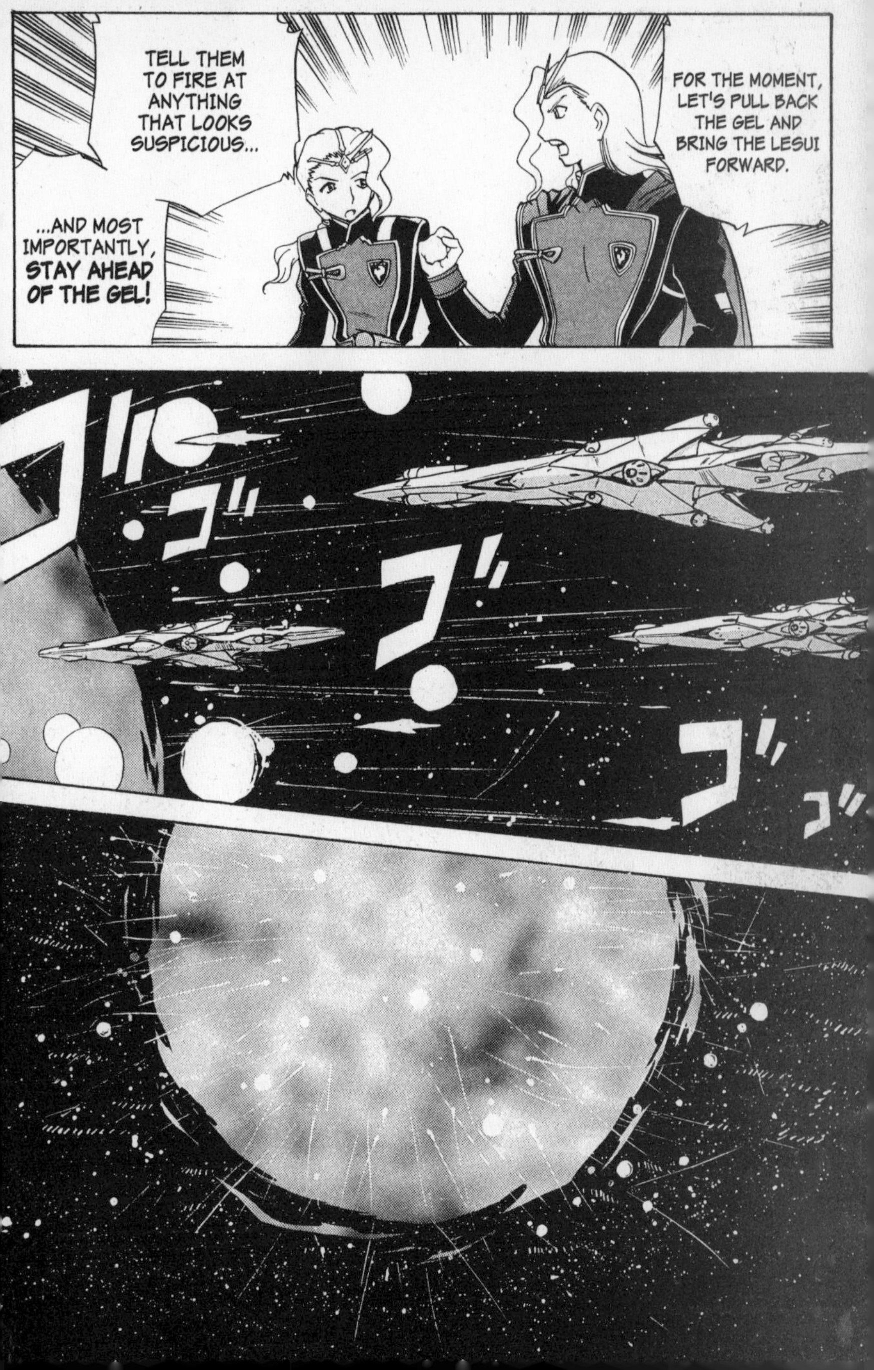
FOR THE MOMENT, LET'S PULL BACK THE GEL AND BRING THE LESUI FORWARD.
TELL THEM TO FIRE AT ANYTHING THAT LOOKS SUSPICIOUS...
...AND MOST IMPORTANTLY, STAY AHEAD OF THE GEL!
ゴ
ゴ
ゴ
ゴ
ゴ

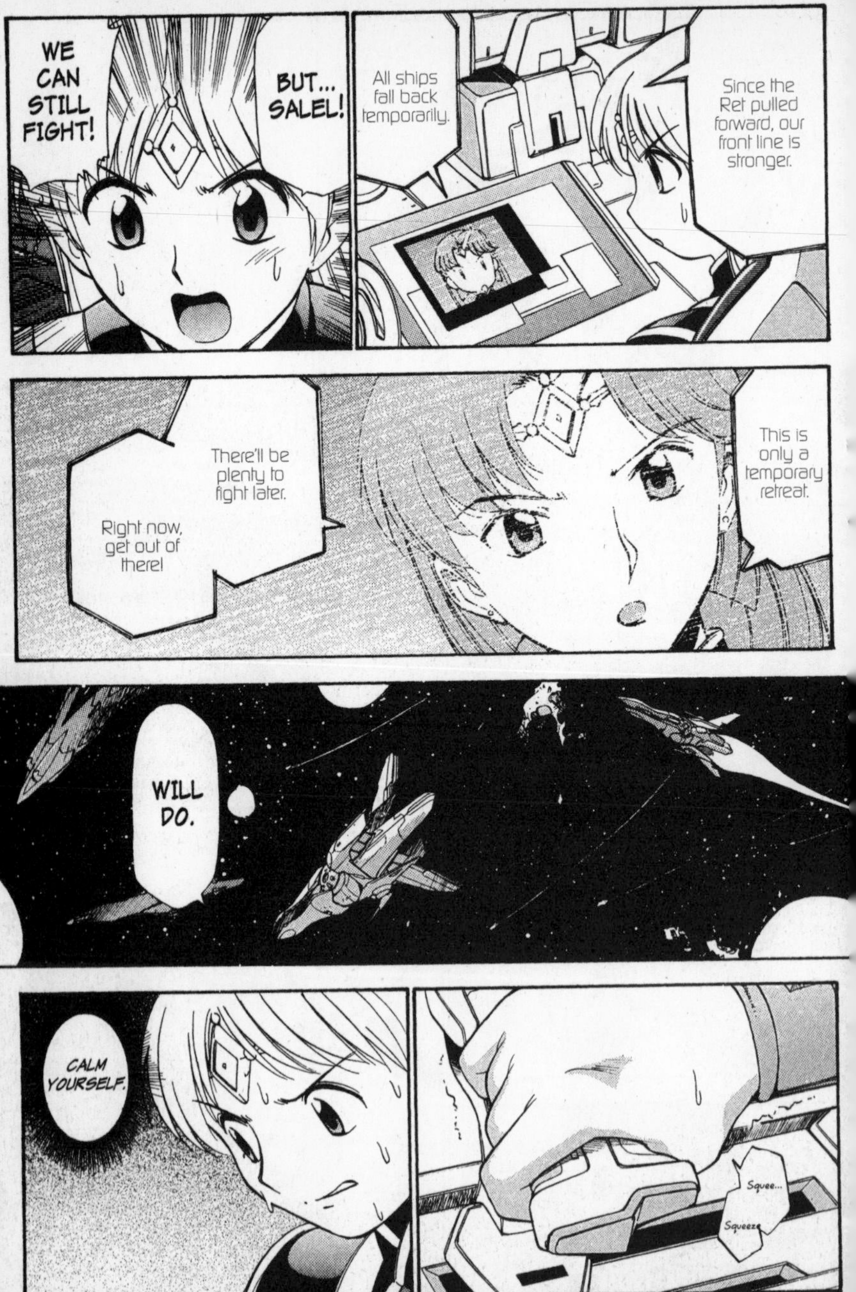
Since the Ret pulled forward, our front line is stronger.
All ships fall back temporarily.
BUT... SALEL!
WE CAN STILL FIGHT!
This is only a temporary retreat.
There'll be plenty to fight later.
Right now, get out of there!
WILL DO.
Squee...
Squeeze
CALM YOURSELF.

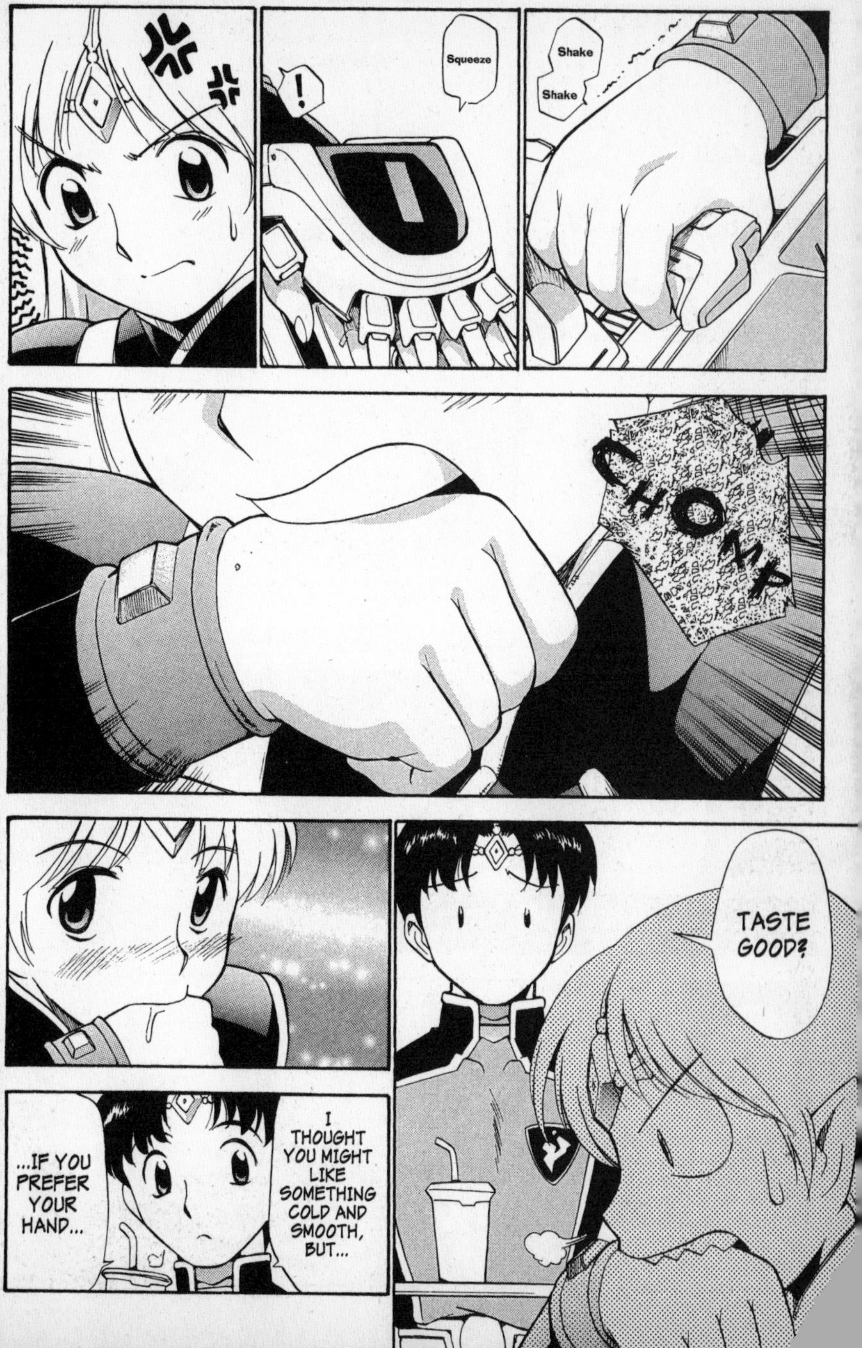
Shake
Shake
Squeeze
!
CHOMP
TASTE GOOD?
I THOUGHT YOU MIGHT LIKE SOMETHING COLD AND SMOOTH, BUT...
...IF YOU PREFER YOUR HAND...

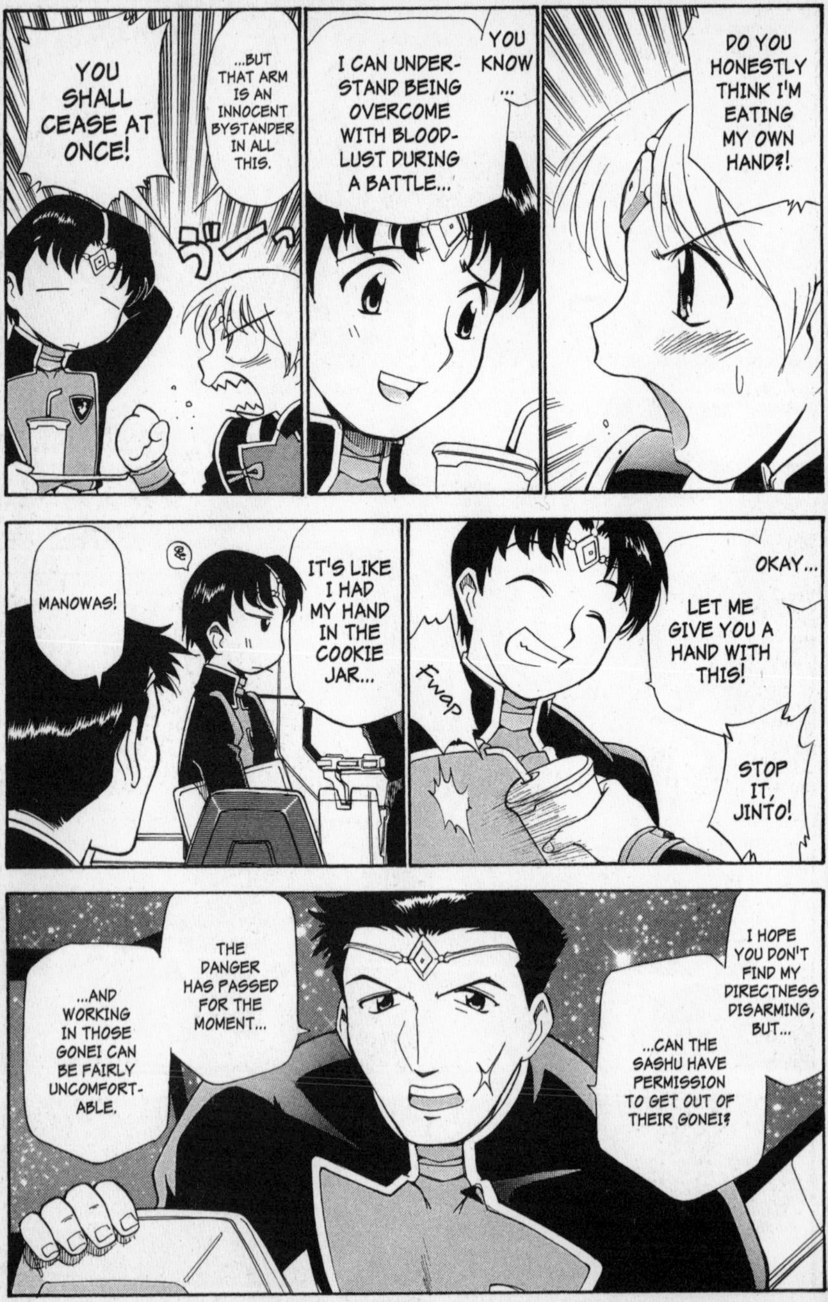
DO YOU HONESTLY THINK I'M EATING MY OWN HAND?!
YOU KNOW...
I CAN UNDER-STAND BEING OVERCOME WITH BLOOD-LUST DURING A BATTLE...
...BUT THAT ARM IS AN INNOCENT BYSTANDER IN ALL THIS.
YOU SHALL CEASE AT ONCE!
OKAY...
LET ME GIVE YOU A HAND WITH THIS!
Fwap
STOP IT, JINTO!
IT'S LIKE I HAD MY HAND IN THE COOKIE JAR...
MANOWAS!
I HOPE YOU DON'T FIND MY DIRECTNESS DISARMING, BUT...
...CAN THE SASHU HAVE PERMISSION TO GET OUT OF THEIR GONEI?
THE DANGER HAS PASSED FOR THE MOMENT...
...AND WORKING IN THOSE GONEI CAN BE FAIRLY UNCOMFORT-ABLE.

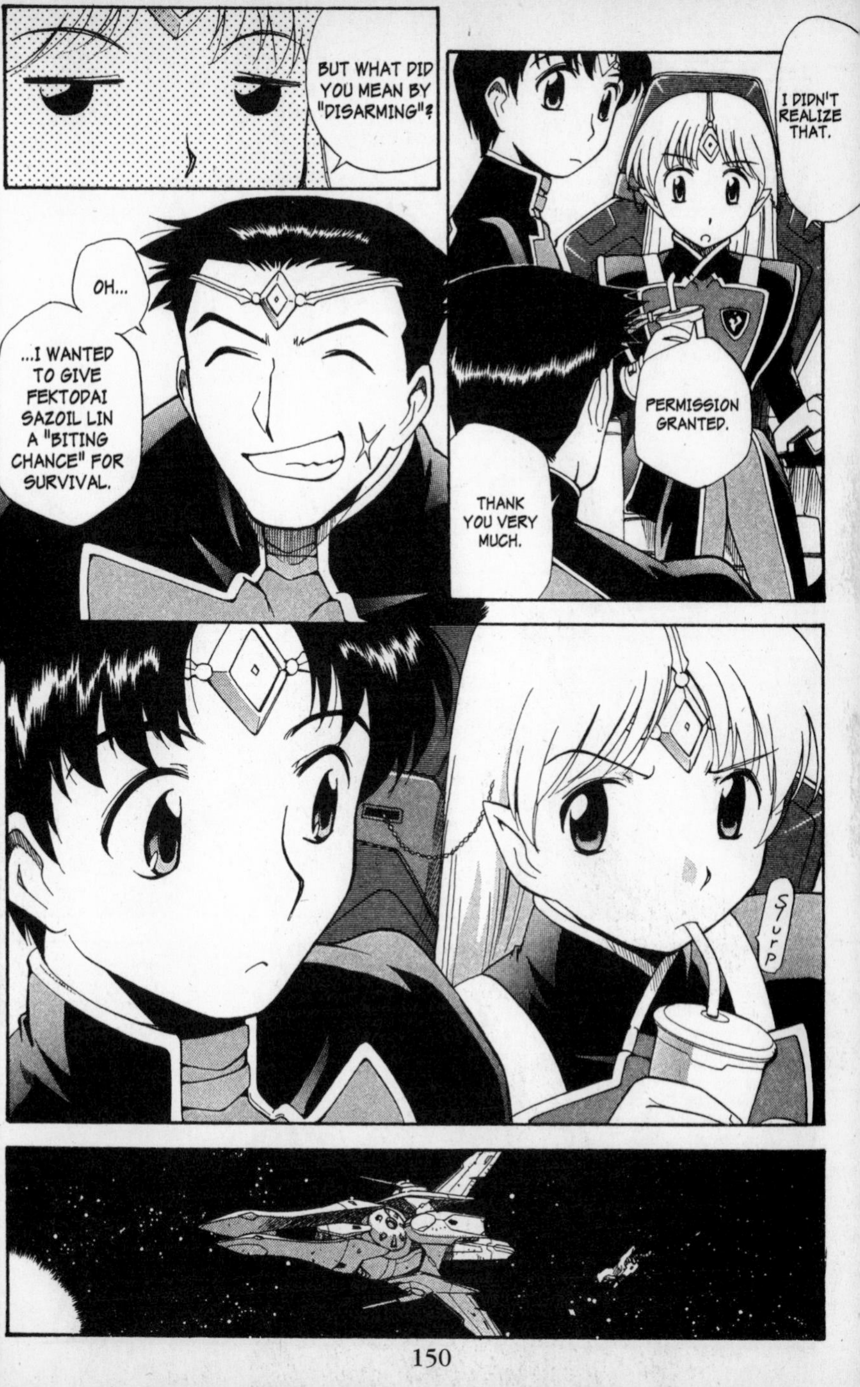
I DIDN'T REALIZE THAT.
PERMISSION GRANTED.
THANK YOU VERY MUCH.
BUT WHAT DID YOU MEAN BY "DISARMING"?
OH...
...I WANTED TO GIVE FEKTODAI SAZOIL LIN A "BITING CHANCE" FOR SURVIVAL.
Slurp

Chapter 8
Escape

DUGSANS

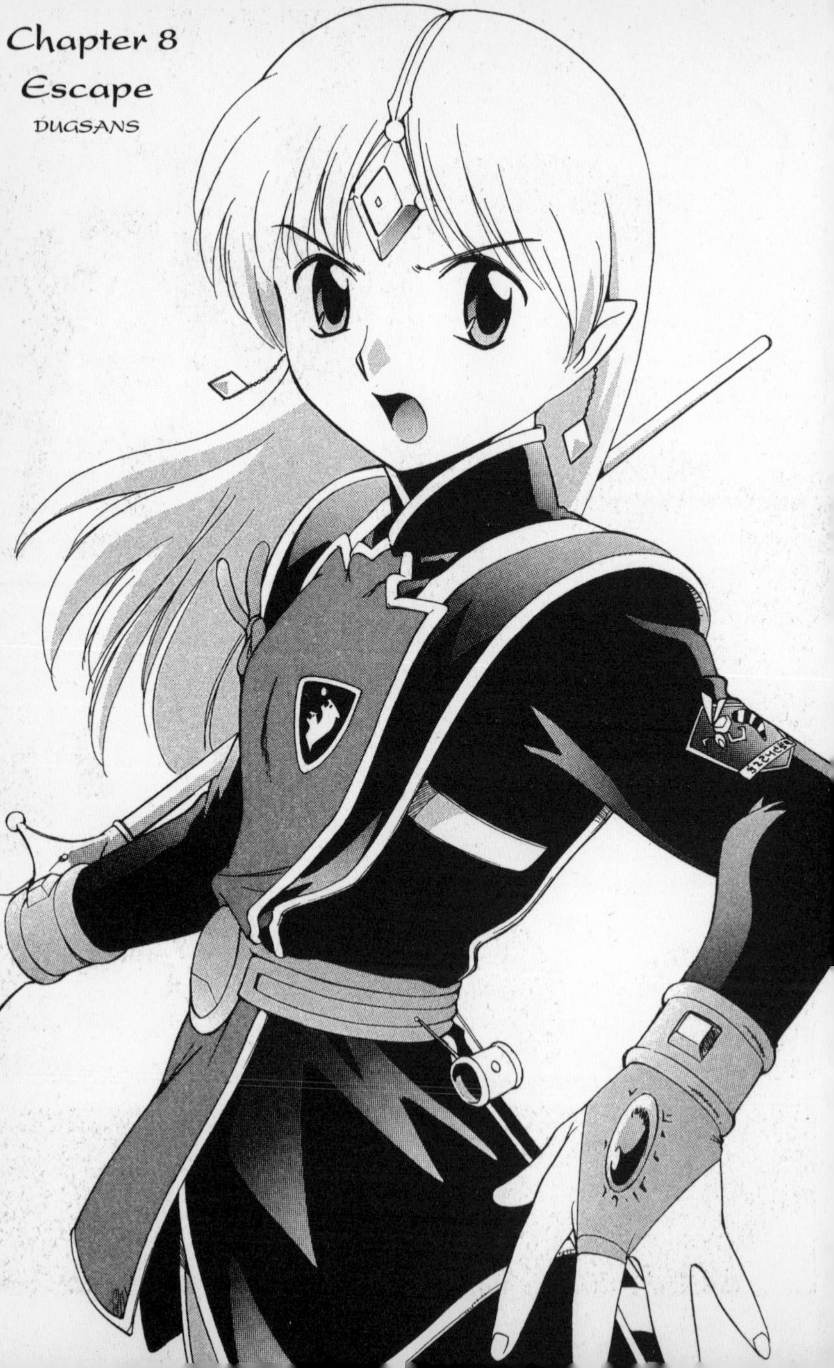

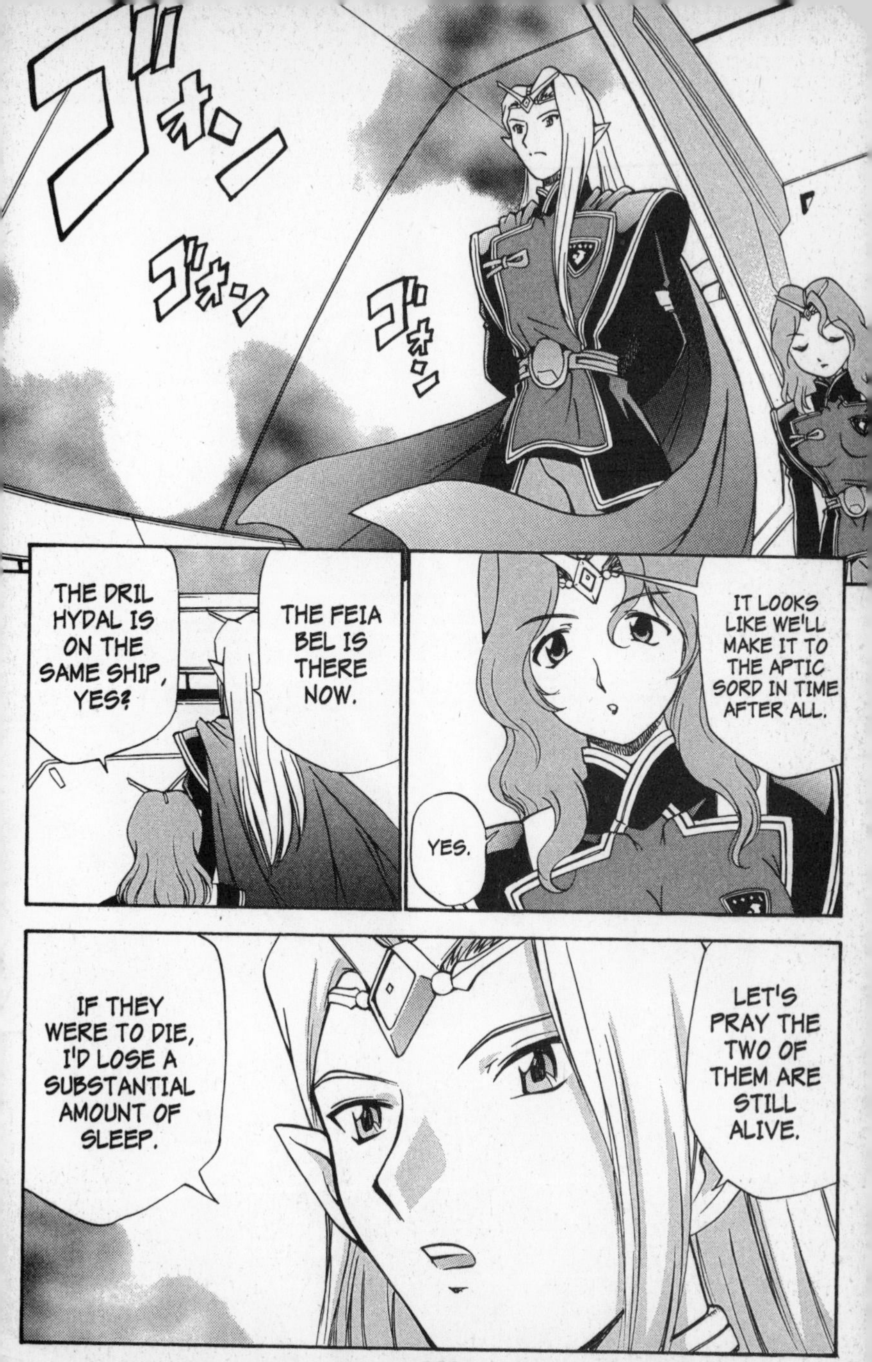
ゴォーン
ゴォーン
ゴォーン
IT LOOKS LIKE WE'LL MAKE IT TO THE APTIC SORD IN TIME AFTER ALL.
YES.
THE FEIA BEL IS THERE NOW.
THE DRIL HYDAL IS ON THE SAME SHIP, YES?
LET'S PRAY THE TWO OF THEM ARE STILL ALIVE.
IF THEY WERE TO DIE, I'D LOSE A SUBSTANTIAL AMOUNT OF SLEEP.

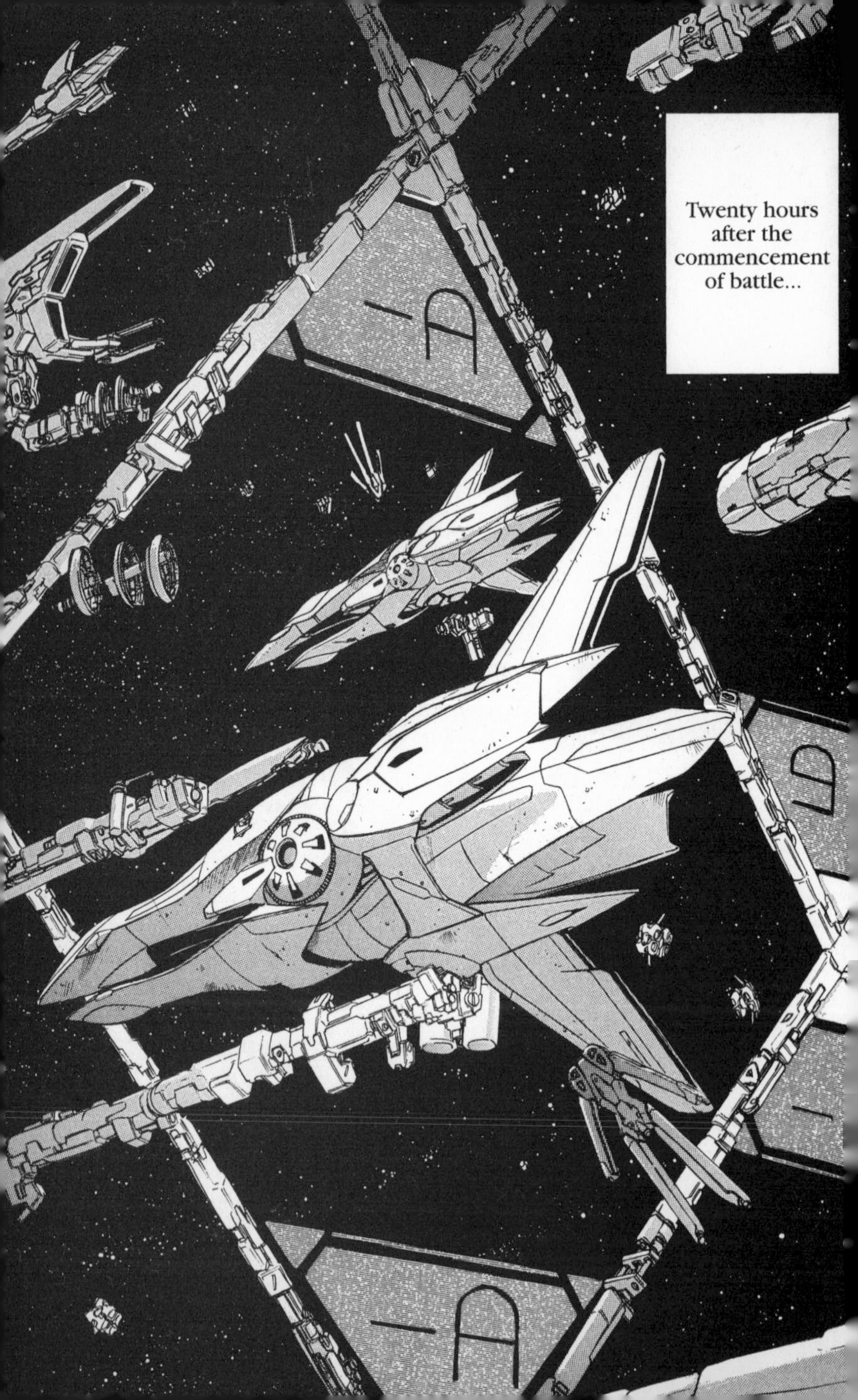
Twenty hours after the commencement of battle...

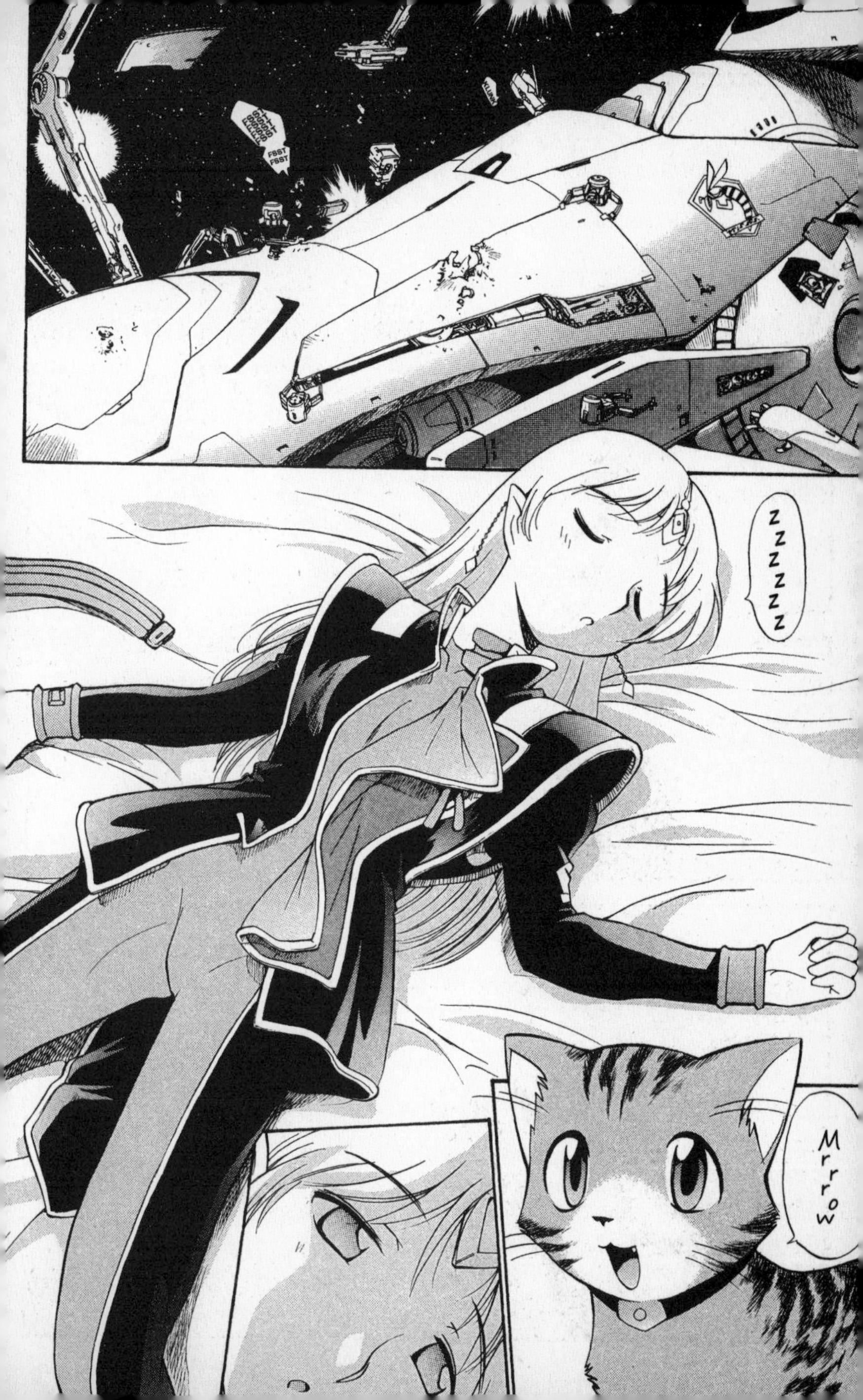
KLUNK
FSST
FSST
ZZZZZ
Mrrrow

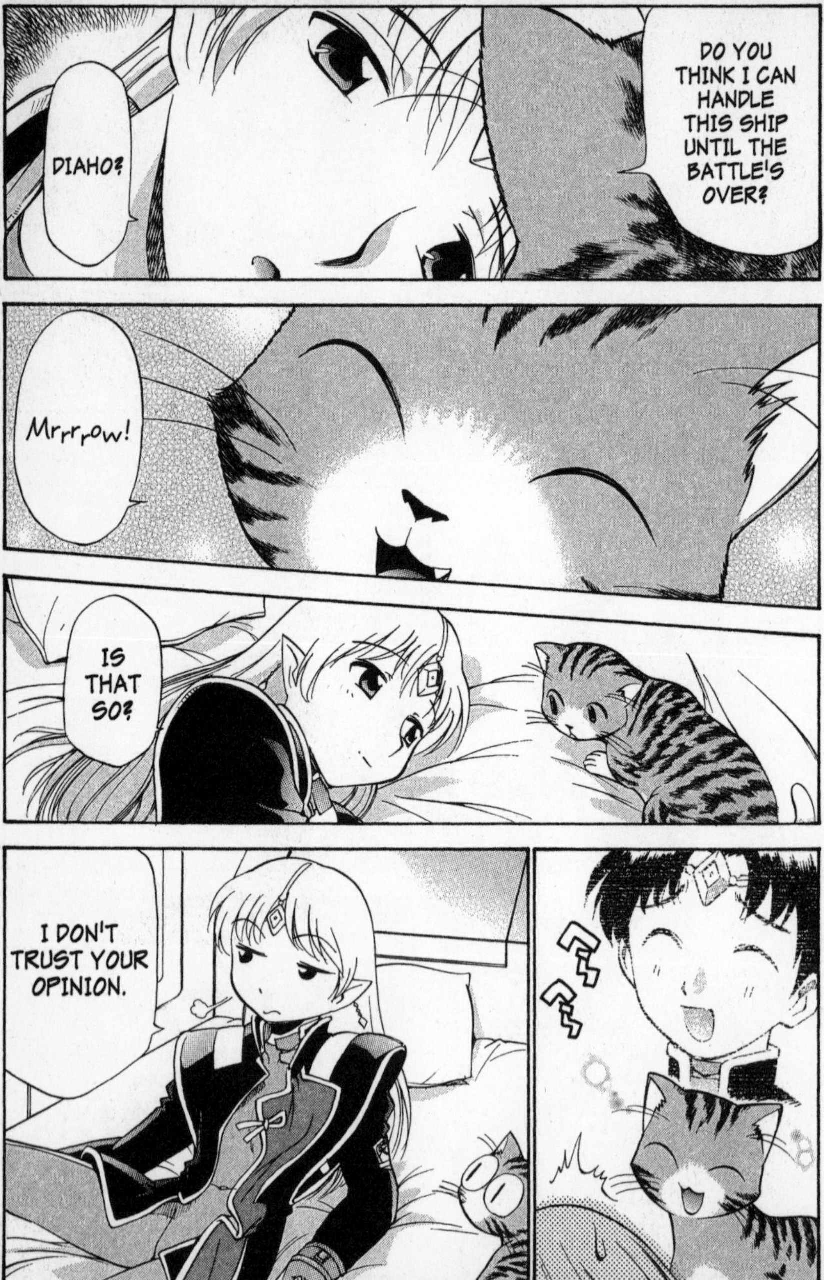
DO YOU THINK I CAN HANDLE THIS SHIP UNTIL THE BATTLE'S OVER?
DIAHO?
Mrrrrow!
IS THAT SO?
I DON'T TRUST YOUR OPINION.

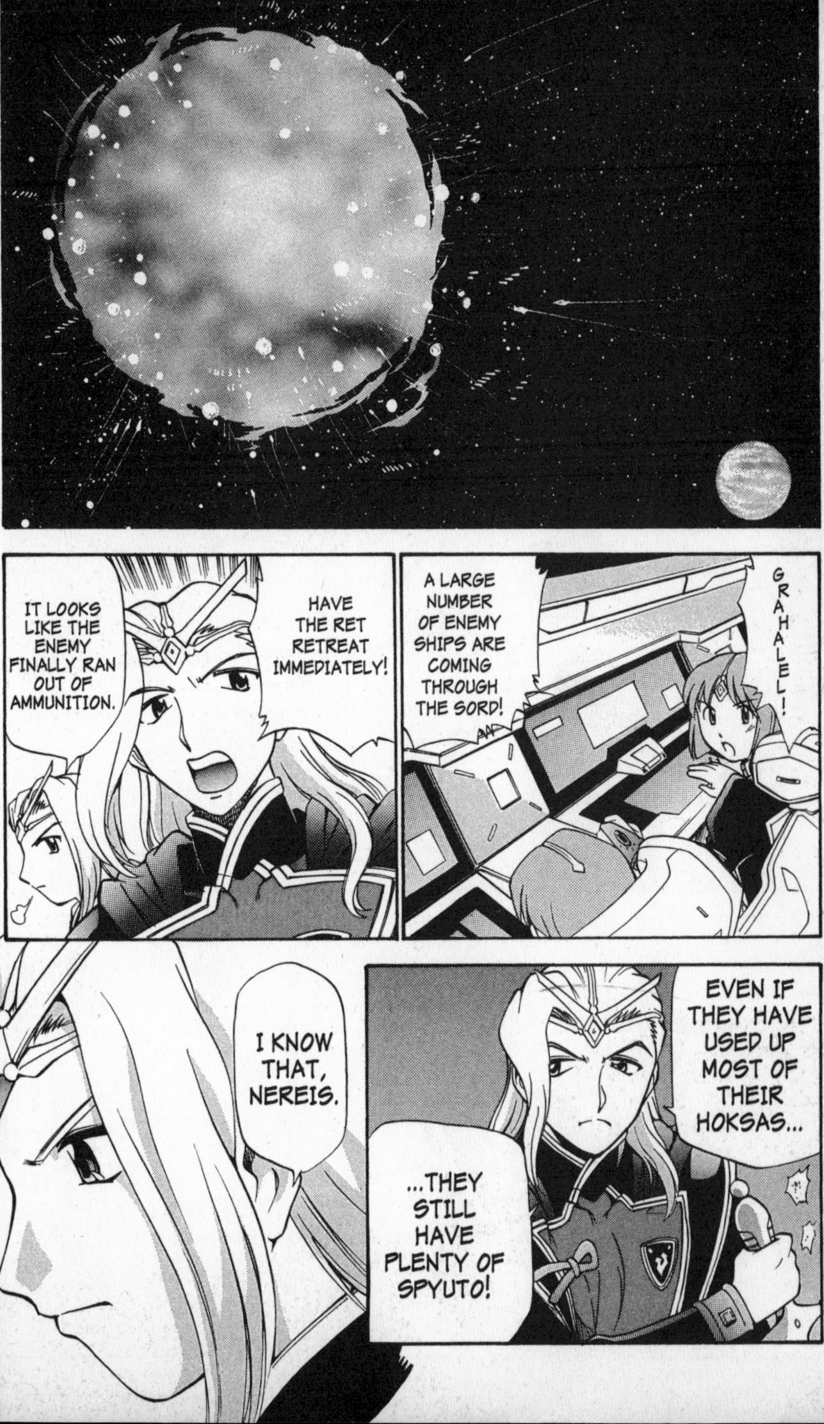
GRAHALEL!
A LARGE NUMBER OF ENEMY SHIPS ARE COMING THROUGH THE SORD!
HAVE THE RET RETREAT IMMEDIATELY!
IT LOOKS LIKE THE ENEMY FINALLY RAN OUT OF AMMUNITION.
EVEN IF THEY HAVE USED UP MOST OF THEIR HOKSAS...
...THEY STILL HAVE PLENTY OF SPYUTO!
I KNOW THAT, NEREIS.

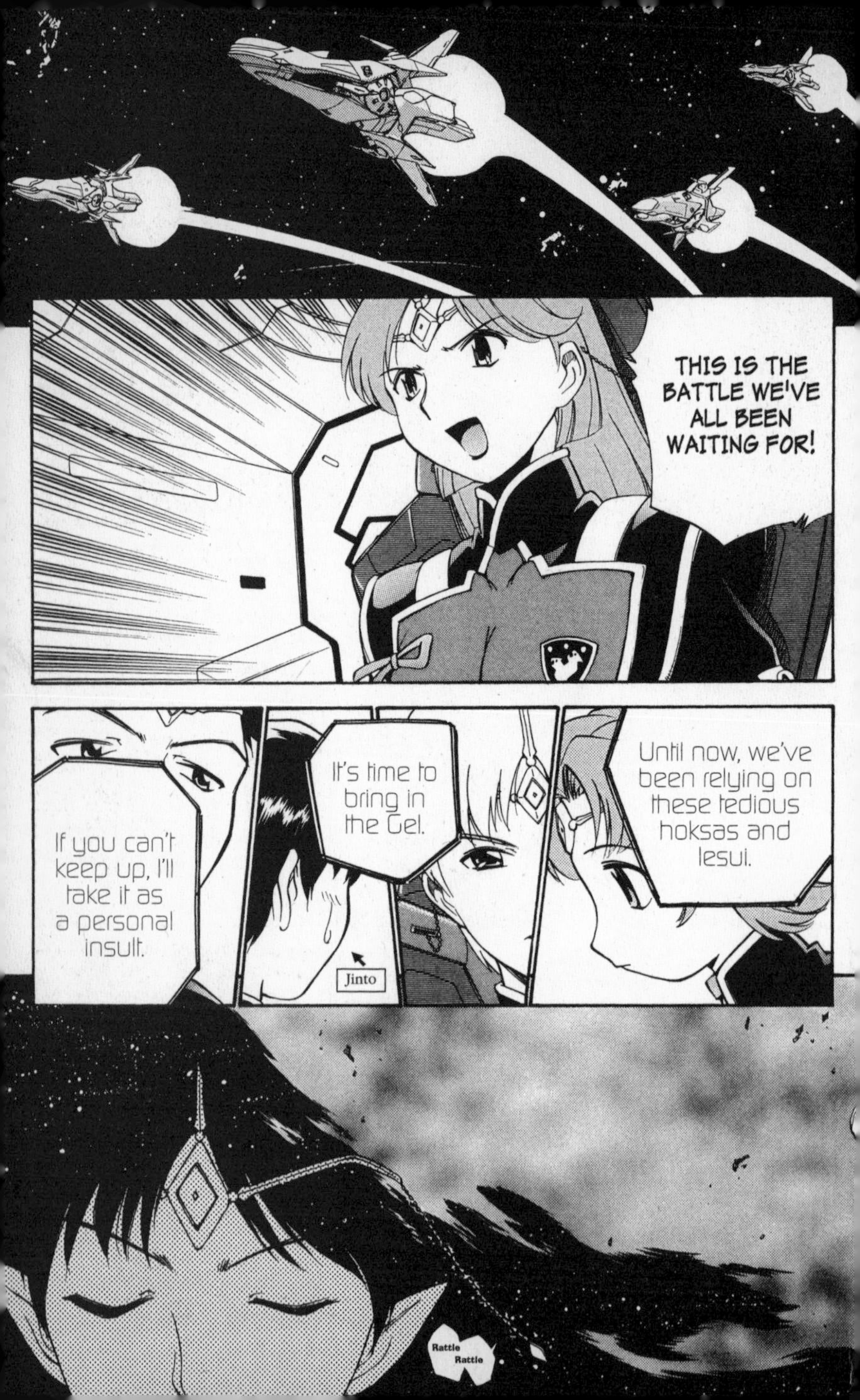
THIS IS THE BATTLE WE'VE ALL BEEN WAITING FOR!
Until now, we've been relying on these tedious hoksas and lesui.
It's time to bring in the Gel.
Jinto
If you can't keep up, I'll take it as a personal insult.
Rattle Rattle

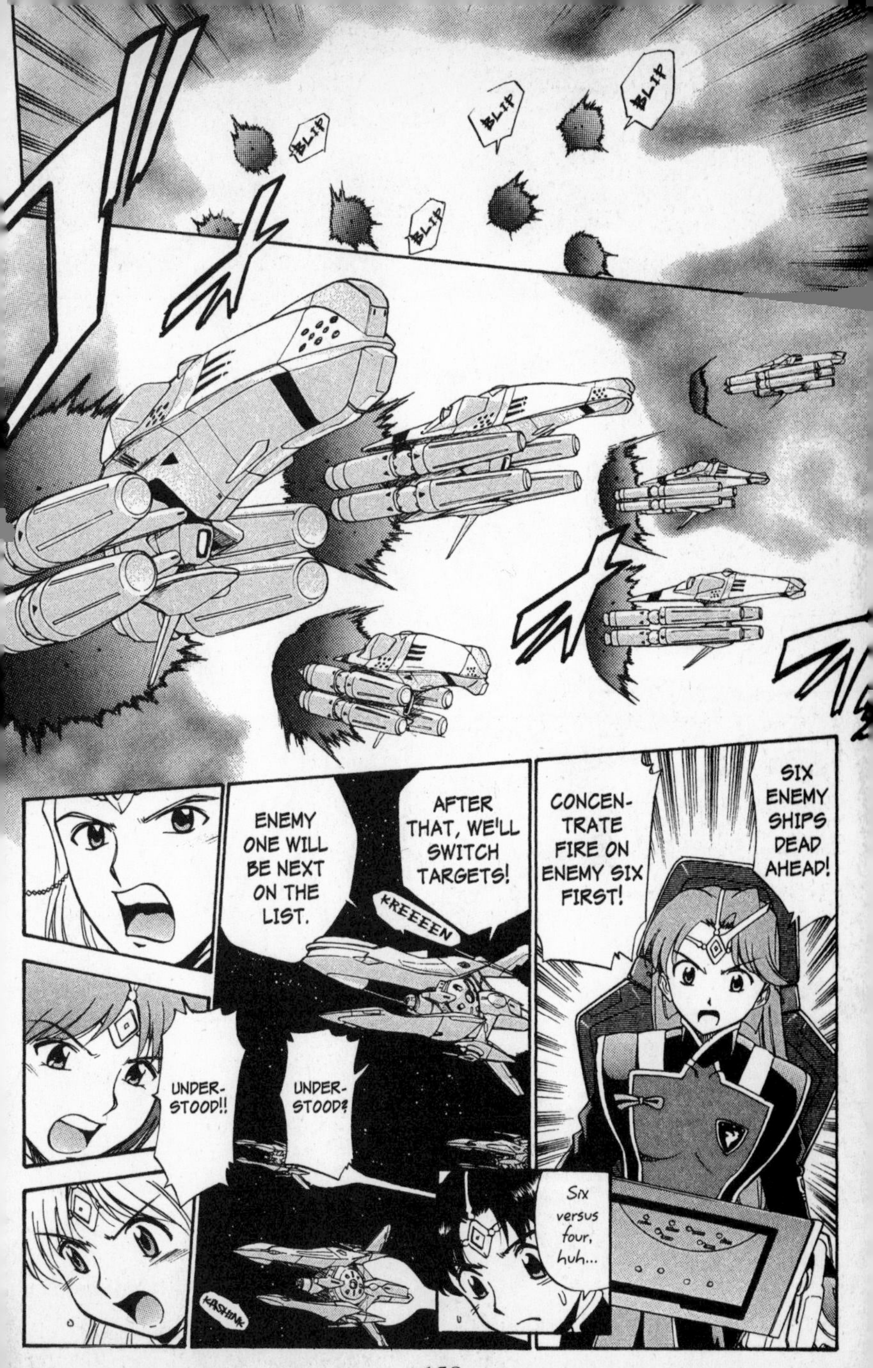
BLIP
BLIP
BLIP
BLIP
SIX ENEMY SHIPS DEAD AHEAD!
CONCEN-TRATE FIRE ON ENEMY SIX FIRST!
AFTER THAT, WE'LL SWITCH TARGETS!
ENEMY ONE WILL BE NEXT ON THE LIST.
KREEEEN
UNDER-STOOD?
UNDER-STOOD!!
Six versus four, huh...
KASHUNK

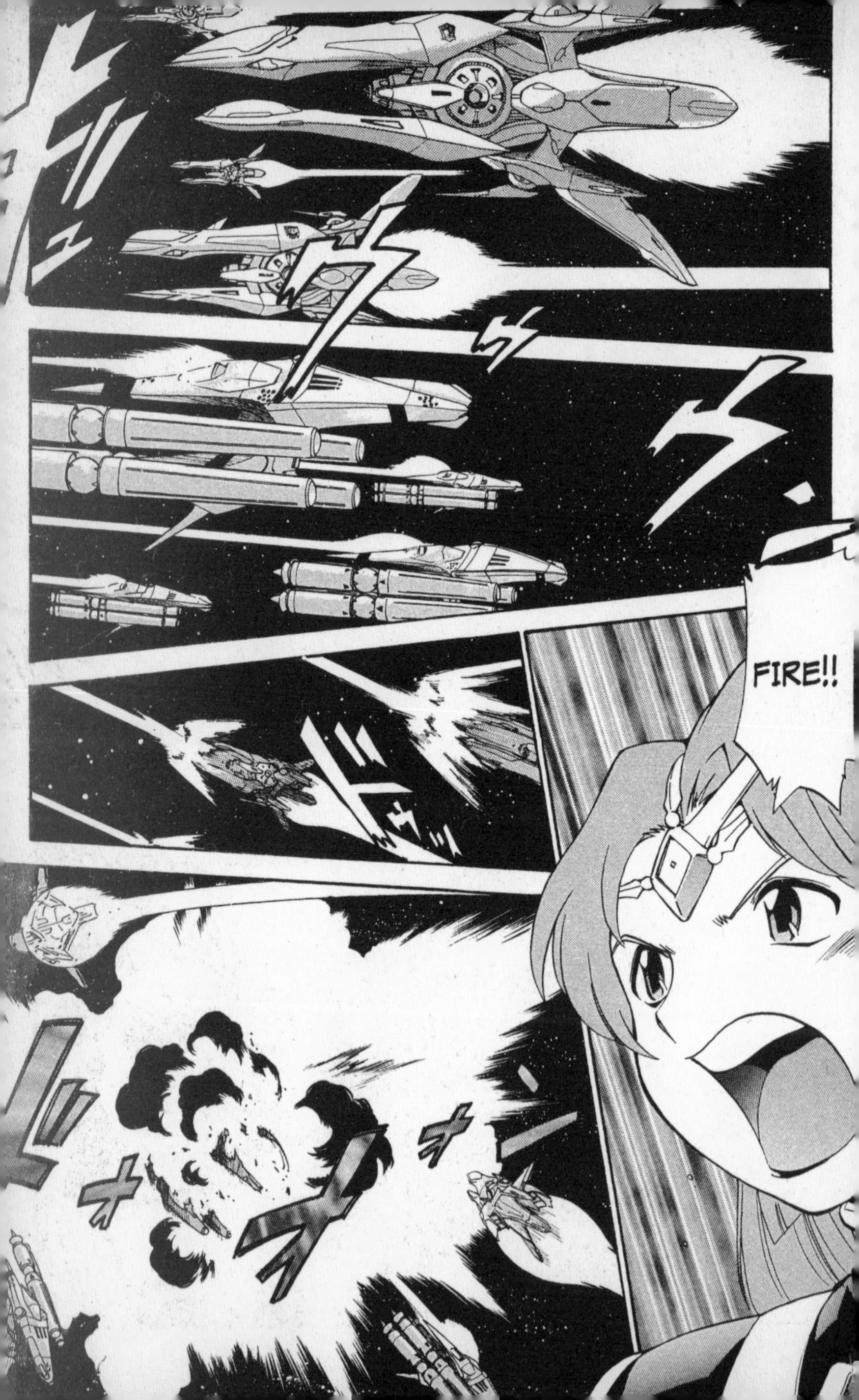
FIRE!!

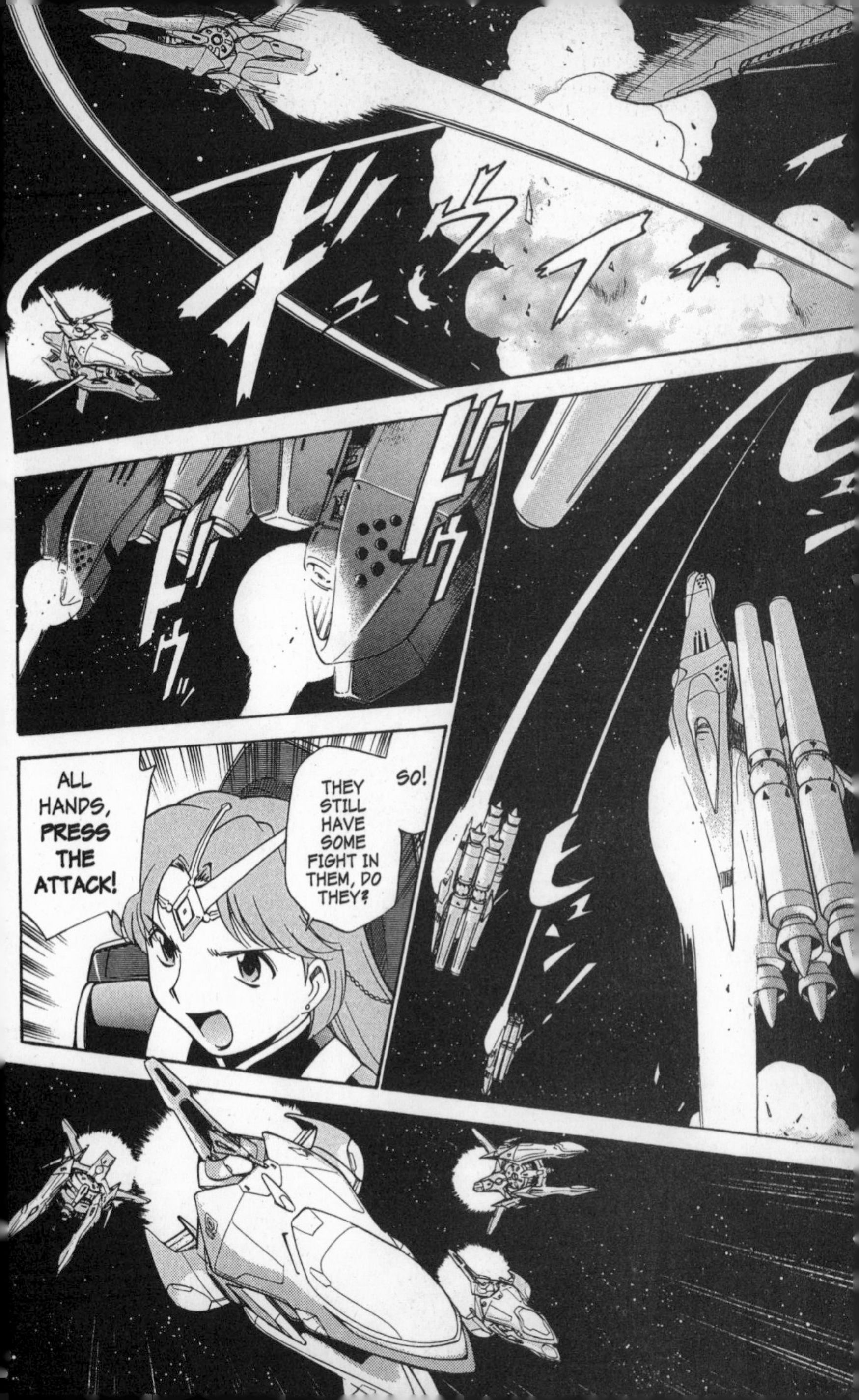
SO!
THEY STILL HAVE SOME FIGHT IN THEM, DO THEY?
ALL HANDS, PRESS THE ATTACK!

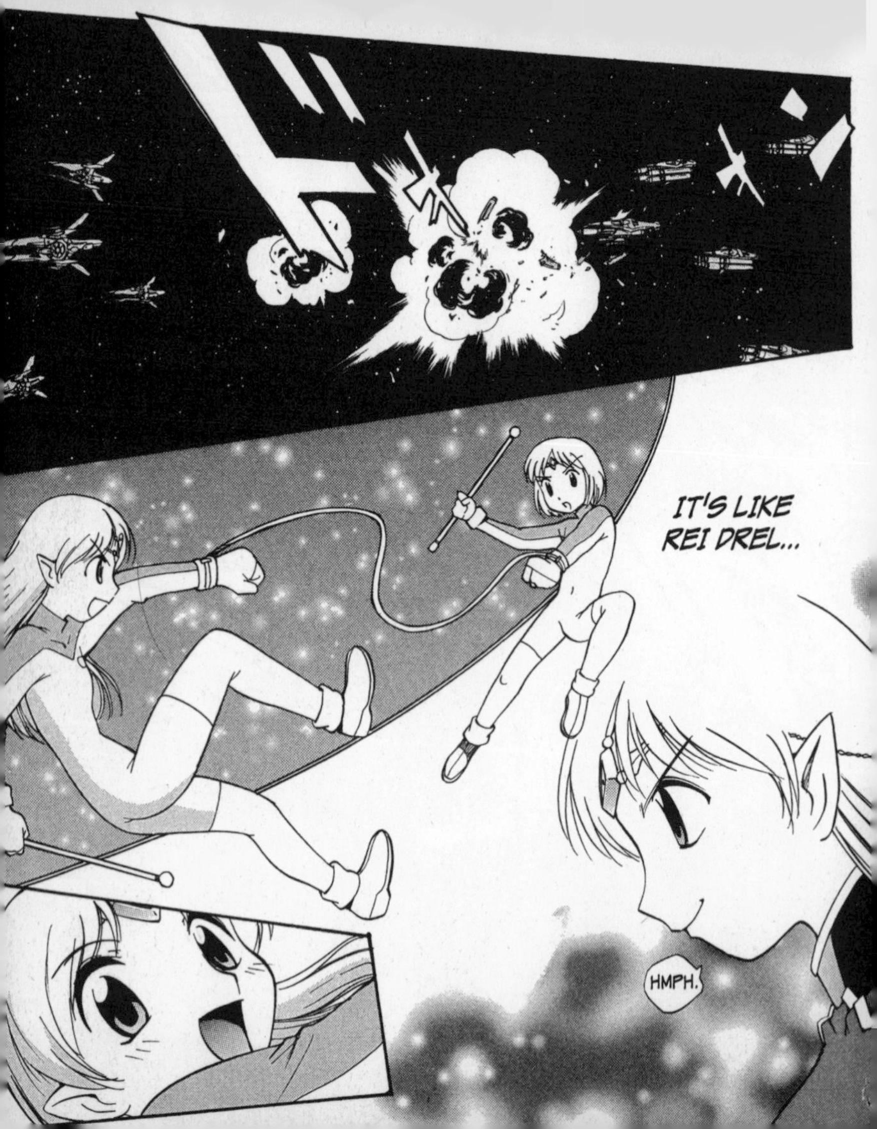
IT'S LIKE REI DREL...
HMPH.

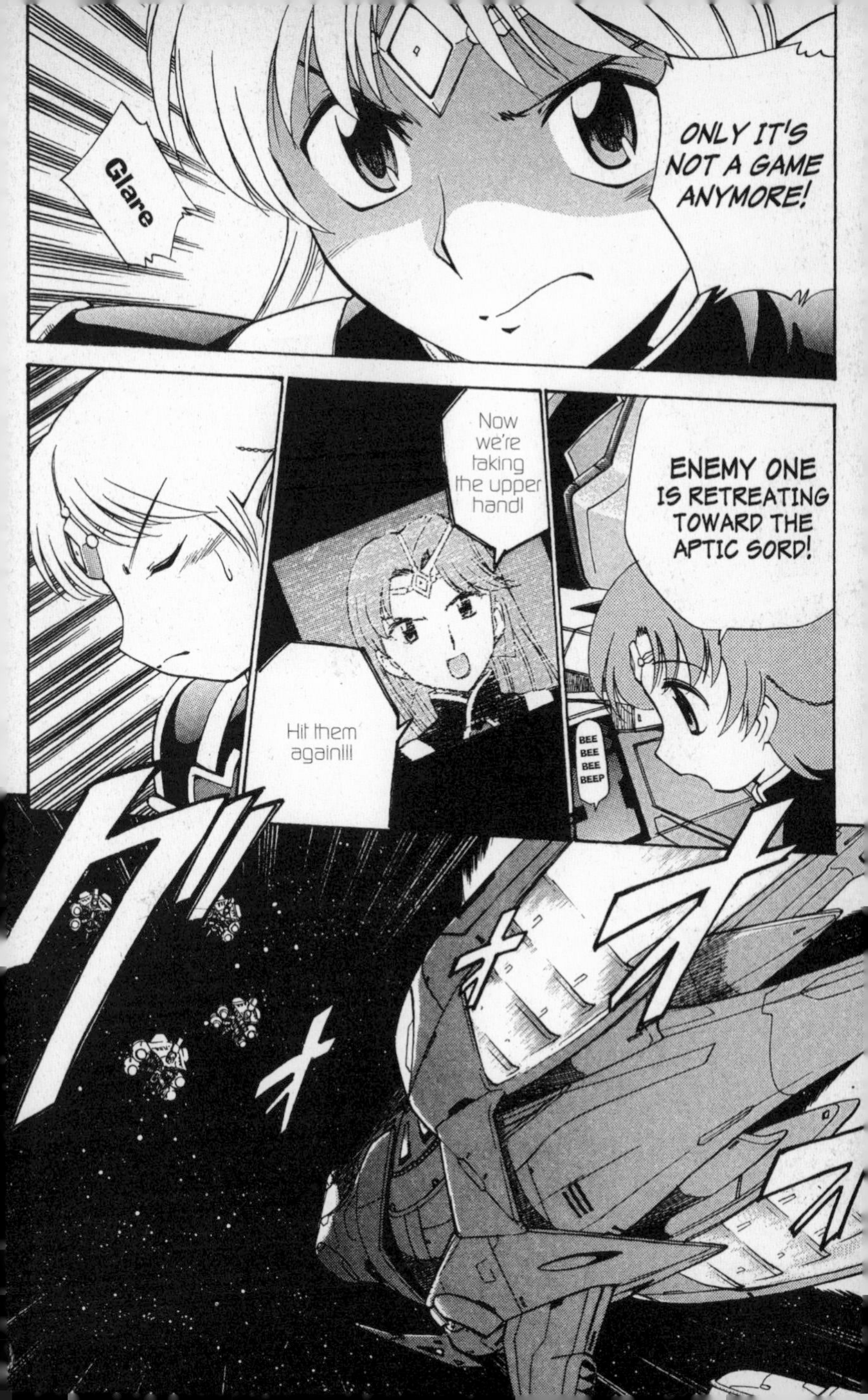
ONLY IT'S NOT A GAME ANYMORE!
Glare
ENEMY ONE IS RETREATING TOWARD THE APTIC SORD!
BEE BEE BEE BEEP
Now we're taking the upper hand!
Hit them again!!!

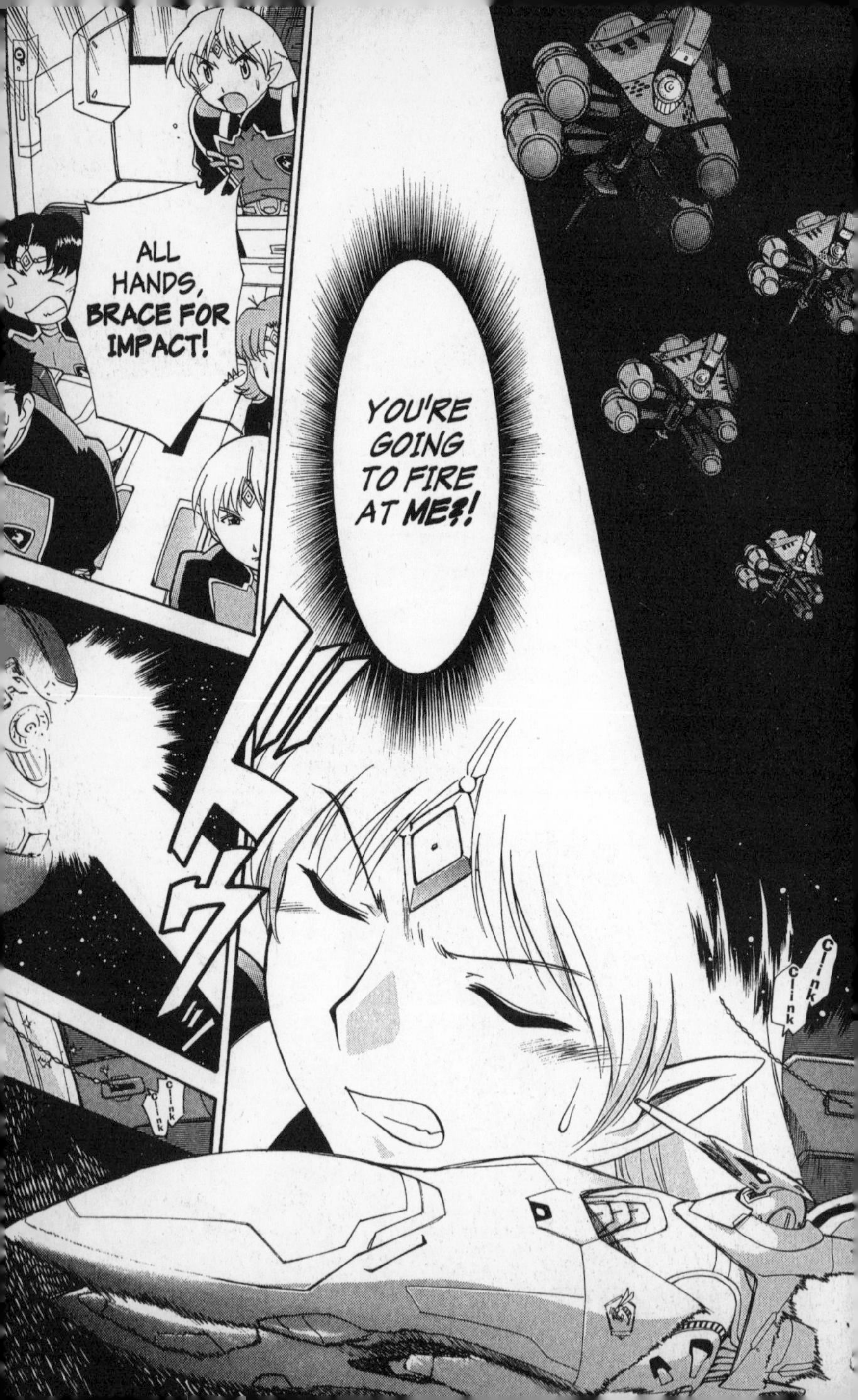
YOU'RE GOING TO FIRE AT ME?!
Clink Clink
ALL HANDS, BRACE FOR IMPACT!
Clink Clink

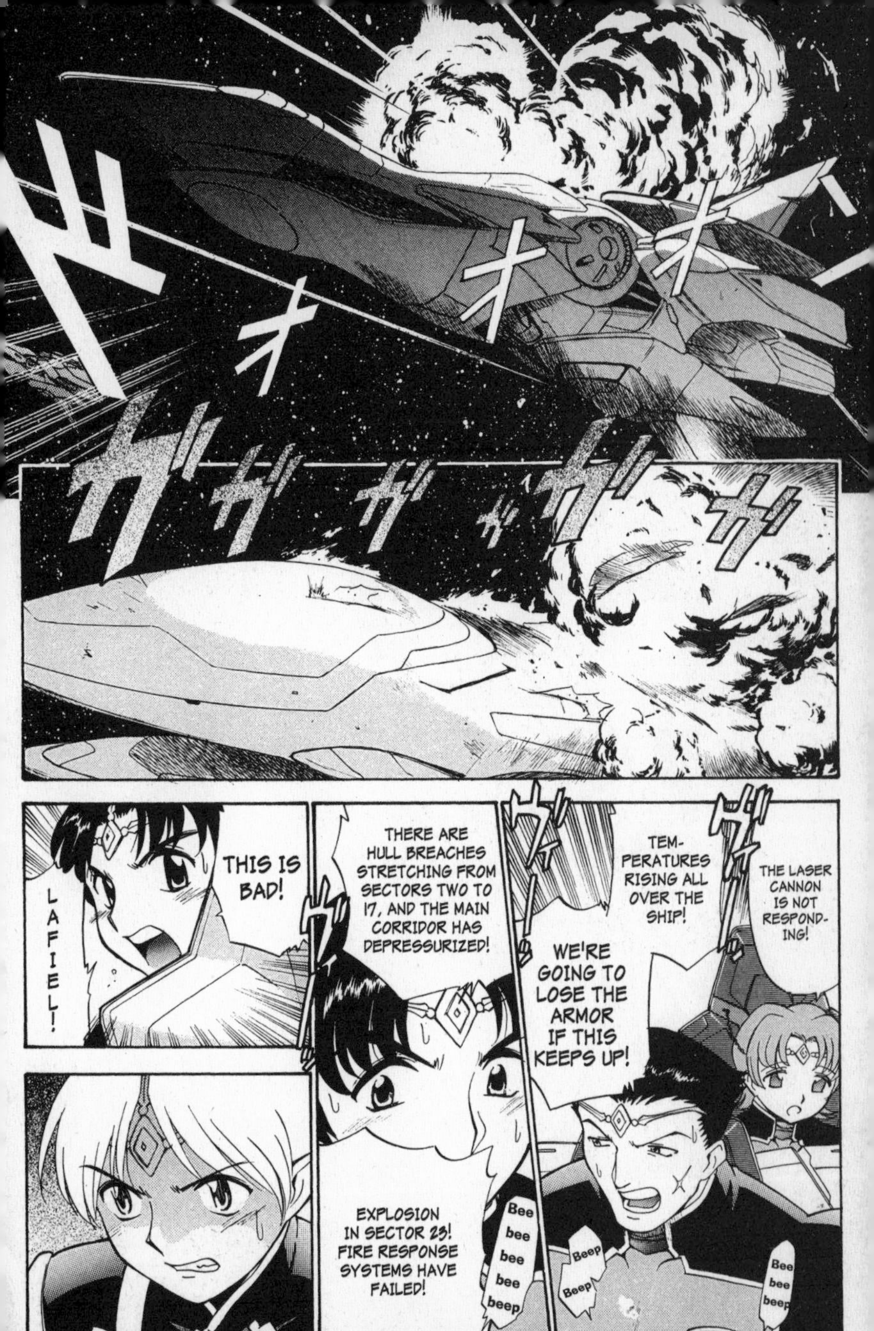
THE LASER CANNON IS NOT RESPOND-ING!
TEM-PERATURES RISING ALL OVER THE SHIP!
WE'RE GOING TO LOSE THE ARMOR IF THIS KEEPS UP!
Bee bee beep
Beep Beep
THERE ARE HULL BREACHES STRETCHING FROM SECTORS TWO TO 17, AND THE MAIN CORRIDOR HAS DEPRESSURIZED!
Bee bee bee bee beep
EXPLOSION IN SECTOR 23! FIRE RESPONSE SYSTEMS HAVE FAILED!
THIS IS BAD!
LAFIEL!

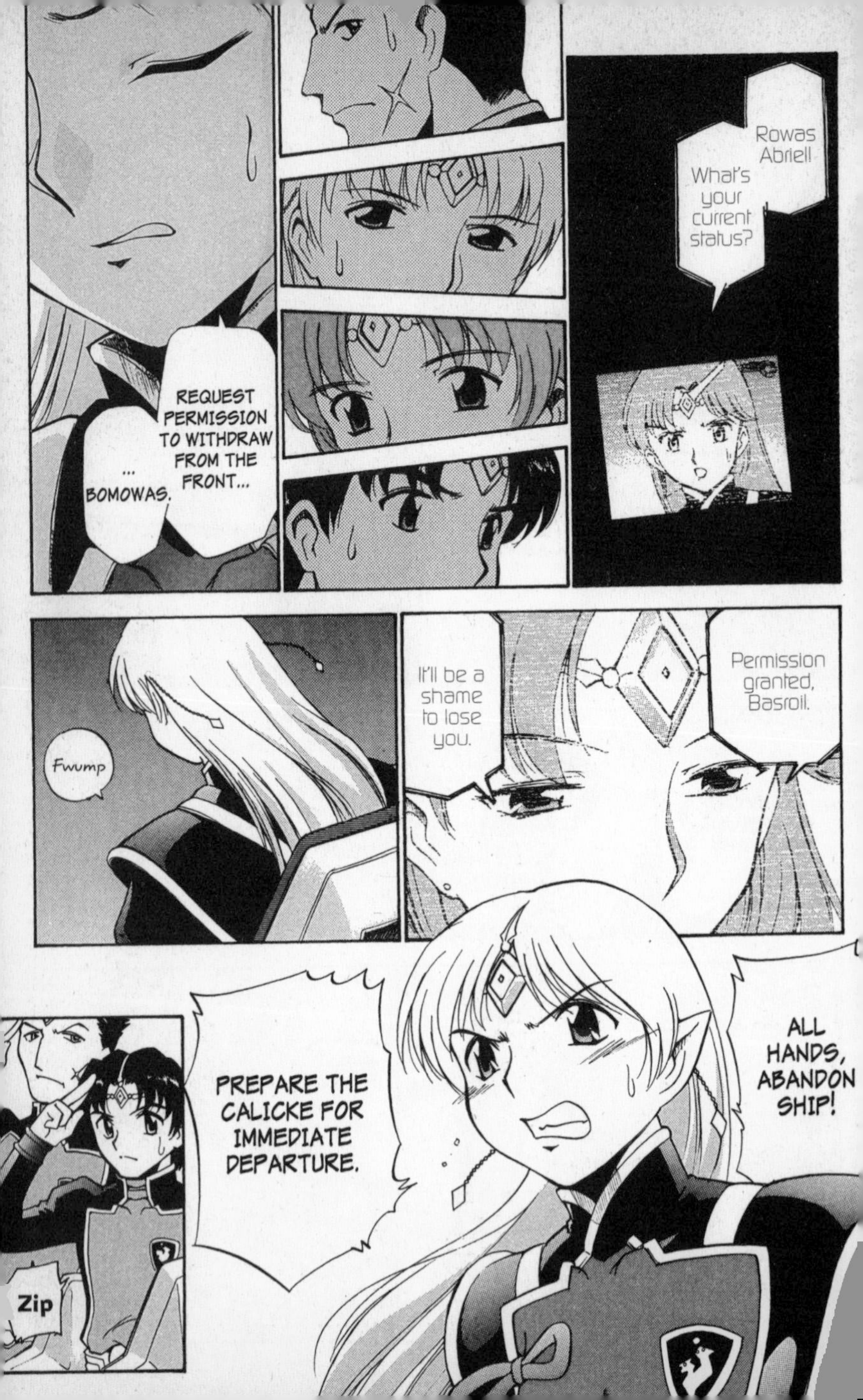

Rowas Abriel! What's your current status?
REQUEST PERMISSION TO WITHDRAW FROM THE FRONT...
...BOMOWAS.
Permission granted, Basroil.
It'll be a shame to lose you.
Fwump
ALL HANDS, ABANDON SHIP!
PREPARE THE CALICKE FOR IMMEDIATE DEPARTURE.
Zip

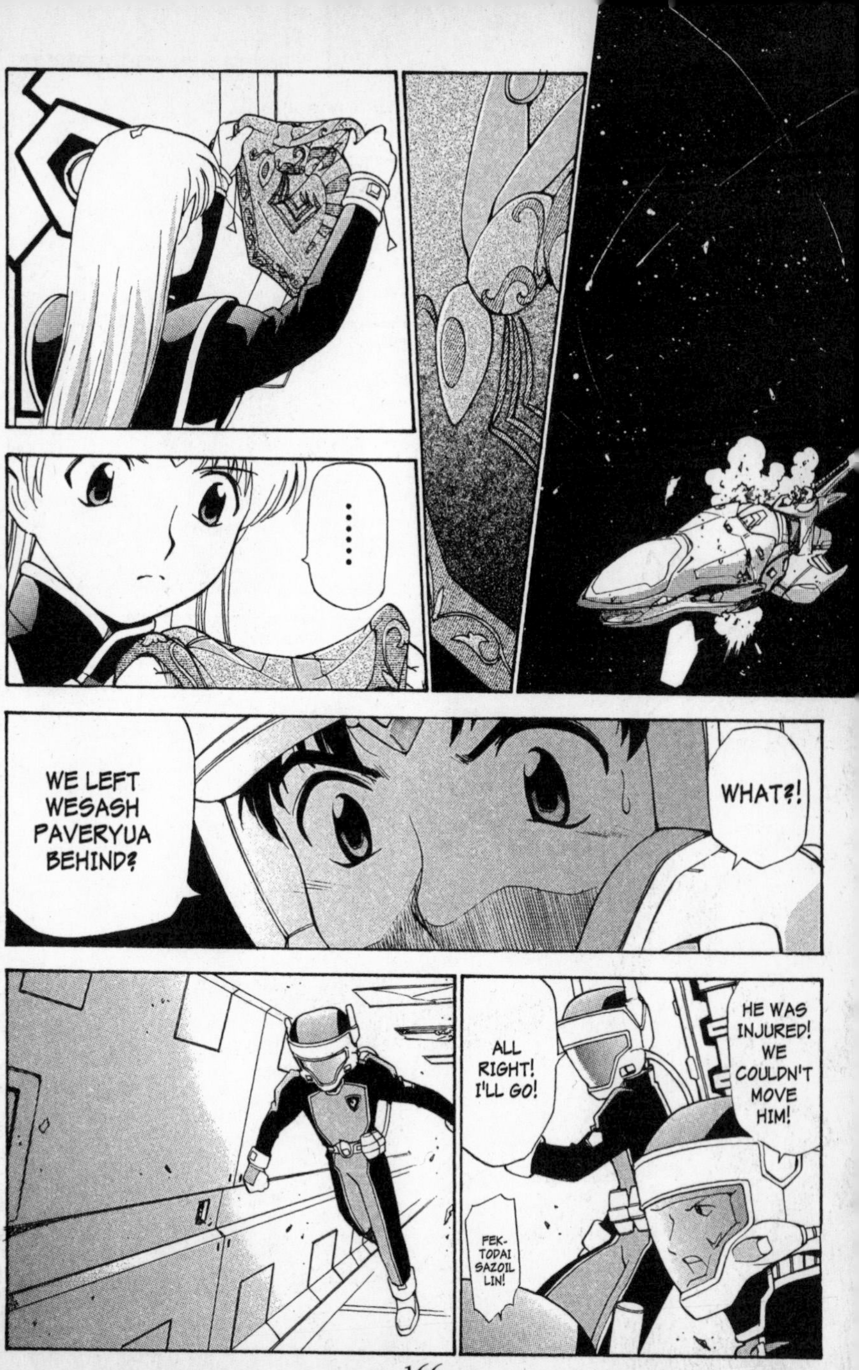
......
WHAT?!
WE LEFT WESASH PAVERYUA BEHIND?
HE WAS INJURED! WE COULDN'T MOVE HIM!
ALL RIGHT! I'LL GO!
FEK-TODAI SAZOIL LIN!

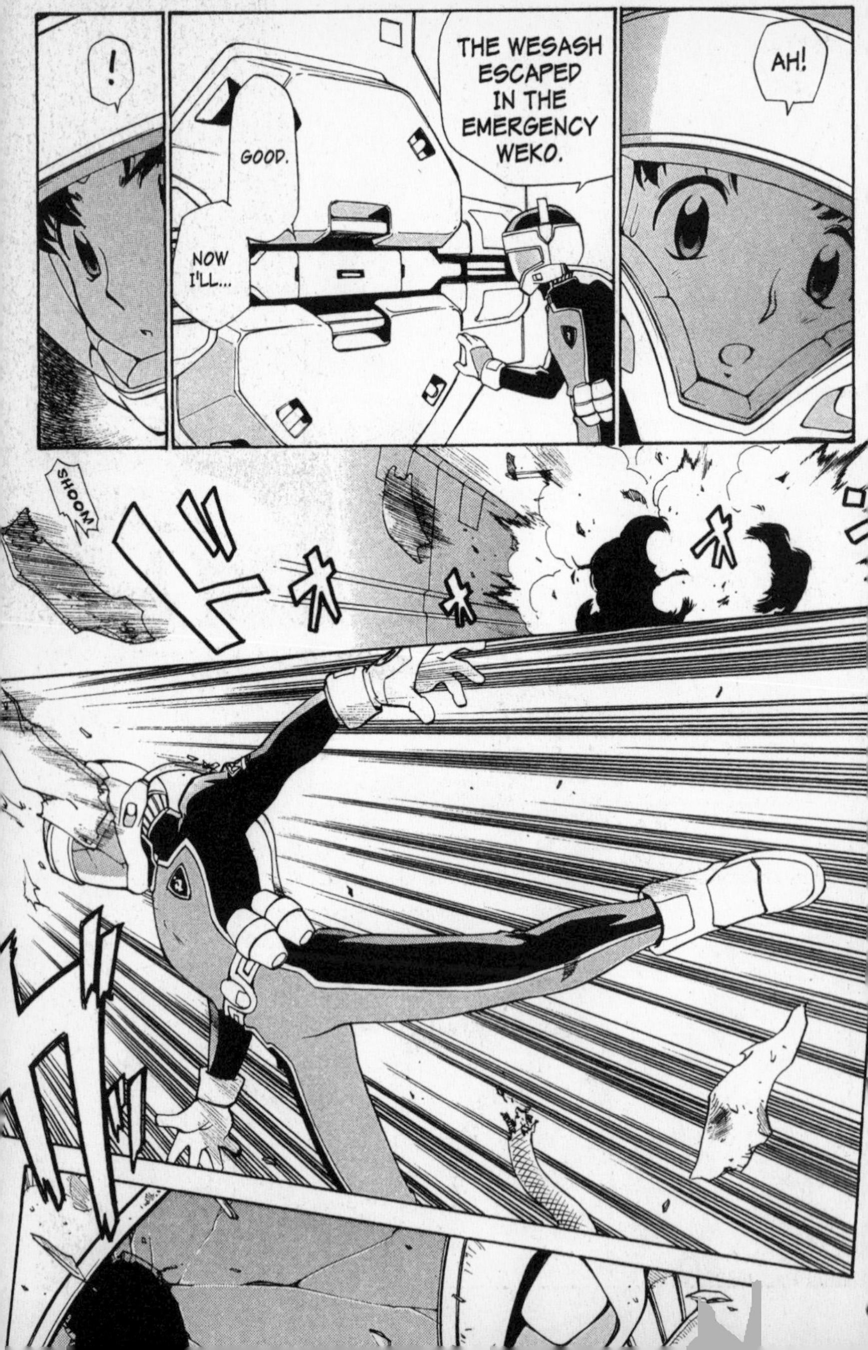
AH!
THE WESASH ESCAPED IN THE EMERGENCY WEKO.
GOOD.
NOW I'LL...
!
SHOOM

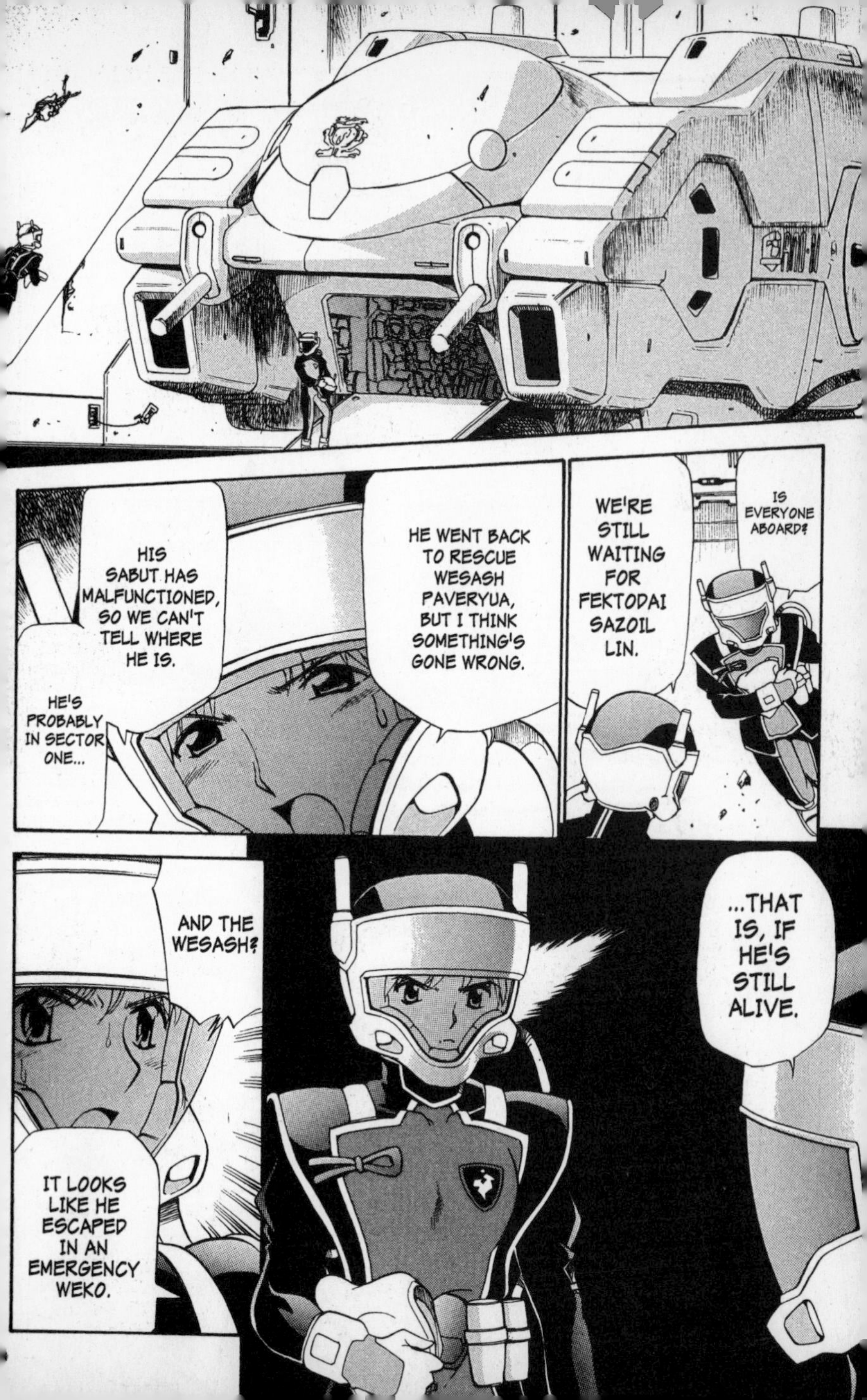
IS EVERYONE ABOARD?
WE'RE STILL WAITING FOR FEKTODAI SAZOIL LIN.
HE WENT BACK TO RESCUE WESASH PAVERYUA, BUT I THINK SOMETHING'S GONE WRONG.
HIS SABUT HAS MALFUNCTIONED, SO WE CAN'T TELL WHERE HE IS.
HE'S PROBABLY IN SECTOR ONE...
...THAT IS, IF HE'S STILL ALIVE.
AND THE WESASH?
IT LOOKS LIKE HE ESCAPED IN AN EMERGENCY WEKO.

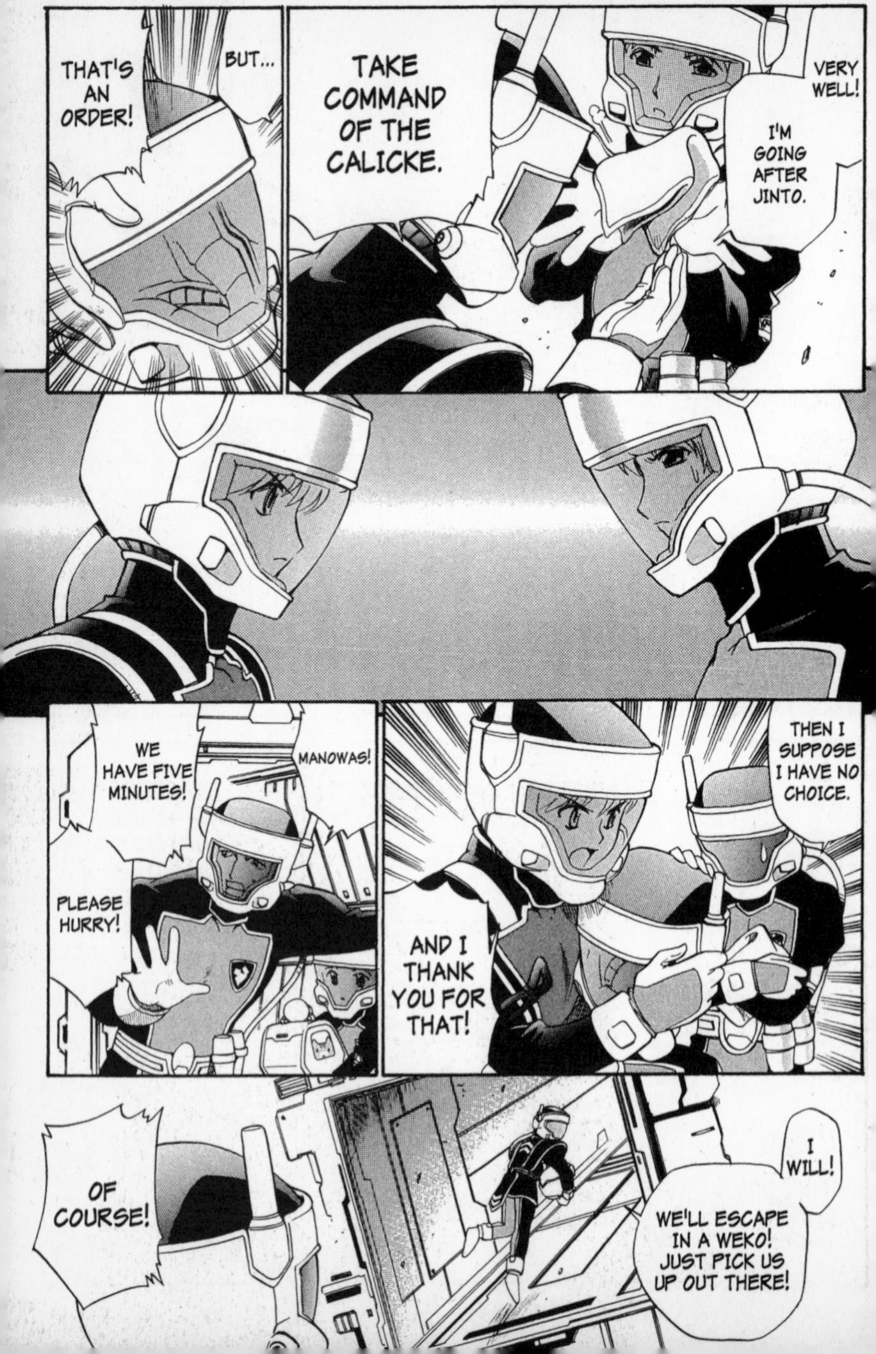
VERY WELL!
I'M GOING AFTER JINTO.
TAKE COMMAND OF THE CALICKE.
BUT...
THAT'S AN ORDER!
THEN I SUPPOSE I HAVE NO CHOICE.
AND I THANK YOU FOR THAT!
MANOWAS!
WE HAVE FIVE MINUTES!
PLEASE HURRY!
I WILL!
WE'LL ESCAPE IN A WEKO! JUST PICK US UP OUT THERE!
OF COURSE!

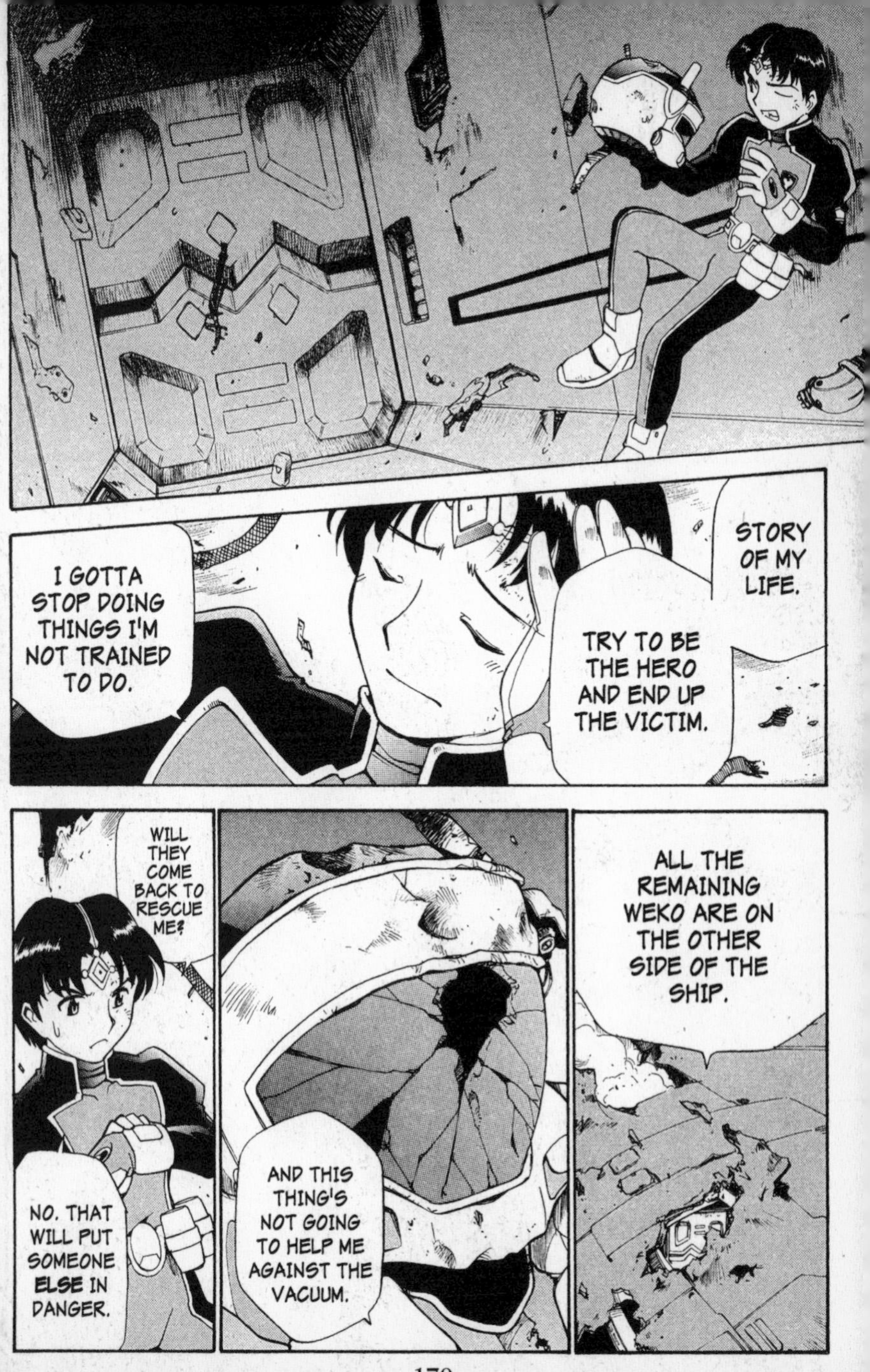
STORY OF MY LIFE.
TRY TO BE THE HERO AND END UP THE VICTIM.
I GOTTA STOP DOING THINGS I'M NOT TRAINED TO DO.
ALL THE REMAINING WEKO ARE ON THE OTHER SIDE OF THE SHIP.
AND THIS THING'S NOT GOING TO HELP ME AGAINST THE VACUUM.
WILL THEY COME BACK TO RESCUE ME?
NO. THAT WILL PUT SOMEONE ELSE IN DANGER.

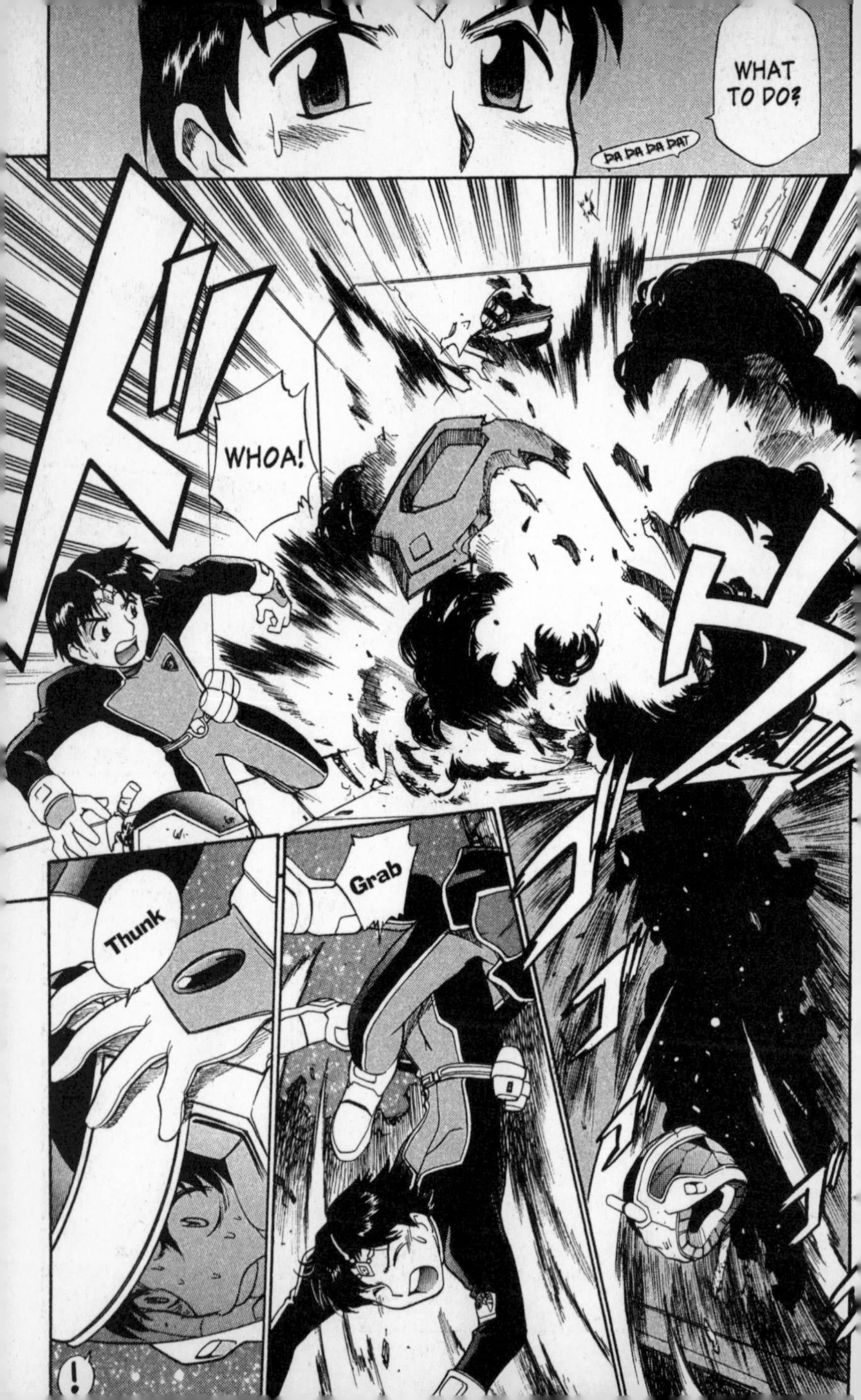
WHAT TO DO?
DA DA DA DAT
WHOA!
Grab
Thunk
!

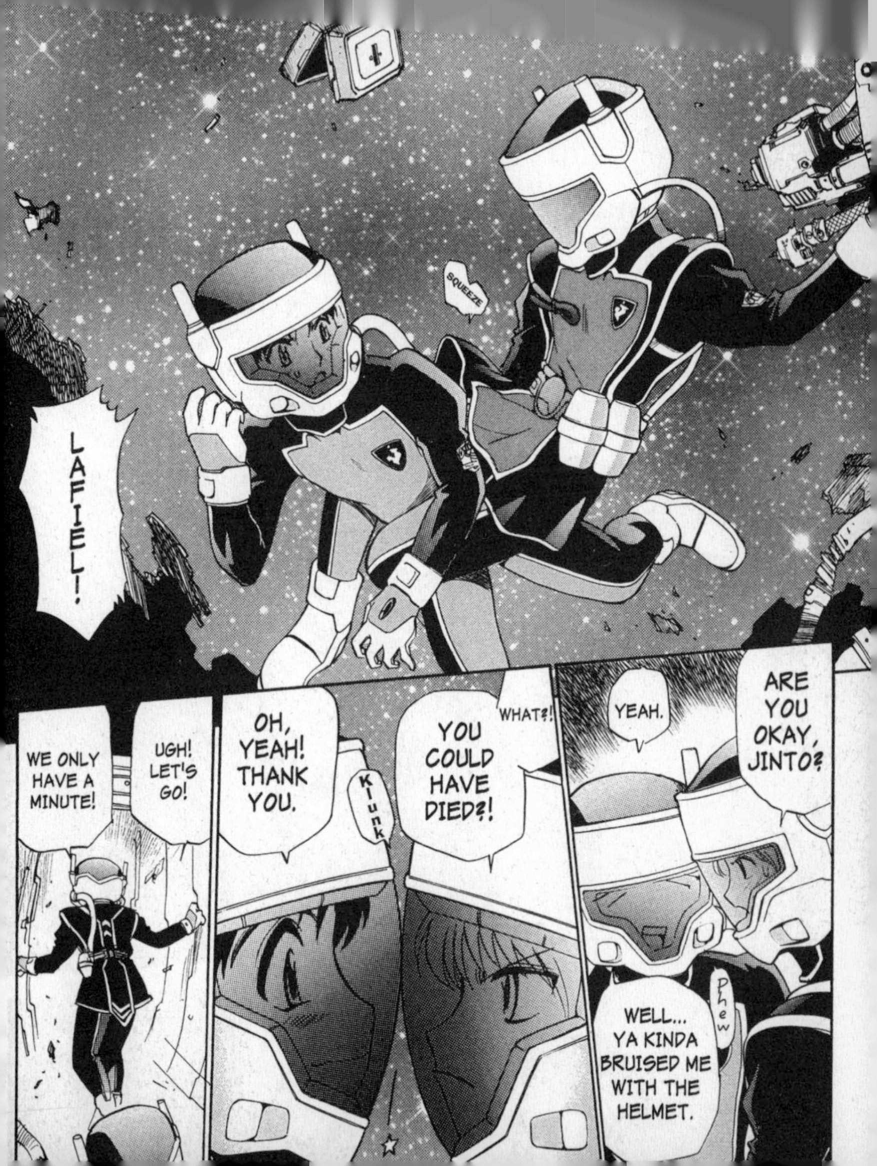
SQUEEZE
LAFIEL!
ARE YOU OKAY, JINTO?
YEAH.
WELL... YA KINDA BRUISED ME WITH THE HELMET.
Phew
WHAT?!
YOU COULD HAVE DIED?!
Klunk
OH, YEAH! THANK YOU.
UGH! LET'S GO!
WE ONLY HAVE A MINUTE!

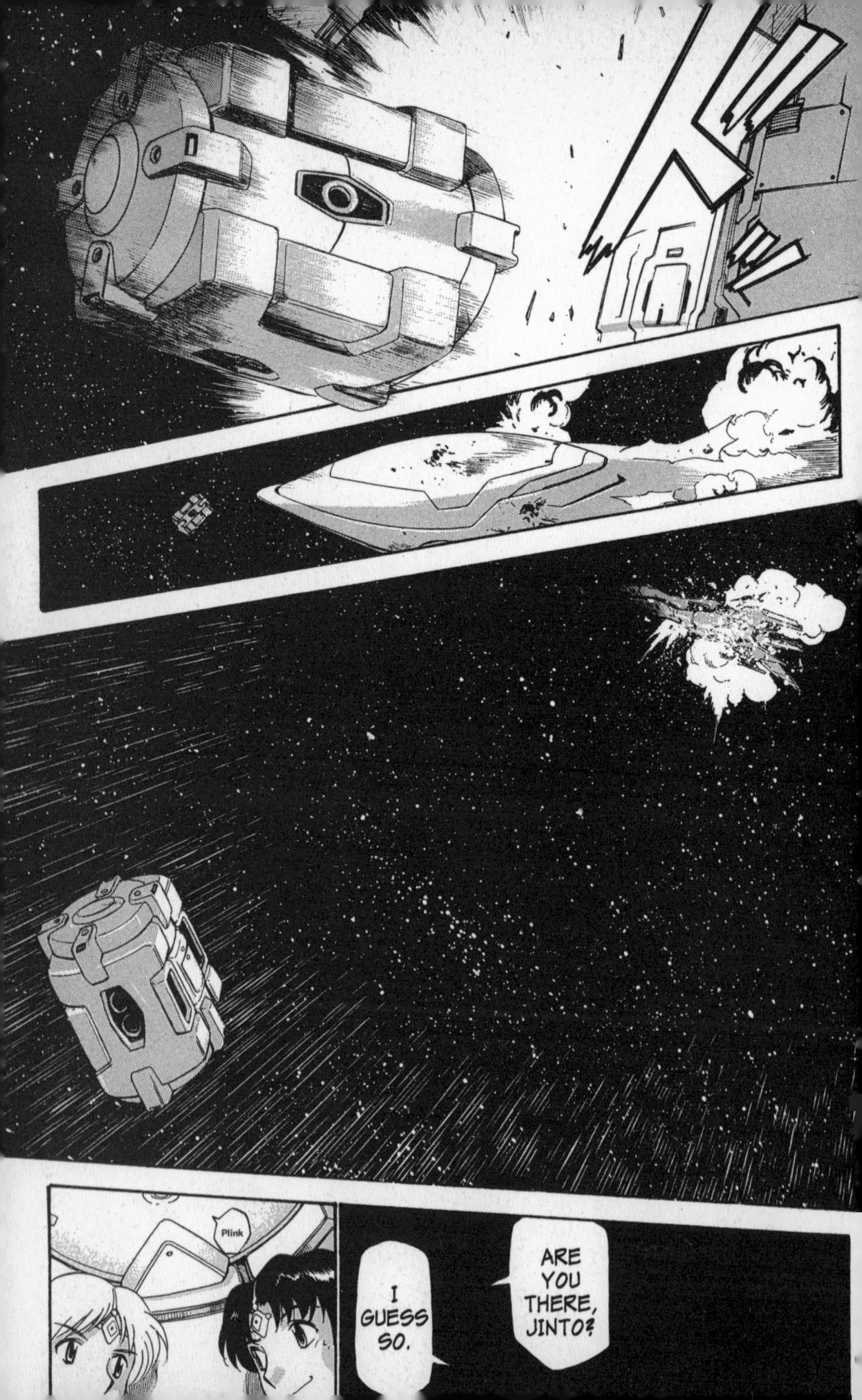
ARE YOU THERE, JINTO?
I GUESS SO.
Plink

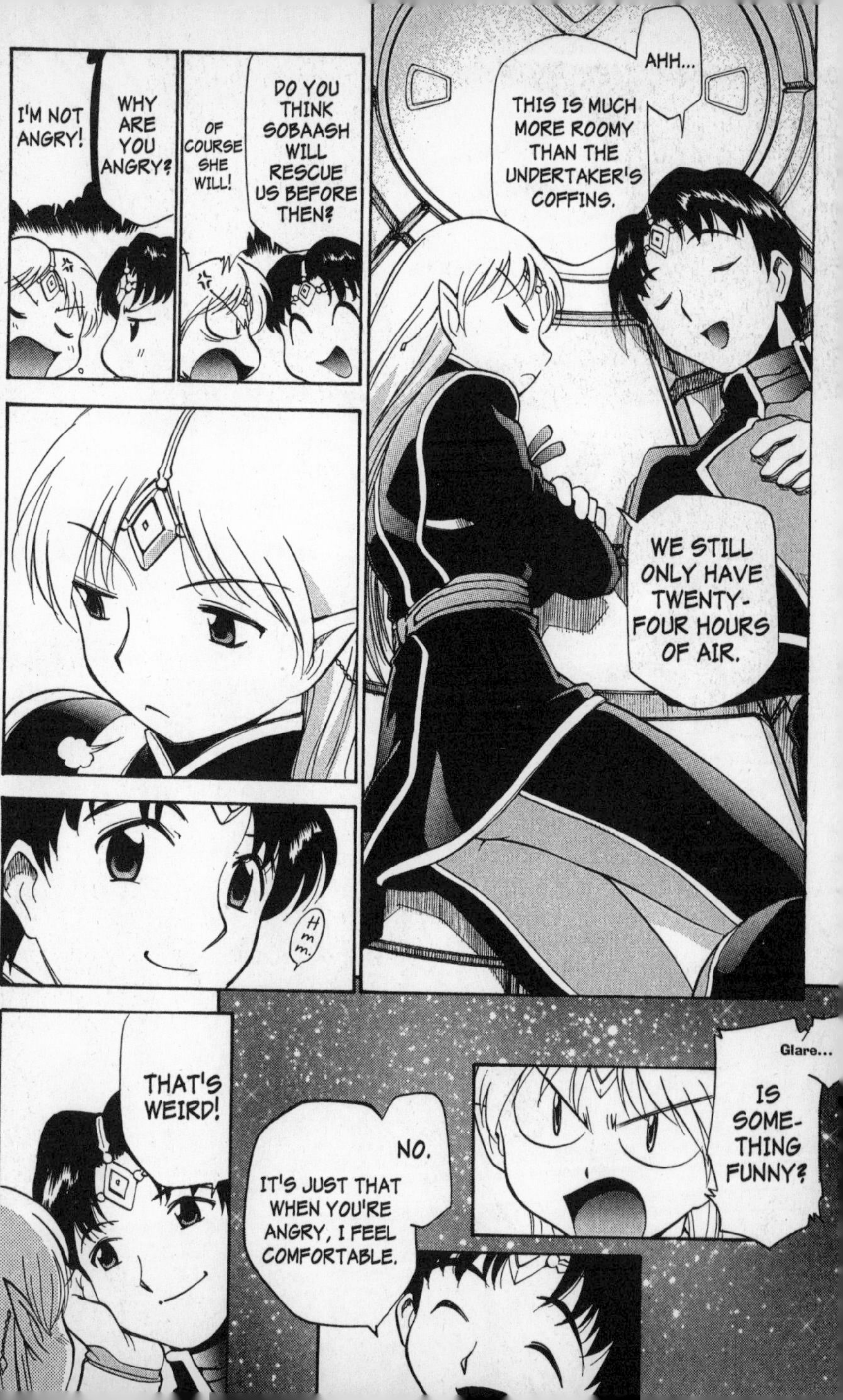
AHH...
THIS IS MUCH MORE ROOMY THAN THE UNDERTAKER'S COFFINS.
WE STILL ONLY HAVE TWENTY-FOUR HOURS OF AIR.
DO YOU THINK SOBAASH WILL RESCUE US BEFORE THEN?
OF COURSE SHE WILL!
WHY ARE YOU ANGRY?
I'M NOT ANGRY!
Hmm.
Glare...
IS SOMETHING FUNNY?
NO.
IT'S JUST THAT WHEN YOU'RE ANGRY, I FEEL COMFORTABLE.
THAT'S WEIRD!

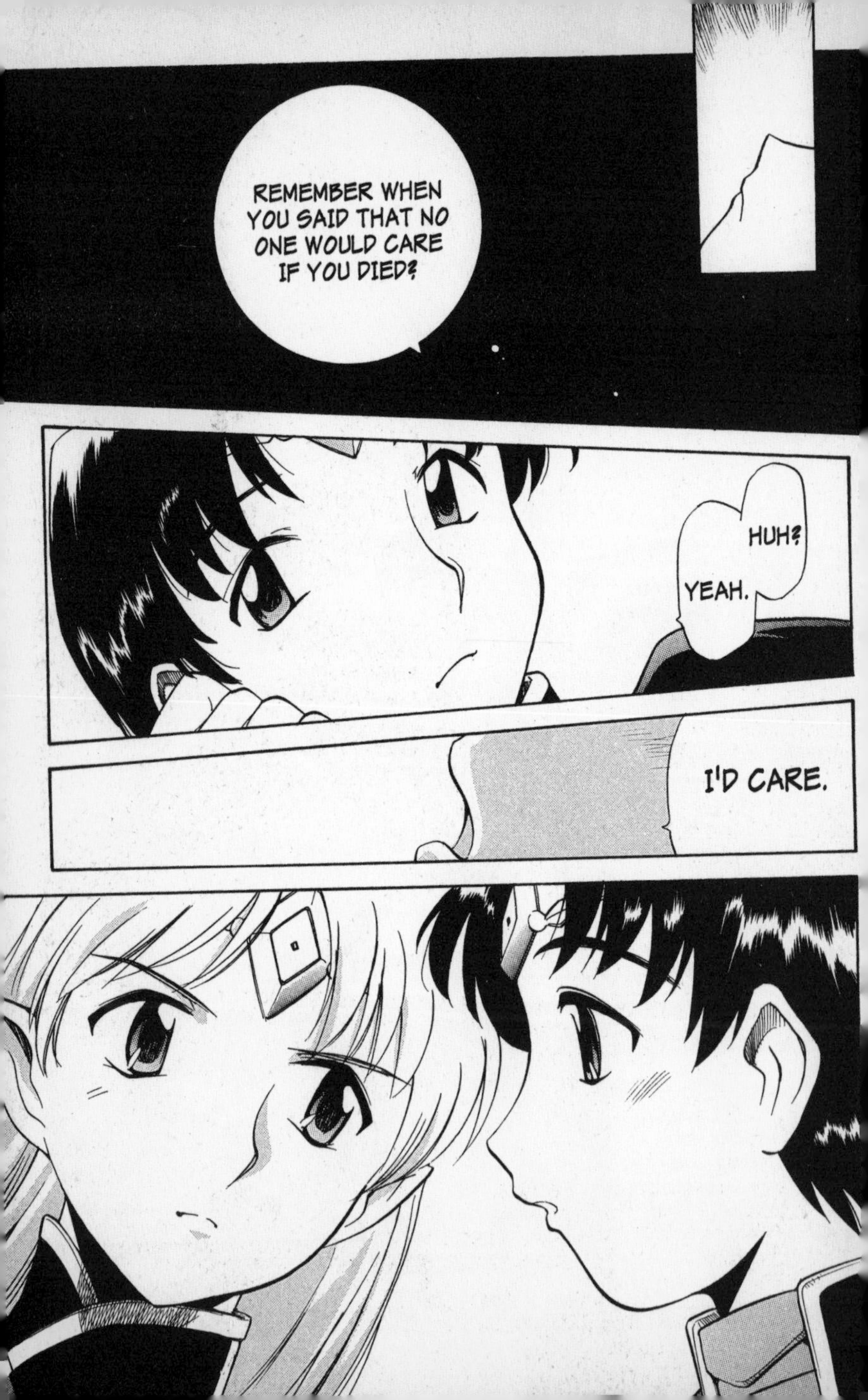
REMEMBER WHEN YOU SAID THAT NO ONE WOULD CARE IF YOU DIED?
HUH?
YEAH.
I'D CARE.

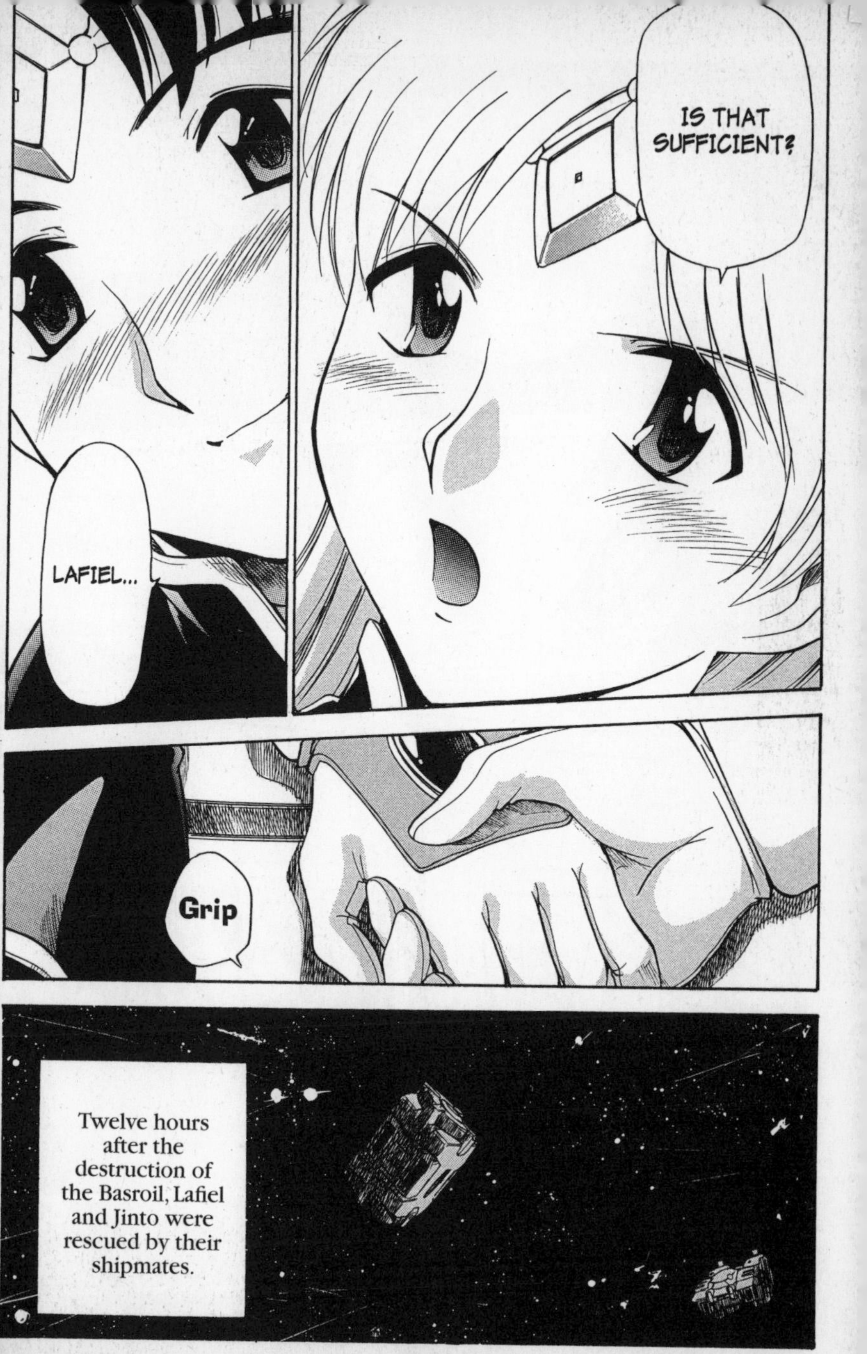
IS THAT SUFFICIENT?
LAFIEL...
Grip
Twelve hours after the destruction of the Basroil, Lafiel and Jinto were rescued by their shipmates.

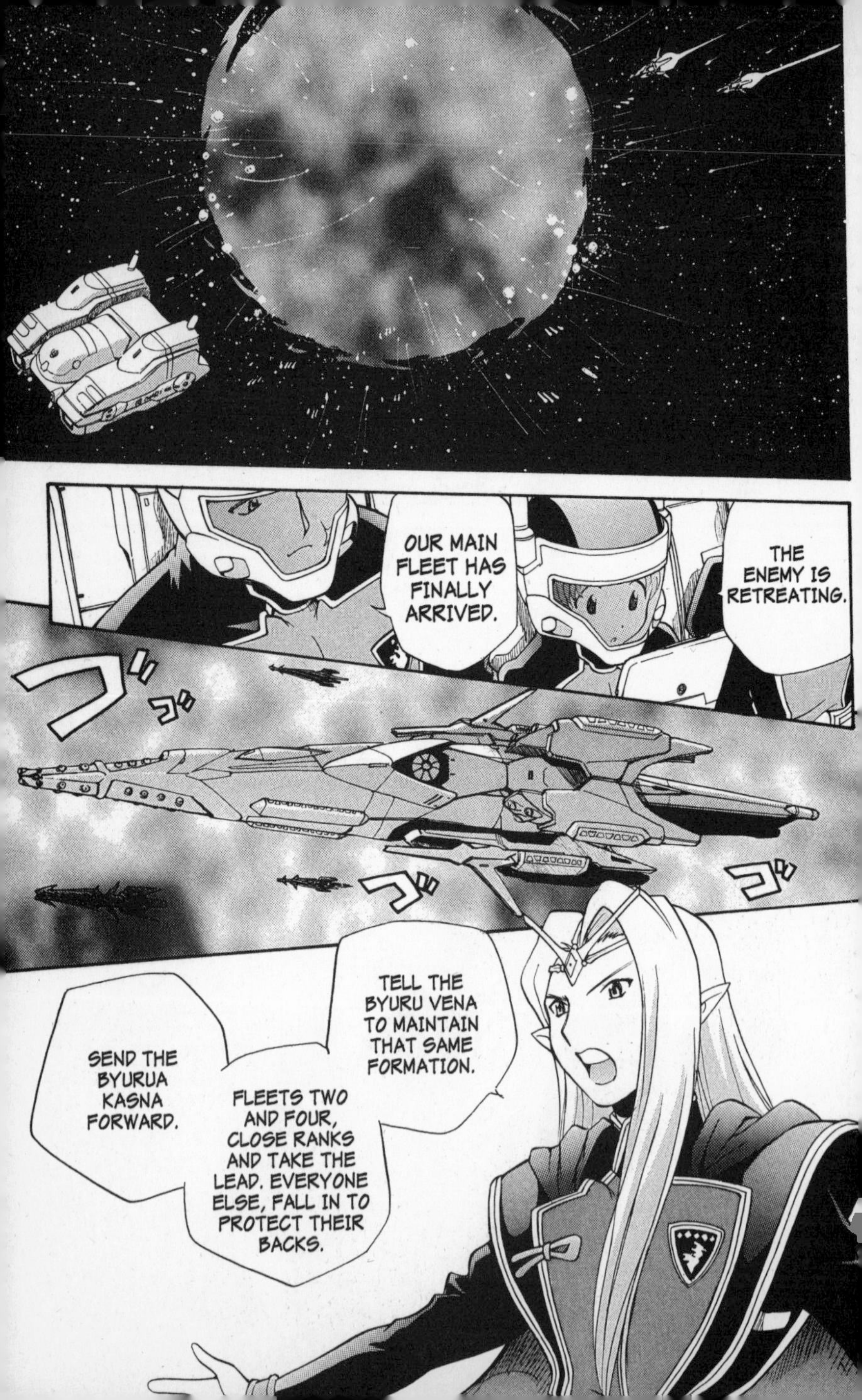
THE ENEMY IS RETREATING.
OUR MAIN FLEET HAS FINALLY ARRIVED.
TELL THE BYURU VENA TO MAINTAIN THAT SAME FORMATION.
SEND THE BYURUA KASNA FORWARD.
FLEETS TWO AND FOUR, CLOSE RANKS AND TAKE THE LEAD. EVERYONE ELSE, FALL IN TO PROTECT THEIR BACKS.

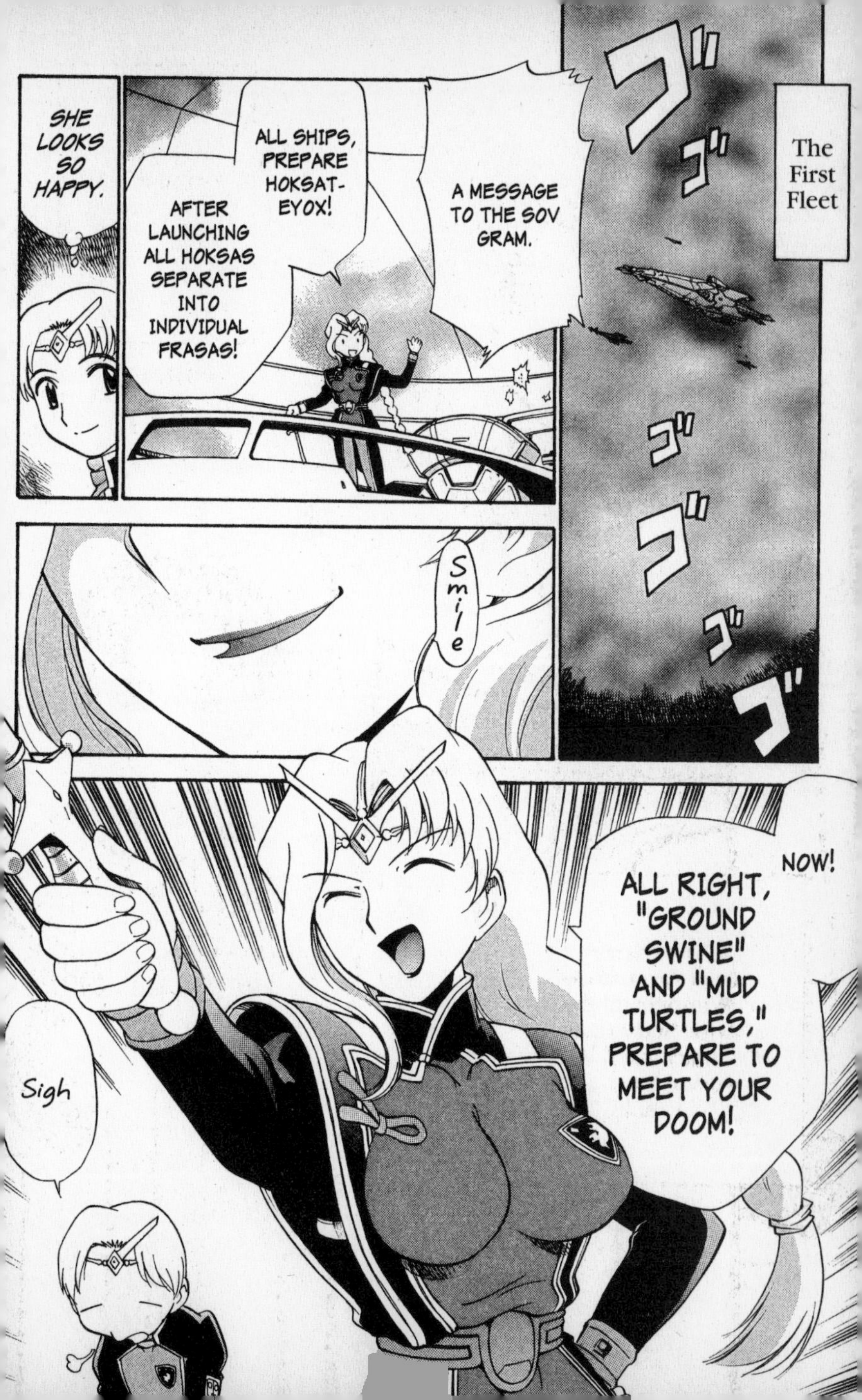

The First Fleet
ゴ
ゴ
ゴ
ゴ
ゴ
ゴ
A MESSAGE TO THE SOV GRAM.
ALL SHIPS, PREPARE HOKSAT-EYOX!
AFTER LAUNCHING ALL HOKSAS SEPARATE INTO INDIVIDUAL FRASAS!
SHE LOOKS SO HAPPY.
Smile
NOW!
ALL RIGHT, "GROUND SWINE" AND "MUD TURTLES," PREPARE TO MEET YOUR DOOM!
Sigh

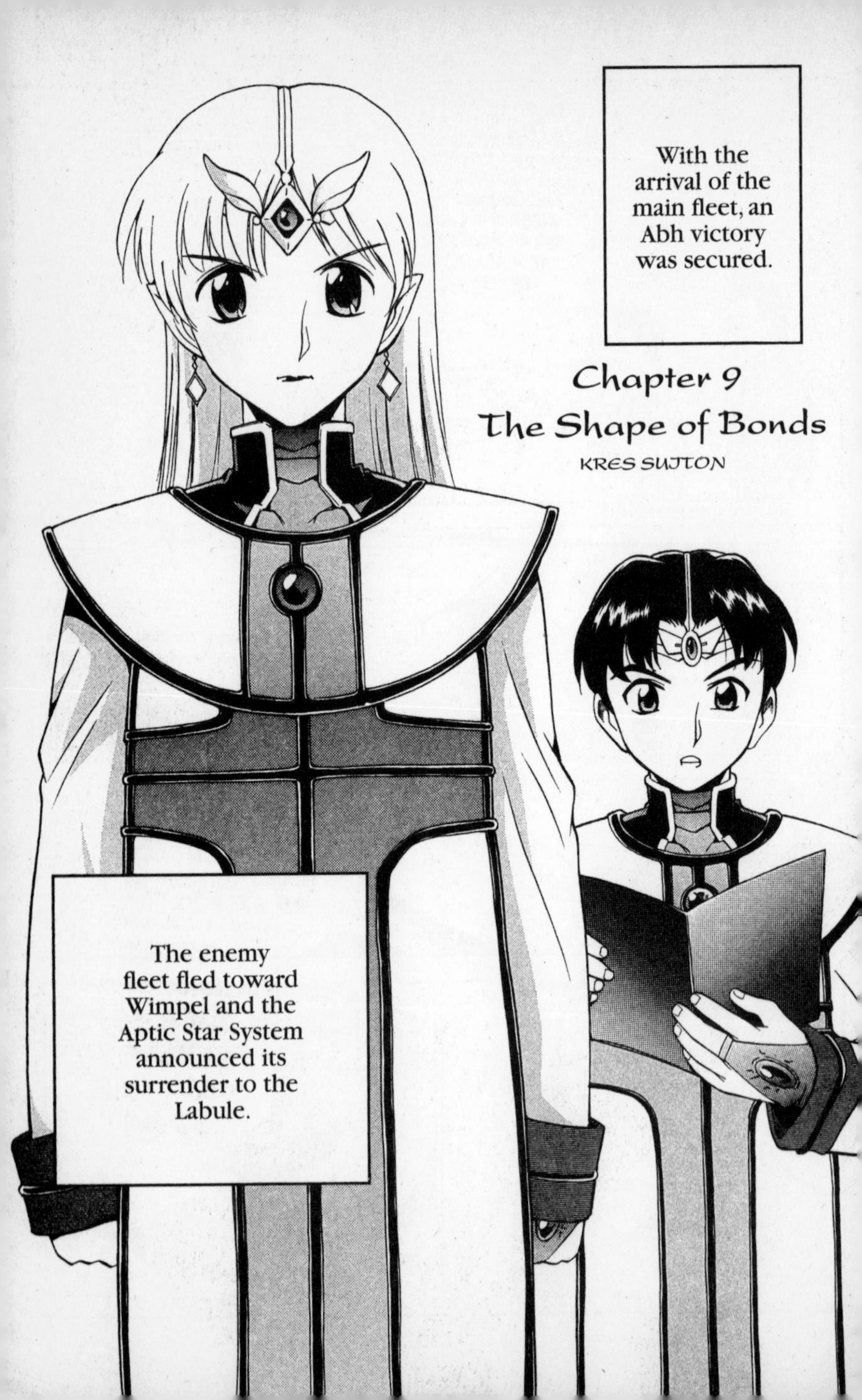
With the arrival of the main fleet, an Abh victory was secured.
Chapter 9
The Shape of Bonds
KRES SUJTON
The enemy fleet fled toward Wimpel and the Aptic Star System announced its surrender to the Labule.

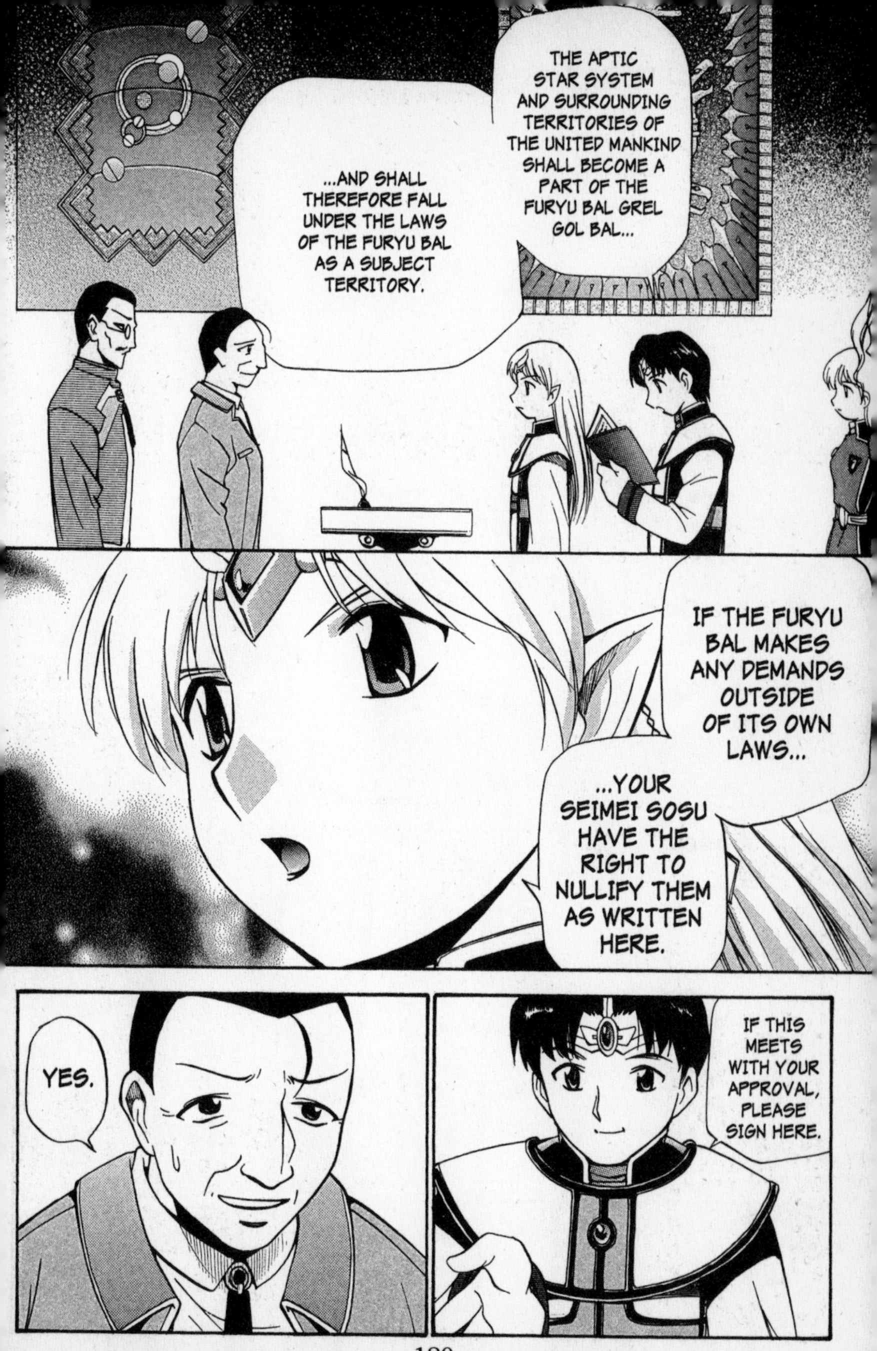
THE APTIC STAR SYSTEM AND SURROUNDING TERRITORIES OF THE UNITED MANKIND SHALL BECOME A PART OF THE FURYU BAL GREL GOL BAL...
...AND SHALL THEREFORE FALL UNDER THE LAWS OF THE FURYU BAL AS A SUBJECT TERRITORY.
IF THE FURYU BAL MAKES ANY DEMANDS OUTSIDE OF ITS OWN LAWS...
...YOUR SEIMEI SOSU HAVE THE RIGHT TO NULLIFY THEM AS WRITTEN HERE.
IF THIS MEETS WITH YOUR APPROVAL, PLEASE SIGN HERE.
YES.

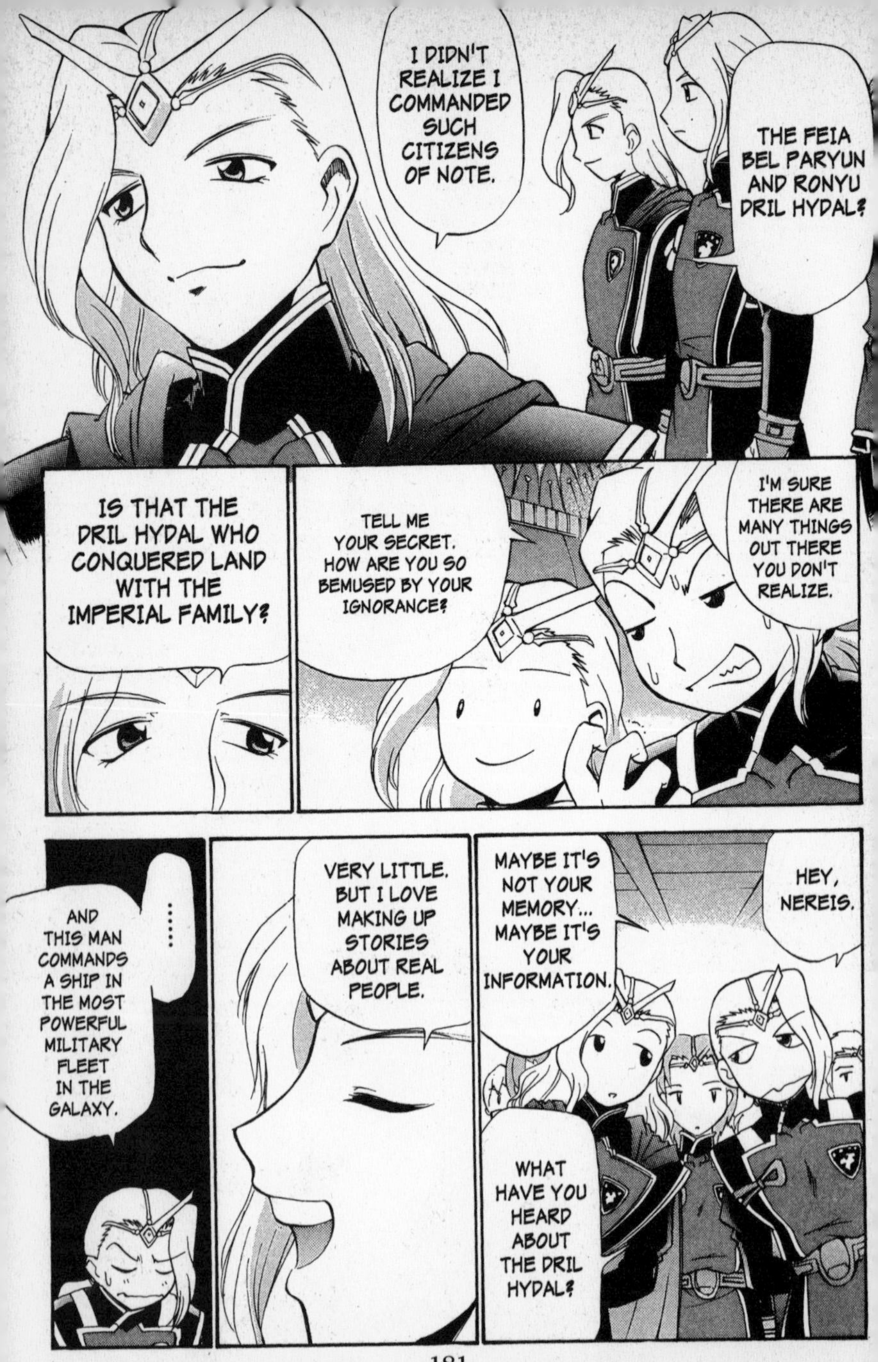
THE FEIA BEL PARYUN AND RONYU DRIL HYDAL?
I DIDN'T REALIZE I COMMANDED SUCH CITIZENS OF NOTE.
I'M SURE THERE ARE MANY THINGS OUT THERE YOU DON'T REALIZE.
TELL ME YOUR SECRET. HOW ARE YOU SO BEMUSED BY YOUR IGNORANCE?
IS THAT THE DRIL HYDAL WHO CONQUERED LAND WITH THE IMPERIAL FAMILY?
HEY, NEREIS.
MAYBE IT'S NOT YOUR MEMORY... MAYBE IT'S YOUR INFORMATION.
WHAT HAVE YOU HEARD ABOUT THE DRIL HYDAL?
VERY LITTLE. BUT I LOVE MAKING UP STORIES ABOUT REAL PEOPLE.
......
AND THIS MAN COMMANDS A SHIP IN THE MOST POWERFUL MILITARY FLEET IN THE GALAXY.

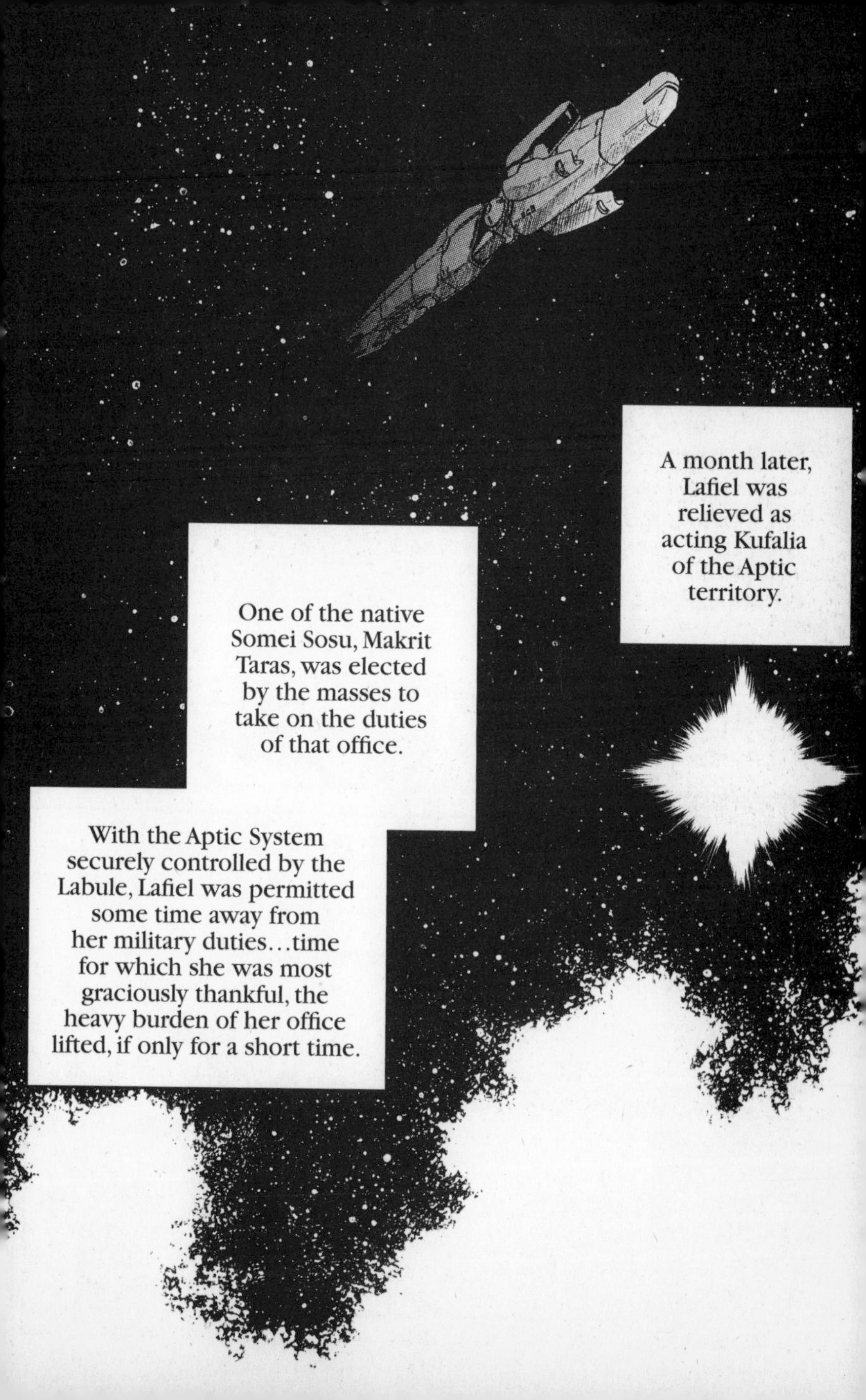
A month later, Lafiel was relieved as acting Kufalia of the Aptic territory.
One of the native Somei Sosu, Makrit Taras, was elected by the masses to take on the duties of that office.
With the Aptic System securely controlled by the Labule, Lafiel was permitted some time away from her military duties...time for which she was most graciously thankful, the heavy burden of her office lifted, if only for a short time.

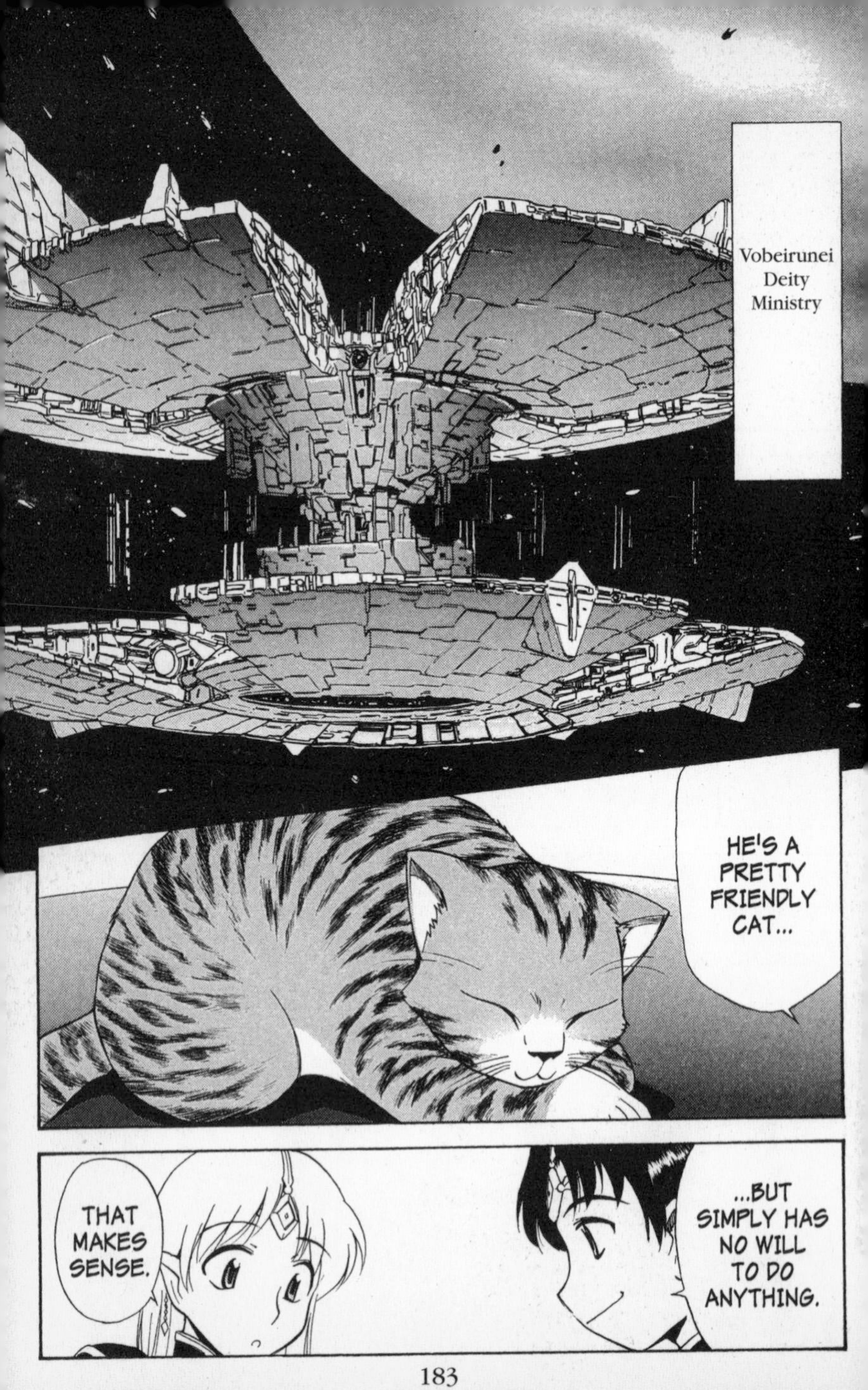
Vobeirunei Deity Ministry
HE'S A PRETTY FRIENDLY CAT...
...BUT SIMPLY HAS NO WILL TO DO ANYTHING.
THAT MAKES SENSE.

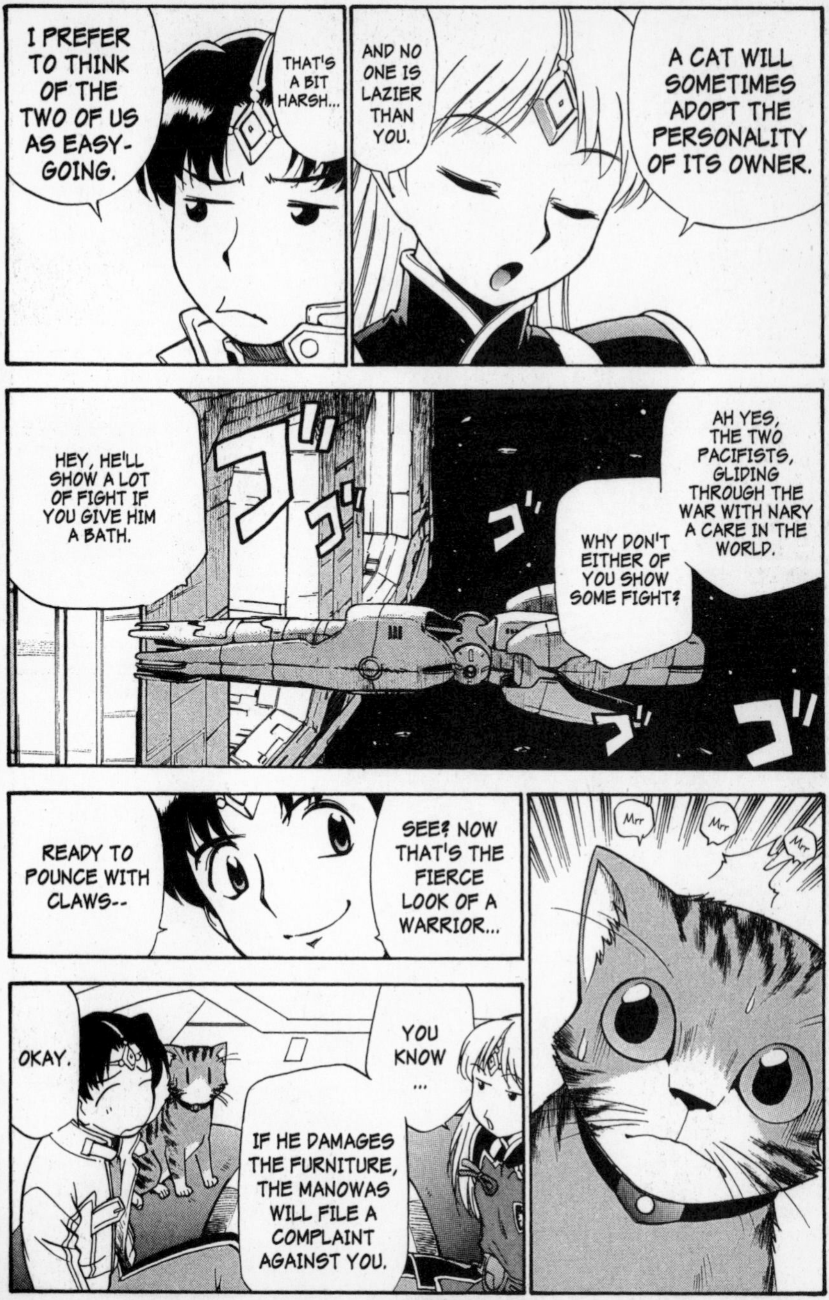
A CAT WILL SOMETIMES ADOPT THE PERSONALITY OF ITS OWNER.
AND NO ONE IS LAZIER THAN YOU.
THAT'S A BIT HARSH...
I PREFER TO THINK OF THE TWO OF US AS EASY-GOING.
AH YES, THE TWO PACIFISTS, GLIDING THROUGH THE WAR WITH NARY A CARE IN THE WORLD.
WHY DON'T EITHER OF YOU SHOW SOME FIGHT?
HEY, HE'LL SHOW A LOT OF FIGHT IF YOU GIVE HIM A BATH.
Mrr
Mrr
Mrr
SEE? NOW THAT'S THE FIERCE LOOK OF A WARRIOR...
READY TO POUNCE WITH CLAWS--
YOU KNOW...
IF HE DAMAGES THE FURNITURE, THE MANOWAS WILL FILE A COMPLAINT AGAINST YOU.
OKAY.

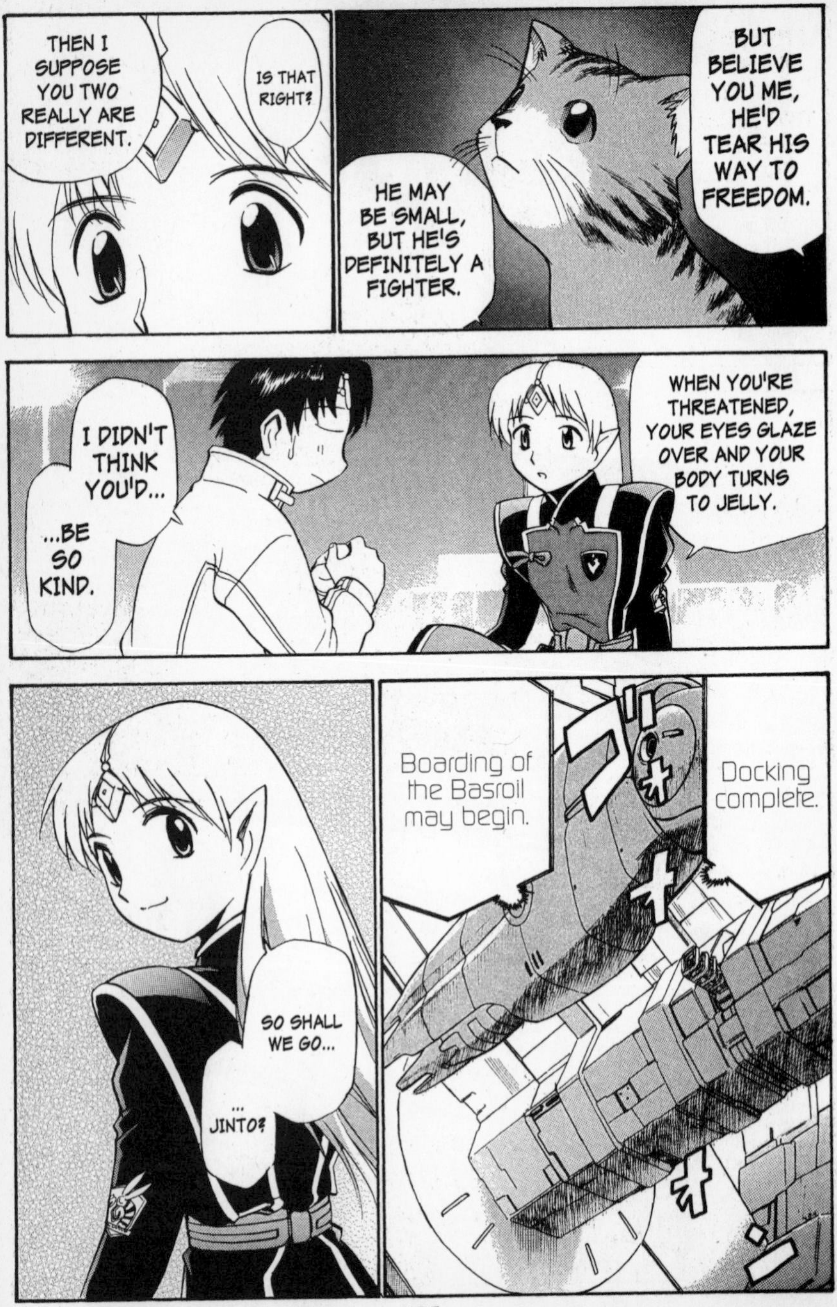
BUT BELIEVE YOU ME, HE'D TEAR HIS WAY TO FREEDOM.
HE MAY BE SMALL, BUT HE'S DEFINITELY A FIGHTER.
IS THAT RIGHT?
THEN I SUPPOSE YOU TWO REALLY ARE DIFFERENT.
WHEN YOU'RE THREATENED, YOUR EYES GLAZE OVER AND YOUR BODY TURNS TO JELLY.
I DIDN'T THINK YOU'D...
...BE SO KIND.
Docking complete.
Boarding of the Basroil may begin.
SO SHALL WE GO...
...JINTO?

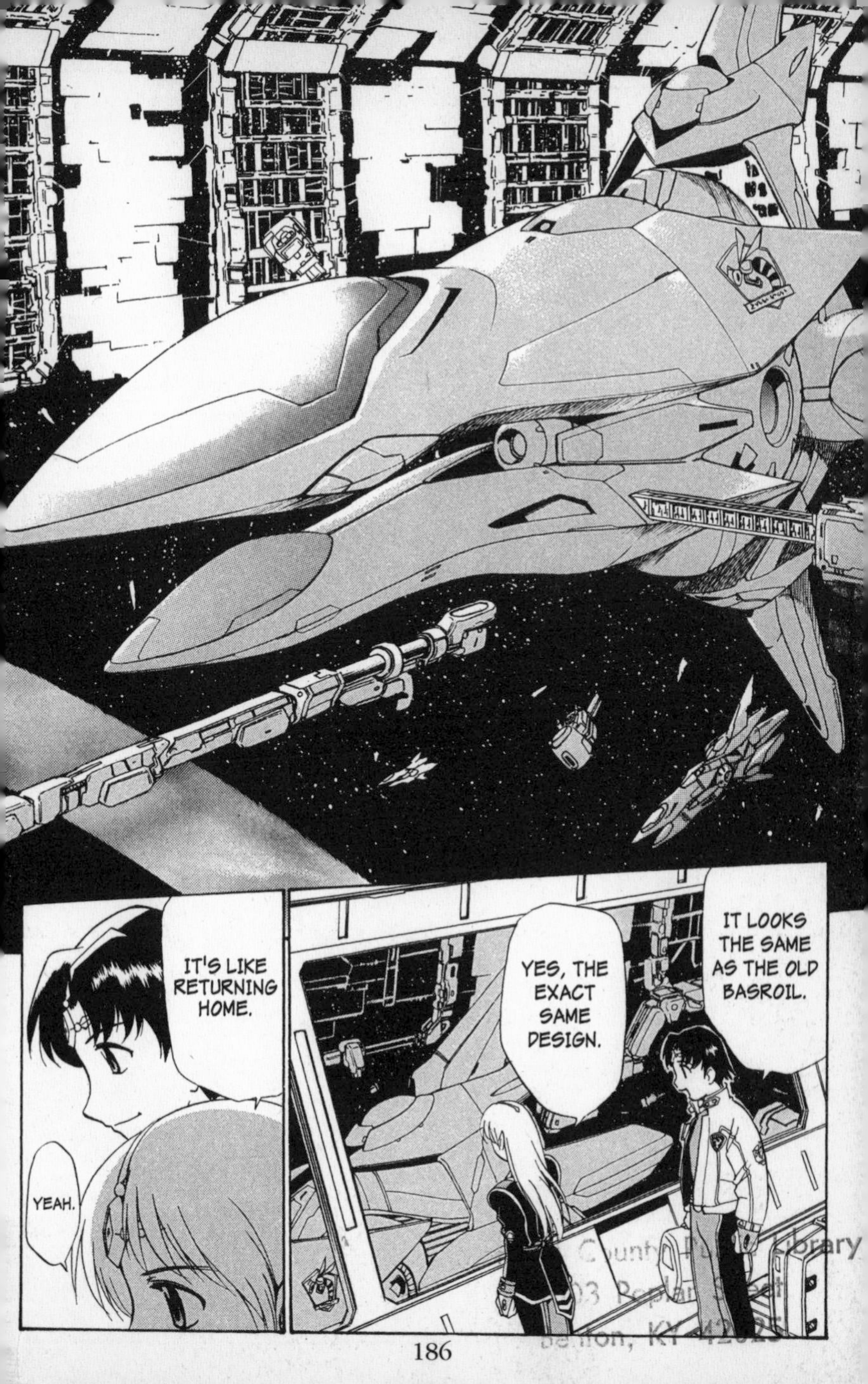
IT LOOKS THE SAME AS THE OLD BASROIL.
YES, THE EXACT SAME DESIGN.
IT'S LIKE RETURNING HOME.
YEAH.

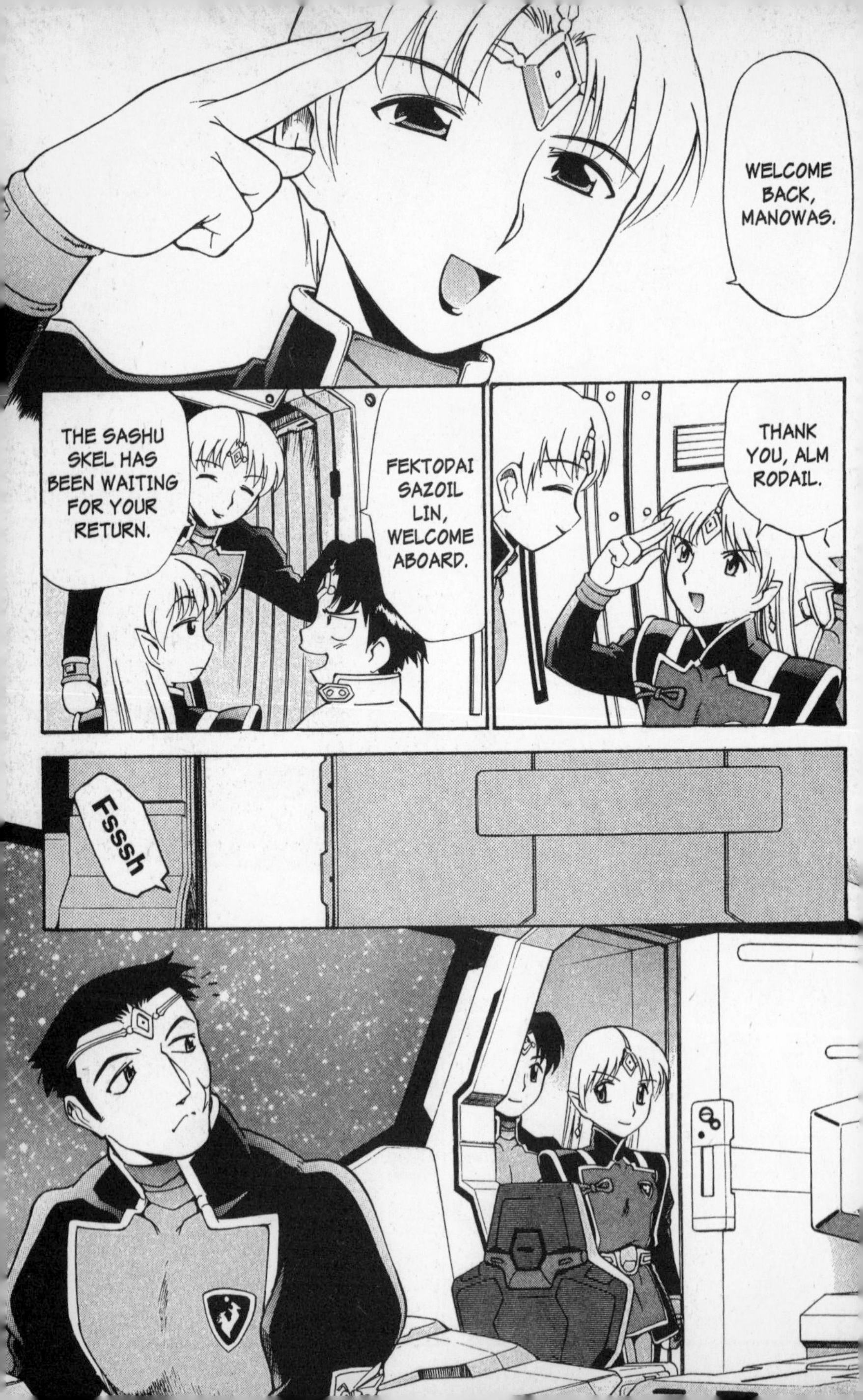
WELCOME BACK, MANOWAS.
THANK YOU, ALM RODAIL.
FEKTODAI SAZOIL LIN, WELCOME ABOARD.
THE SASHU SKEL HAS BEEN WAITING FOR YOUR RETURN.
Fsssh

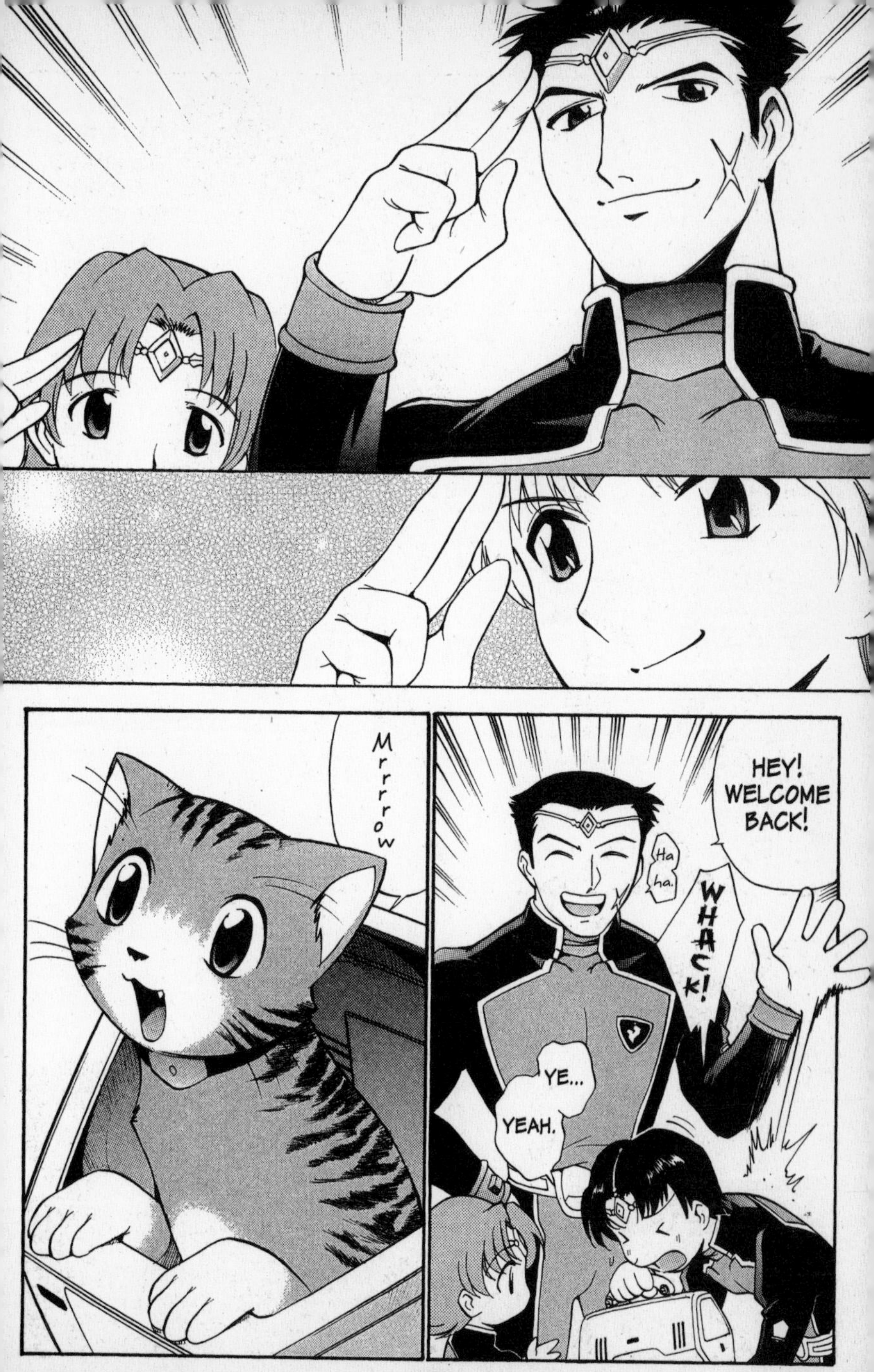
HEY! WELCOME BACK!
Ha ha.
WHACK!
YE... YEAH.
Mrrrrow

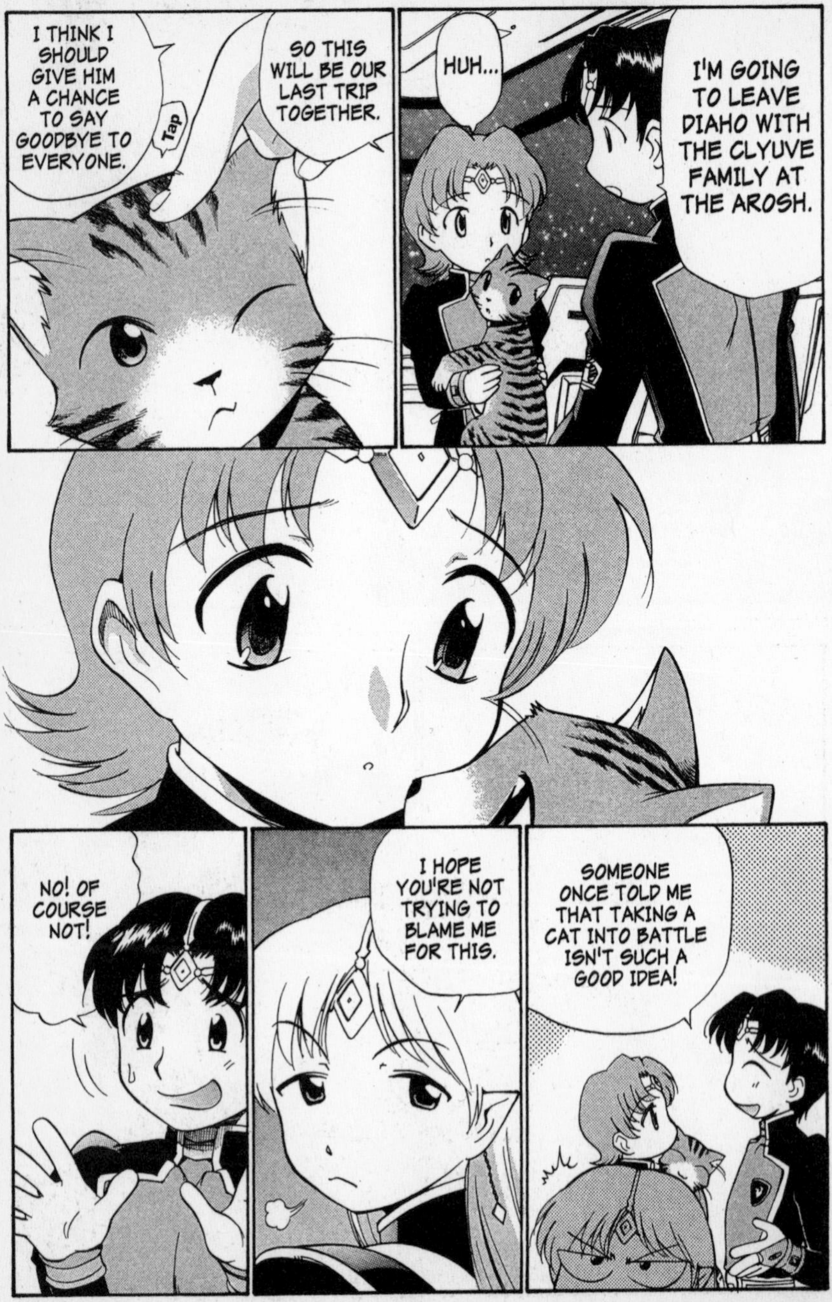
I'M GOING TO LEAVE DIAHO WITH THE CLYUVE FAMILY AT THE AROSH.
HUH...
SO THIS WILL BE OUR LAST TRIP TOGETHER.
I THINK I SHOULD GIVE HIM A CHANCE TO SAY GOODBYE TO EVERYONE.
Tap
SOMEONE ONCE TOLD ME THAT TAKING A CAT INTO BATTLE ISN'T SUCH A GOOD IDEA!
I HOPE YOU'RE NOT TRYING TO BLAME ME FOR THIS.
NO! OF COURSE NOT!

は は は は は

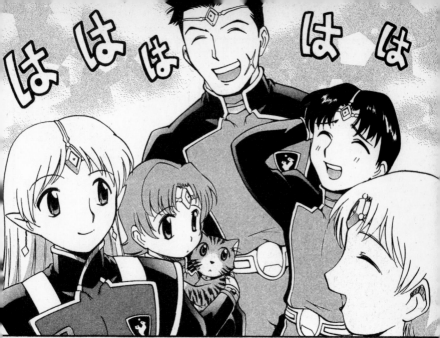

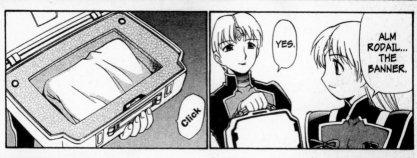

Click

YES.

ALM
RODAIL...
THE
BANNER.

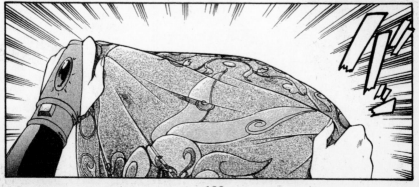

190

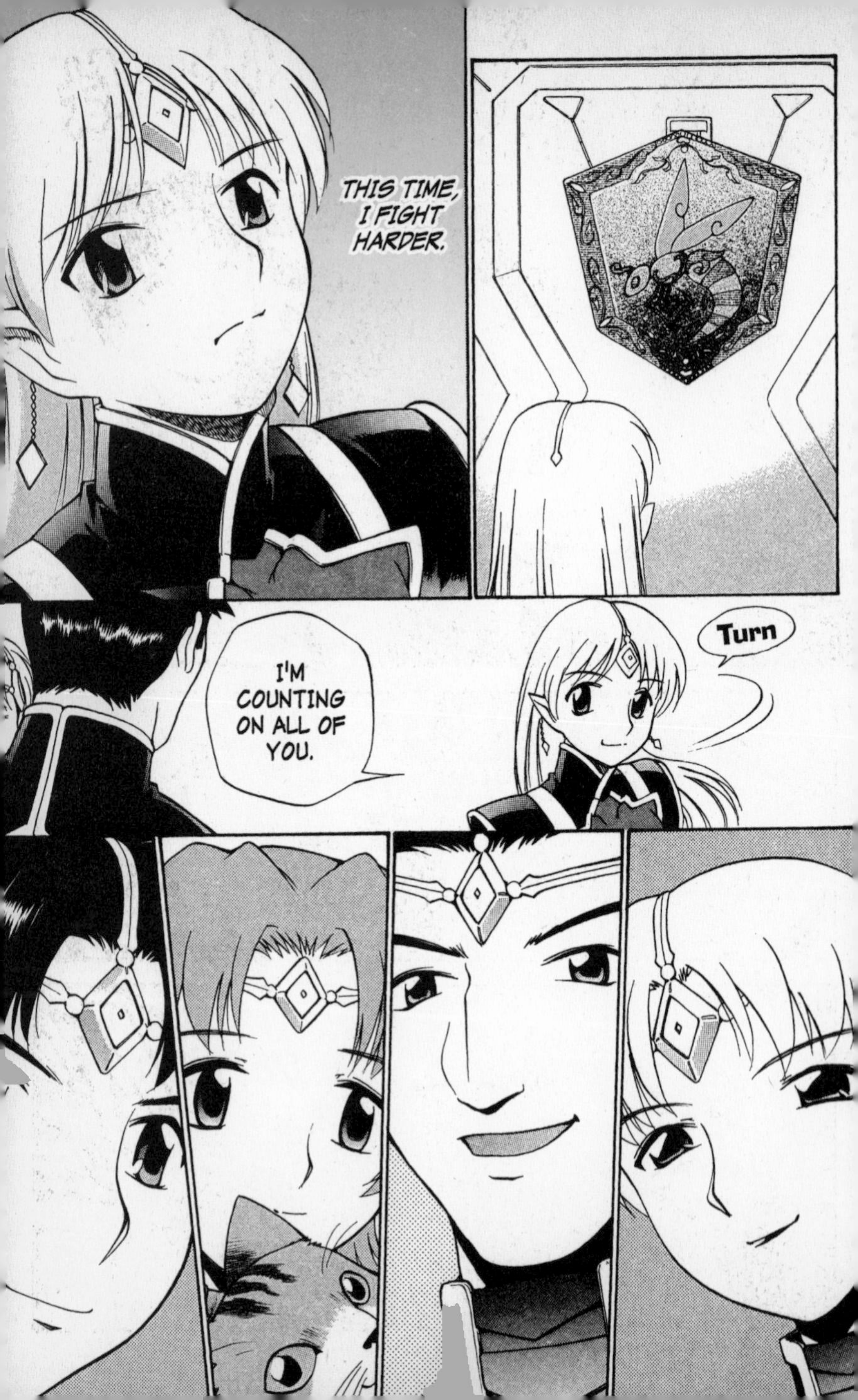
THIS TIME, I FIGHT HARDER.
Turn
I'M COUNTING ON ALL OF YOU.

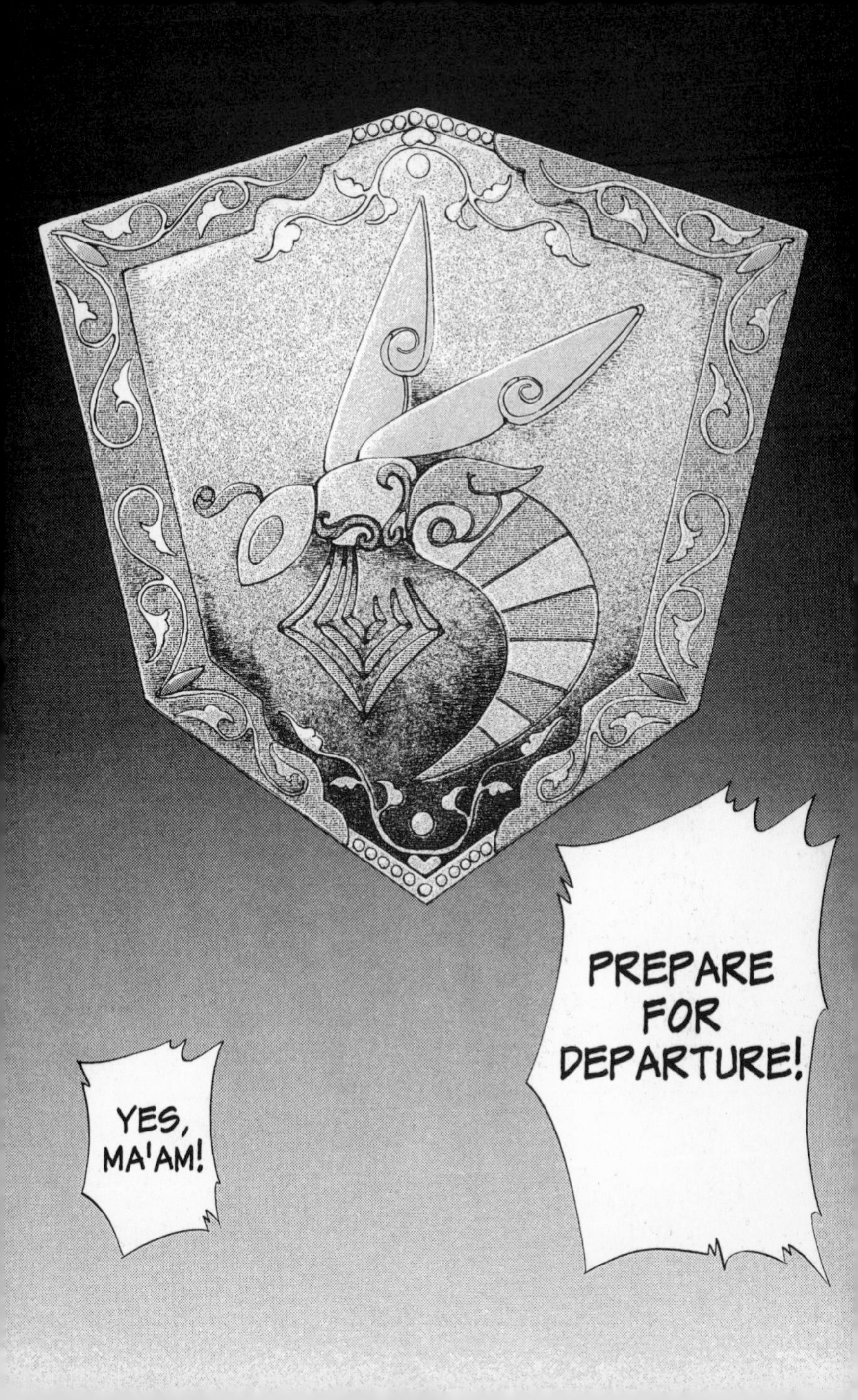
PREPARE FOR DEPARTURE!
YES, MA'AM!

Epilogue

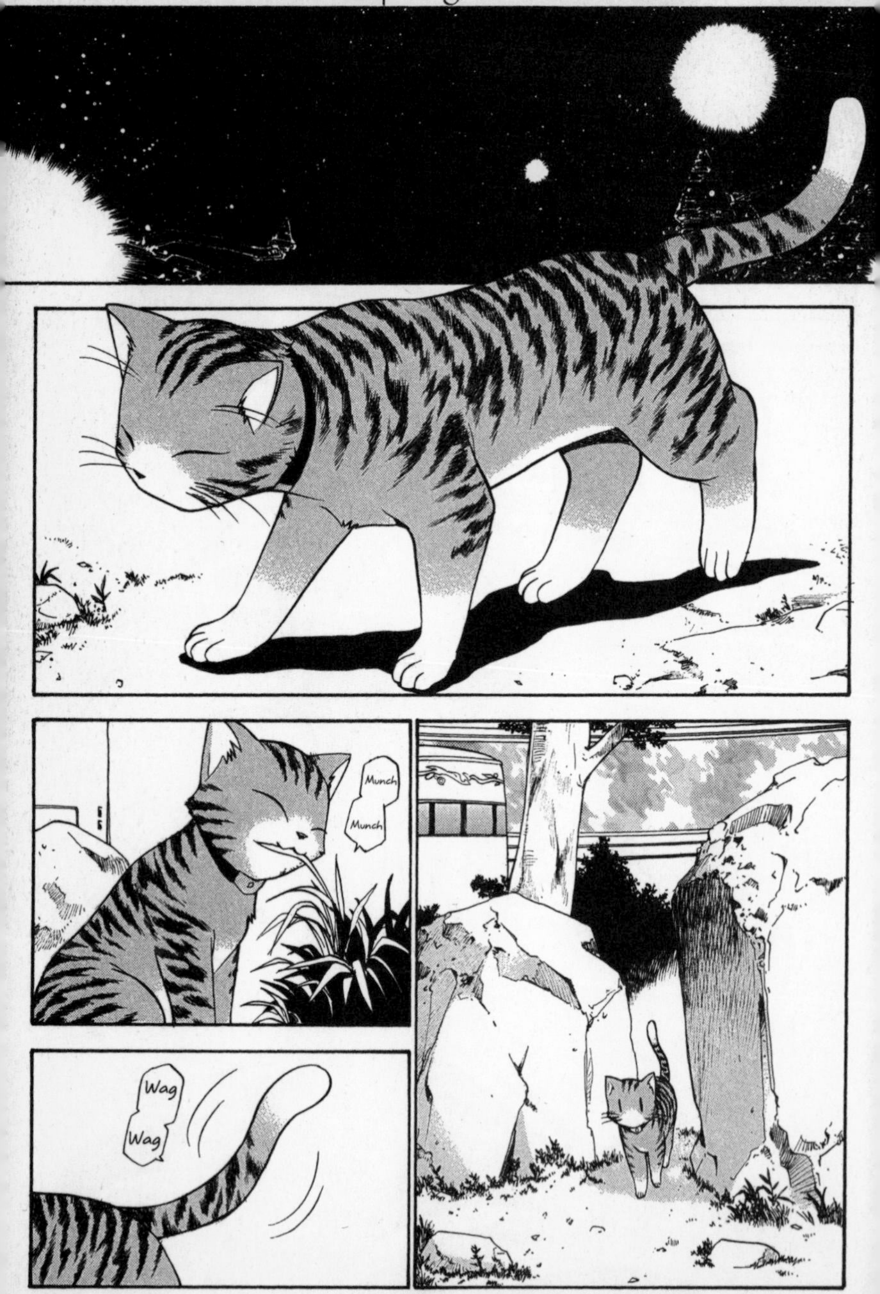
Munch
Munch
Wag
Wag

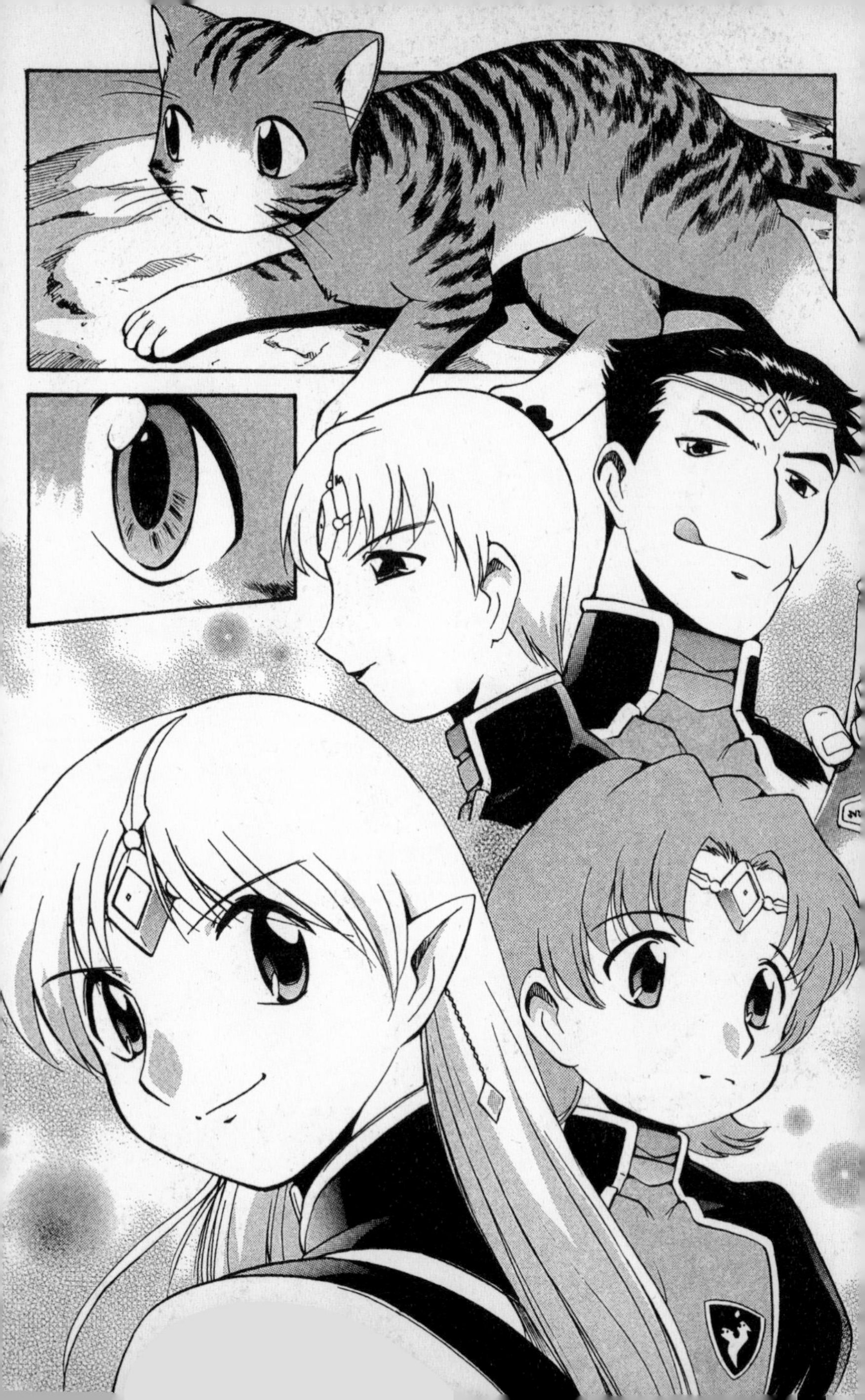

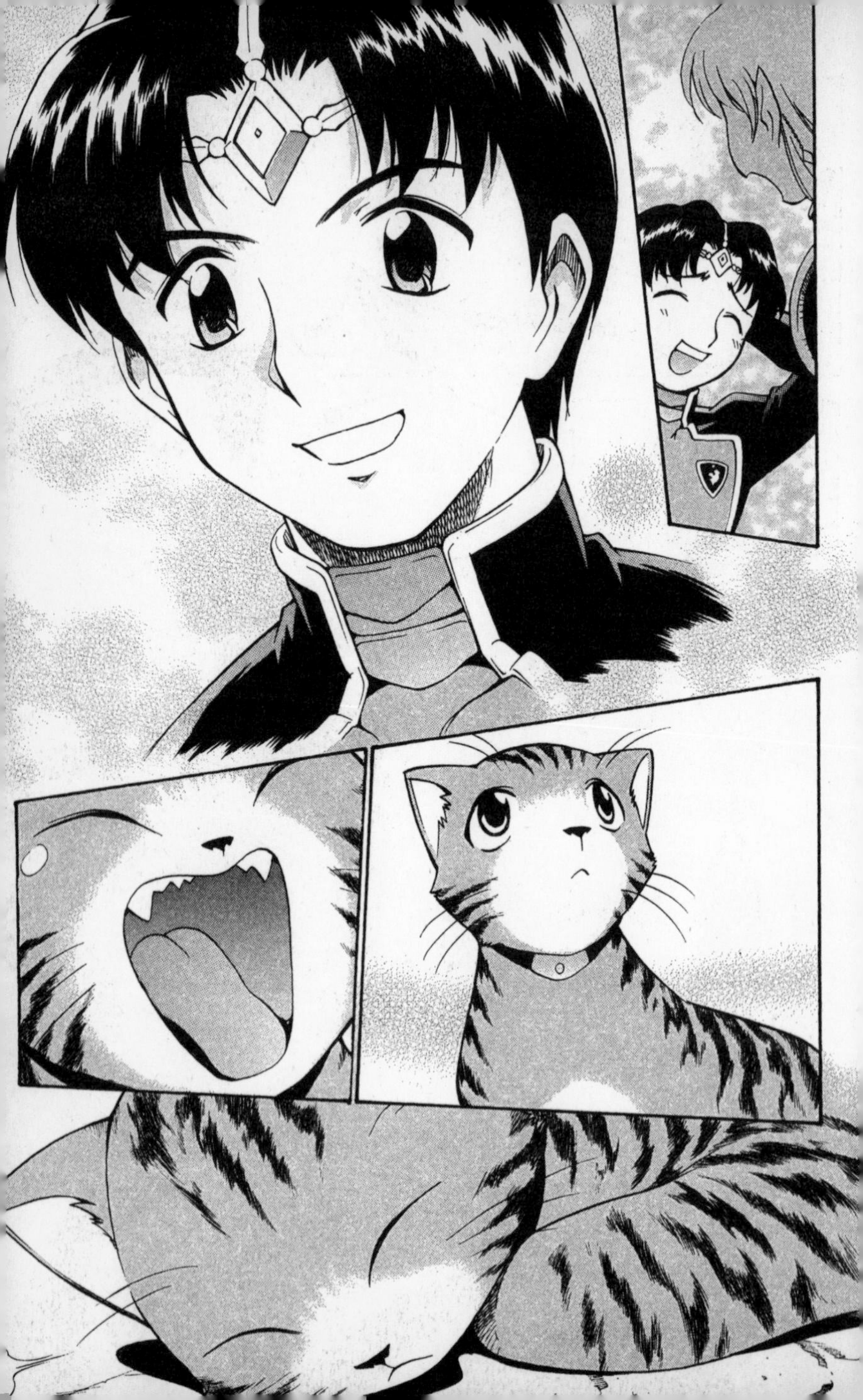

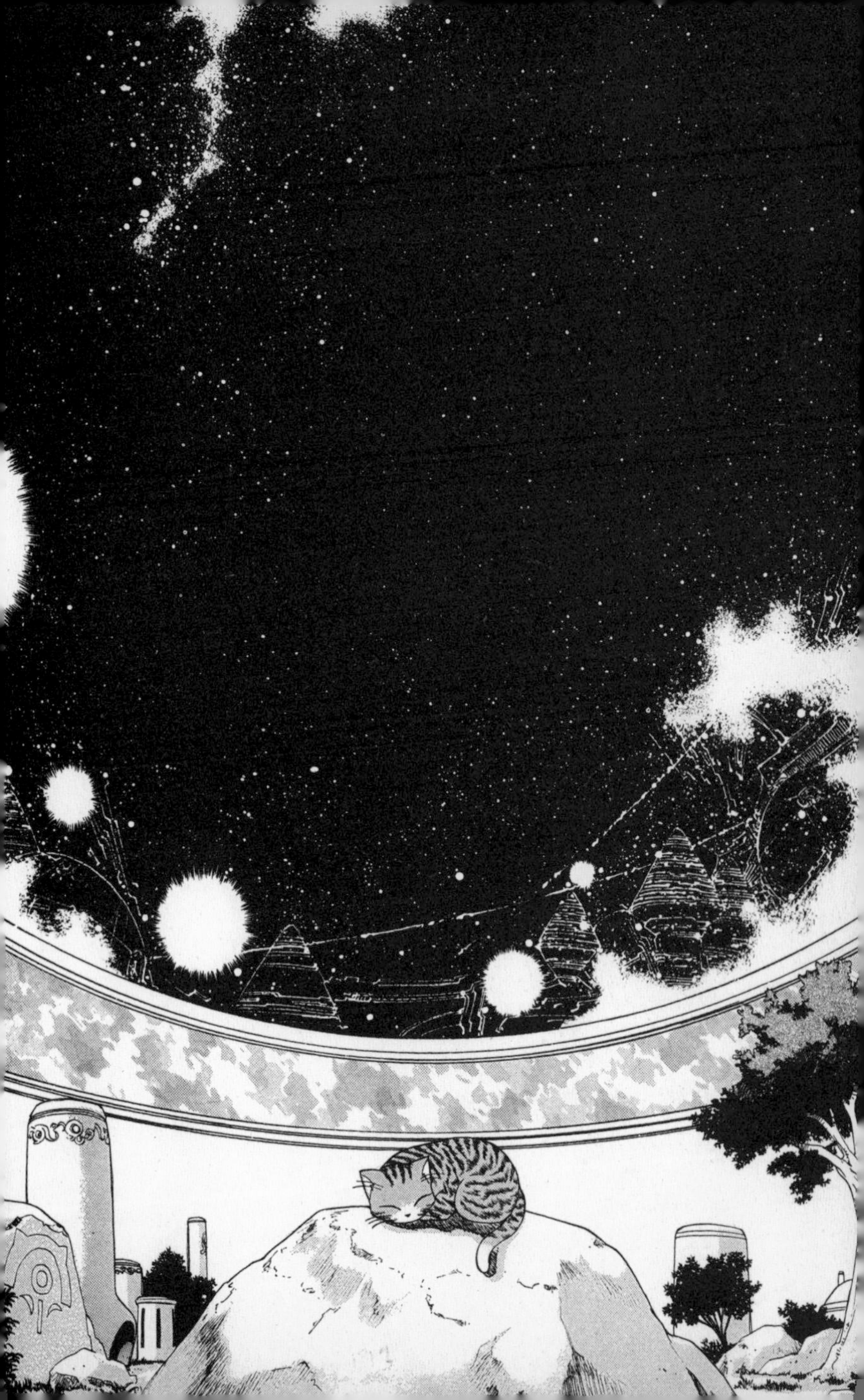

Banner of the Stars
The Shape of Bonds
The End

ABH DICTIONARY

laishakal wek sodal aptical Battlefield at the Aptic Gate

lakney hoka orbital station

lekle senior navigator

lenyu ranks

lenyuju antiproton cannon.

lesui Patrol Ship

libyun territories held by a dril

longia transport shuttles

lope a sliced Abh fruit similar to a lemon

lyum baroness

manowas captain of a gel, a military position

nahen surface world

nahenud lander (pejorative term)

nif duchess

onyu idiot

opsei main engines

pelia transport ship

rei drel an Abh contest that resembles jousting

ret battle ships

ro starship hatch

rodail officer

rojyu lady

ronyu a term of respect reserved for nobility

Rowas Deca-Commander, an Abh military rank

ryuf baron

sabut pressure suit helmet

salel suyum ashal squadron commander

sashu crew

sashu skel Second Aviator

sates gol hoksa space-time mines

seimei sosu territorial representatives

shutium Deity Ministry

soporuka battle

sord gate into or out of planespace

Sord Aptical Aptic Gate

sov battle unit

sov gram Main Fleet

soyala green tea

soyasa black tea

spenu labural Fleet Admiral

spunej Empress

subyut nuclear fusion canon shots

sune noble title

sunesbuga ship's defense shield

suumeid a pacifist philosophy held by the Federation of Hania

syuf ashal gona fourth assault unit

syuf ashal kasna first assault unit

spyuto nuclear fusion bombs

teal nom peach tea

usem scouts

vok lanyu laser cannons

wass kasalel chief of staff

weko escape pod

wesash rank of Crewman

yadbiru squadron

yadbiru ashal battleship squadron

yadbiru usem reconnaissance squadron

yalulug prince

yazu facility

SEIKAI TRILOGY

Abh a race of humans genetically engineered to live in the vacuum of space. Abh have twice the lifespan of unmodified humans, blue hair, pale skin and heightened brain functions. *adj.* having the quality of Abh.

alek lead ship

alm rodail navigator

alpha mabral uniform

Arosh capital

Bomowas Hecto-Commander, an Abh military rank equivalent to a Fleet Captain

byuru fleet

byuru gona Abh Fourth Fleet

byuru kasna Abh First Fleet under Frode Spoor

byuru luna Abh Fifth Fleet

byuru mata Abh Second Fleet

byuru vena Abh Third Fleet

calicke small transport ship

dadeocks normal space, as opposed to Fwas.

daz the vacuum of space and home of the Abh

dril an Abh noble, equivalent to a Count

Dril Hydal Count Hyde, Jinto

dugsans escape

egyulf electromagnetic cannon

fasenzel member of the royal family

feia bel viscountess

feia grahalel Royal Commander, equivalent to a Commander-in-Chief

feia laltonel Royal Highness

fektodai aviator

fektodai sazoil Supply officer

fektodai skem line wing aviator

fitlashos first blood

frasas space-time clusters, usually carrying ships of mine (hoksas)

frode admiral

Furyu Bal the Empire

Furyu Bal Grel Gol Bal Humankind Empire Abh

Fwas planespace

gahol bridge

garyush baronial residence

gel an assault ship

grel gol bal Humankind

gol lyutcos space-time separation

gol putalos space-time fusion

gonei pressure suits

gosk vassals

grahalel supreme commander

guragaf sov headquarters

gyuk lobrot Remembrance Dinner

hoksas mines

hoksateyox mine barrage

kadbyuru squadrons

kasna first

kres suiton the shape of bonds

kufalia territorial governor and ambassador

kufazet operation

Kufazet Leniv Operation Phantom Flame

Labule Abh Star Forces

lafek gunana spectactular insanity, an affliction suffered by the Bebaus family

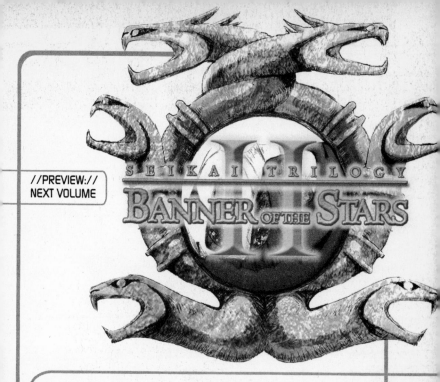

//PREVIEW://
NEXT VOLUME

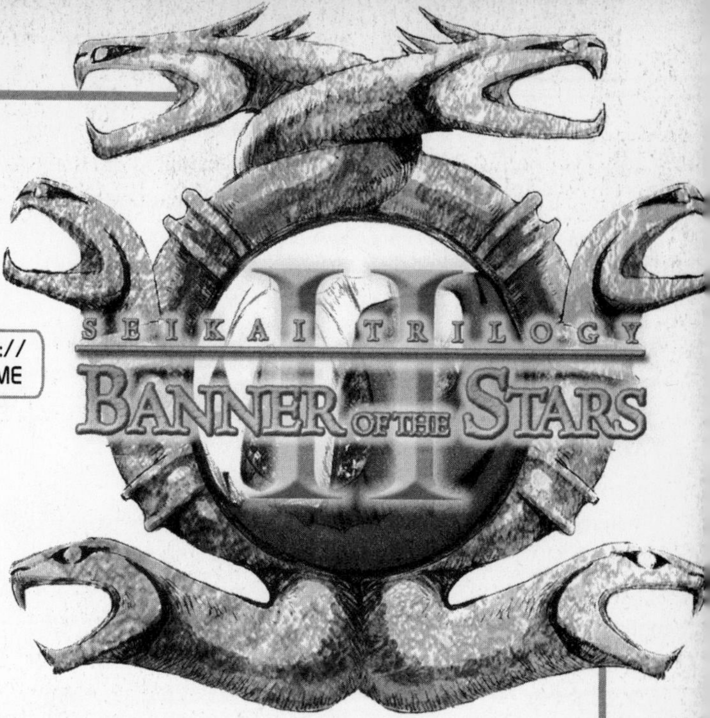
SEIKAI TRILOGY
BANNER OF THE STARS
III

With the success of Operation Phantom Flame, the Abh Empire has found itself in control of vast amounts of territory once controlled by its enemy, the United Mankind. As the Empire begins a new operation to mop up the remaining resistance, Lafiel and Jinto find themselves placed in the role of Territorial Ambassadors on the planet of Lobnas II. The Abh find dealing with surface worlds distasteful enough, but complicating matters further is the fact that Lobnas II is a prison planet whose population disagrees on the best future for their newly liberated world. When the United Mankind returns in an attempt to reclaim Lobnas, an angry revolt leaves Jinto stranded in the chaos, leaving Lafiel in the unenviable position of choosing between Jinto, the man who has been her savior and friend for so many years, and saving her ship from an encroaching enemy fleet.

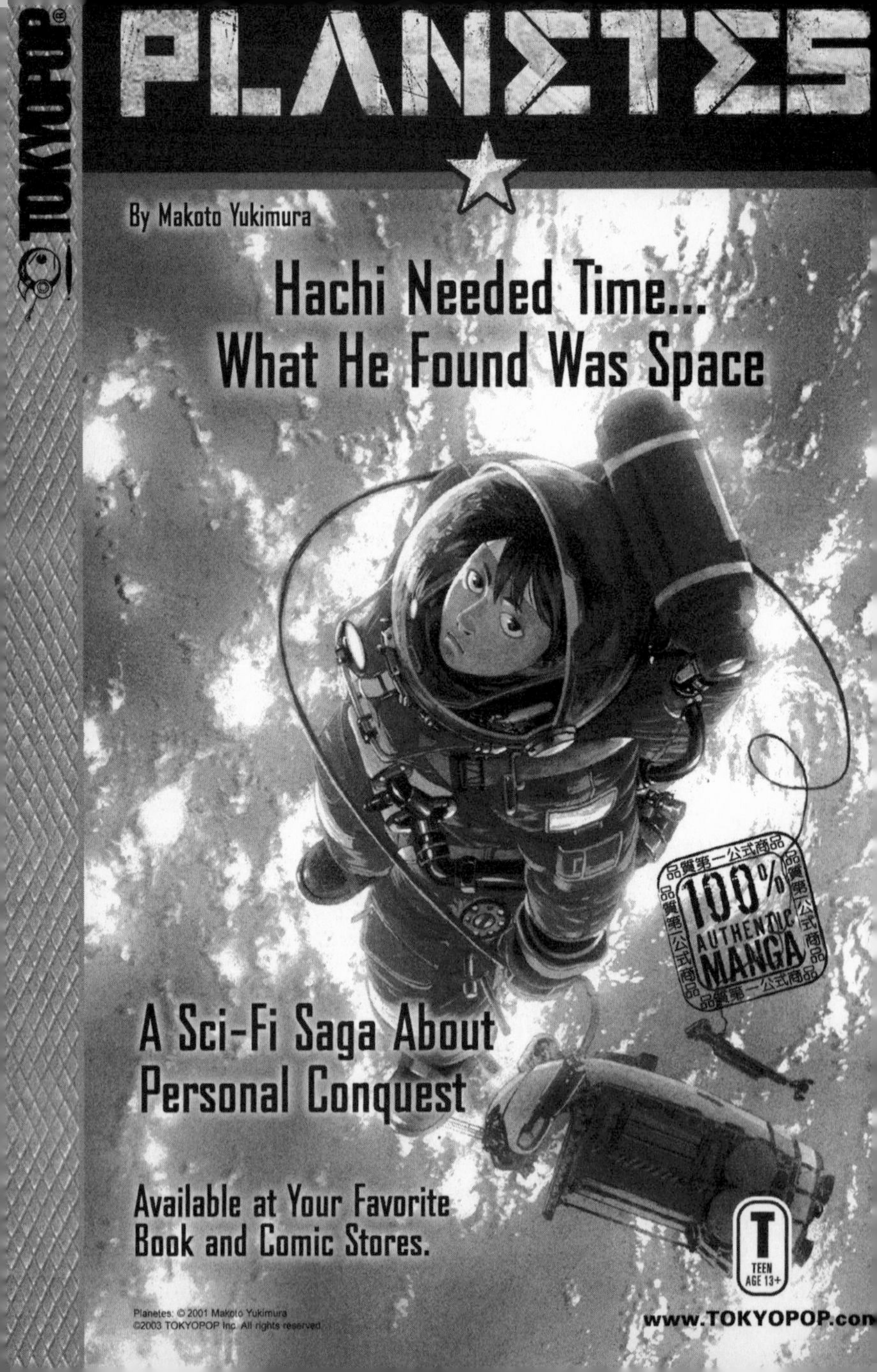
TOKYOPOP
PLANETES
By Makoto Yukimura
Hachi Needed Time...
What He Found Was Space
100% AUTHENTIC MANGA
A Sci-Fi Saga About
Personal Conquest
Available at Your Favorite
Book and Comic Stores.
T
TEEN
AGE 13+
Planetes: © 2001 Makoto Yukimura
©2003 TOKYOPOP Inc. All rights reserved.
www.TOKYOPOP.com

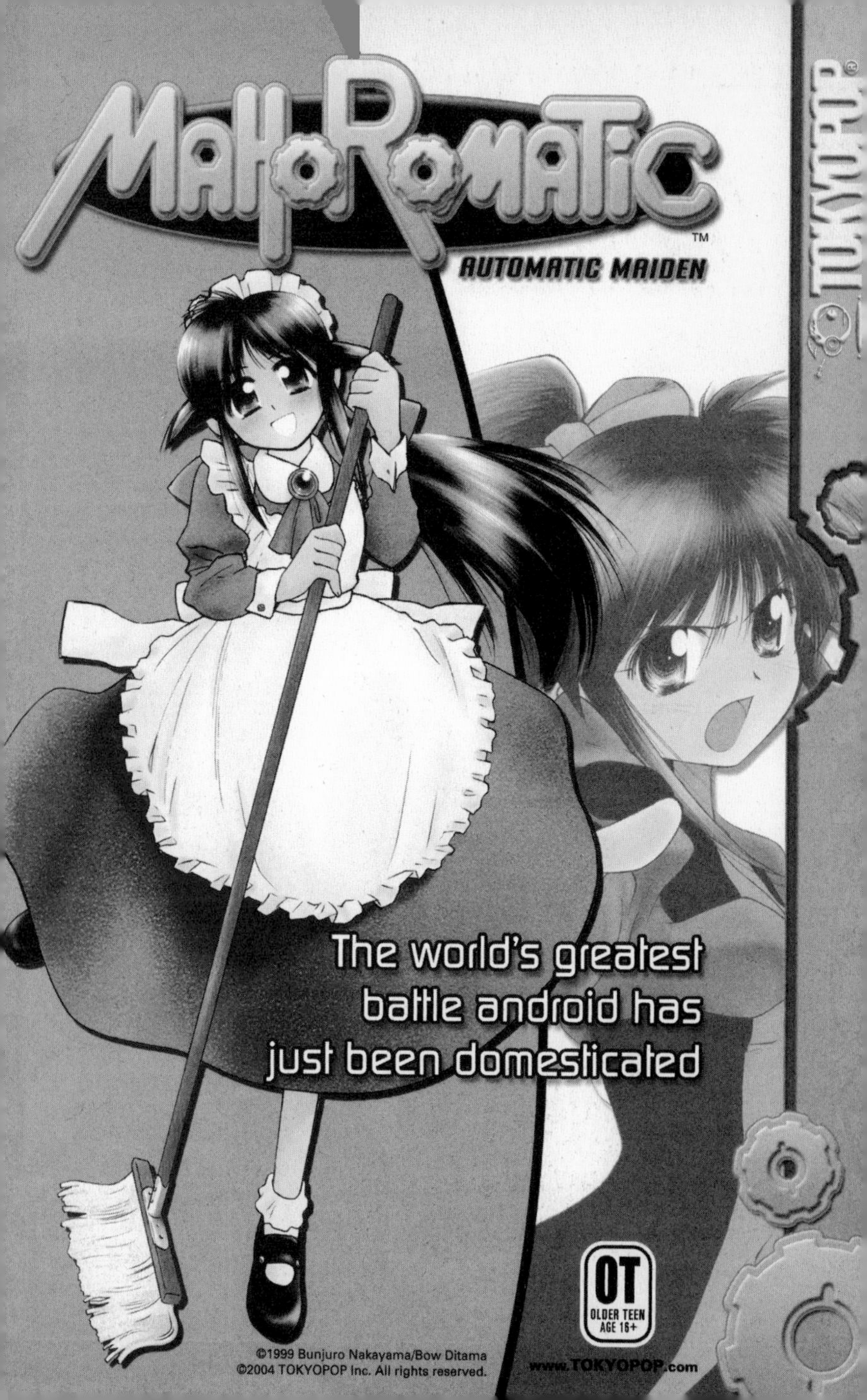
MAHOROMATIC™
AUTOMATIC MAIDEN
TOKYOPOP®
The world's greatest battle android has just been domesticated
OT OLDER TEEN AGE 16+
©1999 Bunjuro Nakayama/Bow Ditama
©2004 TOKYOPOP Inc. All rights reserved.
www.TOKYOPOP.com

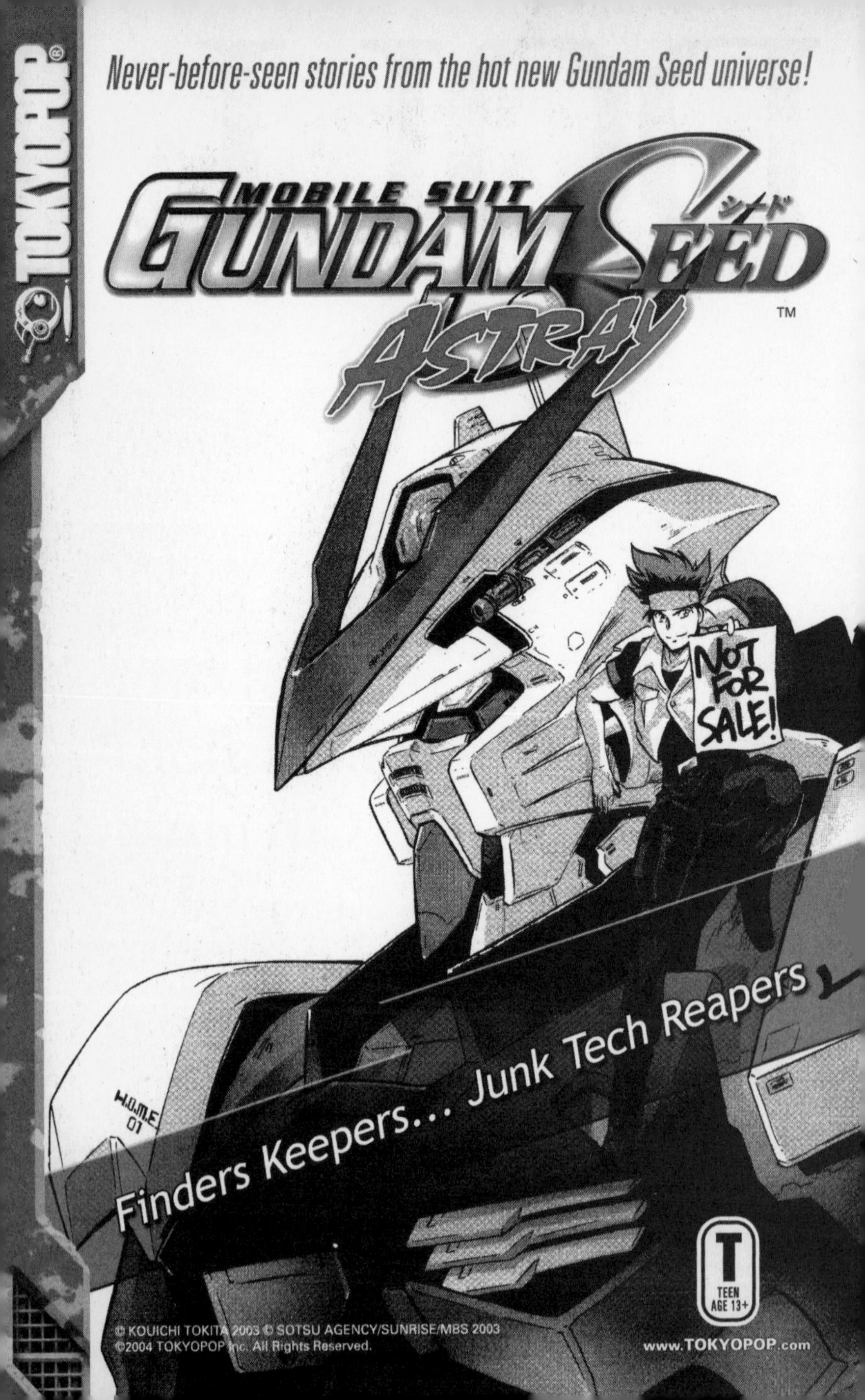
TOKYOPOP®
Never-before-seen stories from the hot new Gundam Seed universe!
MOBILE SUIT
GUNDAM SEED
シード
ASTRAY
TM
NOT FOR SALE!
H.O.M.E 01
Finders Keepers... Junk Tech Reapers
T TEEN AGE 13+
© KOUICHI TOKITA 2003 © SOTSU AGENCY/SUNRISE/MBS 2003
©2004 TOKYOPOP Inc. All Rights Reserved.
www.TOKYOPOP.com
TOKYOPOP

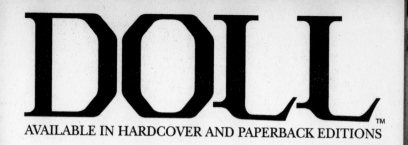

DOLL™

AVAILABLE IN HARDCOVER AND PAPERBACK EDITIONS

Love,
Compassion,
Circuitry.

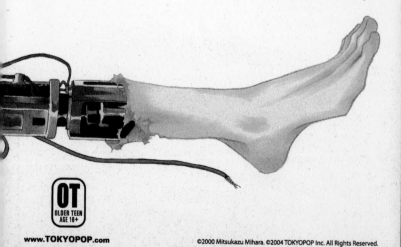

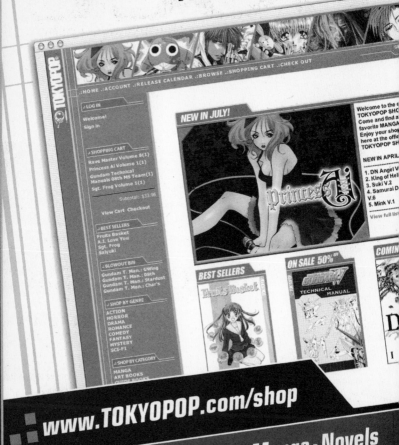
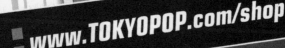